Staging Deaf an

Andy Head • Jill Marie Bradbury

Staging Deaf and Hearing Theatre Productions

A Practical Guide

palgrave
macmillan

Andy Head
Rochester Institute of Technology
Rochester, NY, USA

Jill Marie Bradbury
University of Maryland, College Park
College Park, MD, USA

ISBN 978-3-031-61445-3   ISBN 978-3-031-61446-0 (eBook)
https://doi.org/10.1007/978-3-031-61446-0

© The Editor(s) (if applicable) and The Author(s), under exclusive license to Springer Nature Switzerland AG 2024

This work is subject to copyright. All rights are solely and exclusively licensed by the Publisher, whether the whole or part of the material is concerned, specifically the rights of translation, reprinting, reuse of illustrations, recitation, broadcasting, reproduction on microfilms or in any other physical way, and transmission or information storage and retrieval, electronic adaptation, computer software, or by similar or dissimilar methodology now known or hereafter developed.

The use of general descriptive names, registered names, trademarks, service marks, etc. in this publication does not imply, even in the absence of a specific statement, that such names are exempt from the relevant protective laws and regulations and therefore free for general use.

The publisher, the authors and the editors are safe to assume that the advice and information in this book are believed to be true and accurate at the date of publication. Neither the publisher nor the authors or the editors give a warranty, expressed or implied, with respect to the material contained herein or for any errors or omissions that may have been made. The publisher remains neutral with regard to jurisdictional claims in published maps and institutional affiliations.

Cover Credit: Izabela Habur/ Getty Images

This Palgrave Macmillan imprint is published by the registered company Springer Nature Switzerland AG.
The registered company address is: Gewerbestrasse 11, 6330 Cham, Switzerland

Paper in this product is recyclable.

To Katharyn, always the spark.
To Brian, who makes it possible.

Acknowledgments

We are grateful to the Office of the Associate Dean of Research at the National Technical Institute for the Deaf, Rochester Institute of Technology for providing financial support to complete the research for this book. Special thanks to Trudy Suggs of T.S. Writing for the many hours she spent transcribing the interviews. We thank the photographers for permission to use their images in the book. Most of all, we are deeply grateful to all of the actors, directors of artistic sign language, directors, interpreters, designers, stage managers, and theatre lovers who agreed to be interviewed for this book—Michael Arden, Erin Auble, Michelle Banks, Michael Baron, Joshua Castille, James Caverly, Brian Cheslik, Aimee Chou, Victoria Covell, Tyrone Giordano, Sacha Glasser, Patrick Graybill, Luane Davis Haggerty, Amelia Hensley, Monique Holt, Aaron Kelstone, Cath Kiwitt, DJ Kurs, McClain Leong, Hayden Orr, Malik Paris, Christopher Robinson, Serena Rush, Joseph Santini, Crom Saunders, Alexa Scott-Flaherty, Howie Seago, Ethan Sinnott, Lindsey Snyder, Teresa Thuman, Alexandria Wailes, and Annie Wiegand. Your knowledge, experience, and insights have been invaluable.

Competing Interests The authors have no conflicts of interest to declare.

Why This Book?

In my first semester teaching at the Rochester Institute of Technology (RIT), I directed a production of a play titled *Love's Fire: Seven New Plays Inspired by Seven Shakespearean Sonnets*. Auditions were held during the first week of classes. Halfway through the open call, a young deaf actor entered the room and gave one of the strongest auditions I'd seen all afternoon. Though she was not the first deaf person I'd met, at the time I was still quite new to deaf culture, I didn't have much experience working with deaf people, and I had *zero* experience directing a deaf actor in a play. RIT is affiliated with the National Technical Institute for the Deaf (NTID). In fact, the two share a campus, so her appearance was not totally unexpected. American Sign Language (ASL) interpreters were present at the audition and helped me communicate with her.

It was apparent this actor needed to be in the show, but I found myself discounting her due to my own shortcomings. As I planned out callbacks, her audition form sat on the table, not quite in the 'yes' pile or the 'no' pile. I had many anxieties about the decision since I knew very little ASL: Would interpreters be sufficient in communicating with her? Would we understand each other? No other deaf actors had auditioned, so how would she interact with an otherwise hearing cast? How could I incorporate her deafness and culture into the play? How would we weave together two languages onstage at the same time? Where should I even begin?

All of the thoughts edging her toward 'no' were my own insecurities. She had come in and auditioned better than almost all other actors that day, and if she was a hearing person, she would've been a clear 'yes.' Not casting her, nor even offering her a callback, would be unjust and unfair on many levels. It would be an incredible disservice to her, to the other actors, to the audience, and even to myself, depriving us all of a very unique, challenging, and cross-cultural artistic experience—especially at an educational institution. I picked up her audition form and looked it over again. I did not know how the coming weeks would unfold; I didn't have answers to the various questions banging around in my brain; I felt there were so many inadvertent mistakes that could be made; I also knew she had to be and deserved to be in the play. I put her form in the 'yes' pile. I had no roadmap for how to include her in the production, but deep down past the insecurities, I knew we would all make it work, as a team, because that's what theatre is about.

I ended up casting that actor and we *did* make it work. The play is actually a collection of seven short plays, and she was involved in four of them, each one in a slightly different way. My worries were unfounded—the cast clicked, she was involved and included, and the show came together. Throughout the process, we changed directions, we backtracked, we fixed and adjusted and tried things in new ways, and eventually we had a production to present to our audience fully in ASL and spoken English, and with captions.

Looking back, I need to credit her with extending to the rest of us her patience, understanding, and forgiveness as she overcame our ignorance. There are numerous things I could have done better in working with that cast. I now have tools and awareness that would have helped me serve that deaf actor more. I have new strategies that would have benefited her, and us all, immensely. That's why we're sharing this book. Theatre like this is happening all over the place, but no one is writing about it. No one is collecting best practices and sharing experiences on a wider scale. Nothing has been codified about what to do or not do. This is the roadmap for people who were like me back in that audition room. It is for people who want to create more accessible productions and be more inclusive of deaf artists and audiences. A guide like this would have relieved so much of the burden that the young actor shouldered to teach me about how to work with her.

—Andy

When Andy first mentioned his idea to write this book, my immediate response was "YES, this is so needed and you cannot write this by yourself." For too many years, integrated deaf and hearing theatre has been led by hearing artists. The National Theatre of the Deaf, established in 1967, was led by hearing individuals until 1993, when Deaf actor Camille L. Jeter became a co-artistic director. The original *Children of a Lesser God* and the 2018 Broadway revival had hearing directors, as did Deaf West's smash hits *Big River* and *Spring Awakening*. The lack of deaf creative input at the highest level often leads to shows that are applauded by hearing audiences and reviewers, but leave deaf patrons dissatisfied at best and excluded at worst. Things are finally starting to change, with a deaf and hearing co-director model becoming more common and deaf directors gaining opportunities to direct outside of Deaf theatre companies. But deaf artists still do not have the same opportunities to direct or co-direct as hearing artists. To Andy's credit, he immediately recognized the importance of collaborative authorship for this topic and invited me to become part of his project.

I am not a theatre practitioner myself, but an avid Deaf theatre-goer who has traveled around the country to see integrated productions for over twenty years. I have many thoughts about what makes for a successful and inclusive experience for deaf audiences, and have published some of my reflections. Andy and I have expanded beyond our own individual experiences by interviewing over thirty deaf and hearing theatre artists, interpreters, and audience members for this project. Their generous gifts of time and knowledge have greatly enriched this book.

—Jill

Until now, hearing theatre artists interested in working with deaf theatre artists have had very few resources to turn to. There are only a few non-academic publications about Deaf theatre in general, such as Stephen Baldwin's *Pictures in the Air: The Story of the National Theatre of the Deaf* (1993), or about integrated deaf and hearing theatre in particular. One of the few books on integrated theatre, Mark Rigney's *Deaf Side Story* (2003), is a narrative account of an integrated production of *West Side Story* at MacMurray College. In addition to being authored solely by a hearing individual, Rigney's book does not offer guidelines for practice. Some guidelines can be found in publications such as Luane Davis Haggerty's *Acting I: Del Sign Takes Stage* (2009), Dorothy Miles and Lou Fant's *Sign-Language Theatre and Deaf Theatre: New Definitions and Directions* (1976), and a handful of doctoral theses. However, these publications are out of date or not widely available. While existing publications on disability theatre, such as Stephanie Barton-Farcas' *Disability and Theatre: A Practical Manual for Inclusion in the Arts* (2018), have chapters on deaf and hearing theatre, these sections are brief and do not include the experiences of deaf theatre artists and audiences.

This book doesn't have all the answers, for every production is a unique experience with unique challenges and triumphs. There are many distinct approaches to doing integrated theatre. What works in one venue, with one cast, and for one community may not work for another venue, cast, or community. Instead, we give you a starting point and a direction to work toward. Throughout the book, we include numerous examples and case studies to help you avoid common pitfalls. Out of our own personal experiences and the interviews we conducted for this book, we have developed three non-negotiable principles that are necessary for successfully producing integrated theatre. These principles are the foundation for practices that ensure your deaf artists and audiences are getting the experiences they deserve.

Ultimately, our book aims to help bridge the gap between mainstream theatre (i.e., predominantly hearing theatre) and deaf artists and audiences. It's written for those who want to create more inclusive and accessible theatre, but aren't sure where to begin. It's also for those deaf designers, directors, actors, and artists who are too often burdened with having to teach and explain and adapt in order to work with hearing colleagues. This book is a guide they can refer people to when working with a new company, producer, or director.

In our current moment, deaf stories, deaf artists, and deaf culture are making a huge splash across mainstream entertainment. Look no further than the 94th Academy Awards in 2022, in which the film *CODA* won not only Best Picture, but also a Best Supporting Actor for Troy Kotsur, the first Deaf actor to achieve this distinction. From the ABC Family series *Switched at Birth* to the Disney+ *Hawkeye* and spinoff *Echo*, deaf characters are regularly appearing on television. The theatre world is also seeing an expansion in roles for deaf actors. In 2022, Alexandria Wailes appeared in the Broadway production of *for colored girls who have considered suicide / when the rainbow is enuf*, James Caverly in Olney Theatre Center's *The Music Man*, and Russell Harvard in the Broadway production of *To Kill a Mockingbird*. Opera companies such as Los Angeles Philharmonic and Victory Hall Opera in Charlottesville, VA are experimenting with using deaf actors in productions. The list is only getting longer. We're witnessing a renaissance in deaf representation, and in many cases, deaf and hearing artists are working alongside each other to create unique and impactful work. Productions everywhere are challenging theatrical norms, shifting audience's expectations, and creating stronger community partnerships in the process. We hope this book supports and expands this shift by educating theatre makers about informed, culturally responsible, and successful practices.

If you are a hearing theatre maker reading this book, we embrace your openness to the idea of working with deaf artists. We want you to have the knowledge and tools to make your integrated production a good experience for all involved. The ideas, opinions, and insights in this book come from a variety of sources, from directors to educators to actors to designers to patrons, some deaf, some hearing, many with long performing arts careers. We've included many perspectives to give you the most information to pull from. This book will help you figure out where to start, how to find the resources you need, and how to set yourself and your team up for success.

Contents

1	Introduction and Framework	1
2	History and Practices of Integrated Theatre	21
3	Laying the Foundation	63
4	Assembling the Cast	103
5	Shaping the Performance	119
6	Seeing the Performance	151
7	Conclusion	181
Appendix A: Excerpts from Interviews		185
Appendix B: Full Interviews		211
Appendix C: Further Reading		307
Index		311

About the Authors

Andy Head (he/him) is an assistant professor at the Rochester Institute of Technology and National Technical Institute for the Deaf. Andy has published two articles in *Theatre/Practice*, has worked professionally as an actor, and is an award-winning director. This is his first book. He completed his graduate work in acting at Michigan State University and is a proud Returned Peace Corps Volunteer.

Jill Marie Bradbury (deaf) is Professor and Director of the School of Theatre, Dance and Performance Studies, University of Maryland, College Park, USA. She received her PhD in English from Brown University. Dr. Bradbury is a five-time National Endowment for the Arts grant-winner, including $25,000 for a DeafBlind Theater Institute. This project resulted in the documentary video, Protactile Romeo and Juliet: Theater by/for the DeafBlind and the collaborative essay "Protactile Romeo and Juliet: Theater by/for the DeafBlind" (Shakespeare Studies 47, 2019). Other relevant publications include "Deaf Theater" (Oxford Research Encyclopedia of Literature, 2024), "Disability Embodiment and Inclusive Aesthetics" (Inclusive Shakespeares: Identity, Pedagogy, Performance, 2023) and "Audiences, American Sign Language, and Deafness in Shakespeare Performance" (Shakespeare Bulletin 40.1, 2022).

List of Figures

Fig. 2.1	"A Performance of *Hamlet* by Deaf and Dumb Actors." (*The Graphic*. Printed by Edward Joseph Mansfield, 1886)	23
Fig. 2.2	Malik Paris (*left*) and Jheovani Montanez as double-cast actors playing Usnavi in *In the Heights* at the National Technical Institute for the Deaf, Rochester Institute of Technology. (Photo: Erin Auble)	34
Fig. 2.3	Declan McHale (*left*) as a voicing Guardian Angel shadowing Samuel Langshteyn as Prior Walter in *Angels in America, Part 1: Millennium Approaches* at the Rochester Institute of Technology. (Photo: A. Sue Weisler, RIT)	36
Fig. 2.4	Tyrone Giordano (left) as Huck Finn and Daniel Jenkins as Mark Twain/Voice of Huck in *Big River* at the American Airlines Theatre. (Photo: Joan Marcus)	39
Fig. 2.5	Howie Seago (*left*) as Friar Lawrence in *Romeo + Juliet* at the Allen Theatre. Voicing is provided by ensemble characters in the scene. (Photo: Chris Bennion)	42
Fig. 2.6	Victoria Covell (*left*) as Sally Bowles and Gabrielle Robinson (*background*) as Sally's interpreter in *Cabaret* at the Rochester Institute of Technology. (Photo: Erin Gallagher)	44
Fig. 2.7	Adelina Mitchell (left) as Marian Paroo and James Caverly as Harold Hill in *The Music Man* at Olney Theatre Center. (Photo: ©Teresa Castracane Photography)	47
Fig. 3.1	*Angels in America, Part 1: Millennium Approaches* at the National Technical Institute for the Deaf, Rochester Institute of Technology. Scenic Design: Erin Auble. (Photo: Erin Auble)	90
Fig. 5.1	Access mechanism placement—Dos and Don'ts. (Graphic: Brittany Castle)	145

CHAPTER 1

Introduction and Framework

ESSENTIAL BACKGROUND

Defining Common Terms

Several common terms should be understood from the start. First, it is a longstanding convention to use *Deaf* (emphasis on the capital D) to refer to people who use ASL and consider themselves part of a minority language community; and *deaf* (emphasis on the lower case) or *hearing impaired* for people who tend to use spoken English and identify with the hearing world. People who identify as Deaf reject the framing of being impaired or having 'lost' something. They see their deafness as a positive and essential part of their self-identity, not as a medical status—as Deaf gain, rather than hearing loss.[1] Such individuals typically socialize primarily with other Deaf people and use ASL, though they may also use spoken language and have hearing friends and family. It is important to realize that Deaf in this context is primarily a statement about identity, not about how much one can hear. People may describe themselves as Deaf and yet have a high level of functional hearing, read lips well, and be able to carry

---

[1] Many hearing people view deafness as a loss. Deaf gain is an outlook that shifts the paradigm of hearing impairment toward viewing deafness as a valued identity. If you are interested in learning more about Deaf gain or any other topics discussed throughout the book, check out the Further Reading section at the end.

on conversations in spoken English in some situations. They may or may not use assistive listening technology, such as hearing aids and cochlear implants. In the Deaf community, *hard of hearing* is sometimes used to describe someone who has sufficient hearing to function easily in the hearing world or who feels they exist between hearing and Deaf worlds. ASL users have a strong preference for the term *hard of hearing* over *hearing impaired*, because they view the latter as a term coined by hearing individuals that cannot be signed easily.

Lower case deaf has typically been used in the Deaf community to describe people who are more likely to use spoken English and to socialize primarily with hearing people. However, this group of people tends to prefer the term *hearing impaired* over *deaf*, because they affiliate more strongly with being hearing, and view hard of hearing as an outdated term. They are more likely to describe their hearing status as a disability,[2] to use assistive listening technology, and to reject the idea that deafness is a defining part of their identity. *Late-deafened* is sometimes used to acknowledge the unique experiences of those who undergo a change in their hearing ability as adults.

Although initially proposed to advocate for an understanding of deafness from a cultural, rather than a medical perspective, the Deaf/deaf binary quickly became perceived as reductive and exclusionary. As more and more people find their way to the community of ASL users later in life, due to the rising prevalence of cochlear implants and the impact of mainstreaming educational philosophies, many find that neither Deaf nor deaf fits how they understand themselves. Deaf Studies scholar Paddy Ladd instead proposes the more inclusive term *deafhood*, understood as "the struggle by each deaf child, deaf family and Deaf adult to explain to themselves and each other their own existence in the world" in ways that may or may not align with clearly identified communities, cultures, or language practices (2003, p. 3). For Ladd, deafhood is a continuum of experiences across auditory, linguistic, and cultural spectrums. Throughout this book, we have adopted Ladd's perspective. We use *deaf* to refer to individuals across the spectrums whose hearing abilities diverge from the norm. Going forward, we use *Deaf theatre* to acknowledge the artistic role of ASL and themes related to the experience of deafness in this particular form of

---

[2] There is a complex debate within the deaf community surrounding the word *disabled*. Many prefer to view themselves as a language minority group. Recognizing the legal protections that come with being considered disabled, however, other deaf people do identify as disabled. Nonetheless, they still reject the notion that disability is a wholly negative condition or experience.

dramatic practice, as well as its cultural importance for the community within which it originated. And, we use *Deaf* when referring to specific theatre makers who we know prefer to identify themselves in this way.

The deaf community contains many individuals with additional disabilities. They may identify as *Deaf+* or *Deaf-plus*. People with vision and hearing disabilities are known as *deaf-blind*. Recently, some in this community have adopted *DeafBlind* as an identity related to, but separate from deafness. Alongside this change, *Protactile* has emerged as a distinct sign language grounded in the unique communication needs of the DeafBlind community, as well as a philosophy promoting DeafBlind autonomy and culture. Protactile is discussed in more detail in Chap. 2—"A History of Deaf and Hearing Integrated Theatre".

Another term commonly used in the deaf community is *CODA*, which stands for Child of Deaf Adults (sometimes *KODA*, for Kid of Deaf Adults). CODAs grow up in both worlds. Their first language may be sign and they may not understand that their audiological status differs from their parents until they begin school. CODAs may share similar experiences such as interpreting for their parents or feeling as though they belong in neither the hearing nor the deaf communities. Other abbreviations have been coined to express family bonds with deaf people and the deaf community, including *SODA* (Sibling or Spouse of Deaf Adults) and *GODA* (Grandchild of Deaf Adults). As adults, CODAs and others who have grown up with deaf family members often feel a strong connection with the deaf world and find careers that keep them within it.

Other members of the deaf community include *sign language interpreters*. Translator is not used to describe people who facilitate communication between deaf and hearing individuals. The Registry of Interpreters for the Deaf defines interpreting as "the act of conveying meaning between people who use signed and/or spoken languages" (Registry, n.d.). In other words, interpreters are there not just for the deaf person but to facilitate communication between users of two different languages. Interpreting requires a number of skills, including high-level fluency with sign language, ability to continually receive and comprehend information in one language, hold information in the mind while making appropriate conceptual choices for the context, and express the information in a different language. Certain interpreting fields require extensive background knowledge for interpreters to facilitate communication effectively, such as medical, legal, educational, and performing arts. Interpreters must also be able to adjust to the communication preferences of deaf clients, which may range from more spoken language-influenced sign language to more 'pure' registers. In addition, there are regional and racial variants of sign language within countries. Interpreters can vary widely in their cognitive abilities, background knowledge, and familiarity with the continuum of sign languages. A newer development is the use of *deaf interpreters* (DIs or CDIs). DIs often work with low-vision or deaf-blind clients, but more recently, have been teaming with hearing interpreters to work in spoken English communication contexts. DIs can also work effectively in situations involving scripts, such as theatrical performances. Working with interpreters will be discussed further in Chap. 3—"Guidelines for Designers".

Audism is another common term in the deaf community. Coined in the 1970s by Deaf Studies scholar Tom Humphries, audism is the belief that the ability to hear and speak makes one superior to those who do not have these abilities (1977). Audism is more broadly used to mean any attitude or behavior that is discriminatory toward or biased against deaf people. Audism can be expressed in institutions and by individuals in a variety of ways. Examples of institutional audism include pulling a deaf child out of classes for speech therapy, which takes time away from learning subject matter content; or not hiring a deaf person to do a job because they cannot speak, even if the job could be done using written communication. Examples of individual audism include expecting the deaf person to read lips and being unwilling to write things down, or having spoken conversations while ignoring what deaf participants need to be included. The prevalence of audist attitudes and behaviors in deaf and hearing integrated theatre was a recurrent theme in almost all of the interviews we conducted. Anyone considering an integrated theatre project should take the time to educate themselves about audism before beginning any planning. See the Further Reading section for suggestions.

Finally, readers should be familiar with language variation within the deaf community. Grammatically, ASL and English are very different languages. ASL grammar is discussed in Chap. 2—"Sign Language Linguistics, Poetics, and Musicality". Many individuals in the deaf community use what is sometimes called 'pure' or grammatically correct ASL. Many others use what linguists call *contact languages*. In the United States, these developed in the 1970s when researchers began to show that ASL was a true language. As a result, the resistance to manual approaches to deaf education (manual = using sign language, oral = speaking and listening) began to break down. Educators concerned with supporting deaf children's acquisition of spoken language developed and popularized language mashups such as *signed English* and *SimCom*. In signed English, ASL signs are used but with English grammar. English words are typically mouthed as well. Because it results from contact between two languages, Signed English is also called *Pidgin Signed English* or *PSE*. Another variant, *Signed Exact English* or *SEE* uses invented signs for articles, gerunds, and other elements of English grammar not present in ASL. It has fallen out of favor and is rarely used. When people both speak and sign at the same time, this is called *SimCom*. SimCom has been popular in educational philosophies for decades because it is thought to provide access to both languages. However, recent linguistic research has shown that when people SimCom, they favor one language over the other. Typically, this is their native language. Most of the time, English grammar dominates sign production when SimCom is used, resulting in degraded access to ASL (Tevenal and Villanueva 2009). Due to their educational experiences, however, many deaf people use SimCom.

Language variation within the deaf community also results from geographical, age, gender, and racial differences. ASL users in the northeastern United States have syntactical patterns that differ from those in the southern United States (Bayley et al. 2011). ASL vocabulary varies across the country, with different regions having their own unique signs for certain words and phrases. SOON is signed differently on the west and east coasts, for example. Generational differences are also present, reflecting language changes over time. One example is the sign for VIDEO. The older version incorporated V and T handshapes, reflecting the days of videotapes. Younger generations produce the sign with only the V or use a sign that mimics the YouTube symbol. Men and women tend to sign differently, as well, with men typically having a bigger sign box. In addition, there are racial variations in sign language use in the United States, such as Black American Sign Language, which developed out of school segregation (McCaskill et al. 2011). Finally, as this discussion implies, sign languages are not universal. Every country has its own sign language.[3] While there is an International Sign Language that is used in settings such as the World Federation of the Deaf meetings, this is an invented *lingua*

---

[3] Because the United States was for a long time the only country where deaf individuals could receive advanced education, ASL has had a significant impact on sign languages in other countries. ASL itself arose from a merging of French Sign Language brought to the country in the nineteenth century by Laurent Clerc, who helped establish the first permanent school for the deaf in the United States, and existing regional signs.

franca. With social media and the Internet, of course, more and more exchanges take place between different national sign languages.

Defining Integrated Theatre

Many complexities exist in the process of taking any play from the script to the stage. All theatre artists know and have lived this fact. Deaf and hearing theatre is a unique genre that adds even more layers to that already elaborate process. Throughout the book we use the term *integrated theatre* to mean a very specific version of deaf and hearing theatre. This kind of theatre and the term itself need some unpacking so that we're all on the same page as we move forward.

Integrated deaf and hearing theatre can take many different forms. This variety makes it complicated to name and define it. Ask thirty different theatre artists to define integrated deaf and hearing theatre and you will end up with many different answers (with various points of overlap). Some people we interviewed favored the words *blended* or *mixed* instead of integrated. Some suggested a moniker that relates to *fusion*. Some preferred to call it simply *theatre*. To further complicate naming and defining integrated theatre, each production is its own entity with unique goals, team members, and audience bases. These factors greatly affect the type and level of integration of each production.

In our view, integrated theatre does not simply cast deaf and hearing actors and use both ASL and spoken English on stage. Instead, integrated theatre creates equality between deaf and hearing personnel, perspectives, and audiences. This is achieved when the production team includes multiple deaf individuals; when their unique contributions and access needs are respected; when the production processes are imbued with principles of deaf culture; when ASL and English are given equal prominence on stage; and when deaf and hearing audiences have equal levels of access to the production.

We want to acknowledge that the words *integrate* and *integration* will resonate differently among readers. They are politically charged words that conjure the mid-twentieth-century Civil Rights Movement in the United States. They bring to mind images of Black children being forced to attend white schools in the American South, of signs imposing racial discrimination at lunch counters, of police dogs and fire hoses being turned on human beings. They remind us that we are still a deeply divided nation reckoning with its history of racial inequality and white supremacy. We respect the legacy of these words.

Another legacy is the long history of discrimination and oppression toward deaf people in the United States. The ASL sign for integration is the same that is used for the word *mainstream*, which refers to the practice of sending deaf children to hearing schools. Until the passage of the Rehabilitation Act of 1973, children with disabilities had no legally recognized right to be accommodated in public schools. Thus, most deaf children attended residential state schools for the deaf rather than their local school. If parents chose to keep their children at home, they made do without services such as interpreters or captioning, relying on their children's ability to lipread. Section 504 of the Rehabilitation Act prohibited discrimination on the basis of disability in programs or activities that receive financial assistance from the federal Department of Education. Public schools thus became obligated to accept and accommodate deaf students. The Rehabilitation Act, followed by the Education for All Handicapped Children Act in 1975, and the Americans with Disabilities Act in 1990, resulted in the growth of mainstreaming. While mainstreaming unquestionably has had benefits, it often results in social isolation (Oliva 2004). Many mainstreamed deaf students who later find their place in the deaf community express a feeling of 'coming home' (Christie and Wilkins 2006).[4]

For successful integrated theatre to occur, this past (and present) must be recognized. In many places, barriers to inclusion and accessibility are still as strong as they've ever been. The long history of discrimination against deaf people and against ASL is one reason why integration in theatre doesn't always translate to true equality. That discrimination is still ongoing. The system itself, on the whole, is still set up for hearing artists and hearing audiences. If a company truly wants to create powerful and successful integrated theatre, it is incumbent on the hearing artists to give space to deaf perspectives. This is especially true of those at the top: the decision makers, the producers, the funders, the directors. Their actions set the tone in an integrated production and what they choose to invest in will affect how everyone else on the team decides to invest their energy too.

---

[4] This is changing in some respects, due to the advances in cochlear implant technology that allow implanted students to interact socially with their peers without mediation by interpreters or captioning.

Deaf/Mainstream Theatre Spectrum

We propose to view the current theatre landscape in the United States on a spectrum ranging from Deaf theatre to mainstream theatre. Others have proposed different continuums. Dorothy Miles and Lou Fant's distinction between sign-language theatre and *deaf theatre* has been particularly influential (1976). For Miles and Fant, sign-language theatre describes productions of texts originally written for spoken theatre, but presented simultaneously in sign language and spoken English. Deaf theatre, in contrast, refers to the presentation in sign language of material adapted to express the experience of deafness or created by deaf individuals. Miles and Fant also emphasize "a logical explanation for the presence of narrators and for the use of sign language by hearing characters" (p. 12). Another classification scheme has been suggested by Donald Bangs, who categorizes productions on a continuum between deaf and hearing cultures as expressed in the production language, performance style, and subject matter (1992).

Our spectrum includes presentation languages and cultural content, but also highlights the ratio of deaf/hearing people in production roles, as well as audience accessibility.

```
|----------------------------------------|----------------------------------------|
Deaf theatre                                                    Mainstream theatre
(deaf-led, for deaf)                                        (hearing-led, for hearing)
```

Prominent Deaf theatre companies exist throughout the United States, where deaf artists bring deaf culture and a deaf aesthetic to the creation of plays, which are intended primarily for deaf audiences. ASL is likely the primary language for the production team and artists are likely members of the deaf community. Pride in deaf culture resonates strongly and the production is shaped by a deaf perspective. Deaf theatre that is made by and for the deaf community and performed solely in ASL, without access for hearing audiences, is to the farthest left of our horizontal scale. This extreme of Deaf theatre by deaf, for deaf, without consideration for hearing audiences, is more of an ideal than an actual practice. Historical research shows that Deaf theatre productions have often sought hearing audiences. Even at Gallaudet in the 1890s, plays were often performed with voicing for hearing members of the Washington, DC community. It is likely that 'pure' Deaf theatre has only existed in the form of skits performed at deaf clubs. Full theatrical productions have almost always had hearing audiences in mind. These productions may include sign language interpreters or actors who speak (or voice) the lines, thereby making the play accessible to patrons who don't know sign language. Depending on how these voices are incorporated, the production may begin to enter integrated theatre territory. In general, productions on this end of the spectrum are more accessible than those on the farthest right because the deaf community has dealt with issues of accessibility for a long time and is therefore better equipped to consider accessibility for everyone in the room.

On the opposite side of the scale is mainstream theatre. This is the dominant form of theatre in the United States—made by hearing artists and consumed by hearing audiences. In most cases, one spoken language (often English) is used throughout the show. To comply with the Americans with Disabilities Act, one or more of the spoken performances may be made accessible to deaf people via ASL interpretation and/or captions. Typically, if interpreters are working or captions are implemented, they exist as an 'add-on' and are set to the side of the stage. This poor placement creates sightline issues for patrons relying on either interpreting or captions, and reduces the quality of actual accessibility. Oftentimes, theatre companies cite high costs and don't offer captions or interpreters for more than one performance in the run of a play, even further reducing accessibility. The accessible performance may also be scheduled on a day when ticket sales are low, such as a weekday evening or holiday evening, which limits the choices for deaf patrons. This form of theatre does not include deaf artists and is not integrated theatre.[5]

More and more common in recent years is a kind of theatre we call 'mainstream*ed* theatre.' The *ed* is important and invokes the practice of placing deaf students in hearing school systems, rather than in state schools for the deaf. This kind of theatre is situated to the left of mainstream theatre.

|--|------------------------------------|-----------|
                                                                         Mainstream*ed* theatre
                                                                      (hearing-led, deaf involved)

[5] Individuals producing mainstream theatre can still benefit from reading this book, especially Chap. 5—"Guidelines for Stage Managers and Front of House Staff".

Mainstream*ed* theatre does include at least one (but oftentimes only one) deaf artist. That person may be an actor, a lighting designer, or a dance choreographer. Any involvement by a deaf artist, even in a hearing-led, hearing-funded, hearing-attended production, touches upon integration in some way. While not integrated theatre as we define it, the presence of this artist on the team initiates (or should initiate) the process of considering language and cultural differences. The actual level of integration depends on many other factors such as the role and background of the deaf artist(s) involved and the goals of the producing organization. But the deaf artist's involvement alone means an exchange of languages, cultures, experiences, and perspectives takes place. Their deaf identity impacts their work and their work impacts the production. The key missing ingredient separating mainstream*ed* theatre from integrated theatre is that while mainstream*ed* theatre may have a deaf artist onstage or backstage, the full production may not be accessible to a deaf audience through ASL or captions. Or, access may be provided, but in ways that create an unequal experience for the deaf audience. Typically, in mainstream*ed* theatre, a deaf actor will sign the lines, while another actor will speak the lines. However, when that deaf actor leaves the stage, there is no one left to continue signing, meaning a deaf audience using ASL will only catch a fraction of the story *when and only when*, that single character is present. While access may be provided in the form of captioning devices or off-stage interpreting, the resulting split visual attention creates inequalities for deaf patrons.[6] Though the deaf actor's presence onstage does create a blended language environment, this is not a fully integrated production.

Integrated theatre as we define it exists in the middle of this spectrum. The exact range of the production depends on several factors. Is it more deaf-led or hearing-led? How many deaf artists are involved? How much decision-making authority do the deaf creatives have? What are the goals of the production? What is the purpose of the integration onstage? What is the culture of the producing theatre company—is it open-minded and inclusive of artists and audiences? Who is the target audience? How is access for the audience handled? What will be necessary for the production to be considered successful?

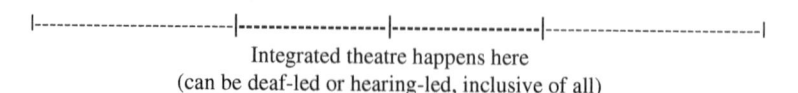

|------------------------|-------------------|------------------|--------------------------|

Integrated theatre happens here
(can be deaf-led or hearing-led, inclusive of all)

[6] This issue is discussed further in Chap. 5—"Dual Staging Models".

In general, common characteristics of an integrated production within this range are:

- The production involves deaf and hearing artists working together toward a common goal.
- The production is inclusive, as well as accessible. All perspectives are included and respected in the decision-making process. Deaf team members are not just given language access to the decision-making but are decision makers themselves.
- The production foregrounds ASL and English bilingualism in the following settings: meetings, rehearsals, shops, fittings, onstage, and backstage. This includes providing an ASL translation of the script and making use of a director of artistic sign language (DASL).
- The production involves a cultural exchange between deaf and hearing worlds that occurs in meetings, rehearsals, shops, fittings, onstage, backstage, and even outside of the theatre setting.
- ASL, spoken English, and open captions are purposefully incorporated into the telling of the story in ways that provide equal access to the production for deaf and hearing audiences.
- There is a purposeful, story-driven explanation of how characters using different languages are able to interact and communicate in the world of the play.
- All deaf characters are played by deaf actors.

A production that includes any one of these characteristics starts a decision-making process about how to best tell the story, how to achieve inclusion for all team members, how to provide access for all audience members, and how to blend two very different cultures. The integration process is woven into the creative play-making process throughout the entire life of the production from initial conception to strike. *This is integrated theatre.* Productions closer to the center of the scale have more equal participation and representation of deaf artists working alongside hearing artists. Though artists may be separated by languages or cultural differences, their equal participation alongside each other is what creates a unified production team.

The very center of the spectrum is perhaps only aspirational. Many deaf theatre makers we interviewed believe they've not yet seen a truly integrated production. Others wonder if it is indeed possible at all.

|---|---|
                        Evenly balanced integrated theatre

    A production at the very center of the scale achieves a delicate balance between deaf culture and hearing culture. The word *balanced* is critical at the center point. It means the production doesn't skew toward either group of people. This balance creates the equality of true integration. This is a production where no artist needs to reorient who they are because they are equally welcome, accepted, and respected. Deaf and hearing participation is evident and equitable at every level. The responsibility for respectful and inclusive communication is shared by all, not seen as the responsibility of the deaf team members. Deaf and hearing artists share directorial responsibilities equally. Responsibilities are also shared on the stage management team. The cast, the backstage crews, the designers, the technicians are all integrated. There is no division within the production—no one has to work to join someone else's world. It's a cohesive and equitable experience during the pre-audition time, auditions, meetings, and rehearsals. Then, both deaf and hearing audiences are welcomed into this unified experience during performances.

    Currently, it's not very realistic for many productions to occur at the very center of the spectrum. There aren't enough formally (or even informally) trained deaf directors, designers, and stage managers across the country to achieve a 50/50 balance on more than one or two production teams at a time. Despite this, hearing theatre companies should make every effort to include as many deaf creatives and crew on the team as possible.

    In summary, we define integrated theatre as:

> A deaf and hearing creative team producing a play bilingually in ASL and spoken English that resonates with and is equally accessible to both hearing and deaf audiences.

    Most integrated productions are planned from the beginning; however, a production can unexpectedly enter the territory of integrated theatre. Perhaps a deaf actor shows up in the audition room of a hearing theatre company and nails their audition. At that point, it becomes the responsibility of the producing company to accommodate their new team member (whether they be actor, designer, stage manager, etc.). Whether the integration is planned or not, our book will explain how to best go about including all artistic team members.

Defining Success in Integrated Theatre

The way to measure the success of a theatrical production varies depending on who you ask. A producer likely has a different definition of success than a director, whose metrics may be different from that of a designer or actor. Audiences exit the theatre with their own view on the success of the show, most times without ever knowing whether the artists involved considered it a success. We asked each of the people we interviewed for this book how they would define success for integrated theatre and we got many distinct answers.

Taking these various perspectives into account, we developed a broad definition of success with which to evaluate integrated productions:

> A production in which all artists feel included, supported, and able to achieve their best work, which then translates to a powerful impact on all audience members.

This definition could be applied to theatre in general, but the words *included* and *supported* are particularly important when a team is working across language and cultural barriers. In this kind of work, it's easy for people to feel excluded or unsupported—and in many cases it's entirely accidental. An integrated production is most likely to achieve success via inclusion and mutual support, when team members, especially those with decision-making power such as producers and directors, are people with *open minds* and *open hearts*. We emphasize this phrase throughout the book because many of the artists we interviewed used those signs when asked what makes for a successful integrated production. The way decision makers approach the process makes a difference for everyone involved. Below are a set of non-negotiable principles which will help start your production on a path to success.

Non-negotiable Principles

In our work of creating integrated plays, seeing integrated plays, and interviewing a wide range of artists who have created or participated in integrated plays, three non-negotiable principles have become apparent. These principles should already be ingrained in an integrated theatre process, so they especially apply to mainstream*ed* theatre on the right end of the spectrum.

1. If the play calls for a character to be deaf, it must be played by a deaf actor. No hearing person should portray a deaf person onstage, period. This goes for television and film as well as theatre. Casting a hearing person to play a deaf character steals the role from deaf artists, who have fewer casting opportunities to begin with. Beyond that, a hearing person without the lived experience of being deaf, cultural competency in the community, fluency of language, and a deep understanding of visual communication, is not able to authentically portray that character. Similar to how one should not cast a white actor to play a non-white character, one should not hire a hearing actor to play a deaf character.

2. When a deaf actor is cast, the leaders of that production must immediately plan to make production inclusive not only for that actor but also for deaf audiences. Creating inclusion means ongoing ASL interpreters need to be hired, as well as a director of artistic sign language (DASL) and, ideally, a deaf consultant. Bringing these experts in early maximizes their impact on the production's inclusiveness. Chapter 2—"Sign Language Linguistics, Poetics, and Musicality" elaborates in more detail on the work of DASLs and deaf consultants. To briefly summarize here, a DASL supports artistic choices involving deaf culture and ASL onstage. A deaf consultant fosters awareness among the production team about deaf culture, ASL, accessibility, and inclusion. When a deaf actor gets a role, word will spread and deaf patrons will attend the show to support their community member. They will expect and deserve to have high-quality access to the play in its entirety. Not providing that equitable experience is audist. Access to the performance should be available in ASL and/or *open* (not closed) captions for the entirety

of each performance and, ideally, the entirety of the run.[7] If the latter is not possible, publicity should clearly identify which performances will be interpreted and/or include captions. Implementing these strategies will help ensure full accessibility for artists and audiences.

3. From the start, high-quality communication must be an imperative. In all aspects of an integrated production, there should be 'equality of communication' between all deaf and hearing people on the creative team—no matter their role. Each individual should be able to express themselves authentically in the language of their choice and be equally received by everyone else in the room. This non-negotiable principle means that all communication is accessible (i.e., received by everyone in the room) as well as inclusive (i.e., available for everyone in the room to join at any time). Especially in theatre to the right of the spectrum, communication may not be made a true priority, leading to an inequitable experience for the deaf artists. Communication as a top priority includes hiring professional, trained interpreters with experience in theatre from the very beginning. It also means that all members of the team are actively engaged in crossing language and cultural barriers on a personal level. Everyone should invest time and energy toward community-building. This involves a willingness to learn and use ASL in meetings, rehearsals, and, perhaps more importantly, breaks or social times. Prioritizing communication is necessary for the entire life of the production. We cannot overstate the importance of equal, inclusive, and accessible communication at every step of the creative process.

Production Case Studies

We have selected four integrated productions that we will use as case studies in the book. This section introduces the case study productions with a short synopsis of each play and provides a rationale for why these specific productions were selected. Examples from these productions will highlight where certain aspects succeeded or did not succeed. A misstep in one

---

[7] Open versus closed captions will be discussed in Chap. 3—"Guidelines for Designers".

area does not mean the entire production was a failure. Instead, the mistake provides a lesson to apply to future productions. No production process is perfect and rarely is any performance perfect. Mistakes are made, things deviate from the plan, setbacks occur, and new paths forward are charted. Live theatre is an ever-changing process and product.

Spring Awakening

In 2015, an integrated revival of the musical *Spring Awakening* by Duncan Sheik and Steven Sater appeared on Broadway and ran for 135 performances. It was produced by Deaf West Theatre in Los Angeles, California under the direction of Michael Arden. The production originally opened at the Inner-City Arts Rosenthal Theater in Los Angeles (2014), later transferring to the Wallis Annenberg Center for the Performing Arts in Beverly Hills (2015), then making its way to the Brooks Atkinson Theatre (2015–2016). *Spring Awakening* was wildly successful in terms of critical recognition and popularity, and is perhaps the most well-known integrated production to date. The musical was led by a hearing director and was envisioned as integrated from the start. A professional production, it went through multiple iterations over several years as it traveled from Los Angeles to New York City. Neither writer worked on the production; however, interviews were conducted with multiple people connected to it. Both writers viewed an archival recording at the Theatre on Film and Tape Archive at the New York Public Library, New York City.

Spring Awakening is a modern rock musical based on an earlier play of the same title by German writer Frank Wedekind. Set in 1891 in Germany, the story focuses on a group of adolescent schoolchildren who are journeying through puberty with unsettled confusion, longing, and rebellion. Melchior Gabor is a brilliant star student, Wendla Bergmann is young and naive, and Moritz Stiefel is just anxious to learn what's happening to him. We follow the stories of these three and those of other teenagers. Their lives and struggles with self-discovery intersect as the young characters encounter physical and sexual abuse, rape, abortion, and even suicide. All the while, their parents and authority figures refuse to help them understand what it means to grow up.

ASL *Midsummer Night's Dream*

In 2018, the Sound Theatre Company (STC) based in Seattle, Washington produced *A Midsummer Night's Dream* by William Shakespeare under the co-direction of well-known Deaf theatre artist Howie Seago and STC founder Teresa Thuman (and with a slightly altered title). This productionced envisioned from the start as an integrated production. As an organization, STC's mission includes embracing a diversity of artists and perspectives. *ASL Midsummer* was their first integrated production; in the years since, they have worked with deaf artists on multiple projects. The production was chosen for its Shakespearean language, in contrast to the other more modern case study productions, as well as its co-director team. Neither writer worked on the production; however, interviews were conducted with multiple people connected to it. Both writers were able to view an archival recording.

A Midsummer Night's Dream is one of Shakespeare's most produced comedies. Set in Athens, it tells the story of young lovers Hermia, Lysander, Demetrius, and Helena. The four flee their parents and escape to a nearby woods. There they are unknowingly caught up in a quarrel between Oberon and Titania—the King and Queen of the Fairies. At Oberon's behest, his servant Puck causes Titania to fall in love with a human, Nick Bottom, whose head is transformed into that of a donkey. Puck also applies a love spell to the Athenian youths, initiating a major reversal of who's chasing who. Eventually all spells are lifted, the fairy royals reconcile, the young lovers find their match, and everyone attends the wedding of the duke to watch a play performed by Nick Bottom and his Rude Mechanicals.

The Music Man

In 2022, Olney Theatre Center in Olney, Maryland, produced Meredith Wilson's *The Music Man*, co-directed by Sandra Mae Frank (Deaf) and Michael Baron (hearing). From the start, *The Music Man* was envisioned as an integrated production. The idea originated in 2017 from Deaf theatre maker James Caverly, who at the time worked at Olney as a carpenter and pitched his concept to artistic director Jason Loewith. Several workshops and creative retreats later, *The Music Man* finally took the stage with a cast of eight deaf actors and eight hearing actors. Caverly himself was cast in the lead role of Harold Hill. The production was chosen because it is one of the most recent examples of an integrated production at a major regional theatre. As another musical production, it also offers opportunities for comparison with *Spring Awakening*. Neither writer worked on the production; however, interviews were conducted with multiple artists from *The Music Man* team. One writer saw the production live and both writers were able to view an archival recording.

The Music Man is set in the fictional town of River City, Iowa in 1912. The story starts with the arrival of Harold Hill, a con man hopping from town to town in the Midwest, duping townspeople into buying musical instruments, and then fleeing with their money. Harold and old friend Marcellus Washburn concoct a scheme to swindle the River City rubes, but are met with suspicion from town librarian and music teacher Marian Paroo. Harold successfully charms the town, all the while sidestepping the school board members demanding to see his professorial credentials. Despite having proof of his lies, Marian, too, is swept up by Harold and his positive effect on the town. As rumors swirl and his ruse begins to unravel, Harold professes his love to Marian and reveals himself as a con man. Instead of escaping, Harold decides to face the music. In front of the angry townspeople, Marian defends him by showing how his actions have actually benefited the town. Harold leads the band in a song and everyone cheers him in the end.

Angels in America, Part 1: Millennium Approaches

In 2021, the Rochester Institute of Technology and National Technical Institute for the Deaf (RIT/NTID) in Rochester, New York produced Tony Kushner's *Angels in America, Part 1: Millennium Approaches*.[8] The production was directed by one of the co-writers, Andy Head. From the outset, this play was envisioned as an integrated production with deaf and hearing actors, stage managers, crew, and production team members. In contrast to the other case study choices, this was an educational theatre production with specific goals about providing performance and backstage opportunities for both deaf and hearing students. Audiences that

---

[8] RIT's School of Performing Arts and NTID's Department of Performing Arts share a unique relationship. The two programs are housed in separate locations, consist of different personnel, and generally serve diverging student populations. However, the two strive to collaborate on multiple projects each academic year. *Millennium Approaches* was one of these joint ventures.

regularly attend RIT and NTID productions are a mix of deaf and hearing people. The director was a hearing director working with a deaf assistant director and DASL. The production was selected as a case study for several reasons including that, as co-writer of this book, Andy could give concrete examples of thought processes, decision-making, and rationale. The other co-writer, Jill, attended the production and can provide a deaf audience member's perspective. As a very well-known play among theatre practitioners, *Millennium Approaches* can serve as a unifying case study example.

Angels in America is set in the mid- to late 1980s. *Millennium Approaches* takes place from October to December 1985, mostly in New York City. The story focuses on the intersecting lives of several main characters. Joe Pitt, a Mormon and a closeted gay man, is married to Harper Pitt, a very isolated woman suffering from agoraphobia and an addiction to Valium. Their marriage splinters while Joe is simultaneously pursued by a fictionalized version of the famous conservative lawyer Roy Cohn. Roy wants Joe to accept a position with the Department of Justice in Washington, DC, where Joe can protect him from mounting legal investigations. At the courthouse where he clerks, Joe meets Louis Ironson, a gay Jewish man who has recently abandoned his partner of four years, Prior Walter, after Prior is diagnosed with AIDS. As Prior struggles with his worsening condition, he is visited by ghosts of long-dead ancestors and an Angel who all proclaim him to be a Prophet.

References

Bangs, Donald. 1992. The Sound of One Hand Clapping: Performing Arts and Deaf People. In *Deaf Studies for Educators Conference Proceedings*, ed. Juanita Cebe, 126–131. Washington, DC: Gallaudet University.

Bayley, Robert, Adam Schembri, and Ceil Lucas. 2011. Variation and Change in Sign Languages. *Sociolinguistics and Deaf Communities*: 61–94. https://doi.org/10.1017/CBO9781107280298.004.

Christie, Karen, and Dorothy Wilkins. 2006. Roots and Wings: ASL Poems of 'Coming Home'. In *Deaf Studies Today! Simply Complex Conference Proceedings*, 227–235. Orem: Utah Valley University.

Humphries, Tom. 1977. Communicating across Cultures (Deaf-Hearing) and Language Learning. PhD diss., Union Institute and University.

Ladd, Paddy. 2003. *Understanding Deaf Culture: In Search of Deafhood*. Bristol, UK: Multilingual Matters.

McCaskill, Carolyn, Ceil Lucas, and Joseph Hill. 2011. *The Hidden Treasure of Black ASL*. Washington, DC: Gallaudet University Press.

Miles, Dorothy S., and Louie Fant Jr. 1976. *Sign-Language Theatre and Deaf Theatre: New Definitions and Directions*. Northridge: Center on Deafness, California State University, Northridge.

Oliva, Gina. 2004. *Alone in the Mainstream: A Deaf Woman Remembers Public School*. Washington, DC: Gallaudet University Press.

Registry of Interpreters for the Deaf. n.d. Home Page. Accessed November 14, 2023. www.rid.org.

Tevenal, Stephanie, and Miako Villanueva. 2009. Are You Getting the Message?: The Effects of SimCom on the Message Received by Deaf, Hard of Hearing, and Hearing Students. *Sign Language Studies* 9 (3): 266–286.

CHAPTER 2

History and Practices of Integrated Theatre

A History of Deaf and Hearing Integrated Theatre

The Roots of Integrated Theatre

Deaf performance has been in existence for as long as deaf people have gathered together in communities, as skits, pantomime, signed songs or poems, and other informal types of drama. The emergence of formal Deaf theatre is associated with the founding of manual schools for the deaf, which began to be organized in the eighteenth century in Britain and other parts of Europe.[1] While some of the earliest accounts of deaf education come from Spain during the late sixteenth century and early seventeenth century, the first formal institutions following the manualist philosophy were founded in France and Scotland (Lane and Philip 1984; Van Cleve and Crouch 1989). The Abbe de l'Epee began teaching deaf students in France sometime between 1755 and 1760, when he established the National Institute for Deaf-Mutes. Thomas Braidwood's Academy for the Deaf and Dumb, the first school for the deaf in Britain, opened in Edinburgh

---

[1] Neither author is aware of any scholarship on Deaf theatre predating the twentieth century outside of the United Kingdom and the United States. We think it likely that Deaf theatre in other parts of the world followed a similar trajectory, but research on this topic is needed. See Further Reading for some resources on contemporary Deaf theatre outside of the United Kingdom and the United States.

in 1760. Thomas Hopkins Gallaudet, Mason Cogswell, and Laurent Clerc established the Hartford Asylum for the Education and Instruction of the Deaf and Dumb, the first permanent school for the deaf (manual or otherwise) in the United States in 1817. Schools for the deaf were established in many other countries during the late eighteenth and early nineteenth centuries. The world's first higher education institution for the deaf, the National Deaf-Mute College (now known as Gallaudet University), was founded in Washington, DC in 1864.

School archives and nineteenth-century newspaper records in Britain and the United States mention theatrical activities organized by deaf schools, suggesting the development of a dramatic tradition centered around these institutions (Lane et al. 1996). In Britain, for example, *Punch Magazine* noted a production of *Henry IV* at the Manchester Deaf Institution in 1865. The spread of formal schooling for the deaf also gave rise to associations that supported the needs and interests of deaf alumni, including socialization and entertainment. Many of these clubs organized full productions, staged readings, and other dramatic activities. For example, the British magazine *The Era* reported on an 1886 production of *Hamlet* by the South London Deaf and Dumb Benefit Dramatic Club. As can be seen in Fig. 2.1, this performance included a voice reader to the side of the stage to provide access for the approximately 600 spectators.

In the United States, schools for the deaf were also important to the development of Deaf theatre. Dramatic activities in sign language were regularly reported on and reviewed by newspapers, showing the wide interest of hearing audiences. In 1870, for example, *The New York Times* published an account of a theatrical benefit hosted by the New York Institution for the Deaf and Dumb that opined, "the performance this season was not quite equal in merit to that of last year" ("Local News"). In 1910, *The Chicago Tribune* reported on the Wisconsin School for the Deaf's staging of *The Taming of the Shrew*, calling it a great success and encouraging further productions ("Promising Invention"). Hearing audience interest in Deaf theatre is evident in other cities, as well. At Gallaudet, theatrical performances began to be organized within a few years of the college's opening. In 1884, students staged scenes from plays in shadow and open pantomime, along with other skits (Tadie 1979). Other student theatrical activities included popular genres such as melodrama, farce, and vaudeville, along with adaptations of well-known plays (Giordano 2016). Nineteenth-century residents of the District of Columbia were very interested in theatrical activities by the deaf, as evidenced by local newspaper

Fig. 2.1 "A Performance of *Hamlet* by Deaf and Dumb Actors." (*The Graphic*. Printed by Edward Joseph Mansfield, 1886)

reports and advertisements of benefit performances on the campus. This suggests that voice access was likely provided for hearing audiences.[2]

Deaf clubs in the United States also organized productions, staged readings, and other dramatic activities. These typically occurred in areas with large concentrations of deaf people, such as Chicago, New York City, Philadelphia, and Washington, DC. In New York City, several amateur Deaf theatre groups formed around the same time and put on regular performances.[3] These productions aligned with trends in hearing theatre, with genres ranging from the classics and Shakespeare, to melodrama and vaudeville, to pantomime and tableaux (Miles 1974).

---

[2] Wylene Rholetter asserts that deaf actors performed primarily for deaf audiences throughout this early period (2016). While this may be true for informal theatrical activities, archival records provide evidence of spoken English readers for formal productions, which suggests they were intended to draw both hearing and deaf audiences.

[3] In France, Henri Gaillard made an unsuccessful attempt to establish the first professional Deaf theatre in 1892 (Miles 1974).

Deaf Theatre in the Early Twentieth Century

Miles observes a shift in Deaf theatre in the period from 1900 to 1930, with a decrease in full-length productions and an increase in comedic, highly visual skits and vaudeville (1974). Within state schools for the deaf, the impact of the 1880 Milan Congress and the rapid spread of oralism likely decimated Deaf theatre.[4] However, significant developments occurred in the community from the 1930s through 1950s. The New York Theatre Guild of the Deaf and the Chicago Silent Dramatic Club were both founded in the late 1930s. In 1942, students from Gallaudet became the first deaf actors to appear on Broadway when they were invited to perform their production of *Arsenic and Old Lace* at the Fulton Theatre.[5] In 1958, under the guidance of then-Gallaudet faculty member Robert Panara, students staged a wildly popular *Hamlet* that was attended by over 700 people (normal attendance was around 250, which suggests large numbers of hearing people turned out for the show). *The Today Show* featured excerpts from the production and interviews with the cast, making this the first appearance of deaf actors on national television (Tadie 1979).

Research on the history of Deaf theatre has been largely focused on white deaf individuals and organizations. Very little is known about dramatic activities in the Black deaf community during the early to mid-twentieth century. None of the published histories of Deaf theatre mention this topic. With the digitization of newspaper archives, more and more information is emerging. For example, while searching digital newspaper archives, Jill came across a 1941 article in *The Chicago Tribune* about a production titled *The White Goddess of the Congo*. This show was produced by the Negro Silent Social Club, an organization unknown in existing Deaf theatre research. Significantly more research is needed in this area.

---

[4] The Milan Conference is a significant moment in international deaf history. At this educational conference, a mostly hearing group of educators of the deaf voted to uphold oralist over manualist educational philosophies. As a direct result of the Milan Conference, many schools for the deaf throughout the world banned instruction in sign language, made teaching speech a primary focus, and purged their staff of deaf teachers.

[5] Tyrone Giordano describes *Arsenic and Old Lace* as the "first public play in sign language to be seen in the United States" (2016). It is unclear what he means by public, since many previous sign language productions were attended by hearing audiences, going as far back as the Philadelphia All Souls' Working Peoples Club's *The Merchant of Venice* in 1894.

Emergence and Effects of the National Theatre of the Deaf

It is likely that both informal and formal dramatic activities organized by deaf people included some hearing people who were part of the community (such as teachers and CODAs). However, the National Theatre of the Deaf (NTD) was the first to integrate deaf and hearing actors for dramaturgical purposes. Founded in 1967 by a group of deaf and hearing individuals, NTD was led by hearing artistic director David Hays. In a break with tradition, Hays used hearing actors, most of whom were sign language interpreters or CODAs, onstage, thus creating the first known instances of professional integrated theatre. Voice actors both interpreted for the deaf actors and played their own roles (Baldwin 1993). The idea that deaf and hearing actors could be onstage together was revolutionary. The deaf-mute character in *Johnny Belinda*, for example, was never played by a deaf actor. Indeed, a 1950 article in the *Wisconsin State Journal* suggested that "the greatest problem" of the play is teaching hearing actors to sign ("Guild Cast"). NTD was transformative in exposing hearing audiences to stage sign language and the artistic capabilities of deaf actors. As Harlan Lane, Robert Hoffmeister, and Ben Bahan write, "In an era when oral education of the Deaf was dominant and ASL denigrated, NTD performances presented to a large audience a language of startling beauty and evident effectiveness, in addition to a cast of witty, smart and attractive Deaf people" (1996, p. 146). It also demonstrated the artistic possibilities inherent in collaborations between deaf and hearing theatre artists.

The success of NTD led to many other companies being established throughout the United States, leading to what has been called "the golden age of Deaf theatre" (Bangs 1989, p. 751). Most only lasted a few years, but a handful managed to survive for ten years or longer. These include Fairmount Theatre of the Deaf (later Cleveland SignStage Theatre) in 1975, also the first resident Deaf theatre company; and New York Deaf Theatre in 1979. Additionally, the Educational Experimental Theatre Program opened at the Rochester, New York National Technical Institute for the Deaf in 1974, while the Callier Theater of the Deaf at the University of Texas, Dallas, was founded in 1978. California State University, Northridge, which established a program for deaf students, also began producing Deaf theatre in the late 1970s. The Circuit Playhouse Theatre of the Deaf, established in Memphis, Tennessee in the early 1980s, was one of the first companies to be composed primarily of Black deaf actors. However, Onyx Theatre, established in 1989 by Black Deaf theatre artist Michelle Banks, was the first to focus on deaf people of color in its mission and programming. Other noteworthy Deaf theatre companies included Spectrum Deaf Theatre in Austin, Texas; Stage Hands in Atlanta, Georgia; Deaf Drama Project in Seattle, Washington; Chicago Theatre of the Deaf; Boston Theatre of the Deaf; Pittsburgh Theatre of the Deaf; and Theatre of Silence in Bozeman, Montana (Mow 1987a). In 1991, NTD veterans Ed Waterstreet and Linda Bove founded Deaf West Theatre in Los Angeles. Deaf West has gone on to become the second most successful Deaf theatre organization in the United States. Indeed, with two Broadway productions and multiple Tony Awards, it might be considered to have surpassed NTD. Regardless of how long-lived or successful they were, all of these companies provided more training opportunities for deaf actors and more exposure to deaf actors and ASL for hearing audiences.

Outside of Deaf theatre organizations, other professional opportunities began opening up for deaf actors. In 1978, Bruce Hlibok became the first deaf actor to appear in a hearing production on Broadway with *Runaways* (Giordano 2016). In 1979, the West Coast Performing Arts Center of the Deaf produced a mixed hearing and deaf *Equus* that also featured one of the first deaf and hearing co-directing teams, Lewis Merkin and Sue Wolf. And Mark Medoff's *Children of a Lesser God*, written for deaf actor Phyllis Frelich, opened at the Mark Taper Forum in 1979. The production moved to Broadway in 1980, leading to Frelich becoming the first deaf person to win a Tony Award in 1981. Deaf audiences turned out in droves to see ASL onstage, despite the fact that spoken English lines were not interpreted for them. *Children of a Lesser God* had a profound impact on the professional opportunities available for deaf theatre artists. As Shanny Mow writes, "Suddenly, deaf actors were in demand for the three roles in national touring companies and repertory theater productions of the play" (Mow 1987b, p. 290).

Integrated deaf and hearing theatre grew over the 1980s and 1990s. The Los Angeles Actors' Theatre production of *Trojan Women* in 1980 featured a deaf and hearing cast. *Since You Went Away*, produced in 1981 by the Creative Center for the Handicapped Theater of the Deaf for Central California, appears to be one of the first musicals with a deaf and hearing ensemble. Another significant production featured Deaf actor Howie Seago, who has become one of the most accomplished professional theatre makers in the United States, in an award-winning performance as Ajax in Peter Sellars' 1986 production of the play. Seago's appearance in the La Jolla Playhouse's *The Tempest* in 1987 is also the first known instance of a deaf actor being cast in a Shakespeare production by a hearing theatre company. In the 1990s, more and more deaf actors gained opportunities to perform in shows put on by hearing theatre companies. While many of these shows featured only one deaf actor, hearing director Colin Cox of the Los Angeles-based Will & Co. cast three deaf actors in his 1994 *A Midsummer Night's Dream*. Will & Co. was also one of the earliest to include multiple sign languages on stage, making use of Mexican Sign Language as well as ASL.

New York City-based Interborough Repertory Theater (IRT) was another early proponent of integrated theatre. Founded in 1986 by Luane Davis Haggerty and Jonathan Fluck, IRT has long focused on the creation of new work. In the early 1990s, Davis Haggerty began offering what she called Del-Sign workshops at IRT, a combination of ASL and Delsarte movement. In 1995, IRT produced *Noises Off*, featuring Deaf actors Michelle Banks, Monique Holt, Iosif Schneiderman, and others. After this show, IRT regularly produced integrated theatre (Davis Haggerty 2007). In 2007, IRT began focusing on development and performance opportunities for deaf artists and audiences (IRT n.d.).

Integrated deaf and hearing theatre rose to new heights with Deaf West Theatre's smash revival of *Big River*. Opening at Deaf West's North Hollywood theatre, *Big River* moved to the Mark Taper Forum in Los Angeles in 2001, Broadway in 2003, and ended with a national tour in 2004–2005. Featuring well-known Deaf actors Phyllis Frelich and Iosif Schneiderman, the *Big River* cast and crew also included Troy Kotsur and Alexandria Wailes, who have gone on to have illustrious careers in theatre and film. The ASL team included NTD alum and accomplished Deaf actors Linda Bove and Freda Norman, along with Betsy Ford and Anthony Natale. *Big River* was nominated for and won numerous awards in Los Angeles and on Broadway, including a Tony for Best Revival of a Musical in 2004. Deaf West repeated its success with *Spring Awakening*, which opened in Los Angeles in 2014 and moved to Broadway in 2015. Many from the *Spring Awakening* cast have become leaders in Deaf theatre and entertainment, including Daniel Durant, Joshua Castille, Sandra Mae Frank, Russell Harvard, and Amelia Hensley. Veteran Deaf actors Troy Kotsur and Marlee Matlin also starred in the Los Angeles and Broadway casts, respectively. Other Deaf theatre artists involved in *Spring Awakening* include Alexandria Wailes as associate choreographer (in what may be the first instance of a deaf person hired for a non-DASL, non-performance role in a Broadway production); Elizabeth Green, Anthony Natale, and Shoshannah Stern as ASL Masters; and Linda Bove as ASL Consultant.

Deaf Theatre in the Twenty-First Century

Although acting opportunities for deaf theatre artists continue to expand in the twenty-first century, growth has been slow in other roles. Despite its emphasis on deaf-centered storytelling, Deaf West's *Big River* and *Spring Awakening* were solo directed by hearing individuals, as were more recent productions of *Fidelio* (2022, in collaboration with Los Angeles Philharmonic) and *Oedipus* (2022). The 2018 Broadway revival of *Children of a Lesser God* also had a hearing director. The 1942 Gallaudet *Arsenic and Old Lace*, which made a one-night appearance at the Fulton Theatre, thus remains the only deaf-led production on Broadway.[6] In regional theatre, however, a co-directorship model has started to spread. Howie Seago co-directed *ASL Midsummer Night's Dream* for the Seattle-based Sound Theatre Company in 2018. Deaf Austin Theatre also adopted the co-director model successfully for *Next to Normal* (2019) and *Cinderella* (2023). Most notably, Olney Theatre Center's 2022 *The Music Man* was co-directed by a deaf and hearing team, Sandra Mae Frank and Michael Baron. The Maryland-based company won three 2023 regional awards for this production, including Outstanding Director, Musical for Frank and Baron; Outstanding Lead Performer, Musical for James Caverly as Harold Hill; and Outstanding Ensemble, Musical. Solo directing opportunities for hearing-centered companies are also starting to emerge. Most recently, Howie Seago solo-directed Deaf playwright Aimee Chou's *Autocorrect Thinks I'm Dead* for Sound Theatre Company in 2023. This paucity of examples shows how far deaf directors have to go to achieve equity with their hearing peers.

Deaf theatre designers also have limited opportunities, although this is due in part to the very small number of trained professionals. Gallaudet faculty Annie Wiegand is one of the only deaf professional lighting designers in the United States, while NTID faculty member Sacha Glasser does lighting design for the institute's productions. San Diego-based Sean

---

[6] The production was directed by Gallaudet student Archie Stack, with assistance from Gallaudet deaf faculty Frederick Hughes and Margaret Yoder. Upon arriving in New York City, the cast rehearsed for three days with Bretaigne Windust, who directed the original Broadway production of the play in 1941 (Tadie 1979).

Fanning, New York City-based Jonathan Mesich, and DC-based Ethan Sinnott (also on the faculty at Gallaudet) are currently the only deaf scenic designers working in professional theatre. Deaf costume and projection designers are even more scarce.

Deaf playwrights have also faced limited opportunities to have their work produced by both hearing and Deaf theatre companies. Throughout its history, NTD has focused on translations or adaptations of plays by hearing authors. NTD has only produced three deaf-authored scripts to date, *My Third Eye* (1971), *Parade* (1975), and *Deafenstein* (2020, 2021). However, not many deaf-authored plays existed prior to the 1970s. Eric Malzkuhn's *Sounds of Silence* (1955) may be the earliest full-length, deaf-centered play in the United States.[7] Douglas Burke, founder of the Dramatics Guild of the District of Columbia Club of the Deaf, wrote several original plays, including *The Good Peddler* (1961), while accomplished actor and director Gilbert Eastman published a deaf-centered adaptation of *Pygmalion*, titled *Sign Me Alice* in 1973. NTD's annual Deaf Playwrights Conference, 1977–1982, offered a unique opportunity for deaf writers to develop scripts (Baldwin 1993). Prior to the passage of the Americans with Disabilities Act in 1990, deaf writers had no legal right to accommodations at writers conferences and retreats. The Deaf Playwrights Conference was one of the only accessible playwriting development opportunities. Notable alumni of the conference included Stephen Baldwin, Donald Bangs, Bob Daniels, Bruce Hlibok, Lynn Jacobowitz, and Shanny Mow (Baldwin 1993). New York Deaf Theatre also ran the Sam Edwards Deaf Playwrights Festival from the 1970s to the 1990s (Conley 2023). In the 1980s, Bernard Bragg published the well-known *Tales from the Clubroom* (1980), co-authored with Eugene Bergman. Also in the 1980s, several of Bruce Hlibok's deaf-centered plays were produced off Broadway, including *Going Home* (1980) and *The Deaf Mute Howls* (1988).

The number of deaf-authored and deaf-centered plays continued to grow in the 1990s, with works created by Bob Daniels, Willy Conley, Terry Galloway, Monique Holt, Raymond Luczak, Howie Seago, and Michele Verhoosky. Daniels' *I Didn't Hear That Color* (1990) was the first play to focus on the Black deaf experience, followed by Michelle Banks'

---

[7] Howard Terry published *The Dream* in 1912, but this play has no deaf themes or characters. Deaf Irish playwright Teresa Deevy wrote many plays at the beginning of the twentieth century and throughout her career. However, Deevy did not know sign language and none of her plays incorporated deaf themes or characters (Conley 2023).

Reflections of a Black Deaf Woman (1996). With Jade Bryant, Banks also co-wrote *Black Women Stories: One Deaf Experience*, an adaptation of stories and poems by Black female writers, for Onyx Theatre in the 1990s.

Today, there are many active deaf playwrights from diverse backgrounds. Conley, Holt, Luczak, and Seago remain active and are joined by Joshua Castille and Jules Dameron; James Caverly and Andrew Morrill; Aimee Chou, Sabina England, Mervin Primeaux-O'Bryant, Rob Roth, and Garrett Zuercher. Under Banks' guidance, VOCA has encouraged the creation of original work by deaf people of color, including Stella Antonio's *In the Eyes of a Deaf Child* (2023) as well as *ISM* (2021) and *ISM II* (2023), a series of monologues created by the VOCA ensemble. However, deaf playwrights rarely have their work produced by mainstream theatre companies. Joshua Castille and Jules Dameron's *What Is Emily Drawing?* (Illusion Theater, 2022) and Aimee Chou's *Autocorrect Thinks I'm Dead* (Sound Theatre Company, 2023) are two recent exceptions. Deaf writers also continue to have limited access to mainstream play development opportunities. Within the deaf community, few opportunities for play development exist. In 1996 and 1998, NTID organized Deaf Creators Play Festivals (DCPF) to support the growth of deaf playwrights. After Bruce Hlibok's death in 1995, his family created an endowed fund at Gallaudet University to offer the Bruce Hlibok Playwriting Competition for students. New York Deaf Theatre relaunched its deaf play festival in 2015 as the Sam Edwards New Play Reading series. In a recent effort to redress the lack of professional development opportunities for deaf playwrights, Peter Cook, Monique Holt, and Aaron Kelstone worked with Deaf theatre companies in the United States and Canada to organize a series of 10-minute play festivals in 2021. Several works from these festivals were selected to be expanded into one-act plays in the relaunched DCPF at NTID in 2022. These are a drop in the bucket, compared to what is available for hearing playwrights.

Protactile Theatre

One very positive recent development has been the growth of Protactile theatre, or theatre by and for DeafBlind people. Protactile (PT) was founded in Seattle in 2007, by aj granda and Jelica Nuccio. While working together at the DeafBlind Service Center, granda and Nuccio began developing ways of communicating with each other directly, without relying on interpreters. This led them to begin thinking about autonomy for

DeafBlind individuals and respect for their unique communication needs. While PT practices are still developing, one of the most important is contact space. ASL uses the space around the body, while PT uses the body itself. Arms, chest area, and legs are used to express linguistic, emotional, and visual information. granda and Nuccio emphasize that PT is not just "a way of explaining things to DeafBlind people that they can't see" but a way of connecting people through shared experiences (2018, p. 14). In 2017, Jasper Norman and Yashaira Romilus developed a PT theatrical adaptation of *The Gift of the Magi* while students in Nuccio's training program. After this experience, Norman and Romilus founded Protactile Theatre and began creating and touring performances for DeafBlind audiences across the country. In 2018, Norman and Romilus collaborated with Jill to produce an adaptation of *Romeo and Juliet* during the Protactile Theatre Institute, funded by a grant from the National Endowment of the Arts and Gallaudet University. In 2019, the three collaborated again on an adaptation of *Rapunzel*. With support from the NEA, the New York State Council on the Arts, and the National Technical Institute for the Deaf, *Rapunzel* was performed at schools for the deaf in New York, Minnesota, and the District of Columbia in 2023.

The Current Moment

Deaf theatre has come a long way since its early days. The increasing popularity of integrated deaf and hearing productions has opened up many new opportunities for deaf actors and DASLs. Although opportunities for deaf directors and deaf playwrights in the mainstream theatre community are still limited, there are signs of growth there also. But Deaf theatre itself faces a number of challenges that make its future uncertain. While Deaf Austin Theatre and VOCA are flourishing, New York Deaf Theatre (NYDT) and NTD are struggling. Neither NTD, NYDT, nor Deaf West offered any public programming in 2023. Many Deaf theatre companies have gone out of business, including Fairmount/Cleveland SignStage, Rocky Mountain Deaf Theatre, and more. As it is for hearing theatre companies, funding is a constant challenge. The 'golden age of Deaf theatre' occurred in part because the federal Department of Education designated significant funds for Deaf theatre for nearly thirty years. After this funding was cut in 2006, companies struggled to replace this source of support (Steketee 2016). Deaf West and NYDT managed to survive, while NTD shuttered its mainstage company and focused on its youth theatre branch.

The closure of NTD's summer acting school, the only professional training program for deaf actors, greatly reduced the development of new talent. The pipeline has also been impacted by declining enrollments at Gallaudet and NTID. This is due, ironically, to the impact of the Americans with Disabilities Act, which mandated that all higher educational institutions receiving federal funds provide reasonable accommodations for students. Suddenly, deaf college students had many choices besides Gallaudet, NTID, and a handful of deaf programs at hearing colleges. The ADA also required K-12 programs to educate students with disabilities in the "least restrictive environment," which was interpreted to mean mainstream programs for deaf students. In addition, an increase in the number of children receiving cochlear implants has led to more parents choosing oral methods and education. As a result, the number of children who are mainstreamed or who attend their local schools as 'solitaires' has shot up, while enrollment at state schools for the deaf has declined, to the point that several have closed. Mainstreamed students often attend hearing colleges as well, thus missing out on exposure to deaf theatre in their school years. Expanded educational choices definitely have positives. And many individuals who were mainstreamed as children later find their way to the deaf community. Nonetheless, these developments have undoubtedly impacted the foundation on which Deaf theatre has historically rested.

Dual Staging Models

Approaches to the integration of deaf and hearing actors have changed over the years. Prior to NTD, access to Deaf theatre for hearing audiences was almost exclusively provided by readers positioned off or to the side of the stage. By utilizing hearing actors who both voiced for the deaf actors and played their own roles, NTD opened up new artistic opportunities in what we are calling *dual staging*. Theatres founded after NTD played with different possibilities. Fairmount Deaf Theatre/Cleveland SignStage Theatre (CSST), founded by Deaf actor Brian Kilpatrick and hearing theatre artist Charles St. Clair, was an early experimenter with dual staging models to accomplish its mission of creating "a cultural adaptation, a union of the cultures of the ear and the eye" (Zachary 1995, p. 130). These experiments included one production with two separate casts, one signing, one speaking, performing simultaneously and side by side on identical sets. In *The Fourposter*, set in a bedroom, deaf actors took center stage while voice actors were visible through family picture frames. For a production of Neil Simon's *Fools*, signing actors had a speaking actor and vice versa, but the language modality of the individual actors changed throughout the performance (Zachary 1995). Several of the dual staging models Fairmount/CSST experimented with are still popular today.

This section covers the most typical approaches for staging integrated theatre, with examples from a variety of shows. A production may use more than one dual staging model during a single performance. Alternatively, productions may use a model that doesn't neatly fit into the categories we outline here, or may create a hybrid version that pulls from different elements of the approaches we discuss. Nonetheless, the models we describe can serve as a starting place for developing an initial concept that fits the unique artistic aspects of each production. The first three models we describe focus on a close connection between a deaf and hearing actor pair. Others may define these approaches differently, but for us, the key element is the use of two actors to portray a single character. These models are double casting, shadowing, and 'voice of'.

Double Casting

Double casting is an approach to integration in which two actors perform the same role onstage at the same time. One deaf and one hearing actor function as two physical representations of the same character—almost like they're looking into a mirror. The two actors equally embody the character, sharing similar blocking, motivation, timing of lines, and reactions. Often their costumes are linked by style, color, pattern, or accessory. In her book *Disability and Theatre*, Stephanie Barton-Farcas refers to this method as co-playing. "My thought behind creating co-playing was to enable not only deaf and hearing actors to act together, but to be able to present the project to a deaf and hearing audience simultaneously. Thus, one deaf and one hearing actor would simultaneously act the same role at the same time" (2018, p. 40).

A recent example from RIT and NTID Performing Arts utilized double casting. In 2022, a production of the musical *In the Heights* directed by Luane Davis Haggerty double-cast all principle and supporting characters, including Usnavi, Vanessa, Benny, Nina, Abuela Claudia, and even Graffiti Pete. Each character was simultaneously played by two actors—one signing and one speaking. With a large-cast musical and many bodies sharing the stage, the production team primarily linked the co-playing actors through costumes. As seen in Fig. 2.2, the two actors playing Usnavi, for example, wore nearly identical outfits. The primary difference between them was the color of their shirts, which were specifically chosen to contrast with actors' skin tones.

As with all the models of integration we discuss, double casting has advantages and disadvantages. The advantages of double casting include the potential to provide equal access for both deaf and hearing audiences;

Fig. 2.2 Malik Paris (*left*) and Jheovani Montanez as double-cast actors playing Usnavi in *In the Heights* at the National Technical Institute for the Deaf, Rochester Institute of Technology. (Photo: Erin Auble)

and for deaf and hearing actors to share the spotlight equally.[8] Double casting creates the opportunity for unique artistic moments when the co-playing actors interact with each other, which can be very effective in terms of character or thematic development. The disadvantages include the difficulty of directing and blocking two performances so that they support, rather than detract from each other. If one actor finishes their lines ahead of the other, for example, or the actors have different emotional registers, the double casting will not succeed artistically. The actor pairs must be willing to work collaboratively to create a cohesive co-performance. Another drawback is that for the hearing audience, their experience of the quality of the deaf actor's performance will be influenced by the quality of the hearing actor's. The issue is inherent in all integrated theatre models that use voicing to provide access to signed lines for hearing audiences. The perception of the deaf actor's performance is inextricably tied to the hearing actor's performance. Double casting can also take away already infrequent opportunities for deaf actors to be in the spotlight. Finally, double casting is expensive, as two sets of actors are required.

Shadowing

In the shadowing model of integration, a deaf actor is paired with a hearing actor or a hearing actor is paired with a deaf actor, but only one of them is the primary actor playing the role. Like a shadow, the secondary actor typically moves with the primary actor and maintains a degree of physical closeness. Compared to double casting, this model keeps the audience focused on only one primary actor instead of both actors as equals. Despite this, shadowing is similar to double casting in that both actors/characters are clearly and logically connected. Oftentimes, shadow characters exist in the world of the play and are costumed, but they may or may not be acknowledged by the primary characters. Shadow characters typically fall into one of two types:

1. The shadow is assumed to be just that: the shadow of the primary character and as such the two actors are playing the same character—albeit only one is the primary focus for the audience.

---

[8] We write potential because the actual implementation may significantly undermine the advantages of the approach to integration in this and all of the models discussed.

2. The shadow is its own autonomous character who acts more as an observer of the action onstage, while being tasked with providing access to the primary character's lines and matching whatever emotion they convey.

In either case, shadows typically do not speak their own independent lines or appear in scenes separate from the primary actor.[9] Fig. 2.3 illustrates the shadowing model as utilized in the National Technical Institute for the Deaf, Rochester Institute of Technology production of *Angels in America: Millennium Approaches.*

The shadow model was used in the RIT and NTID Performing Arts production of *Angels in America, Part 1: Millennium Approaches.* The

Fig. 2.3 Declan McHale (*left*) as a voicing Guardian Angel shadowing Samuel Langshteyn as Prior Walter in *Angels in America, Part 1: Millennium Approaches* at the Rochester Institute of Technology. (Photo: A. Sue Weisler, RIT)

---

[9] Shadow casting is different from shadow or zone interpreting, in which interpreters are placed on the stage to provide voicing for deaf actors. The interpreters may be dressed in black or in costume, but they are not actors taking on the role of a character.

director and assistant director created a staging concept called the Host of Guardian Angels, which followed the latter type of shadowing.[10] During the performance, a group of shadow actors inhabited the stage to provide accessibility to audience members. Some of these actors were tasked with providing a voice for signing characters, like Harper Pitt. Other actors were tasked with providing sign language for speaking characters, such as Roy Cohn. These Guardian Angels maintained close proximity to the primary actors but limited their physical movements to reduce distraction. They did not present a mirrored image of the primary character as in double casting. Instead, each was their own independent character with specific costumes, movements, and intentions. As a group, the Guardian Angels shared a similar costuming look and similar physical characteristics, such as how they stood, sat, and moved. These choices reinforced cohesion among the group of angelic characters. Individually, they were united with their primary actor in expressing lines. However, as separate characters, they developed their own, unique perspective on the action in each scene. During blocking, signing shadow actors were situated on higher levels of the set, still near the primary actor but positioned to avoid sightline conflicts. Voicing shadow actors typically stood just upstage of the primary actor or sat near them without blocking the signing. In both cases, the shadow actors followed the acting impulses of the primary actors.

The shadowing model has a number of benefits. It allows for more focus on the primary actor, while still providing access within the world of the play. This can be more artistically cohesive than interpreters seated off stage, for example. If the primary actors are hearing, deaf shadow actors provide close proximity access. This is ideal and reduces the problem of split visual attention. However, there are some potential drawbacks to the shadowing model. For hearing audiences, the perception of the deaf actor's performance is still tied to the hearing actor's performance. Another issue is the possibility of obstructed sightlines. Hearing shadow actors can likely be heard from anywhere onstage, especially if they're using a mic. Therefore, it's relatively easy for them to stay upstage of the primary actor. However, a deaf shadow actor needs to be seen by the audience and this may affect how they are blocked around the primary actor. When using the shadowing model, directors need to ensure the audience always has a clear view of the signing actor.

The shadowing approach may also limit access for deaf audiences. Due to cost, hearing theatre companies typically will only provide voicing

[10] This conceptual choice is detailed further in Chap. 3—"Pre-audition Period".

shadows for deaf actors. Without signing shadows for the hearing actors, however, the production's accessibility for deaf audiences is detrimentally impacted. In some productions, no form of access to spoken English lines is provided for deaf audiences at all. In others, access is provided via interpreters, captioning placed to the side of the stage, or handheld captioning devices. This creates the problem of split visual attention, when deaf audiences must 'ping pong' their gaze between the stage and the access mechanism. In this situation, deaf audiences inevitably lose a bit of the story each time the dialogue shifts between a character speaking on stage and a character signing on stage. If the shadowing model is used only to provide voices for deaf actors, careful attention should be given early in the process to how access for deaf audiences is provided for lines delivered by characters who are not shadowed.

'Voice Of'

Another approach to pairing deaf and hearing actors is the 'voice of' approach popularized by Deaf West Theatre. Linda Bove and Ed Waterstreet founded Deaf West Theatre intending to create a strong deaf center (Giordano 2016). Access for hearing audiences was originally provided by offstage voicing accessed via headsets. Within a few years, however, Deaf West began placing speaking actors onstage or above stage, later adopting what artistic director DJ Kurs calls the 'voice of' approach. In this model, hearing actors playing characters onstage provide voicing for deaf actors. This approach has some similarities to how we define the shadowing approach, in that deaf and hearing actors are paired together. One main divergence is that the actor playing the 'voice of' character is also portraying *their own character separately*. As shown in Fig. 2.4, one example of this is in *Big River*, where Deaf actor Tyrone Giordano played main character Huck Finn. The Voice of Huck was played by hearing actor Daniel Jenkins, who also played Mark Twain. Though there is an established connection throughout the musical between Huck and the Voice of Huck, Mark Twain is a separately scripted character with his own character development and lines. In our view, this distinction is what separates 'voice of' from shadowing. 'Voice of' characters also speak their own lines and appear in scenes separate from the actor they are voicing for. Shadow actors only appear with their assigned primary character. Depending on the production, there may be a clear dramaturgical reason for the 'voice

Fig. 2.4 Tyrone Giordano (*left*) as Huck Finn and Daniel Jenkins as Mark Twain/Voice of Huck in *Big River* at the American Airlines Theatre. (Photo: Joan Marcus)

of' to be assigned to a certain character. In other cases, it may not be made explicit why these two characters are connected.

The 'voice of' approach can be more artistically cohesive than shadowing, because the voicers exist as scripted characters in their own right. This approach works well with plays that have narrators or to which a narrator can be added. In Deaf West's *Big River*, Mark Twain was both narrator and 'voice of' Huck. However, the challenge then emerges of providing access to the narrator's own lines. Not every play can logically accommodate a narrator, either. Finally, conflicts can arise when the 'voice of' character also has its own lines in the same scene.

Double-casting, shadowing, and 'voice of' models of integration emphasize unity and connection between hearing and deaf actor pairs. They require financial resources and willingness on the part of actors to work together closely. Other models of integration allow for more fluidity and cost savings in how language access is provided, by moving away from consistent pairing. These models are discussed next.

Disconnected Persona

In this model, much less connection exists between characters/actors compared to the models already discussed—hence 'disconnected.' This model functions more pragmatically than others, with accessibility as the main goal and dramaturgical considerations having less or little importance. The audience's attention is focused on one physical body onstage while accessibility is provided through a second body somewhere else. In accomplishing this, one actor is assigned to provide voicing or signing for another actor and their main task is to interpret that primary actor's choices. The connection between these deaf and hearing actors is practical, rather than character-driven. The assignment may be consistent throughout the play or it may be opportunistic, making use of whoever is available within a given scene to provide language access. This model is often used when the primary actor is deaf. In our experience, the disconnected persona approach has three main variations.

1. The disconnected persona actor cannot be seen by the audience (if voicing) or is onstage but not acknowledged in the world of the play. The audience is expected to pretend the person is not really there. If a deaf actor is the primary actor, then a voicing actor speaks the lines away from the stage focal point—this could be a less prominent onstage position, the offstage wings, a hidden place in the set, or even from the audience. When the primary actor is speaking, typically there is a stage position where the disconnected persona signing actor can be easily seen. This location may be built into the set, or as a second level upstage, or off to either side of the stage. Because the audience needs to see the signing actor for accessibility, this actor remains present throughout the scene but is removed from the story.[11]
2. The disconnected persona actor exists onstage as a minor or ensemble character, but their voicing support is masked or hidden so the audience doesn't know where the voice is coming from. In this scenario, one disconnected persona actor may voice for multiple signing characters.

---

[11] This staging can create access issues for deaf audiences, however, due to the lack of proximity between the voice and sign actors. This issue is discussed further in "Artistic Challenges and Issues".

3. The disconnected persona is a collection of voicing actors who take turns as the voice when it's most convenient—a kind of voicing by committee. In this scenario, actors switch off voicing responsibilities depending on who can most easily take over the voice and remain obscured from the audience.

In each of these variations, the actor taking on the disconnected persona must align their performance with that of the primary actor by matching their emotions, choices, and impulses.

The disconnected persona model was used in Seattle-based ACT Theatre's 2019 *Romeo + Juliet*. Deaf actor Joshua Castille played Romeo and Deaf actor Howie Seago played Friar Lawrence. Voicing for both was provided by several different actors, usually whoever was on stage with Castille and Seago at the same time. Fig. 2.5 shows the use of the third variation of the disconnected persona model. In many scenes, this was Mercutio or a member of the Montague family. In other scenes, an actor would come near the stage to voice (the production was in the round).

One advantage of the disconnected persona model is that it can give the deaf actor more ownership over the role and the performance. If the audience doesn't know where the voice is coming from, it's not attached to any particular actor. The deaf actor doesn't have to share the spotlight. The deaf actor can also assert ownership of the voicing. For example, in Deaf West's 2022 *Oedipus*, several deaf actors visually gave permission for the voice actors to begin voicing by looking back at them. This concept worked because of the status differences between the characters portrayed by the deaf actors and the characters portrayed by the hearing actors. Other advantages of the disconnected persona model include lessening the financial impact of providing access, by making double use of actors cast as minor or ensemble characters. Finally, the disconnected persona role is more flexible than the other models already discussed, because lines can be divided between multiple minor characters.

This flexibility does have potential drawbacks, though. Using multiple actors to provide voicing for one character may be perceived negatively by hearing audiences. For example, Michael Shurgot writes in a review of *Romeo + Juliet* that having multiple voice actors for Romeo undermined his coherence as a character for hearing audiences (2019). Another drawback is that the disconnected persona approach may be more likely than other models to draw on actors in the existing cast, rather than bringing in actors who have prior knowledge of ASL, to provide access for deaf

Fig. 2.5 Howie Seago (*left*) as Friar Lawrence in *Romeo + Juliet* at the Allen Theatre. Voicing is provided by ensemble characters in the scene. (Photo: Chris Bennion)

audiences. If a director is choosing from 'who's available,' this can be an accessibility barrier. Not all actors have the aptitude to quickly learn and accurately produce sign language. Even with intensive practice, actors without prior knowledge of sign language are unlikely to master essential features such as facial expressions, intonation, and correct prosody. This may result in the stage ASL being difficult for deaf audiences to understand.[12]

---

[12] This issue is discussed further in "Artistic Challenges and Issues".

Interpreter-Characters

In this model, hearing characters interpret for a deaf character. The interpreter role may be a logical element of the story or a new character may be created with the sole purpose of interpreting for a deaf character. Another version of this approach is when a hearing character in the story temporarily steps into an interpreting role for a deaf character. Overall, this dual staging approach occurs more often in plays with one deaf actor in an otherwise hearing cast. The deaf character needs to communicate with hearing characters onstage and an interpreter-character facilitates that communication. This approach differs from shadowing, 'voice of,' and disconnected persona models in that the interpreter-character's role is not primarily envisioned as providing access for the audience. Instead, the interpreter-character mediates communication between characters in the play, which may also happen to provide access for the audience.

In the 2018 RIT and NTID Performing Arts production of *Cabaret*, Sally Bowles was portrayed as a deaf character. The Kit Kat Klub was envisioned as a place where deaf and hearing people could mingle, sheltered from the oppressive German government. Cliff Bradshaw was played as a hearing character by a hearing actor. When Sally and Cliff first met, Cliff knew little sign language and so an interpreter facilitated their early conversations. The directing team took the interpreter relationship a step further and had Sally's interpreter always present with her, thus providing accessibility for all non-signing characters (and audience members). Because many of Sally's musical numbers occur in the club with her performing to that night's actual theatre audience, her interpreter became one of the Kit Kat Girls who danced right along with her, speaking every line and singing every song, but always giving Sally the primary spotlight, as illustrated in Fig. 2.6. A backstory was invented to explain both their relationship and how this new character operated in the rest of play.

When relying on the interpreter-character approach, it's important to establish who the interpreter is and who are they interpreting for. It's also essential to keep that relationship consistent. Under these conditions, the audience knows what to expect from that specific character/relationship. Suppose a new character unexpectedly starts to interpret for a deaf character. Audiences will be jolted by this sudden change in storytelling.

There are several potential pitfalls with this approach. First, if the actor cast is not fluent in sign language, this choice will not be believable for deaf audiences. And if the interpreter-character is also being used to

Fig. 2.6 Victoria Covell (*left*) as Sally Bowles and Gabrielle Robinson (*background*) as Sally's interpreter in *Cabaret* at the Rochester Institute of Technology. (Photo: Erin Gallagher)

provide access for the deaf audience, the lack of fluency in ASL will create an inequality between the deaf audience's experience and the hearing audience's. Another possible issue with this approach is what happens when the deaf character leaves the scene. If their interpreter also exits, the audience is left without anyone signing onstage. When this occurs, another mode of access must be provided. If not, then access for the deaf audience is negatively impacted.

For example, in the 2019 Broadway production of *King Lear*, Deaf actor Russell Harvard played the Duke of Cornwall. As he was the only deaf character in the play, the role of Cornwall's aide in Shakespeare's original play was expanded to include interpreting for Cornwall. The aide, played by Michael Arden, signed all the spoken lines to Cornwall and voiced Cornwall's signed lines for the other hearing characters. Though the aide was present for Cornwall's scenes, it did not make dramaturgical sense for him to be present for all scenes. So, the scenes without Cornwall were only accessible to deaf audiences via GalaPro captioning.[13] This access approach created the problem of split visual attention that we discussed earlier.

Simultaneous Communication (SimCom)

Simultaneous Communication, or SimCom, is the term for when a person signs and speaks at the same time. At first glance, this may seem to be the best mode of integration: one actor who can both speak and sign their lines simultaneously. However, as mentioned in Chap. 1, ASL and English are their own unique languages with distinct grammatical structures and it is incredibly difficult to communicate effectively in both modes at the same time.[14] Due to the complexity of using two languages at once, a person attempting to SimCom will generally favor their native language. The secondary language will become fragmented and difficult to understand. Actors tasked with SimCom do have the benefit of memorizing and rehearsing their lines. They're not using two languages at once on the fly and so they can make adjustments in an effort to clearly communicate in both. But even when well-rehearsed, beyond acting in two languages at once, actors also will be following the blocking patterns, performing their stage business, and remaining open to reacting to the impulses of their scene partners. That's a lot for one mind to manage all at once.

While SimCom may be useful onstage in certain specific and limited situations, it often results in unequal access for deaf audiences. Hearing actors who SimCom are usually not fluent in ASL. Their sign production is likely to be unclear and they are likely to be missing essential semantic features such as facial expressions. Additionally, voicing in English means that actors cannot include mouth morphemes, which convey important semantic information. Add in the dominance of English syntax over ASL syntax and the result is usually signing that is barely comprehensible for deaf patrons. Because of this, we suggest very careful consideration among members of the artistic team about using SimCom in a production. Be mindful of how SimCom fits into the story, how often characters are using SimCom, and the background of the actors being asked to SimCom. If

---

[13] GalaPro is a handheld captioning device that scrolls a few lines of text at a time. The positives and negatives of GalaPro are discussed in Chap. 5—"Guidelines for Stage Managers and Front of House Staff".

[14] The grammatical structure of ASL is discussed in more detail in the next section of this chapter.

SimCom is used, we strongly recommend using open captions as well to support deaf audience access.

To return to the *Cabaret* example: throughout the story, Sally and Cliff spend months together in an intimate relationship. It made sense to the directing team that Cliff would begin to learn sign language from Sally, which would reduce the need for an interpreter between them. Not to mention it eventually became awkward for Sally's interpreter to be present in their scenes. The actor playing Cliff was a hearing person who already knew ASL, so he could sign more comfortably than Cliff could reasonably learn in the span of a few months. One misstep of the team is that Cliff was eventually tasked with SimComming his lines in addition to interpreting for Sally. While this might have made sense in the context of the scenes and worked for the characters, it did not work for all audiences. The actor playing Cliff was a hearing person with English as his first language, and any discrepancies in his SimCom favored English while hindering ASL. This is not to condemn the extreme hard work of that actor, but rather to point out a gaffe in the overall concept. Were all lines communicated in both spoken English and ASL? Yes. Were they communicated as clearly as possible? No. This decision ultimately limited equal language and story access for the deaf audience, thus negatively impacting their playgoing experience. The decision was in opposition to one of our non-negotiable principles, because it did not fully prioritize communication for the entire audience.

Signing-Centered

There's a noticeable trend happening recently in integrated productions to perform certain roles, moments of roles, or even entire scenes only in ASL, without voicing. In these situations, captions are used to provide accessibility for non-signing audience members. This method, which we call signing-centered, allows deaf performers to fully take the spotlight without being tethered to a voice.

This model has many positives. Any approach to syncing sign and voice onstage asks both actors to modify themselves to fit the other person. They're asked to slow down or speed up, to pause or to skip ahead, in order to stay aligned with their partner. This game of catch up can easily take priority in an actor's mind. They start worrying, "Am I in tandem with my partner?" instead of thinking about their character's motivation or obstacles. Because ASL and English are separate languages, it's impossible to sync up one hundred percent of the time. Audiences may interpret timing discrepancies between two actors as mistakes—when, in fact, they're not. Finally, there are many, many opportunities for hearing actors to take the spotlight. Adopting this approach is one way to remove burden and restraint from deaf actors and put them squarely center stage.

One potential downside of this model for hearing audiences is that they are asked to take in two sources of visual information—the actor's signed performance and the captioning. While deaf people hone this skill in various ways, such as watching television with closed captioning, most hearing people don't. Some hearing audiences may dislike this additional cognitive burden.

The Music Man at Olney Theatre Center in 2022 (Fig. 2.7) utilized the signing-centered model to great effect. Many scenes occurred throughout

Fig. 2.7 Adelina Mitchell (*left*) as Marian Paroo and James Caverly as Harold Hill in *The Music Man* at Olney Theatre Center. (Photo: ©Teresa Castracane Photography)

the play where two characters—either both deaf or one deaf, one hearing—communicated using only ASL, without voice. Marian Paroo and Harold Hill, Marcellus Washburn and Harold Hill, and Mayor Shinn and Harold Hill all communicated in this way. All the while, captions were provided upstage center for non-signing audience members to follow along. One must give a lot of credit to Olney for taking this approach and situating so many conversations only in ASL.

Theatre companies may be reluctant to take the signing-centered approach, fearing that hearing audience members, who make up the majority of patrons, may not attend without full voice access to the production. The smash success of Olney's *The Music Man* proves that hearing audiences are willing to take on this challenge. The production sold out multiple shows, was featured on national news, and won multiple regional theatre awards.

Not providing access to signed lines can also be used to great artistic effect. For example, in Ravi Jain's 2019 *Prince Hamlet*, Deaf actor Dawn Jani Birley played Horatio, who narrated the entire play. At times, Birley signed without voicing or captioning. Reviewers commented on how the silence made them recall the lines themselves and the power of silence to convey emotion (Bradbury 2022). However, hearing directors sometimes make the mistake of withholding access to spoken lines for artistic effect. For example, the 2015 Red Theatre Chicago production *R+J: The Vineyard* framed the strife between the Capulets and the Montague families as a clash of communication modalities. The Capulets stress speaking and lipreading, while the Montagues use ASL. Hearing director Aaron Sawyer opened the play with members of the Capulet family speaking, but these lines were not accessible to deaf audiences via offstage interpreting or captioning. In a post-show conversation with one of the authors, Sawyer said he wanted deaf and hearing audiences to have the same experience of exclusion. While this was a novel experience for hearing patrons, deaf people live this experience every day of their lives. We strongly believe that artistic decisions should never remove or impair communication access for deaf audiences.

Sign Language Linguistics, Poetics, and Musicality

The obvious difference between spoken and signed languages is that the former is auditory while the latter is visual. Spoken languages also tend to be linear in structure, while sign languages are more synchronic—inflecting a series of signs with simultaneous linguistic markers that are as essential to the creation of meaning as the signs themselves.[15] Sign language thus requires signers to use multiple parts of their bodies simultaneously and their audiences to perceive these synchronic elements, as well as the linear progression of signs used. The importance of this difference in temporality between spoken and signed languages cannot be overstated when it comes to staging integrated deaf and hearing theatre. This section briefly overviews important aspects of sign language linguistics, poetics, and musicality that are central to staging.

Sign Language Linguistics

A sign is composed of four elements: handshape, orientation, movement, and location. ASL handshapes have descriptive labels such as V, bent O, flat O, etc. For example, the ASL sign for INTERRUPT uses the open B handshape on both hands.[16] Orientation describes the placement of the handshape in relation to the signer—is the palm up or down? Facing the signer or away from the signer? For INTERRUPT, the non-dominant hand has the palm oriented toward the signer while the dominant hand is perpendicular to the signer.

Movement refers to whether the hand is stationary or moving during the sign; whether the movement is done once or repeated; and the direction of the movement. For example, a single movement bringing the dominant hand between the thumb and the index finger of the non-dominant hand means INTERRUPT, while a double movement means ANNOY. Movement can also function as an adverb, to describe the intensity of an action or feeling. If something is really annoying, for example, the movement will be bigger and more forceful than if something is moderately annoying. As mentioned in Chap. 1—Section "Essential Background", movement also has gender and racial elements. Research has shown that male-identifying sign language users tend to sign bigger than female-identifying users, while Black sign language users in the United States tend to sign bigger as well.

---

[15] This synchronic nature is one reason that it is impossible to fully capture sign language in written form, although various systems have been proposed.

[16] English words for ASL signs are typically written in all capital letters, to indicate that the English word and the ASL sign are not exact equivalents. These are called glosses.

Signs can also have directional or nondirectional movement. ANNOY and INTERRUPT are non-directional signs because their position doesn't move to express interaction between people (or other entities). A directional sign is GIVE (made with the flat O handshape), which can be moved in different directions to create meanings such as 'you give me' versus 'I give you.' Location refers to where the sign is made in relation to the signer's body. For example, ANNOY is located in the breast area. Signs can be located on the brow or ear, near the eye or mouth, on the shoulders, arms, legs, or hands, away from the body, and so on. Almost any part of the body can be a location.

Non-manual markers, such as facial expression, body positioning, and other bodily inflections carry important linguistic information. Facial expressions conveying grammatical information include eyebrow and eye movement, mouth shape and movement, and even nose movements. Raising or lowering the eyebrows in conjunction with a sign, for example, can change whether a signer is asking a question or making a statement—'Are you annoyed?' versus 'I'm annoyed.' Eye gaze can be used to express role shifts and status relationships, as well as to point at things. In addition to culturally specific types of mouthing, sign languages have conventionalized mouth shapes that carry specific meaning. These vary across sign languages. In ASL, for example, mouthing FISH adds the meaning of 'finished' to a sign. However, many sign language users also incorporate mouthing of English words. This is generally seen by linguists as deviating from the formal rules of sign language and has been the subject of sometimes acrimonious discussion between those who wish to promote and preserve a 'pure' language variant versus those who accept non-standard variants.

Body positioning is another important non-manual marker. Head movement is used in sign language to express a range of grammatical elements such as negation, temporality, and emotion, as well as perspective (where the speaker is in relation to large or small objects, for example). Turning the shoulders one way or another can be used to show role shifts, changes in who is speaking, or choices between options (this or that); while hunching the shoulders in different ways can express indifference or lack of knowledge. Posture and body movement also add descriptive meaning.

Sign space is another key grammatical element. The space in front of and behind the body can be used to express temporality (past, present, and future) as well as to create what linguists call constructed action. This means that events are narrated through gestures. Many native sign language users are gifted mimics and can communicate information simply by gesture. Visual narratives are also created using depiction, the sign language equivalent of 'show, don't tell.' Depiction uses linguistic features such as classifiers, role shift, and the space around the signer to act out events and actions. Classifiers are handshapes representing specific nouns that can be manipulated to show action. For example, the index finger handshape and the V handshape held upside down can be used as classifiers to represent a person walking. The classifier movements describe how the person is moving—slowly, quickly, smoothly, awkwardly, uphill, downhill, etc. More classifiers can be added to show interaction with physical space—the upside-down V can walk over the arm to show crossing a bridge, for example. Through role shift, the signer can become the person walking—the signer can look around or mime peering under a bridge.

Sign Language Poetics

Although sign languages typically have smaller vocabularies than spoken languages, they are endlessly creative in how the individual signs are combined with other linguistic features to create nuanced meaning. This is equivalent to inventing completely new words in spoken languages. Creativity is prized in artistic sign language. Audiences will react appreciatively to seeing a new, particularly ingenious way of expressing an idea or describing an action.

While depiction and mime are central, artistic sign language also makes use of visual equivalences of sound-based poetic techniques such as rhythm, rhyme, and onomatopoeia, as well as poetic devices such as metaphor and symbolism. Rhyme may be created through repetition of handshapes, while rhythm can be expressed through pacing, sign size and intensity, body movement, and repetition. Onomatopoeia is created through unique mouth morphemes that express visual equivalents of sounds, such as BAP, POW, WAA, etc. Sign language also has its own unique poetic techniques such as visual vernacular (VV). VV is a type of artistic expression that uses cinematic elements, including shots, views, and angles, coupled with time distortion, personification, gestural language, and onomatopoeia. Video editing is also a common element of VV. For example, Ace Mahbaz's "Game Over" includes short clips from each video game scene depicted. Joel Ortiz's "Water Flow" uses color for artistic effect, while Douglas Ridloff's "Transients" adds white outlines to the performed imagery.

Deaf communities have unique genres of literature that play with the formal features of visual languages. Handshape stories are short compositions with constraints on what handshapes may be used and in what order. Number stories, for example, must use signs with the same handshapes as the numbers 1–10 in that order. No other signs may be used. ABC stories are similar, but use the handshapes of the alphabet in A-to-Z order. Classifier stories are another type of creative sign language. In these stories, only classifiers, and sometimes only one classifier, can be used to express the story.

Sign Language Musicality

Sign language musicality is a relatively new area of research in sign language poetics. Contrary to popular belief that deaf people exist in a world of silence, many deaf people enjoy listening to music, dancing to music, and making music. While music is generally understood to be an inherently auditory art, focused on vocal or instrumental sound, it can be defined in visual terms. We might, for example, adapt *Encyclopedia Britannica*'s definition of music as 'An art concerned with combining *visual* elements for beauty of form or emotional expression, usually according to cultural standards of rhythm, melody, and harmony' (Epperson 2023). Deaf artist Rosa Lee Timm, Deaf scholar Jody Cripps, and others have recently begun exploring how sign language has visual equivalents of auditory-based musical concepts. As discussed above, rhythm can be created visually through pacing, sign size and intensity, body movement, and repetition. Signers can follow a set beat, create tempo through the speed of the signing, add stresses by emphasizing certain signs, and play with how long movements are held to create varying durations. Harmony can be created by using multiple signers. Texture can be created using various visual elements in addition to signs, such as imagery, graphics, light, color, and overlaying visual elements via video editing.[17]

---

[17] Melody, the rhythmic ordering of low and high pitches, is one musical concept that needs more research to determine its visual equivalent. Pitch is based on the vibration of sound waves. Does sign language have pitches? Would light waves be the equivalent? If so, it would seem that the visual equivalent of pitch would be color. But, this doesn't seem to quite capture the musical effect of melody.

Several forms of sign language music exist. The first is purely visual signed music, with no auditory elements. The second is original music created by deaf artists that uses both auditory and visual elements. The third is sign language translations of sound-based music. In integrated theatre, the third form is most commonly seen. Integrated musicals are very popular and integrated opera is becoming more common.

To sum up, sign languages have unique linguistic, poetic, and musical elements that can differ significantly from those of spoken languages. These aspects create unique artistic challenges in staging deaf and hearing integrated theatre. If you are new to integrated theatre, having a basic understanding of sign language linguistics, poetics, and musicality will help you understand these issues, which are discussed in the next section. It will also help you to better understand the work of the director of artistic sign language, who has primary responsibility for aligning the two very different languages.

Artistic Challenges and Issues

Issues with Casting and Representation

A number of artistic challenges arise in working with deaf and hearing actors. Some are specific to stage productions while others are broader in nature. One of the most long-standing general issues is the casting of non-deaf actors to play deaf characters. As mentioned in "A History of Deaf and Hearing Integrated Theatre" of this chapter, deaf actors were not cast for deaf roles on stage until the 1960s. Even after NTD's success made the artistic capabilities of deaf actors evident, directors in film, television, and the performing arts continued to cast hearing actors for deaf roles. In the 1970s, NTD actor Audree Norton was reportedly denied a role on an ABC series because the director preferred to work with actors who could speak (Schuchman 1999). After she made this public, the deaf community organized protests. In the 1990s, the casting of a hearing actor to play a deaf character in the film *Calendar Girl* led to demonstrations as well (Giordano 2016). As seen in the National Association of the Deaf's list titled "Hearing Actors Who Have Stolen Deaf Roles," deaf actors have frequently lost out to hearing actors (NAD n.d.). And the problem persists today. In the 2019 film *Sound of Metal*, two of the main deaf characters were played by hearing actors, while Marlee Matlin had to threaten to quit the film *CODA* in order to get deaf actors cast in deaf roles (Clarke

2021). Also in 2021, CBS announced that it had cast a hearing actor to portray deaf character Nick Andros in the upcoming remake of *The Stand* series. In contrast to film and television, the live theatre industry has done a better job of casting deaf actors for deaf roles over the past decade, possibly due to the influence of the inclusive casting movement.

Reasons for choosing hearing over deaf actors typically include 'star power' and inability to find a skilled performer who fits the role. Directors may also cast hearing actors because it saves the cost of interpreters, although admitting this would be a violation of equal employment law in the United States. The primary reasons for choosing deaf actors for deaf roles relates to authentic representation and equity. While it is sometimes difficult for non-disabled individuals to understand, people with disabilities often see their conditions as a central facet of their identity. They may view being disabled positively, even while experiencing impairment effects, or physical aspects of the disabling condition that are painful, limiting, or otherwise undesirable. Actors with disabilities thus see casting able-bodied actors as 'cripping up' or an inauthentic form of representation.

Many deaf people also see themselves as a language minority and as part of a distinct culture. Thus, casting a hearing actor to play a deaf character constitutes inauthentic representation because the hearing actor does not have the necessary fluency or cultural competency for the role. Casting a non-native speaker to play a French character would be critically panned; so why is it acceptable to cast a non-native user of ASL to play a deaf character who uses ASL?

Equity is another important reason to cast deaf actors in deaf roles or in roles where characters use sign language. These are among the few acting opportunities open to deaf actors, as they are rarely considered for roles that are not initially written as deaf. When directors cast hearing individuals who are fluent in sign language as deaf characters, as happened with CODA Paul Raci in *Sound of Metal*, the small pool of available roles for deaf actors shrinks even further. Without opportunities to perform, deaf actors will not be able to develop the 'star power' that leads to additional opportunities. This is why we strongly advocate that roles which require signing should go to a deaf person. There may be some rare situations in which the production concept or the available pool of deaf actors necessitates casting hearing actors who know ASL. But in general, directors should be creating more opportunities for deaf actors, not taking them away.

Issues with the Portrayal of Deaf Characters

Another general issue is the use of inaccurate and stereotypical portrayals of deaf persons and sign language onstage, on screen, and in the mainstream media. This is a problem rooted in deeply ingrained cultural narratives of disability. People with disabilities are depicted as tropes, rather than individuals, as helpless victims in need of pity, as heroes or superheroes conquering their physical limitations, or as villains whose outward deformity manifests as inward character/personality flaws. Disability stereotypes are also used as plot devices, representing the disabling condition as an obstacle to be overcome. Scholars David Mitchell and Sharon Snyder have coined the phrase *narrative prosthesis* to describe the symbolic or metaphorical use of disability in artistic works in ways that demean the lived experience of people with disabilities (2001).

Stereotypes of deafness include social isolation, inability to appreciate or enjoy music, having the ability to lipread effectively in any situation, and the ability of assistive listening technology to provide full access to sound. These cultural narratives around deafness are either inaccurate or fail to recognize it can be a valued socio-cultural identity. We strongly encourage directors to avoid dramaturgy and characterizations employing such reductive and negative representations of deafness. Instead, directors should work with the director of artistic sign language to infuse their integrated productions with the experience, language, and visual aesthetics of the deaf world. This does not mean that the disabling aspects of deafness can never be depicted or that characters must always perceive their deafness in a positive light. Deaf people are not monolithic and neither is the experience of deafness. We are, instead, advocating for portraying deaf characters as individuals, rather than as metaphors or symbols, and for being aware that social and cultural factors are far more disabling than the physical condition of deafness.

An example of this type of portrayal can be found in NextStop Theatre Company's 2014 *Richard III*, directed by Lindsey Snyder and featuring Deaf actor Ethan Sinnott. Productions of *Richard III* almost inevitably demonstrate narrative prosthesis and disability simulation, with able-bodied actors hobbling around stage, decked out in prosthetic devices and humps that outwardly show Richard's internal deformity. Snyder's production rejects this symbolic use of disability to explain Richard's villainy. The audience sees how prejudice and discrimination against aberrant bodies influence Richard's psychology and behavior. But the presence of other deaf characters and moments when they communicate directly with Richard through ASL suggest that the handicapping element of his disability comes from social barriers, rather than from personality flaws (Bradbury 2023).

Artistic Challenges Onstage

Moving from broader concerns to issues specifically linked to stage productions, one key challenge is the interplay of spoken and signed languages in live performance. Unlike two spoken languages that might compete for auditory attention, the different modalities of spoken and signed languages allow them to occur simultaneously. However, it is extremely difficult to achieve a seamless blend of languages onstage. As discussed earlier in this chapter, spoken and signed languages have very different grammatical structures. The amount of time needed to express the same lines in spoken language and sign language may not be the same. This can make aligning the languages challenging. The fact that scripts are almost always composed in written English first and then translated into sign language also complicates the alignment. Some concepts, imagery, or metaphors in the written script may be difficult to express clearly in sign language. But the director of artistic sign language and translation team must ensure the time needed to produce the signed lines closely matches the time needed to speak the lines. This constraint limits the translation choices, which may impact the intelligibility of the translation itself.

In integrated theatre that is primarily hearing-led, directors should be wary of allowing spoken language to dominate to the extent that the signed language becomes secondary. This can create inequalities for the deaf audiences. For example, if there is a particularly knotty translation problem, directors could reach out to the playwright or publisher to request permission to modify the language. Directors who are not fluent in sign language should also avoid imposing a vision of what the sign language translation should look like. In this respect, NTD is a case study in what not to do. Founding artistic director David Hays, who was hearing and did not know ASL, promoted a highly artistic form of stage ASL that followed the spoken lines as closely as possible. But deaf audiences found this approach difficult to understand (Bangs 1989). Hays and later artistic directors, also hearing, defended this style by arguing that NTD is theatre *of* the deaf, not theatre *for* the deaf (Dale 1985). In other words, NTD targeted hearing, not deaf audiences. To avoid creating this type of inequity in audience experience, we advocate that hearing directors leave all translation decisions to the director of artistic sign language.

It can be helpful, though, for directors to have a basic understanding of some issues related to the translation choices. First is the question of what type of sign language to use overall and for various characters. As discussed in Chap. 1—"Essential Background", a wide range of signed communication exists within the deaf community in the United States—from signed English to 'pure' ASL. And sign styles are influenced by age, region, gender, nationality, and race. The type of sign used onstage should be an artistic decision that correlates with how the character is conceptualized. To the extent possible, the translation team should be composed of individuals who represent these backgrounds, so that culturally authentic translations can be created. For plays set in earlier periods, very little information about historical sign language use exists. Different approaches can be taken. The translation may make use of a more formal or gestural register, to suggest a difference from contemporary language usage. Or, the translators may decide to keep the language modern to support easy access for deaf audiences.

Similar choices may be made with regional dialects and foreign languages. For example, if a play has both spoken Spanish and English, the director may want to use a Spanish sign language along with ASL. This decision may make artistic sense, but deaf audiences may dislike not being able to understand the foreign sign language. It may be perceived as a lack of access, rather than an artistic effect. To avoid this, the translation team may decide to simply use ASL throughout. Or, if the foreign sign language is used, the English translation might be given in captions. A captioned note such as "[foreign sign language]" could also provide context for the audience and reduce potential confusion or frustration. Another option is to modify stage signing to suggest a linguistic difference, while still allowing it to be understood. For example, the translation team might use more gestural signing to represent that a foreign language is being used. These approaches can also be used in captioning plays or scenes where the use of a foreign spoken language is central to the dramatic situation.

Finally, fingerspelling is difficult to read at a distance and should be avoided as much as possible. In smaller venues, more fingerspelling may be acceptable.

With respect to the performance of the translation, any non-signer who will sign on stage needs to have an innate capability for gestural expression. Some actors are better at this than others. Directors should work with the director of artistic sign language to cast with that quality in mind. The production schedule must also ensure that actors who are not fluent in sign language have the time for intensive language learning. Correct sign production, facial expression, and prosody are essential for making the stage sign language intelligible for Deaf audiences.

Uniquely Challenging Scenarios

Narrowing our focus even further, integrated productions of musicals and classical or early modern plays present a number of unique challenges. With musicals, three different communication modalities must be aligned—spoken, signed, and musical. It is essential that the music director work closely with the director of artistic sign language to ensure that the musical score and the stage signing are aligned. This may entail making small modifications to the score, such as adding or holding notes, and is an area where musical directors must trust the ideas, advice, and judgment of their deaf team members. Additionally, elements of sign language musicality must also be integrated into the translation and performance. If a song includes both solo and ensemble performance, it must be carefully staged so that deaf audiences can follow transitions between performers. For example, if the ensemble is placed on stage left and a soloist on stage right, this creates the problem of split visual attention. Placing the ensemble and the solo signer close together will make it easier for deaf audiences to follow. Performers can use gestures to direct the audience's attention between ensemble and solo sections. Lighting can also be used for this purpose. Finally, a system of cues must be used to help deaf performers follow the music during rehearsals and performances. This cueing can be visual, such as a raised hand or specific action with a prop, or physical, such as a touch on the back or an unobtrusive squeeze by a hearing actor. For operas, a system of visual cueing is essential since operas tend to have minimal stage movement that deaf actors can rely on. Additionally, if the opera is performed in a language that is not English, the deaf performers will not be able to rely on recognizing mouth shapes made for certain English words.

Classical and early modern plays present unique challenges because of their highly poetic language. Integrated productions of Shakespeare are relatively common, but approaches to translation vary widely. Some directors of artistic sign language prefer to follow the Shakespeare text closely, while others favor conceptual alignment over adherence to the original language. To understand what this means, let's look briefly at two translations of Hamlet's most famous soliloquy, 'to be or not to be.' How might one translate these lines: "Whether 'tis nobler in the mind to suffer / The slings and arrows of outrageous fortune, / Or to take arms against a sea of troubles, / And by opposing end them?" If following the Shakespeare text closely, the translation might try to capture the imagery of slings, arrows, and arms. We might gloss this as: BETTER WHICH? SUFFER BAD LUCK ARROWS, SLINGS HIT-ME? READY, PROBLEM WAVES-APPEAR-OVER-ME, FIGHT FIGHT WAVE-OVERWHELM, DIE? In this example, the gloss is keeping close to the original language in Shakespeare's text. Or, the translation might instead focus on the key concepts in the lines and drop the Shakespearean language in favor of imagery that makes more sense in ASL. An example of this can be found in Deaf actor John McGinty's 2020 translation, which he shared on Facebook. This translation can be glossed as: MAYBE GO-AHEAD THINK-OBSESS-PONDER FALL-INTO (or DROWN), HELP ALL PROBLEMS UP-TO-NOW PUSH-AWAY, SOLVE. In this example, the imagery of weapons and a sea of troubles has been replaced with the central idea of Hamlet's neurosis and suicidal ideation.

In addition to deciding on an overall translation approach, the director of artistic sign language and translation team must find visual equivalences for puns, double entendres, homonyms, and other sound-based literary devices. Sign language poetics can be used to parallel the artistry of Shakespeare's language. Translators must be selective, though, as it is not possible to reproduce all of the dense wordplay in Shakespeare's text without negatively impacting the intelligibility of the translation. Artistry and clarity must be balanced. Translators must also decide how to handle poetic meter, especially when used to distinguish between high and low class characters. Iambic pentameter does not map well onto the grammatical structure of sign language. But sign registers can be used to express differences in character status. Another issue not generally discussed is mouthing. Mouthing English words is common in everyday sign language use, so many deaf actors also do this when they perform. However, mouthing should be governed by artistic choices. Mouthing in sign language productions of Shakespeare's plays raises questions of which discourse register should be used.

In this chapter, we have outlined information that will help you undertake integrated theatre. As with other art forms, Deaf theatre and integrated deaf and hearing theatre have a rich history to appreciate. Being cognizant of the unique opportunities and challenges of combining two very different languages and cultures onstage will help you develop your initial concept, have productive discussions with your director of artistic sign language and actors, and produce a show that is equally accessible to both deaf and hearing audiences. Being aware of stereotypical representations of deafness and ethical considerations related to casting deaf and signing roles will also benefit your approach to staging. With this expanded knowledge, you are now ready to dive into the actualities of staging integrated deaf and hearing theatre.

REFERENCES

"A Promising Invention". 1910. *Chicago Daily Tribune*. May 26, 1910.

"About Bruce Hlibok". 2021. Accessed November 15, 2023. https://www.brucehlibok.com/

Baldwin, Stephen C. 1993. *Pictures in the Air: The Story of the National Theatre of the Deaf*. Washington, DC: Gallaudet University Press.

Bangs, Donald. 1989. What Is a Deaf Performing Arts Experience? In *The Deaf Way: Perspectives from the International Conference on Deaf Culture*, July 9–14, 1989, Gallaudet University. Ed. Carol J. Erting et al., 751–761. Washington, DC: Gallaudet University Press.

Barton-Farcas, Stephanie. 2018. *Disability and Theatre*. New York: Routledge.

Beutel, Paul. 1977. Everyone Should See Spectrum's 'A Play of Our Own.' *The Austin American Statesman*. November 16, 1977.

Bradbury, Jill Marie. 2022. Audiences, American Sign Language, and Deafness in Shakespeare Performance. *Shakespeare Bulletin* 40 (1): 45–67.

———. 2023. Disability Embodiment and Inclusive Aesthetics. In *Inclusive Shakespeares: Identity, Pedagogy, Performance*, ed. Sonya Loftis Freeman, Mardy Philippian, and Justin P. Shaw, 25–42. New York: Palgrave Macmillan. https://doi.org/10.1007/978-3-031-26522-82.

Clarke, Cath. 2021. 'Deaf Is Not a Costume': Marlee Matlin on Surviving Abuse and Casting Authentically. *The Guardian*, August 6, 2021.

Conley, Willy. 2023. *Plays of Our Own: An Anthology of Scripts by Deaf and Hard-of-Hearing Writers*. New York: Routledge.

Dale, Steve. 1985. National Theatre of the Deaf Puts Quality as Primary Goal. *The Chicago Tribune*, March 1, 1985.

Epperson, Gordon. 2023. Music. *Encyclopedia Britannica*. Accessed October 16, 2023. https://www.britannica.com/art/music.

Giordano, Tyrone. 2016. Actors. In *The SAGE Deaf Studies Encyclopedia*, ed. Genie Gertz and Patrick Boudreault, 5–8. Thousand Oaks: SAGE Publications. https://doi.org/10.4135/9781483346489.

granda, aj, and Jelica Nuccio. 2018. Protactile Principles. Accessed November 15, 2023. https://www.tactilecommunications.org/Documents/PTPrinciplesMoviesFinal.pdf

"Guild Cast Learns New Way to Talk". 1950. *Wisconsin State Journal.* April 23, 1950.

Haggerty, Luane Davis. 2007. *The Little Train that Could: The Story of Interborough Repertory Theater.* Self-published.

Interborough Repertory Theater. n.d. History. Accessed November 15, 2023. https://irttheater.org/

Lane, Harlan, ed., and Franklin Philip, trans. 1984. *The Deaf Experience: Classics in Language and Education.* Cambridge: Harvard University Press.

Lane, Harlan, Robert Hoffmeister, and Ben Bahan. 1996. *A Journey into the Deaf-World.* San Diego: DawnSignPress.

"Local News in Brief". 1870. *The New York Times.* May 21, 1870.

Miles, Dorothy. 1974. A History of Theatre Activities in the Deaf Community of the United States. MA thesis, Connecticut College.

Mitchell, David, and Sharon Snyder. 2001. *Narrative Prosthesis: Disability and the Dependencies of Discourse.* Ann Arbor: University of Michigan Press.

Mow, Shanny. 1987a. Theater, Community. In *Gallaudet Encyclopedia of Deaf People and Deafness,* ed. John Vickery Van Cleve, vol. 3, 288–289. McGraw-Hill Professional.

———. 1987b. Theater, Professional. In *Gallaudet Encyclopedia of Deaf People and Deafness,* ed. John Vickery Van Cleve, vol. 3, 289–291. McGraw-Hill Professional.

National Association of the Deaf. n.d. Hearing Actors Who Have Stolen Deaf Roles. Accessed November 15, 2023. https://www.nad.org/hearing-actors-who-have-stolen-deaf-roles/

Rholetter, Wylene. 2016. Arts, Performing. In *The SAGE Deaf Studies Encyclopedia,* ed. Genie Gertz and Patrick Boudreault, 48–51. Thousand Oaks: SAGE Publications. https://doi.org/10.4135/9781483346489.

"Rhythmic Music to Aid Negro Pantomime". 1941. *The Chicago Tribune.* May 18, 1941.

Schuchman, John S. 1999. *Hollywood Speaks: Deafness and the Film Entertainment Industry.* University of Illinois Press.

Shurgot, Michael. 2019. Reprising ASL at ACT: *Romeo and Juliet* at A Contemporary Theatre. *Scene: Reviews of Early Modern Drama* 1 (4): 1–8.

Steketee, Martha Wade. 2016. *NEA Roundtable: Creating Opportunities for Deaf Theater Artists.* The National Endowment for the Arts.

Tadie, Nancy Bowen. 1979. A History of Drama at Gallaudet College. PhD diss., New York University.

Van Cleve, John Vickery, and Barry A. Crouch. 1989. *A Place of Their Own: Creating Deaf Community in America.* Washington, DC: Gallaudet University Press.

Zachary, Samuel J. 1995. Cleveland Signstage Theatre: America's Professional Resident Theatre of the Deaf. In *A Deaf American Monograph,* 127–133. Silver Spring: The National Association of the Deaf.

CHAPTER 3

Laying the Foundation

Pre-audition Period

No amount of planning is too much when it comes to creating a play with an integrated team of deaf and hearing artists. Success in rehearsals and performances is built upon the firm foundation created during the pre-audition period. The more time and care go into this phase, the more benefits you will reap in the days to come. We define pre-audition as the time before auditions take place when actors have not yet entered the process. Others may call this pre-production. This is the period for a directing team to develop their concept, share that major guiding idea with the design team, and begin ushering the show down its unique path.

The Directing Team

One of the most important decisions—one that will directly affect the production every day going forward—is the composition of the directing team. In creating integrated theatre, it is essential for the directing team to include the perspective of both deaf and hearing individuals. The reasons for this are many but boil down to the fact that each person is a representative of their culture. Within the United States, deaf culture is a subset of a majority culture, with its own values, rules, norms, and aesthetics. As the dominant group of the population, hearing directors already bring their

© The Author(s), under exclusive license to Springer Nature Switzerland AG 2024
A. Head, J. M. Bradbury, *Staging Deaf and Hearing Theatre Productions*, https://doi.org/10.1007/978-3-031-61446-0_3

own lens, assumptions, and characteristics to the project. It is very difficult to step outside of that perspective however much a hearing director may wish to do so. Deaf people have cultural competencies and lived experiences that hearing directors do not; they see and understand things happening in the creative process that hearing directors cannot. If you are creating a play with both deaf and hearing artists, for both deaf and hearing audiences, then the production should be shaped equally by deaf and hearing lenses. Together, this team is responsible for the entire production, beginning with creating the initial concept that will guide it. The more balanced the directing team, the more balanced the production will be as well.

The director relationship can take many forms, especially considering the full spectrum of integrated theatre that was detailed in Chap. 1—"Defining Integrated Theatre". Most common iterations are co-directors; director and assistant director; and director and director of artistic sign language. We advocate for co-director roles whenever feasible to create as much equality as possible between the production leaders. The dynamics of the relationship are as unique as the people filling those roles; however, some broad ways to look at each relationship are as follows.

Co-directors

In a co-director relationship, the two directors share equal weight and equal responsibility for all artistic decisions. A working relationship like this is centered near the middle of our spectrum. There is an equilibrium of hearing perspectives and deaf perspectives coming together. The traditional view of the director's role is 'the one who steers the ship.' Co-directors must navigate how they arrive at artistic decisions *together* and develop a shared way of working. There is much more give than take in this kind of collaborative relationship. In fact, many people we interviewed stated a correlation between the flexibility of a hearing co-director (or director) and the overall success of the production. For any hearing person working on the production, but especially the hearing co-director, entering the production with an *open mind* and an *open heart* to your deaf colleagues will pay dividends throughout the process. This means a willingness to accept the ideas of others, admit when your ideas don't work, and even advocate for the ideas of your deaf team members to the larger production team.

The co-directors, like any directing team, are faced with a series of initial conceptual questions.

- Which characters are hearing?
- Which characters are deaf and where do they fit on the deafhood continuum?
- If characters traditionally thought to be hearing people are now deaf, how does deaf culture enter the story?
- How are the characters able to understand each other if they're using different languages?
- Is there a dramaturgical reason for the unique communication environment within the story?
- How is the audience able to understand everything happening onstage?

Initial brainstorming sessions may occur months before auditions begin. Solidifying a plan that both directors have agreed upon will lead to more successful auditions because there is a clear vision for how each character fits within the story. Once the directors share their concept with the rest of the team, the two of them should be involved together at every step along the way: at production meetings, at meetings with individual designers, at further brainstorming sessions, at auditions and callbacks, at rehearsals, at tech week. When creative disagreements occur, which is inevitable, it helps to take a pause, then come back together. Ultimately, both directors want to produce a powerful and enjoyable show for audience members. For any sort of creative disagreements, you should always remember our third non-negotiable principle and consider how communication onstage is being affected. As you will see in our case studies, making communication the top priority will almost always lead to a more successful production for all artists and audiences. Think about the various creative solutions to a problem and go with the one that keeps communication front and center. For hearing co-directors (and directors) this is a moment to practice having an open mind and an open heart.

It can't be overstated how challenging it can be to find co-directors whose creative visions jive together. All artists have their own aesthetic. Some co-directors will have aligning or overlapping ones, while others will have conflicting aesthetics. We suggest really taking the time to find a co-director team that can work well together. As a reminder, if a hearing co-director doesn't know ASL, then interpreters should be present at all meetings. In the best situation, ongoing or designated interpreters will be working on the production from start to finish.

Director–Assistant Director

In a director–assistant director (or director–associate director) relationship, the director is viewed through the traditional theatre lens and has the final say for artistic decisions on the production. The assistant director is there to support the director's vision. In order to create as much balance as possible on this team, if the director is hearing, we advocate for a deaf assistant director, and vice versa. In integrated theatre, for all decisions, beginning with developing the concept, the director should include the assistant director as much as possible. This is true whether the production is more deaf-led or more hearing-led, but it is especially important the more the production exists to the right of the integrated theatre spectrum. Hearing-led productions involving deaf actors should prioritize including a deaf directing perspective from the beginning to generate a more authentic concept that works for both deaf artists and audience members. Together, the director and assistant director will answer the same set of initial conceptual questions, thinking through which characters are deaf, which are hearing, and how they all fit into the story cohesively. To truly benefit from having this assistant director, the director must approach their relationship with cultural humility.

As much as possible, the assistant director should attend all production meetings and design meetings; should be involved in the translation of the script into ASL (if the assistant director is deaf); should be present at auditions and callbacks; should regularly attend rehearsals; should be encouraged to give feedback notes directly to both designers and actors; and should consistently be asked their opinion. If the assistant director is deaf, their thoughts on translation, stage sign language, deaf identity and culture, and anything related to visual communication for actors or audience should be respected. To ignore the advice of a deaf person in these areas is to engage in audist behavior. A deaf assistant director may work directly with deaf actors without the director present. Conversely, a hearing assistant director may work directly with hearing actors without the director present. Again, ASL interpreters should be scheduled and confirmed for every step along the way. Whether the assistant director is deaf or hearing, they cannot adequately contribute to the team unless quality communication is a top priority. You've invited them to join your team, now you need to make sure they have what they need to succeed. This begins with communication. Finally, a deaf assistant director should not be the only deaf member on the directing team. In addition to the assistant director, we recommend hiring a director of artistic sign language and a deaf consultant. See Chap. 3—"Director of Artistic Sign Language" for a detailed discussion of this.

What is the difference between an assistant director and a co-director? At the surface, much of the work appears to be the same. The difference is not only in title, however. A co-director takes on more weight of artistic responsibility. They are equally tasked with creating a cohesive production. An assistant director supports the director, but does not share that same weight of responsibility. This may be due to experience level, time commitment, or where the show is centered. Perhaps a deaf-led production wants the show to land more on the left side of the spectrum. In this case, a hearing assistant director is hired to support the deaf director and bring their hearing lens, but the deaf director ultimately has the final say in decision-making.

Director-DASL

In theatre happening further to the right, that is, mostly-hearing-led, a director–director of artistic sign language (DASL) configuration is most common. The role of the DASL will be detailed later in this chapter, but in brief, they provide a knowledgeable and experienced perspective on what's happening onstage. The director has the final say on decisions, but it is the DASL's role to make sure the story is working for both deaf actors and audiences. A DASL should be hired as soon as a director makes the decision to work with deaf actors or sign language. Hiring them is only the first step. A DASL can only be as helpful as the director will allow. A director who doesn't heed the advice of a DASL will not be making an accessible or inclusive show. As early as possible, a director should sit with the DASL and develop the initial concept for the production. The DASL will be able to provide invaluable input on how deaf characters can fit into the story, how to make the rehearsal process work for actors, and how to make the performance successful for audiences. The DASL should be involved in all design meetings, as costumes, set, and lighting can significantly impact the visibility of sign language on stage. To reiterate, this is the place where a director's open mind and open heart allows the production to truly flourish by accepting the ideas, advice, and suggestions of their deaf colleagues.

It sometimes happens that a production is not planned to be integrated, but one or two deaf actors audition and are cast. At a minimum, the company should immediately hire a DASL. In this situation, the pre-audition period did not include discussions about how to integrate deaf characters and sign language into the story. Those decisions must now be made in a very short time. All aspects of the pre-audition process must be reviewed from the perspective of access and inclusion not only for the new deaf actor(s) but also for the deaf audience that is guaranteed to show up when a deaf actor appears onstage. Scenic, lighting, costume designs should be reviewed with a careful eye toward visual language access. The earlier a DASL enters this process, the better. But at a minimum, they must be involved before rehearsals begin.

In summary, whatever the production, whatever the dynamic and the working relationship that is established, it is critically important—especially for a hearing person or a predominantly hearing theatre company—to bring on deaf leaders early in the process and to accept their input with an open mind and open heart. We cannot state this often or strongly enough. These should be some of the first decisions made: Who is the deaf director, co-director, assistant director, or DASL? What other deaf artists are supporting the production in leadership roles? If you find yourself in a situation where you are now unexpectedly working with deaf artists, you need to pause to consider: What is their role in the story? How can you best fit them into your production and your process? If you are in this situation and don't know where or how to seek out deaf leaders, we recommend the following starting points:

- Look for interest groups on social media, such as the National Deaf Theatre Society on Facebook, or for hashtags such as #ASLtheatre.
- Find and follow deaf creatives on Instagram and TikTok.
- Do a web search for deaf actors and Deaf theatre in your area.
- Reach out to deaf organizations or schools in your area.

Creating an Initial Concept: *Angels in America, Part 1: Millennium Approaches*

Using one of our case study productions as an example, we will walk through one possible process for developing an initial concept. For *Millennium Approaches* at Rochester Institute of Technology, the production was led by a hearing director with a deaf assistant director (AD). The AD also took on the responsibilities of a DASL. Pre-audition work started in April of 2021. At that time, the director and AD began meeting regularly to answer the initial conceptual questions. Auditions occurred in August 2021.

Which Characters Are Hearing?
From the beginning, *Millennium Approaches* was planned as an integrated production. Because much of the story focuses on the lives of two couples (Prior and Louis, Harper and Joe) the directing team wanted the couples to be 'integrated' with one deaf character and one hearing character in each. Making two of these four principal characters deaf created a stronger balance of representation onstage. It allowed the deaf actors to more authentically portray the characters, and beyond that, added new layers to the story being told. To decide which of these four characters should identify as hearing and which as deaf, the directing team first looked at the specific textual demands for all characters and then at each character's individual given circumstances.

Immediately, one character emerged as a definite hearing person. The character Roy M. Cohn is based on the real-life Roy Cohn, who was a hearing man. It felt inappropriate to portray this actual person as deaf, when he was not. We felt Roy must be hearing in the play just as he was in life. To add to this, Roy's first scene involves essentially a three-page monologue over phone calls. Making him deaf would create a series of creative problems that would then have to be solved, beginning with the opening scene.

Once it was established that Roy was a hearing character, the directing team analyzed his *interaction web*—a term used for all the characters Roy came in contact with throughout the story. The first major point on Roy's web is Joe Pitt. During the story, Roy's character has considerable influence on Joe. For them to truly connect, the directing team felt strongly that Joe needed to be a hearing person as well. Even putting their relationship aside, Joe occupies the prominent position of chief clerk at the Federal Court of Appeals and, back in 1985, this position would have likely been held by a hearing person.

Two other major points on Roy's interaction web are his doctor, Henry, and his Republican crony, Martin. Roy is described as a cagey person, and with no known deaf contacts in the play, it is plausible that he would only choose a doctor with whom he could speak directly. Thus, Henry needed to be a hearing man. A similar justification was made for Martin, who knows secrets about Roy's legal troubles and also cajoles Joe into working for the Justice Department. Again, Roy would need someone he could talk with openly. For that to happen, the team believed Martin needed to be a hearing man.

Could a different justification be made for Roy, Joe, Henry, or Martin to be deaf? Of course. Each directing team has reasons for coming to whatever decisions are made. For the production of *Millennium Approaches* at RIT, this is the path that was chosen. The main point in describing how the production answered this particular question is that each of the character relationships was analyzed in detail and a rationale was developed for how every character was envisioned in the play.

Which Characters Are Deaf and Where Do They Fit on the Deafhood Continuum?

Millennium Approaches is written with characters that are hearing by default. Transforming any character who is written as hearing into a deaf character can introduce creative problems that must be solved for the choice to be believable.

Take Harper Pitt as an example. The directing team's strong desire to have integrated couples meant that if Joe is a hearing character, his wife Harper is a deaf character. Harper is written as an isolated character who rarely ventures out of her apartment. *Millennium Approaches* begins in 1985, a time before the American with Disabilities Act was passed. ASL interpreters were not yet a guaranteed constitutional right. This was also a time before cell phones and the Internet were ubiquitous. The directing team believed that making Harper deaf would add more complexity to her isolation. In the script, she relies on Joe for nearly everything. In the context of this production, that would now include communicating with the outside world. One creative problem that arises with this change is that Harper spends most of her days listening to the radio. The first approach to solving this was successful. The director wrote to the publishing company and requested to change Harper's radio program to a television program. Fortunately, they granted the request and allowed a few key lines to be slightly modified.

Having made this decision, the directing team then needed to investigate Harper's interaction web. The primary point on her web is Joe, and in the team's vision, her relationship with Joe was made possible because of his knowledge of ASL (which we'll explain in more detail soon). Another vital point on her web is Mr. Lies. Mr. Lies is an interesting case because he's an imaginary character. Due to spending so much time alone and taking massive amounts of Valium, Harper dreams up people to converse with. As Harper is deaf, the directing team believed Mr. Lies—being her own creation—would believably be deaf as well.

To return to Joe, in this concept he was already established as a hearing character. With a deaf Harper, the directing team wanted a Joe who could believably sign with her in their scenes. This meant the production needed a hearing actor who could speak lines with Roy and sign lines with Harper. Conceptually, this meant needing to develop a reason why Joe even knew sign language in the first place.

To answer this, the directing team started looking into the history of deaf individuals in both Utah and the Mormon Church. Harper and Joe are originally from Salt Lake City, and being members of the Mormon Church is a strong facet of their given circumstances. As far back as 1884, before Utah had even gained statehood, the Utah Schools for the Deaf and Blind were established. In 1917, Ogden, Utah—not far from Salt Lake City—established a deaf branch of the Church of Jesus Christ of Latter-day Saints. Ogden is also home to one of the Utah Schools for the Deaf. Additionally, important aspects of the Mormon religion include missionary work, converting non-believers to Mormonism, and fostering a tightly knit community. It's conceivable that Joe, through his church life, would have been exposed to deaf Mormons from a young age—one of them being Harper. The script does not explicitly state how Joe and Harper met and so a character background was developed to fit the concept.

To strengthen Joe's background with sign language, he was envisioned as a Child of a Deaf Adult (CODA). His mother, Hannah Pitt, appears in three scenes of *Millennium Approaches*. The directing team posited that if Joe was raised by a mother who used ASL, he would have learned sign language from her growing up. This upbringing would allow him to believably communicate with Harper in the play. Readers familiar with *Millennium Approaches* will quickly point out that one of Hannah's few scenes occurs over a phone call with Joe in which he confesses that he is gay. Investigating Harper's interaction web has now sparked questions about Joe's interaction web. A new creative challenge to solve has also popped up: How does the phone call work if Hannah is deaf?

To answer this, the directing team examined Hannah's interaction web, which includes the character Sister Ella Chapter. They share one scene at the end of Act Two in which they look out over Salt Lake City from Hannah's back deck. In the scene, Ella says to Hannah, "You're about the only friend I got," indicating a closeness between them—despite Hannah's cold demeanor (Kushner 2013). To the directing team, this meant the scene could occur in ASL because Ella, being Hannah's close friend, could believably know enough ASL to converse with her. With that in mind, Ella became the solution to the phone call with Joe. A moment was engineered onstage where Hannah got Ella on the phone to interpret the call with Joe. Prior to the existence of relay services for the deaf, relying on hearing friends and neighbors to interpret phone calls was common. In addition to being historically accurate, this choice made such a vulnerable scene in the play even more so because it was entirely filtered through Ella. All of Joe's spoken lines were signed by Ella and all of Hannah's signed lines were spoken by her, allowing the phone call to take place. The full scene, as written, happened onstage, albeit through this new lens. Again, is this the solution other production teams would arrive at? Maybe not. This directing team brainstormed options, looked at the various characters' interaction webs, and created a situation in which the scene could actually unfold in both ASL and spoken English—for the benefit of both the characters and the audience.

To wrap up this particular section, answering the initial questions can become like a set of dominoes falling over—one decision triggers the next, which triggers the next, which triggers the next. You look at one character who is now envisioned as deaf and say, who *else* does this affect, who else is in their web, and how do they now believably interact? Roy's web connects to Joe, whose web connects to Harper and to Hannah, who connects to Ella. In a separate way Joe's web also connects to Louis, who connects to Prior. Harper also connects to Mr. Lies and to Prior, who connects to Belize, who connects back to Louis. Every one of these connections must be logically worked through and the directing team must follow the outcomes of their decisions.

How Are the Characters Able to Understand Each Other If They're Using Different Languages?
Of all the questions on the list, this is one of the most essential questions to answer. The world that is created onstage must make sense for the characters living in it. The concept must be accessible to all of them or it won't work. If moments in the play are not accessible to all of the characters, then those moments must be *performed that way* on purpose as part of the concept.

In *Millennium Approaches*, the directing team matched characters who could use the same language. From a casting standpoint, this decision put more work on the actors playing Joe and Louis. As stated, Joe signed with certain characters while speaking to others. Much like Joe, Louis was envisioned as a hearing man who knew ASL. He spoke with certain characters, like Joe, and signed to others, like Prior, who was envisioned as deaf. Much like the answer to the question of how Joe knew ASL, a specific backstory was developed for Louis. In the same way Harper's interactions with various characters were defined, the same process was completed for Prior. Doing this detailed work and sifting through each interaction web helped establish how every character could communicate with and understand all other characters they met throughout the story. This created consistency in communication on stage.

In *Millennium Approaches*, having certain characters who could communicate in both ASL and spoken English solved several problems. At the same time, it did not make sense that *all* characters would be able to do this. This meant when characters using different languages met, the directing team needed to solve how they could understand each other, which was accomplished in a variety of ways.

One example is Emily, a hospital nurse. In Act Two, Prior is hospitalized as his condition worsens. Emily's first scene is with Louis while Prior is asleep in the hospital bed. Because both Emily and Louis were envisioned as hearing characters, it meant their lines to each other were spoken. An unconscious Prior did not need the lines signed to him. As will be discussed in more detail soon, communication was still accessible for the audience via open captioning and the Guardian Angels.

Later in the play, Emily has a scene where she is alone with Prior. For this interaction, using the interpreter-character model, a separate character was invented. The new character worked as a nurse in the hospital, knew sign language, and could informally interpret for Prior and Emily. This choice involved a bit of historical anachronism, as it wasn't until after the ADA was passed in 1990 that hospitals were legally responsible for providing interpreters. The audience was asked for a bit of suspended disbelief and the interpreter-character made the conversation between Emily and Prior possible. Similar to the Hannah-Joe phone call, the two portrayed the entire scene in the presence of a new character who slightly altered, but did not obstruct, the scene. To the directing team, their exchange occurred in a way that made sense in the world of the play and for the audience.

Within the story, there are also times when a lack of access to one of the languages used onstage makes dramaturgical sense. One example of this happened in Act Three. After learning that Harper has disappeared and Joe is in the hospital, Hannah flies to New York City. Leaving the airport via bus, she mistakenly gets off in the Bronx instead of in Brooklyn. Alone at night and lost, she meets a character named Homeless Woman. Since Hannah in this production is deaf, we decided that Homeless Woman is a hearing person. This created a situation where neither character fully understood the other. The scene is already written for their conversation to be a struggle. The script includes moments when Hannah speaks to Homeless Woman and does not get a response, and other times when Hannah talks to herself. The stage directions call for Homeless Woman to "turn to the empty air beside her and begin to berate it" and have a conversation with a person she has hallucinated (Kushner 2013). Hannah and Homeless Woman spend the first half of the scene unable to connect at all. It's not until near the end of their interaction when Hannah loses all patience and forces Homeless Woman to help her that they actually share any dialogue of substance. At this moment, the directing team utilized a combination of gesture, lipreading, and passing written notes back and forth for Hannah to get the information she needed. So, throughout the scene, each character was not truly accessible to the other and it was *purposefully* decided to have their scene performed that way. Doing so added another layer of complexity to Hannah's frustrating journey in New York City. Again, as will be discussed in a later section, communication was still accessible for the audience via open captioning and the Guardian Angels.

Is There a Dramaturgical Reason for the Unique Communication Environment Within the Story?
Answering this question is the first step to making sure your artistic choices are clear to your audience. There are two approaches in addressing it. First, with some productions, such as *Spring Awakening* and *The Music Man*, the director and/or dramaturg use space in the program book and in the lobby display to explain their concept. They 'front-load' the audience with contextual information to better understand how their play will function. Michael Arden's director's note for *Spring Awakening* connects his production to the 1880 Milan Conference, where oralism was determined to be the best educational method for deaf students. At performances of *The Music Man*, lobby materials explained how co-directors Michael Baron and Sandra Mae Frank envisioned the town of River City, Iowa in the vein of nineteenth-century Martha's Vineyard where hearing and deaf people lived together in a very close-knit, bilingual community.

Other productions will make no mention of their conceptual choices, but instead hope the characters, relationships, and storytelling are clearly communicated to the audience through their concerted work during the production process. *Millennium Approaches* took this latter route. Was the audience explicitly told that Joe was a CODA? No. However, the directing team believed the audience would see that his mother was deaf and understand that's how he knew sign language. On the other hand, one character whose backstory was perhaps not as clear to the audience was Louis. How did he acquire his working knowledge of sign language? Audiences were not explicitly told his backstory, but the clues were there. The first scene of the play takes place at the funeral of Sarah Ironson, Louis' grandmother. The entire scene is a eulogy given by Rabbi Isidor Chemelwitz. The decision was made that Sarah—an unseen character in *Millennium Approaches*—is deaf, and a deaf actor was cast as Rabbi Chemelwitz. A backstory was developed that Sarah taught some sign language to Louis as he grew up. Later in life, Louis met Prior, a deaf man, and the two started a relationship. Louis' knowledge of ASL was then called upon every day in his four-year relationship with Prior. This decision was well thought-through, incorporated into the character, and provided a dramaturgical reason for how Louis and Prior could believably interact in ASL. This backstory was not explained to the audience, and so they didn't know the specific world that had been created. Instead, the production relied on the interactions between the characters, and allowed the relationship to speak for itself in the overall arc of the story.

How Is the Audience Able to Understand Everything Happening Onstage?
Once the characters understand each other and the dramaturgical rationale of each scene has been established, this essential question must be answered. Not only should the world of the play make sense for the characters living in it, but from a language standpoint, it should be accessible to your mixed deaf and hearing audience. You, as a directing team, have already resolved how the characters access language in the world of the play. Now you must decide how the audience has access to both languages on stage.

In the concept for *Millennium Approaches*, audience language accessibility was initially a harder nut to crack than character language accessibility. To solve this, the directing team took the largest conceptual leap by creating what was called the 'Host of Guardian Angels.' In the play, the Angel is a prominent character who visits Prior in Act One and Act Two via her voice, before arriving physically (in a tremendous way) in Act

Three. In the text, the Angel is referred to as a Principality. This led the directing team to explore the notion of angelic hierarchies. Principalities are found in the lowest order, below angels like Seraphim and Cherubim, but still above Guardian Angels, who are at the very bottom of the hierarchy.

Conceptually, it was decided that the Angel had sent before her a Host of Guardian Angels to watch over the characters in the play. This meant that actors were added to the cast to portray Guardian Angels and shadow principal characters like Prior and Harper. Functionally, these shadow actors either spoke or signed the lines for their assigned characters. If the principal character spoke a line, the Guardian Angel signed it, and vice versa. This created access to both languages for the audience. The Guardian Angels were always present when their principal character was present to provide language access.

It's imperative in integrated theatre that language access be considered from the beginning, not added on at the end. How directing teams approach this will depend on the production itself and what makes sense for that specific show.

In addition to considering how spoken English and sign language would both be presented onstage, the directing team decided from the very beginning to use open captions throughout the entire show. The captions were integrated into the set design and were projected center stage just above the actors' heads. The team made the decision to use all three modalities for several reasons. First, not all deaf people know or use sign language. One common mistake many hearing people make is to assume that if someone is deaf, it automatically means they know or are fluent in ASL. Using captions in addition to sign language gives these individuals access. Second, many student actors at NTID come from oral backgrounds and are learning sign language. Their stage signing may lack the clarity of native users. Captioning preserves accessibility for deaf audiences in this situation. Third, the use of captions can benefit many hearing people as well. During the performance of a play, there may be times when a line is not heard due to the actor's volume, too much activity onstage, audience response such as a laugh or clap, sound effects or underscoring, or many other factors. In these moments, hearing audience members can look to the captions to confirm or clarify lines that may have been missed. For these reasons, the use of captions has become standard in all NTID Performing Arts productions. And as this production was co-produced by NTID, captions were planned from the start.

If Characters Traditionally Thought to Be Hearing People Are Now Deaf, How Does Deaf Culture Enter the Story?
Deaf culture was manifested in different ways throughout *Millennium Approaches*, both large and small. Harper and Joe interacted in ways that are typical in the deaf community. For example, to get each other's attention, they would stomp on the floor or touch a shoulder. As another example, the directing team believed that Harper was not as formally educated as Prior, and though both were signing onstage, their signing registers were different to reflect that educational difference. In a similar way, Belize was made into a deaf character, and his signing reflected Black American Sign Language, a variant of ASL that developed among Black communities in the United States due to the segregation of schools based on race.

To return to the Hannah-Joe phone call, the directing team decided that though Hannah was deaf, her late husband had been hearing, and so their house would have a landline phone. A light was installed on the prop phone to indicate to Hannah (and the audience) when the phone was ringing. The light functioned in the same way a flashing doorbell or smoke detector works within a deaf household. The practice of having a neighbor interpret a call, as Ella did for Hannah, was common before relay call services, FaceTime, and videophones. In 1985, accessibility devices such as TTYs were expensive and not every deaf person had one (Jill did not get her first TTY until the late 1990s). All of these are examples of how deaf culture became ingrained in the world of the play. Because the actors playing these characters were deaf, they could imbue their characters with their perspectives and experiences, resulting in more authentic performances.

In answering the initial conceptual questions for *Millennium Approaches*, the directing team always focused on how the characters communicated onstage and how their lines were communicated to the audience. If a scene or a character did not satisfy both of these objectives in a clear, logical way, the directing team revisited the drawing board and envisioned it differently. In fact, many of the examples just given were not the original vision, but were the product of evolving ideas, open communication, and artistic trust. This conceptualization process occurred over months from April to August so that by the time of auditions, there was a very clear understanding of how every character was envisioned in the story.

Guidelines for Designers

After the directing team answers the initial questions and has a developed concept, it's time to meet with the full design team. This section gives helpful considerations for designers when working on an integrated production.

First Production Meeting

For the first production meeting, it's crucial to have as much balanced representation on the team as possible. An integrated production at the center of the spectrum would include multiple designers working in tandem in each area. Perhaps the production has an integrated team with different deaf and hearing designers who have various deaf and hearing assistant designers. For example, the scenic designer is hearing but has a deaf assistant, while the costume designer is deaf with a deaf assistant, while the lighting designer is a hearing person. The specific makeup of the team is not critical because, with the possible exception of sound design, any design area can be handled by a deaf or hearing person.[1] The primary goal is that your team has a diverse mix of individuals.

Working with ASL Interpreters

Remember that high-quality communication is a non-negotiable principle for integrated productions. Communication must be accessible and inclusive for the entire team. With this diverse mix of team members, it's vital to have ASL interpreters present at all meetings from the start. Ideally, the same interpreters are assigned to the production from the very first day to the very last. By being involved from day one, interpreters will be familiar with the goals of the production, the people and positions involved, the terminology used, the concept, the planning and scheduling of meetings and rehearsals, and the context of the work—all of which allow them to do their job better. New interpreters joining late in the process bring the same learning curve as replacing an actor in the middle of rehearsals. That

---

[1] Because many deaf people have some ability to hear, it is not impossible for a deaf person to work as a sound designer. Sound can also be represented visually on various types of equipment.

person will not have the necessary information and context to immediately do their best work, so everyone's work will temporarily suffer.

Interpreters should be acknowledged as people and considered part of the larger creative team. However, there should be clear boundaries about what they are and are not responsible for. Interpreters are there to facilitate communication. They are not there to teach sign language or be an expert on deaf culture and deaf people. It is helpful if all theatre artists understand these responsibilities and avoid asking interpreters to step out of role. There should also be enough interpreters for the number of people in the room. As an example, a one-hour production meeting should have at least two interpreters. While some interpreters are willing to work solo for assignments an hour long or less, having multiple interpreters allows for 20-minute rest periods, which help interpreters avoid repetitive stress injuries and stay mentally fresh. A four-hour long rehearsal should have at least two interpreters in each room where deaf people are working. Each performance should have at least two to three backstage interpreters, ideally with one in each wing, and one floating around as needed.

When including interpreters on your production, several things will aid them in facilitating fluid communication among the group.

- Book interpreters far in advance. Oftentimes, requests for interpreting services are made at the last minute, which means interpreters may not be available. Or, the available interpreters may not be the best suited for the job due to their background, knowledge of theatre, and level of skill. Interpreters have different areas of specialization, such as business, medicine, or the arts. An interpreter who does not typically work in the theatre industry will not have knowledge of common terminology, practices, people, or contexts. More specific to an individual production, they likely won't know the script, characters, name signs, translations, designs, blocking, etc. and therefore will be interpreting from a major gap in context. Avert this dilemma—plan months in advance and secure interpreters early.
- Request to have the same interpreters throughout the entire process. This is called ongoing or designated interpreting. Just like any team member, being present from the beginning will give the interpreters valuable context for what the group is discussing. Without pertinent context, it's likely that information will not be effectively conveyed. When this happens, most often the deaf people in the room do not have effective access to the conversation. Know that if new interpreters

join at any point later in the process, all team members, but especially deaf team members, will be negatively impacted while interpreters catch up to the rest of the team.

- Once interpreters have been attached to the production, they are now part of your team. Include them on all communications with the team, including but not limited to emails, meeting notes, agendas, and reminders. Check to see how much information will be helpful to them and what communication channels will work best. Send a list of the names, pronouns, and photos of each person and their role on the team to ensure the interpreters know who's who. Provide them with notes or presentation materials before meetings. Give them a copy of the script. In fact, they might end up needing several printed scripts throughout the process for note taking. Make sure your production stage manager has their contact information in case there are any last-minute changes to meeting times, dates, or locations.
- Several days before each meeting, reconfirm times, dates, and locations with the interpreters to make sure they will be there.
- Realize that interpreting is not a word-for-word translation of a conversation. As we've said, ASL and English are distinct languages. It takes a different amount of time to express an idea in each. A long sentence in English could be summed up in a quick ASL sign, whereas one English word might need unpacking to properly express it in ASL. This means when someone has finished making a point, the interpreter may not be finished. Good interpreters also build in 'lag time' of ten to twenty seconds, so they are purposefully behind the person who they're interpreting. Lag time allows them to receive a more complete thought before they begin to interpret. In hearing culture there's a tendency to jump in as soon as someone else is finished talking. This creates a disadvantage for any deaf team members because they're still waiting to get the information. Add a few moments for the interpreter to finish before the next person starts begins talking.
- At meetings, always follow visual communication rules. First, establish and follow a turn taking system for group discussions. Turn taking can help keep in mind the interpreter's lag time. Another reason for a turn taking system is that conversations can easily become animated, with many people tossing out new ideas rapidly and talking over each other. Crosstalk such as this makes it nearly impossible for

an interpreter to fully and accurately interpret everything that's being said and who is saying it. This excludes deaf people from the conversation. A simple hands-up turn-taking system allows everyone to know who has the floor next and creates opportunities for deaf people to participate equally.
- Identify yourself when you have the floor. This is helpful because deaf participants will be looking at the interpreter and not you. When you say your name, the deaf team members will know who is speaking. Regular interpreters will learn who everyone is, of course, but when people actually say their name, they create time for the interpreter to name whoever is speaking.
- When using presentation materials such as a PowerPoint, limit the use of words on the screen and pause with each new slide to allow time for everyone to look at it. A hearing person can look at the slide while you continue presenting. A deaf person must look at the interpreter when you are presenting and can't look at the slide at the same time. Pausing to see the slide first will help everyone stay together. You should also pause if you are referring to an element on the slide.
- This last one may seem self-explanatory but it's surprising how often it comes up. Do not stand in front of the interpreter or visually block them in any way from the people who need to see them.

Working with Deaf People

When working with a deaf team member through an interpreted conversation, it's important to maintain eye contact with the person you're speaking to. Yes, the interpreter is present, but they are not the focus of the conversation. Information flows back and forth through an interpreter as you talk to your teammate. Look at them when they talk to you. Eye contact is supremely important in deaf culture. It shows that you are listening to someone and respecting what they have to say. In deaf culture, breaking eye contact when in a conversation is considered rude. Hearing people respond to sound. When the interpreter begins to speak, you may be tempted to look at them. If this happens, simply apologize and return to your teammate. Look at them when they are communicating and look at them when you are communicating. Doing so shows that you are in conversation with them. A faux pas of many hearing people new to working with interpreters is to talk to the interpreter. Speak to the deaf person, for that is who you are really addressing.

Key Points in Design

This section provides several key points to keep in mind as designs begin moving forward from the first production meeting. No matter the makeup of the directing team, we highly recommend getting opinions from the deaf members on the team as designs progress. Ask for feedback from deaf directors, co-directors, assistant directors, DASLs, designers, design assistants, and even stage managers. For designs that heavily influence actors, such as costumes, communicate with deaf actors to make sure the designs work for them. There are multiple ways designs can aid or hamper an integrated production. Use these guidelines when creating your design.

Scenery

- One very important scenic consideration is the size of the venue. The farther away signing actors are from the audience, the harder it becomes to catch what is being signed. In larger venues, to provide the best access to signing onstage, design more simplistic scenery that limits visual distractions behind signing actors. Consider the color, pattern, and design of all upstage walls and flats. Paint treatments that are colorful, patterned, visually busy, or similar to actors' skin colors may impede signing comprehension from the house. Establishing areas in the scenery where signing actors can be easily spotted will help audiences follow the story. This is especially important if the stage is crowded with actors' bodies. In these cases, deaf audiences won't initially know where to look or who to focus on and moments of the story may be lost. For more intimate venues with smaller house sizes, a designer has more freedom to experiment with the color, pattern, and design of scenic elements because audiences are closer to the stage and can more easily see signing actors.
- Another important scenic consideration is eliminating sightline obstructions. The signing onstage needs to be seen by both the actors and the audience. The main center stage playing space should be open and free of anything that would block sightlines. Any scenic pieces that move on and off should not create new sightline obstructions. In general, the scenic design should give the director options for where actors can be clearly seen onstage. A particularly helpful tool is the use of levels. Designing a set that includes multiple heights at which actors can be seen will give the director more options for

blocking. Having multiple seating options onstage (such as chairs, benches, blocks, or ramps) adds even more possibility for levels. These various options help avoid sightline barriers onstage. The use of levels may also be helpful depending on the rake of the audience. For houses with slight rakes, action played closer to the front row is often obstructed for patrons sitting in the back of the house because they can't see over the heads of the patrons in front of them. Levels onstage can raise the height of actors to also fight against issues such as this. Keep in mind, however, that stairs with more than one or two steps or levels with a large step up/down may cause deaf actors to look down for safety. This will break their attention from what is happening on stage and may create blocking problems.

- Take time to think about the location of captions. The best use of captioning onstage is when it is purposefully integrated into the set. Identifying a placement that is at the appropriate height and size is the first step. We suggest as close to the action as possible and just over the actors' heads. This will limit the distance an audience member's eyes need to travel from the action to the captions. In theatres with multiple seating levels, it can be challenging to find a captioning placement that works for all. In this situation, designated seating for deaf audiences can be used to determine the best placement. Captioning placement is further discussed in Chap. 5—"Guidelines for Stage Managers and Front of House Staff". The design of the captions themselves should be completed by the projection or captions designer, in consultation with deaf team members. However, the location should be driven by meetings between the director and scenic designer, also in consultation with deaf team members (such as a deaf consultant).

- Occasionally, scripts call for lines or action happening offstage to be received by characters onstage. Approaching these moments should be done in conversation with the director. Scenery should be designed in such a way to help show what is happening offstage. For example, if a character is signing or speaking offstage, how does the audience receive this communication? How do the characters onstage receive this communication? Designing the set to display this communication is one possible way to approach the moment. For example, in Shakespeare's *Twelfth Night*, Malvolio is imprisoned in a dark room and questioned by Feste. The set for Peter Novak's *Twelfth Night in ASL* (2006) included a trap door in center stage. The actor's hands protruded through the trap so that Malvolio's signing was visible to the audience.

Costumes

- For any signing actors, choose costumes that contrast with their skin color. Darker skinned actors should be dressed in lighter costumes, particularly on top where the majority of their signing will occur. Conversely, lighter skinned actors should be dressed in darker tops. With all tops, it is important to consider the signing box. The signing box is the space in front of the body, from about forehead to stomach, where many signs are created. Busy designs or patterns in the signing box detract from the visibility of the signing. A better place for such patterns and materials is lower on the body. Small patterns may work in the signing box. Again, the size of the venue should be taken into consideration. Seek the input of deaf eyes, such as the DASL or deaf consultant, before using patterns.
- Be cautious of using sparkly or reflective materials, such as sequins or rhinestones in costumes and accessories. The reflected light flashes will make it hard to see the signing. Similarly, be cautious of using bright white clothing, as it will reflect light and make it difficult to focus on signing actors. Instead, use off-whites.
- In general, avoid costumes that will restrict movement or facial expression, unless they are being deliberately chosen to support the story. Clothing should not impede finger, hand, wrist, arm, neck, or shoulder movements. Use of gloves should be very limited and purposeful, as they significantly impact the intelligibility of stage signing. Bracelets, rings, and even fingernails can also be visually distracting. Additionally, facial expressions convey a lot of meaning in signing and so the face should not be covered or blocked—again, unless it is being intentionally done to support the story. This applies as well to hair pieces, masks, or hats that may obscure the face. Hair styles may also impede reception of information communicated by facial expressions. When possible, hair should be styled off the face.
- When designing wigs, head coverings, hairpieces, or makeup, consult with individual actors about their assistive listening technology, such as hearing aids or cochlear implants. Cochlear implant devices are placed on the ear and the back of the skull. If deaf actors will be wearing their assistive listening devices onstage, costume elements should not interfere with them.

- When the time comes for costume fittings with actors, always have an interpreter present no matter how long or short the fitting.
- If you are applying makeup to a deaf actor and you need to communicate, wait until their eyes are open to do so.

Props

- The main consideration here is to be cognizant of the fact that signing actors need their hands to communicate. Many signs can be conveyed with one hand. In a comedic scene, part of the comedy might be trying to communicate despite having a handful of props. Props can also be put down or handed to another character to sign a line, then taken back up again. The primary takeaway is to remember the importance of having available hands.

Lighting

- This may seem obvious, but first make sure all lighting onstage is bright enough for signing to be seen clearly from all seats in the house. Some lighting design choices purposefully put actors or scenery in shadow or utilize vibrant color hues. More abstract lighting such as this can be effective so long as signing clarity isn't sacrificed. In scenes that take place under low light or extreme colors, consider how the signing is affected. Can it still be seen clearly from the audience? If not, then it isn't an effective lighting choice for integrated theatre. Hearing lighting designers should not rely on their own judgment here. Ask the DASL or deaf consultant.
- A halo effect can be created on signing actors by positioning lighting instruments upstage of them at a high angle. This extra splash of high, upstage lighting illuminates the actor's perimeter and makes them stand out more onstage. The lighting effect pops the actor's body and highlights their signing. When using this technique, remember to add appropriate front lighting to highlight their facial expression as well.
- Especially in plays or musicals with a large number of people onstage at the same time, lighting can be effectively used to highlight where the signing actors are located. Remember that a deaf audience needs to first find who is signing before they can take in the lines that are being communicated. Lighting can make this identification process quicker by spotlighting the actor audiences need to look at. Even a

slight bump in lighting intensity will draw the eyes of the audience to the right focal point.
- As noted in "Scenery," the production may be implementing captions onstage in the scenic design. The lighting designer needs to be aware of caption placement. Lighting can unintentionally wash out captions.
- Backstage areas should have appropriate cue lights installed for deaf actors. They may not be able to hear or see what is happening onstage and need a cue light to tell them when to enter. The cue light can be triggered by a stage manager or assistant stage manager.
- Make sure there is appropriate blue lighting in all backstage and offstage wing areas. This is helpful for anyone who has difficulty seeing in dim places, but also makes signing backstage more easily seen. In performances that call for costume quick changes or speedy scene changes, having the appropriate blue lighting backstage allows all crew members and actors to clearly see and communicate with each other.
- When tech week arrives, make sure to create a stopping signal. Typically, in mainstream theatre, when a rehearsal run needs to stop, someone will call out "Hold!" For your integrated production, build in a visual signal that is the equivalent of calling for a hold. This is a two-step process. First, how do individuals, such as an actor or designer or director, visually signal for a hold? Then, how do you convey the hold to the entire team? Amongst your team, decide what the visual equivalent is for calling hold and make sure everyone knows this signal. To convey the hold to everyone, establish an unmistakable indicator such as a full stage of red light. Then, when anyone calls a hold or shows the visual signal, the light board operator can quickly punch the hold light cue, indicating to everyone that a hold has been called. Once these visual stop signs have held the run, immediately bring up house and work lights so that everyone can gather to discuss the hold.
- See "Sound" for connecting sound effects with lighting effects.

Projections

- Similar to the guidelines in "Scenery," limit moving projections behind signing actors. It's very easy for these movements to impede signing comprehension from the house.

- When creating captions, use only one to two rows of text per caption. To determine font size, sit in the very last row of the theatre and read the text. Your smallest acceptable font should be whatever can be comfortably read without any squinting or straining to see. Get a variety of perspectives on the sizing as everyone's eyes are different. Use a darker background color with a lighter color font. Perspectives on this differ, but generally an off-white text works well. The beginning of each new line should indicate which character is speaking. Add blank captions when there are significant pauses onstage. Be cautious of accidentally giving away a joke or surprise too soon in the captions.[2]
- Consider using creative captioning, in which the captioning design matches the style of the show and reflects characterization and tone. Creative captioning is a relatively new development, but some preliminary research suggests that audiences respond positively to it (Glover 2021). Design and placement guidelines for creative captioning have been developed by Ben Glover (n.d.).
- Include brief descriptions of any important sound cues, music, or underscoring. Creative captioning can also be used to provide visual access to sound design.
- Be thorough when creating the captions to ensure there are no errors or inaccuracies in the text.
- See "Sound" for connecting sound effects with projection.

Sound

- Any purposeful sounds or effects onstage should have a visual equivalent. Examples include: thunder accompanied by a lightning effect, a doorbell accompanied by a blinking doorbell light, a ringing phone accompanied by a flashing phone light. For any sounds that can't be conveyed via lighting, think about how they could be conveyed physically onstage or via projections. Also consider how captions can be used to describe sounds.
- For any music, utilize speaker placement to create vibrations that can be physically felt by audiences. Large bass speakers with subwoofers can send sound vibrations to audience members through the stage floor. Some companies have experimented with attaching subwoof-

---

[2] More guidelines and a helpful checklist can be found on the StageTEXT website: https://www.stagetext.org/for-venues/resources/

ers to seating platforms in order to create more vibration for deaf audiences to feel. Some theatres have provided balloons for deaf audience members to hold, allowing them to feel the vibrations. Vibro-tactile vests have also been developed that allow deaf audiences to physically experience music.
- An additional tool when using music is establishing a visual representation of the music. This could be a person playing it live—perhaps a musician with a harp or banjo or piano—or a graphic representation. It could be using music videos (with captions) during pre-show, post-show, or intermission. The director and DASL can work with the sound designer to embed other visual representations of the music into the staging. This might make use of sign language musicality, dance, or other visual representations of the quality of the music. This is an area that has been neglected in integrated theatre. More experimentation is needed, especially in musical theatre.

Bringing It All Together

These guidelines are meant to help designers be aware of best practices for designing in an integrated production. As with all theatre, the team also needs to create one cohesive theatrical world onstage. Designs should fit together stylistically and complement each other. Your first production meeting gets the ball rolling on creating this world. After the meeting there may be follow-up meetings with individual designers before additional production meetings take place. As the team goes forward, always keep in mind the third non-negotiable principle—high-quality communication is an imperative. Remember to foster inclusivity with all deaf team members and to maintain accessibility in all future meetings. Equal, inclusive, and accessible communication must be cultivated at every step of the creative process. Finally, whenever possible, give precedence to the input of the deaf team members. Remember that they are the experts on visual communication and deaf culture.

Key Points in Design: *Angels in America, Part 1: Millennium Approaches*

Initial design conversations for *Millennium Approaches* began with scenery and took place far in advance of auditions. The play was originally scheduled for the spring of 2021 but, due to COVID-19, it was postponed until the fall of 2021. Conversations with the scenic designer started in the summer of 2020. The priority list for the scenic design included: (1) maximizing the Angel's physical entrance into the story, (2) making scene transitions fast and efficient, (3) incorporating both projection and caption surfaces, and (4) including multiple levels for blocking. The director and scenic designer met approximately once a month for brainstorming sessions during the summer and fall months of 2020. At this point, a deaf assistant director (AD) and DASL had been identified, but was unable to attend these initial meetings and later ended up stepping down for personal reasons. Scenic ideas and rough design sketches had been shared with the AD/DASL but were not able to be further developed before their departure. A new deaf AD/DASL came onboard in spring 2021. Though scenic conversations had continued and the design was much more developed, the new AD/DASL viewed sketches as soon as he joined and began providing feedback.

Millennium Approaches was performed in a proscenium house with nearly 450 seats. NTID's Panara Theatre is unique in having been designed for deaf audiences. In addition to a steep rake, all seating faces center stage. These physical elements make designing for integrated productions easier. For *Millennium Approaches*, a single, stationary wall spanned almost the entire stage and provided most of the background. Cut into the wall were two arched entryways. These could be closed via sliding panels that doubled as projection surfaces. Rear projections were displayed independently on each entryway's sliding panel. Front projection was used to display captions on the wall. The captions appeared on a horizontal area just above the archways. Several scenes also included moments of front-projected imagery spanning the wall. Downstage of the entryways was a large platform with a wrap-around step. Between the entryways, in the center of the platform, rested four moveable, 3-foot stage cubes. Downstage of the wall, stage space was free of sightline obstructions and provided multiple playing areas—either on the platform, the wrap-around step, or on the stage floor itself. The set was painted with a combination of warm grays and browns, which both represented the look we wanted and offered a neutral, non-distracting background for signing actors. *Millennium Approaches* is a three-act play with twenty-six scenes taking place across various locations. The set itself was a unit set that allowed the assorted scenes to take place anywhere on it. Smaller furniture pieces were moved off and on to specify the location of each individual scene. See Fig. 3.1 for a view of the completed set.

Fig. 3.1 *Angels in America, Part 1: Millennium Approaches* at the National Technical Institute for the Deaf, Rochester Institute of Technology. Scenic Design: Erin Auble. (Photo: Erin Auble)

As the scenic design developed, the projection designer was introduced to the projection locations and surface options within the set. When the arched entryway panels were closed, the projection designer used these areas to great effect. Projections were developed to specify each location throughout the play. For example, Harper and Joe's apartment was established by projections within the stage right entryway; Roy's office gave a glimpse of the New York City skyline that spanned both entryway surfaces; Prior and Harper's shared dream/hallucination received a projection treatment that was front-projected onto the entire wall; in a split scene taking place at both an elegant NYC bar and in Central Park, front projections on the wall established where the both bar and where the park each existed onstage; Harper's imaginary Antarctica was a full stage projection of swirling ice and snow. Captions were displayed throughout all of these examples.

The arched entryway panels were also used to project pre-recorded characters. In the script, the Angel first visits Prior with only her voice. Because Prior was deaf, a visual projection of the Angel was created. The actor playing the Angel was recorded and then various digital distortions were applied to the video. The goal was to maintain her signing clarity without entirely revealing her appearance to the audience, which allowed her full reveal to be preserved until the finale, while also making the character accessible to Prior (and the audience). The actor playing Prior then performed his scenes with the pre-recorded Angel projected on the entryway surfaces. Other non-physical characters such as Mr. Lies, Ethel Rosenberg, and the ghosts of Prior's long-dead ancestors were also played as projections on these panels. As the panels became so essential to the storytelling, the director frequently met with the projection and scenic designers to ensure these pieces of the production fit together seamlessly. Once the new AD/DASL joined the team, he began attending production meetings, was brought up to speed with all conversations, and provided valuable feedback about making these elements work for deaf actors and audiences.

The director, scenic designer, and projection designer on the *Millennium Approaches* team were all hearing people. During the pre-audition process, all were cognizant of keeping designs fluid until feedback from deaf team members could be given. In the case of this production, the AD/DASL was one of the few deaf members of the production team, albeit one with a lot of influence in creative decision-making. Once identified, this new person was present for as much of the process as his schedule allowed. The director took great care not to move forward until the AD/DASL had reviewed ideas and given feedback. Other team members were genuinely open to this feedback and made adjustments as necessary.

DIRECTOR OF ARTISTIC SIGN LANGUAGE

What's in a Name?

The term *director of artistic sign language* (DASL) is relatively new to the theatre scene, gaining traction in the mid-2010s.[3] Before DASL became the preferred title, a person doing this work might have been referred to as an ASL Master, ASL Coach, or Sign Coach. Much like a fight director or intimacy director, a DASL is an expert who supports the production in a specific way. The duties of the role are still evolving and being codified. Whereas the responsibility of an ASL Coach was very specific—observe and assess the signing onstage—the responsibilities of a DASL cover much, much more than this. Including the word *director* highlights the

---

[3] Some people pronounce DASL as *dazzle*. We prefer to use the acronym itself: D-A-S-L.

fact that a DASL is ultimately responsible for developing a key part of the production—the performances of the signing actors.

From the moment a production is conceived of as integrated or a deaf actor is cast, a DASL should be hired. This person should be deaf. Directors might be tempted to hire a hearing person who is fluent in ASL, such as a CODA or interpreter for this role. Doing so is considered unethical in the deaf community. Yes, it is easier for hearing directors, as well as cheaper, to hire someone hearing to be a DASL. But this takes jobs from deaf individuals who are not only just as qualified, but bring authenticity through lived experience of deafness and reliance on visual communication. This gives them insights hearing people lack.

From the moment they assume the role, the DASL should be integrated into the process. The most important factor for a DASL's success is to have the acknowledgment and respect of the director. How a director treats a DASL will influence how the rest of the creative team treats the DASL. The work of a DASL cannot be effectively done without being seen as an equal by all other team members. Their work *is* equivalent to the work of all principal designers and directors. They need others to trust their expertise and experience, and be willing to collaborate throughout the production process. Hearing directors and others whose involvement in the production falls within the DASL's realm of experience engage in audism when they do not respect the perspectives and recommendations of the DASL.

The Role of the DASL

There is currently no standardized training for DASLs. That is starting to change as more training opportunities are being offered. But for now, artists working in this role have mostly developed their understanding of their responsibilities through their experience—a kind of trial by fire. This means interpretations of what a DASL actually does can vary widely depending on who you ask. However, as more and more deaf performers work in theatre, film, and television, the need for DASLs and DASL training is ever-increasing. We have interviewed a handful of prominent DASLs and created the following section based on their ideas, experiences, and opinions.

A DASL can take on many responsibilities. However, they primarily focus on the representations of deaf culture and use of ASL onstage, and the creative decision-making that affects those two things. To do this, a

DASL must be a full collaborator in supporting the director's vision. In many ways, the DASL role is similar to the dramaturg role. But, their responsibilities go beyond that to include translation, coaching and directing the actors using sign language, and advising on every aspect of the staging that impacts the visibility of the stage signing.

Being a DASL requires an immense amount of time, energy, and commitment. It is an everyday role, not someone who pops in to observe a few rehearsals and give a few notes. Their role is much more than only advisory. A DASL should be involved during pre-auditions, auditions, rehearsals, and tech week, all the way up to opening night. Unfortunately, a DASL must also be prepared to face resistance from others on the team. This may come from a director, a designer, or even actors, who either don't fully understand the DASL's role, or feel that this person is not really needed, or disagree with their choices. It's easy to underestimate how crucial this role actually is in integrated productions. There is so much work for a DASL to accomplish that we even recommend more than one DASL. A team is able to divide the many responsibilities and therefore do better work for the production. Let's look at the production process via the DASL role.

Meeting with the Director

As soon as a DASL is hired, they should meet with the director to learn about the show itself. This meeting should take place as far in advance as possible. If signing actors are already cast, the DASL should meet them as soon as possible. Some DASLs may also want to meet with the production interpreters to begin developing that working relationship. When meeting with the director, the DASL is there to learn about their vision. This includes asking questions about the script, the specific concept for the production, crucial background information on the team and/or process, how characters are envisioned, and how sign language and deaf culture contribute to the story. The stage sign language should match the characters appropriately and the DASL can learn how best to achieve that through this meeting.

The relationship between a DASL and a deaf director compared to that with a hearing director will look different, especially if the hearing director is new to working with deaf artists and deaf culture. Deaf directors typically view DASLs as partners and collaborators. They will discuss and share ideas about the characters, translation choices, and designs. When working with a hearing director new to deaf people, the DASL typically must make decisions by themselves. They are seen as the deaf expert in the room and are left to figure out what works and what doesn't. Because the director does not know any better, they will generally accept what the DASL says in regard to deaf people and culture. This puts a lot of pressure on the DASL to speak for an entire community and is another reason we advocate for multiple DASLs when possible.

Work on Their Own

After meeting with the director, the DASL will begin their own creative process. This is approached differently by different people, but shares similarities to other team members on the production. A scenic designer takes certain information away from the first production meeting and tackles their area of the play: the scenery. For a DASL, this period typically involves a deep analysis of the script and the characters, paying particular attention to the characters who will be signing. This includes any signing deaf characters, but also other characters who interact with them. The DASL is beginning to lay the groundwork for translating the play from English into ASL (or other signed language). They will consider how the characters are envisioned as deaf or signing persons, how their signing is produced; why certain signs may fit better than others; where the characters are from and how cultural ties impact their signing choices; how given circumstances such as class, gender, and race may affect their signing; and how relationships may affect their signing. It's very analytical work, at times akin to that of a dramaturg. While working through the script in this way, the DASL should continue to meet with the director to refine their ideas and further develop the characters.

Translation Period

Once there is a clearer view of the characters, the DASL can begin translating the script. This period begins an ongoing process that may evolve when actors are later added. Typically, translations will continue to grow and change throughout rehearsals as more is learned about the story and characters. Translation is another period when having a team of DASLs is extremely beneficial because the process itself is very complex with many ways to approach it. Consider the amount of work involved in taking *A Midsummer Night's Dream*, or *Angels in America*, or *Spring Awakening*, and translating all of the nuance and metaphor and imagery into an entirely new language. That's a tall order for any one person to do alone and the end product will be much stronger if there are multiple creative minds at work. We strongly recommend hiring at least one other translator to work with the DASL. A team of three to four is ideal, depending on the complexity of the play or musical. Having a DASL team will also allow for cultural competency in different dialects, racial/ethnic identities, and subcultures.

Translating a script into ASL means creating a completely new script, which typically takes on one of two (or sometimes both) forms. It may either be written down in what is called a gloss script, or it may be video recorded, or both. A gloss is like a shorthand translation of ASL. Because ASL is a visual-gestural language and not a written language, the notations in a gloss script don't capture everything that's being signed.[4] Due to this, a gloss leaves room for interpretation because two actors looking at the same gloss might express it in different ways. For this reason, once a translation draft is complete, a DASL will oftentimes create a video script. For actors, seeing lines signed is more helpful than trying to interpret them from written text. But a gloss can be more useful as a quick reference in rehearsals. Either way, it's important for the DASL and translation team to keep documentation of their translation. The gloss and/or videos will eventually be given to the actors, but also will be kept for future use. They may be shared with an understudy, or used to teach a new actor stepping into an existing role, or called upon if a show is remounted.

The ASL scripts are a guide for actors to begin learning their lines. Depending on the specific production, the DASL's approach, and the actors involved, there may be more or less freedom for the actors to develop their own translations. For example, a seasoned DASL working with less experienced actors may complete much of the translation prior to rehearsals and then give the ASL script to the actors. A DASL working with more experienced actors may come in with specific ideas for certain moments but also see what the actors bring to the table. In some professional productions, actors are given a video script and expected to follow it without variation. In our work at NTID, the ASL script is typically a starting point and the DASL and actors continue developing the translation together. Directors who are new to integrated deaf and hearing

---

[4] Various systems have been proposed for capturing sign language in writing, but none have really caught on.

theatre should discuss with the DASL which approach will serve their production best. However, we strongly recommend NOT expecting deaf actors to do full translations of their own lines themselves during the rehearsal process. This takes time away from the deaf actor's work to memorize lines, learn blocking, and develop their character, creating inequities between the deaf and hearing actors.

The more time a DASL has to translate a script, the better. In an ideal world, they would be given months to translate prior to rehearsals and a team of people to work with. The process of translation includes not only signing what is being stated in the dialogue but, just as importantly, matching signing choices and signing style to the envisioned characters. Coming to decisions about this involves everyone on the translation team bringing their ideas, backgrounds, and experiences to the process. There can be much debate and deliberation to arrive at the best translation draft.

Auditions

Many people interviewed for this book stated that DASLs should absolutely be attending auditions when deaf actors will be cast. However, it is not currently common for theatre companies to have DASLs in the audition room. We advocate for them to be present. If they are not there, who is assessing the signing ability of those auditioning? Oftentimes when signing actors audition and there is no deaf directing team member present, an ASL interpreter is asked to pass judgment on auditionees. This puts that interpreter in a very difficult situation. It's absolutely not their job to evaluate the actors who have come into the audition room. They are there to interpret, that is it. Because the number of interpreters is limited, relying on an interpreter's judgment potentially also creates an unfair power dynamic within the deaf community. Additionally, if the director is a hearing person, they will naturally respond to what they hear. There is a risk that they may rely on their perception of the interpreter's voicing, rather than on the acting ability of the person auditioning. All of these situations place the deaf actor at a disadvantage. Having the DASL present during the audition means that deaf actors will be evaluated on their strengths as actors and their fit with the director's vision. The DASL can also evaluate hearing actors who will be expected to sign for their potential ability to express themselves through visual-gestural language. The director will get the final say about who is offered a role, but the DASL's recommendations should be weighed heavily in those decisions.

Production Meetings and Design Process

As production meetings occur and designs are developed, the DASL should have the same access to all principal designers as the director does. We recommend the DASL attend all production meetings as well as any individual meetings that involve the director. If this is not possible, the director should report ideas back to the DASL to gauge their impact on the signing and representations of deafness onstage.

Throughout the process, the DASL should be allowed to give feedback on different design elements, such as scenery, costumes, and lighting. As stated in the "Director of Artistic Sign Language" section of this chapter, all of these designs have the ability to positively or negatively impact the visibility of signing onstage. The DASL is there to provide knowledge and experience about what works and what doesn't. If the lighting is too dim, they should be able to point that out and have an adjustment be made. If the costume color does not contrast enough with an actor's skin color, they should be able to point that out and have an adjustment be made. Remember that they, too, are there to support the director's vision and the success of the production. Just as importantly, they are also there to make sure the story is working for deaf actors and the performance is working for deaf audiences. They're looking at not only the signing itself but how all the things onstage come together in one picture. No matter the look or the design, it is possible to achieve a certain vision while still making that vision accessible.

First Rehearsal

The first rehearsal is the time to introduce the DASL to the entire cast and make sure their role is clearly understood. At this rehearsal, it's important for someone to discuss with the cast what is necessary to create an inclusive and accessible environment for this production. The DASL *can* give input here, however, we advocate for a separation of responsibilities. The DASL can do a lot, but the more responsibility that rests on their shoulders, the less time they can devote to their primary responsibility for what's happening on the stage. Therefore, for this crucial cast conversation, we recommend hiring a separate deaf consultant. Later we will expand on the role and responsibilities of a deaf consultant.

Ongoing Rehearsals

As we've said, the DASL should be involved daily at rehearsals and that starts with tablework. In fact, we've found that in integrated productions with multiple actors performing the same role, doing tablework and translation work together is incredibly effective in creating offstage bonds and onstage chemistry. While this work is happening, typically the director is leading the rehearsal and the DASL is right there to add input. The DASL will only have as much authority as the director allows them to have. Directors must prioritize giving DASLs time to provide feedback to actors. When giving notes, a director who allows time and space for a DASL to also give their notes will create a more equitable and successful process.

There may also be times when a DASL is working on translation with actors separately from the director. Working on translation requires a lot of time. It is more than just polishing the signs the actors are using. The DASL will explain why they want to see certain lines signed in certain ways and how the translation was developed to enhance the director's vision. They will help the actors incorporate the signing into their own bodies and make adjustments that may feel more natural to that specific actor. As mentioned previously, the DASL and actors may work on the translation together. This gives the actors freedom to bring themselves to the role while also maintaining consistency in the translation. The DASL gives the actors feedback on their stage signing, just as a voice coach gives actors feedback on how they deliver their spoken lines. During blocking rehearsals, DASLs will also view the stage from different angles and consider how to establish the best sightlines for audiences. Their input on blocking choices and the use of stage space is essential. A deaf or signing actor cannot see how their own signing appears onstage and so the DASL helps make their signing clear, visible, and readable throughout the house.

As rehearsals progress, a DASL will function as a primary support person for both director and actors. The DASL is there to figure out the best way to help all of the actors work together to support the director's vision. They will advocate for the things they see that need to be altered. They will want to be involved in any conversations regarding the signing actors. They will communicate with the design team. They will continue developing characters with the actors. They will work with understudies to make sure those actors are ready to go on if needed. Their list of responsibilities feels almost endless!

Interpreted Performances

If the production is using performance interpreters for audience accessibility, in addition to the stage signing, the DASL may also help screen which interpreters are chosen. On top of that, they may work with the interpreters (much like they do with actors) to emphasize certain signs or ways of signing something during the performance. The ASL script that was created along the way can also be given to these interpreters to use. However, there's not a consensus yet on how much a DASL should be involved in this area. Time spent on audience accessibility may be time taken away from what is happening on stage. We advocate for a deaf consultant taking on this responsibility for audience accessibility instead of the DASL.[5]

The Role of a Deaf Consultant

If the DASL is an everyday role focused on the art that's being created onstage, then a deaf consultant is a more limited role focused on establishing accessibility and inclusion *within* the production and performance process. They are there to support deaf actors or team members during their work on the show, by leading culture and communication workshops, for example. They can also consult on interpreter or captioning placement, designated seating for deaf audiences, and provide training for box office staff to become comfortable communicating with deaf patrons. A DASL can undertake this work, but their role should be focused on the artistic rather than accessibility elements of the production. We recommend separating these two roles, if budget permits. Another reason for hiring a deaf consultant is that they can come in later in the rehearsal process to provide another set of 'deaf eyes.' Because the DASL is enmeshed in the production on a daily basis, it is hard for them to step back and see with fresh eyes. A deaf consultant will be unfamiliar with the translation and staging, and can therefore catch elements of both that may be unclear or not accessible to deaf audiences.

---

[5] We do, however, advocate for hiring a DASL to work with the interpreting team providing access for mainstream theatre production, where no stage ASL is involved.

The first rehearsal is a great place to bring in a deaf consultant to 'onboard' everyone. They may lead any number of workshops or training sessions focused on topics such as working with deaf people, introduction to deaf culture, basic sign language, how to work with interpreters, setting up a backstage cue system, front-of-house accessibility, or best seating for deaf patrons.

To reemphasize, hiring a deaf consultant who focuses on the workplace experience and audience accessibility separate from a DASL who focuses on the storytelling experience allows both of those individuals to do their jobs better.

Key Team Member

As you can see, the work of a DASL is all-encompassing. For an integrated production, they are one of the most critical team members. They are not simply consultants or tutors. They do much more work than a vocal or dialect coach. They are likely more present than a fight or intimacy director, or even dramaturg. The level of their involvement puts them on the same rung as an assistant or associate director. One of the most crucial aspects that leads to a DASL's success is making sure they and everyone else understands their role. They may be willing to take on more responsibilities than listed here and if they do, they should be paid for that additional work.

Director of Artistic Sign Language: *Angels in America, Part 1: Millennium Approaches*

As we've said, for *Millennium Approaches* at RIT and NTID, the production's assistant director also took on the responsibilities of DASL. As AD, he met with the director regularly for pre-audition brainstorming. As DASL, he was already in the room for those meetings. This was a benefit of having one person take on both roles. The downside is that it put a ton of work and pressure on the shoulders of a single person. In hindsight, asking the AD to take on so much work was not fair to him and he should have had additional support. Many conversations around this topic took place after the show closed. We encourage you to learn from our mistake and hire the appropriate people to ensure your show's success.

The translation period for *Millennium Approaches* was led by the AD/DASL and involved four other individuals: the director and three deaf artists with long careers in Deaf theatre. The translation team was purposefully diverse to reflect the background of the characters and included identities such as queer, Black, Jewish, female, and male.

Prior to meeting in person, the team divided the work of translation by character, with each team member taking several characters and roughing out their translations. Questions were asked about how the characters were envisioned. Joe being a CODA and Prior a culturally deaf man from a wealthy and educated background meant that each of them came to ASL in a different way. Translators needed to know this information to begin approaching the characters. During the in-person meeting, the team worked through each scene of the play over three full days. Translators would 'perform' their characters and others would watch to give feedback, analyze sign choices, discuss signing style, and make adjustments. Additional discussions ensued with every scene and character. It was critical for the director to be present and weigh in on characters or answer questions. When the scene's translation was ready, it was recorded. Later, the AD/DASL took those recordings and re-recorded them in a more neutral way, depicting the signing but removing any acting performance. He wanted to avoid a situation where actors took on the characters in the way they were portrayed by the translators. Instead, actors should focus on the correct expression of ASL and come to their *own* conclusions about the performance of the character.

The AD/DASL attended auditions and callbacks and helped cast the show. When rehearsals began, he was available to work through the translation with each of the signing actors. In doing so, he used his re-recordings as well as created new clips when the translation was adjusted to match the actors' natural signing registers. As the director moved through tablework with actors, the AD/DASL was across the room working through each scene's translation with other actors. Just like the characters, actors all come to ASL in different ways. Some are born deaf in families with strong ties to the deaf community and ASL as their native language. Some are hearing who know ASL because they have deaf family members. Some, both deaf and hearing, have only started learning ASL more recently. The AD/DASL assessed each actor's skill and comfort with ASL to meet them on their level. Some actors picked up the translation right away and even had suggestions for how certain lines could be signed. Some actors needed more one-on-one support and met with the AD/DASL often to work on their lines.

During blocking, the AD/DASL attended rehearsals regularly and would jump in to give feedback. If he wasn't present, scenes would be recorded and sent to him. When rehearsals returned to that specific scene, he would watch it before we made any further progress. Over the course of the first few blocking rehearsals, a set of staging ideas that fit the concept of the show was developed and these existed as a framework for approaching each scene. Early blocking work for integrated productions can be slow, as you must develop the principles by which your production exists physically onstage. Once the ideas were set, blocking work moved much more fluidly. These ideas are detailed further in Chap. 5—"The Rehearsal Process".

One scene in particular was quite a blocking challenge. Act 2, Scene 9 is written as a split scene between Harper/Joe and Prior/Louis. Other split scenes in the play move back and forth gradually, allowing the characters to share a long moment before crossing to the other scene. This split scene is accompanied by the stage directions, "This should be fast. No freezing; even when one of the couples isn't talking, they remain furiously alive." This scene jumps back and forth every few lines. A hearing audience can still be watching Harper/Joe when the scene switches to Prior/Louis and keep following the story. But because the deaf audience needs a little bit of lag time to redirect their visual attention, the directing team had to establish a series of physical cues onstage to pull focus when the scene jumped between couples. For blocking the scene, the director asked the AD/DASL to take charge of dictating how it should unfold, where the actors should stand for optimal sightlines, and how physical cues should be depicted. It was a reversal of roles as the AD/DASL led blocking while the director observed and offered feedback. In the end, it was one of the most successful scenes of the play—in spite of the difficulties with staging it—because of the collaborative spirit invested into it.

References

Glover, Ben. 2021. *How to Use Creative Captioning with Icarus Theatre*. Accessed November 15, 2023. https://www.youtube.com/watch?v=V4TQrZKBKGE

———. n.d. *Guidelines*. Creative Captioning. Accessed November 15, 2023. https://creativecaptioning.com/guidelines/

Kushner, Tony. 2013. *Angels in America, Part 1: Millennium Approaches*. New York: Broadway Play Publishing.

CHAPTER 4

Assembling the Cast

THE AUDITION PROCESS

The directing team is set, the concept for the story is solid, the vision of the characters is fully fleshed out, the production team has met and work is progressing. Soon performers will be introduced into the mix. This chapter will help plan for their arrival from announcing auditions to casting.

Announcing Auditions

As with any general theatre auditions, the announcement will contain dates, times, locations, and important character information. For an integrated production, several additional pieces of info should be included. First and foremost, make it clear that you are seeking deaf actors. A simple tagline such as "Looking for deaf actors" puts the message out there. Next, explain the specific characters who these actors might portray. You've spent months developing a concept and now is the time to share the vision with your potential acting pool. Identify which characters are deaf in your concept. Include other important info such as the characters' background, signing style, whether the actor needs to be able to speak as well as sign, and how you envision them communicating with others in the play. The more information you provide, the better prepared

© The Author(s), under exclusive license to Springer Nature Switzerland AG 2024
A. Head, J. M. Bradbury, *Staging Deaf and Hearing Theatre Productions*, https://doi.org/10.1007/978-3-031-61446-0_4

auditionees will be. Finally, to expand your talent pool, consider allowing video auditions. Many deaf actors are willing to travel for roles.

Beyond characters, provide information about the audition process itself. It helps actors to know what to expect when they arrive. Make it clear that you've already booked interpreters for the auditions and callbacks. Give contact information for someone who can answer any audition-related questions. If you plan to provide any sides in ASL, include information that too (we'll discuss ASL sides more fully soon). If you are accepting self-tapes, give clear instructions. Let actors know if you prefer videos to be captioned or if you want someone off screen speaking the lines in tandem. All actors benefit from receiving as much information as possible but this is especially true for deaf actors auditioning for a predominantly hearing theatre company. If you are in doubt about what information to include, err on the side of more.

Lastly, in addition to any written announcement, we advocate for also releasing this information in ASL. With the advent of social media, spreading video content is just as easy as sharing written content. ASL is a visual-gestural language and posting your announcement in a video allows that language to be expressed. It also demonstrates to potential actors that you're invested in accessibility and inclusion. As a starting point, you can use the audition video to advertise your casting call. Beyond that, the video is an effective way to introduce your team. If your production has a deaf director, co-director, or assistant director, they can introduce themselves in their own language via the visual medium. The more deaf leaders a video showcases, the more deaf actors will see what kind of production you're creating. The information and introductions you want to share can easily be made into one longer single video or split into several videos released separately. If you do make an audition video, remember to caption it.

ASL Script at Auditions and Callbacks

Prior to auditions, it is likely that your translation team will have a completed draft of the ASL script—especially if you've planned for an integrated production. Instead of waiting until after casting to share this script, why not make it available to actors for auditions and callbacks? If you plan to use specific sides from the written script, you can just as easily share those same sides translated into ASL. It's another signal that the production has prioritized accessibility and inclusion.

Some deaf actors will prefer to translate lines themselves. It's generally expected that professional deaf actors can read an English script and translate it on their own. That said, as we've described, translation is a process that takes time to work through. An actor with ASL as their first language has to read the English script, internalize the meaning and content, then reproduce it in a second language. The more time an actor has to work through this, the better translation they will produce. Additionally, as we've said, an idea in English can be expressed many different ways in ASL and vice versa. Therefore, providing the ASL script will exhibit how your team is envisioning the characters, the signs you've chosen, and the ways you're approaching certain lines.

In many audition settings, it's assumed that actors will arrive with their own pre-prepared monologues. However, if you do plan to provide any audition monologues or sides to actors, consider providing that same material in ASL as well. Providing an ASL script is a strategy to help level the playing field. A hearing actor with English as their first language can pick up the text, read it, and perform it. For the deaf actor, there's always an added step of translation. An ASL script can help eliminate that extra step, creating more equity in the audition process.

Establishing the Environment

In the same way as hearing actors, deaf actors are in the room because they want the role. They want to perform. They want to be a person just like everyone else at auditions. It's your job to remove as many barriers as possible from the audition experience. It shouldn't be on their shoulders to educate the people sitting on the other side of the table about deaf people, deaf culture, or ASL. It shouldn't be on their shoulders to request an interpreter. It shouldn't be on their shoulders to speak for an entire community. They want to walk into the room and focus on their art. The environment that you create is what will best allow them to do that. Auditions are your chance to represent yourself and your company well and to start your production on the right foot with the actors. What follows is a checklist to ensure you're establishing the best environment for deaf and hard of hearing actors:

- Prioritize communication by securing enough interpreters for all auditions and callbacks.
- Arrange for deaf members of your directing team, including the DASL, to be in the room.

- Educate yourself on deaf culture, the deaf community, and basic ASL if you haven't already done so.
- Establish a vision for the show and a plan for how deaf actors will be involved, then be ready to explain this if asked.
- Bring openness and flexibility in regard to actors' communication needs.
- Address any accessibility needs or concerns that are expressed in the moment.
- If you make any mistakes, accept responsibility and apologize, then keep moving forward.
- Allow for more time in the audition than you normally would, given that you are working in two languages.
- Harness your spirit of collaboration and demonstrate that you are invested in working with the deaf actors.

We are assuming that if you are planning for an integrated production, you *are* invested in this work. Auditions are your first opportunity to demonstrate that to potential actors. Completing each item from the list above will send a message to deaf actors that you have appropriately and adequately planned for their arrival. For additional help in setting up auditions, you should look to your deaf directing team members, DASL, and/or deaf consultant. Each production is a unique endeavor and these people will be sensitive to the needs of deaf actors while assisting you in preparing for your specific audition process.

Interpreters at Auditions

As discussed in Chap. 1, making communication the top priority will lead to a more inclusive and successful production. That is true when working with the directing team and the designers during the pre-audition period and it is just as true when you arrive at auditions and callbacks. If you expect to have deaf actors attending auditions, you need to have interpreters available, no ifs, ands, or buts. There should be at least one interpreter in each room where a deaf person may be interacting with a non-signing person.

If your audition includes any cold readings with a scene partner, make sure there is a deaf person available to read with deaf auditionees. The reader should not be the interpreter. Interpreters are there to interpret, not perform as a scene partner. We recommend hiring someone specifically as your signing reader, just as you would have a specific speaking reader.

If you plan to have interpreters voice when deaf auditionees perform a monologue or scene, provide the interpreters with the appropriate text beforehand. Interpreting from ASL to spoken English isn't a one-for-one word exchange and without knowing the lines, the interpreters will not be able to speak them as written. Don't expect the interpreter to perform the character. They will interpret the intent of the deaf actor but, again, they are not there to act.

Provide music stands for deaf actors and for interpreters. This will allow them to set down any paper scripts and have their hands fully free for signing. Another strategy is to project the script onto a nearby wall, perhaps behind the directing team, so that the actor (and interpreter) can see the script and keep their hands free all while facing the directors.

Auditions and callbacks have a vastly different feel than production meetings. At meetings, you were likely seated. During auditions, there is much more physical movement happening. The director may be up on their feet. Actors are coming in and out of the room. Stage managers and assistant stage managers move about. For callbacks, that activity is amplified. Along with this kind of active work comes the need for taking breaks. It's important to think about the breaks you are giving to the people in the room and how these breaks are handled. Typically, when breaks happen, people scatter, leave for the bathroom, go out into the hall, etc. Oftentimes people keep working or discussing certain relevant topics. Plan to have enough interpreters available so that one of them can keep interpreting throughout the break period if important conversations are happening. If no one is interpreting these vital conversations, the deaf actors (and team members) will be excluded. Additionally, just like actors, interpreters need to take appropriate breaks to do their best work. This is one reason why multiple interpreters are hired for longer assignments. They typically take turns every twenty to thirty minutes to ensure they're staying fresh and to avoid repetitive stress injuries. Another reason for hiring multiple interpreters is that during these breaks, interpreters are often still working. Good interpreters will function as a team, supporting the person currently interpreting if something is missed or misunderstood and ensuring they each get proper break times.

While on the topic of interpreting, you should never discuss the cost of interpreters in front of deaf actors (or other deaf team members, for that matter). Yes, there are costs associated with making your production more accessible and inclusive. Yes, that is a fact your theatre will have to manage. When planning for an integrated production, you have to build these costs into your budget from the beginning. An integrated production will call for new budget lines associated with hiring interpreters, consultants, and additional team members. Do your research beforehand so you can accurately forecast what the cost will be. Holding all production values constant, integrated productions can cost anywhere from twenty to forty percent more than a non-integrated production, depending on how many deaf individuals are involved. Understand that interpreters have to make a living, too, and offer them reasonable compensation. Don't expect them to do the work pro bono or at a reduced rate because your theatre is a non-profit. If interpreters are able or willing to give a non-profit rate or volunteer their time, they will offer it. Don't try to cut costs by hiring the cheapest interpreters or by trying to get away with fewer interpreters. Quality communication between deaf and hearing participants will make or break your integrated theatre production. If you need to cut costs to make the production happen, find other budget lines to reduce. Above all, do not mention or complain about the costs of interpreters in front of deaf artists. Doing so reduces their presence to a cost. It says to them that the price of accessibility is more important than the artistic value they have to contribute. It says there's an additional burden to having them there. They already know there's an additional cost. They don't need you putting that in their face.

Callbacks

Callbacks present an excellent opportunity to test out some of your conceptual ideas. You will likely be using this time to situate the right actor in each role, see the chemistry between different actors, and evaluate how different combinations of people appear together onstage. In addition to those priorities, use callbacks to experiment with your integrated concept. If your vision includes scenes with different signing and non-signing characters interacting, see what that looks like. See what works and what doesn't. See how various actors respond to the concept you've envisioned. There is plenty to be said for a talented actor and there's even more to be said for a talented actor who is also an open-minded, flexible acting partner willing to cross cultural and language barriers to connect with another actor. This is your chance to see how actors interact as characters *and* as human beings. Of course, the acting is important. But in an integrated production, the way people work together across barriers is *just* as critical. You will need a cast that can come together as a cohesive unit. Callbacks can tell you who is willing to bridge the gap and who isn't.

If possible, we suggest holding a brief introductory session at the start of callbacks. It's likely that you will have hearing actors in the room who are unfamiliar with deaf culture and have never interacted—much less acted—with a deaf person before. Again, we recommend speaking to your deaf directing team members, DASL, and/or deaf consultant to devise a workshop or training that outlines fundamental knowledge. If there's not a time when all actors will be together for such a session, short training videos could be made and shared with actors prior to their arrival at callbacks.

If you provide sides to actors prior to callbacks, that is another opportunity to share the ASL script. If you are providing sides after actors arrive, it's still possible to share videos digitally, though the time is now past for the ASL script to be effectively used to prepare for an audition. In this case, actors will need to translate on their own lines on the fly because they won't have time to internalize the ASL script.

Remember to provide your interpreters with the sides before callbacks begin. It's likely they will be working throughout callbacks so make sure to request enough interpreters. Again, there should be at least one interpreter in each room where a deaf person may be interacting with a non-signing person. In the case of any scenes where a signing actor and a non-signing actor will be reading together, you should have two interpreters available in the room for the actors. For example, a signing actor is stage right and will be communicating to a speaking actor who is stage left. One interpreter will be behind the signing actor. When this actor signs, the interpreter will voice. The other interpreter will be behind the speaking actor. When this actor speaks, the interpreter will sign. This provides both actors with the best level of accessibility during the scene. Ideally, a third interpreter will be in the room so that someone is near the director to interpret. That's a lot of interpreter fees, we know. But this goes back to one of our non-negotiable principles—make quality communication a top priority. Cut costs in other places if you have to. A splashy set will not make or break an integrated production. Communication access will.

Help, a Deaf Actor Just Showed Up Unexpectedly!

Much of what we've covered up to this point has been related to planned integrated productions. What should you do if you're a predominantly hearing theatre company holding auditions for a production and a deaf actor walks into the room? First, take a deep breath. Deaf people interact with non-signing hearing people often and they're adept at navigating these interactions. Some actors may reach out ahead of time to give you a heads up they're coming. If this happens, you should try to secure interpreters. Despite how difficult it may be to find last-minute interpreters, you should still try to get at least one there.

Other actors may decide at the last minute that they want to take a shot at your audition and arrive unexpectedly. In these instances, your willingness to work hard to communicate, despite the challenges, will be your most effective tool. A hearing person without any knowledge of ASL can still make a genuine effort to connect with a deaf person—both inside the audition room and in life in general. After you've taken that breath, ask them how they prefer to communicate. Many hearing people assume that all deaf people can read lips effectively, but this is not always true. Only about twenty to forty percent of spoken English can be understood through lipreading even in the most ideal conditions. Lipreading ability is highly contextual. Background noise, unfamiliarity with the topic of the conversation, poor lighting, and even facial hair can all impact the deaf person's ability to lipread. The number of speakers is important also. A deaf person might lipread fluently in a one-to-one conversation, but be at a loss in a three-way conversation. Do not assume lipreading is effective for a deaf person in any given situation unless they tell you it is.

Deaf people may prefer to write back and forth via paper or cell phone or a nearby whiteboard. If writing, be clear and to the point. They may prefer using their voice to communicate their needs. Voicing can be a very sensitive topic for deaf individuals, due to negative experiences with speech therapy. Avoid asking deaf people if they can speak. If they do choose to voice, also avoid commenting on the quality of their speech. Deaf people may use a hearing aid or cochlear implant and be able to hear you fairly well with these assistive devices. Or they may ask you to use gestures or body language to show them what you want. With any of these examples, give them as much eye contact as possible. Whatever shape the conversation takes, make the exchange about them and allow their preferences to guide the interaction. Practice demonstrating your open mind and open heart.

Once their audition has ended, if you choose to call them back, you should get interpreters for callbacks. We urge you to communicate directly with the deaf person and ask for a list of their preferred interpreters. Not every interpreter is a good fit for every deaf person. And not every interpreter is equally qualified. At this point, it may be difficult to hire a co-director, assistant director, DASL, or deaf consultant prior to callbacks but it doesn't hurt to reach out to the local deaf community. Depending on where your production is occurring, you may have a variety of resources to utilize. Harness the power of social media in your area to see who's out there. Search for any deaf associations or deaf schools in your city. See if there are any ASL courses being taught at local schools or colleges. Ask your nearest interpreting agency or accessibility service provider how to get in touch with local deaf people. You never know what new partnerships may be formed.

Casting

Once auditions and callbacks have been completed, you will sit down with your directing team to cast the roles. If you have planned for an integrated production, ideally all of the roles as you've envisioned them can be rightfully cast by the actors who auditioned. Any decisions made regarding deaf or signing actors should be strongly influenced by the DASL or other deaf directing team members. A hearing director may like certain aspects of an actor, but if that director is not a native signer, they should respect deaf opinions about which signing actors can play the signing characters. You can't simply cast any deaf person to play a deaf character. Trust your deaf collaborators to make the best decision in this area. Doing so now will save a lot of headache down the road when an actor doesn't truly fit the character. If you are unable to cast the show as originally conceptualized despite having deaf actors audition, you may have to reach out to your local deaf community to seek people or you may have to alter the way you've envisioned certain characters.

If you have not previously planned for an integrated production but are now planning to cast a deaf actor, we cannot overstate how important it is to hire other deaf team members as quickly as possible. At the very least you should hire a DASL to bring a deaf perspective to the artistic side of the process and a deaf consultant to focus on accessibility during the process.

A Different Kind of General Audition

One model for accessible auditions has been practiced by Seattle-based Sound Theatre Company (STC). In the past, they've experimented with reserving one day during general season auditions specifically for artists identifying as deaf or disabled. In addition to offering an array of accessibility options, from a wheelchair-accessible space, ASL interpreters, tactile interpreting for DeafBlind actors, sighted guides, Braille transcripts, and large-print materials for blind or low-vision actors, their model reframes the audition process to break down the power dynamics typically found in an audition room. Their goal of human-centered auditions displays the values of the company by signaling to artists that they want to provide a more tailored audition experience. It shows they are not only prepared for a variety of performers who want to audition but actively seeking them out. A theatre company that advertises accessible auditions such as this removes the burden on the performers to do extra work to get accessibility. STC has also invited other Seattle theatre representatives to join them on this particular audition day. Doing so has multiple benefits—strengthening bonds in the local theatre community, giving deaf and disabled artists a chance to audition for more companies at the same time, and sharing what different companies are working on. For those companies, they're introduced to a whole set of new artists that they've likely never worked with before.

Whether or not you've fully conceptualized an integrated production, hosting a day of auditions like this notifies the public of your accessibility plans, gives your company a chance to see a wide range of performers that you might not have seen otherwise, and provides a chance to build stronger relationships within your own local theatre community.

Guidelines for Actors

Working Across Boundaries

Callbacks will likely be the first time that deaf and hearing actors are interacting during the production. For hearing actors working in an integrated production, success stems as much from their ability to connect as a human being as it does from their skills in portraying a character. Placing communication as the top priority means that members of the team are actively engaged with crossing language and cultural barriers on a personal level. Everyone shares the responsibility of fostering a team-first mentality. Everyone invests time and energy toward community-building. This involves a willingness to learn and use ASL in meetings, rehearsals, and, perhaps more importantly, breaks or social times. This section gives helpful guidelines for actors when approaching callbacks, and later rehearsals, for an integrated production.

A Few More Terms

From the outset, we want to establish a distinction between the words *counterpart* and *scene partner*:

- *Counterpart* is the term we use to describe an actor with whom another actor is simultaneously performing a role. Counterparts appear in many of the previously discussed approaches to dual staging, but primarily in double-casting, shadowing, and 'voice of' pairings. These models define a specific connection between two actors onstage and so, for each of them, the counterpart is clear. For disconnected persona and interpreter-characters, though the connection between actors is less direct, the term counterpart still applies because in both models, two actors are performing the character together. Counterpart as a term is meant to signify just that—two people together making one character. Therefore, it loses some of its usefulness in two specific situations: (1) when the disconnected persona model takes a voicing-by-committee approach, and (2) when the interpreter-character model doesn't pair one interpreter-character to one specific character, but has them interpreting as needed. In both of these scenarios, there is one primary actor who works with *multiple* counterparts throughout the play. In rehearsal, we would still use *counterpart* in both situations, albeit with more explanation about which counterpart we're referring to.

- *Scene partner* maintains its traditional definition. This includes all the actors portraying different characters within a given scene. In integrated productions, a scene includes a variety of primary actors, counterparts, and scene partners. How all of these actors interact onstage will be based upon the concept for the production.

This section discusses concepts and strategies that can be applied to working with counterparts and scene partners together or separately.

Counterpart

All actors have worked with various scene partners across their careers. Since the role of scene partner is more understood, we will first focus on the role that may be more foreign: the counterpart. The process of creating a character requires dedication and creativity. To bring those ideas into a rehearsal room demands vulnerability and flexibility. There are just as many entry points to this process as there are actors. When a second actor is added in the development of a single character, the creative act is altered. Two perspectives, two aesthetics, two approaches, two languages must be blended to tell the singular story. It is a very complex process to bring two actors together into one character.

For hearing actors, the number one greatest asset in this commingling is your personality. Not your ability to make bold choices, nor your magnetic stage presence, nor your trained vocal or physical instrument. For an integrated production, your skill in connecting as a human being trumps your talent onstage. The ability to enter the process with an open mind and open heart is key. No amount of acting technique can assist in overcoming language and cultural barriers the way generosity and a spirit of collaboration can. Of course, acting talent is an important component. However, in this situation, it takes a backseat.

Educate Yourself

As soon as it is known that a production will include deaf actors, hearing actors should begin educating themselves. Ideally, the production is offering some sort of informational session or workshop. This may or may not happen for callbacks. If it does, great! You should attend and really take in the information that is being shared. If not, refer back to Chap. 1 and also use the power of the Internet to help you out. There is plenty of information out there for you to get a basic understanding of the dos and don'ts when working with deaf people. Auditions and callbacks are already a nerve-wracking time, so preparing yourself for how to best interact in this situation will only help you feel more ready. If you feel nervous about working with a deaf person, this sort of knowledge gives you more confidence when coming to callbacks. Even learning ASL for "Hi, my name is ___, how are you?" will help you initiate a connection.

Show Cultural Humility

If someone doesn't respect deaf people as people, they will never respect them as artists. As much as you can during the craziness of callbacks, reach across the gap to connect with deaf actors in the room, especially those you are assigned to read with as counterparts. Show that you are making an effort to connect. Try out that ASL you just learned. Allow them to take the lead. Go further than just meeting them halfway and it will make a difference that will be apparent when you read together.

It's a common experience for a deaf person to be talked over by hearing people. During callbacks, we suggest that you take a 'wait and see' approach. Many actors are ready to jump in with creative solutions to onstage problems or to answer questions posed by the director. This may be even more so during callbacks when ideas are bubbling up from each corner of the room and everyone wants the role. The aim in these situations is to be helpful in solving an issue or to express your creativity in discussing the scene. Rather than jump right in immediately, another approach is to step back, observe, and be attentive to your counterpart. Defer to their idea first. See how they want to proceed in the scene. Don't assume you know the best way to support them. Allow them to take the lead.

If you find that you have questions about deaf people, deaf culture, or ASL, ask a deaf person. Don't ask the interpreters. This is inappropriate and audist. The interpreters are there to facilitate communication, not as experts on deafness, deaf culture, and ASL. Hearing individuals involved in the production who may be familiar with these topics should also defer to deaf people's lived expertise. Initiating a simple exchange about your questions may help connect with your counterpart before it's your turn to read together.

On Your Feet

When it comes time to read with your counterpart, you have to expand your awareness beyond yourself. In callbacks, especially if you're unmemorized, it can be easy to have your face stuck in the script. Depending on the director's concept and the dual staging model used, there may be a sense of synchronization you want to achieve with your counterpart. To do this you have to be open to them *in addition to* being open to your scene partner(s). Here are some pointers to keep in mind:

- Don't stand in front of a signing actor whether they're a counterpart or scene partner.
- Don't stand in front of any interpreters in the room.
- Keep your counterpart in your line of sight and use eye contact to check in with them.
- Decide with your counterpart who is leading the start of each line.
- Watch your counterpart and begin speaking each line when they start signing.
- Don't obscure your mouth with the script. For deaf people who can lipread, this is an important way to follow where you are in the script. Due to lag time, a deaf actor using an interpreter may also want to be able to see when you start and finish speaking.
- Even if you don't know ASL, try to read your counterpart's body language and energy to get a sense of pacing.
- Be careful of getting too far ahead of your counterpart in the scene. Often deaf people will mouth English words when signing. You can lipread to help keep an eye on where they are in the lines (bonus—this will help you develop empathy for how difficult and mentally taxing lipreading is).
- If your scene partner is signing, wait for them to finish their line before you start your next line. Occasionally, someone voicing for them may finish first. Resist the urge to start your line and keep your focus until your scene partner has completed the line.

It's very easy to spot when counterparts are in or out of sync with each other. It takes time for counterparts to develop confidence in staying on the same page with one another. In a frenzied callback setting, it may not be possible to develop this confidence and shared timing. In-scene mistakes may cause awkwardness to bubble up. As best as possible, let this go, maintain focus on your counterpart, and keep your chin up.

Once You Have the Role

Congratulations, you're in the cast! Perhaps your counterpart was someone you met at callbacks or perhaps not. Either way, many of the lessons from callbacks can be applied to your rehearsal process. Again, prioritizing your connection with your counterpart as a fellow human and actor will help establish a stronger foundation for the two of you to work from.

- Always remember eye contact.
- Throughout the rehearsal period, find time to work one on one with your counterpart. Try this without an interpreter, just the two of you engaged together making it work.
- At the first rehearsal, make sure you clearly understand the director's concept, the dual staging model(s) that will be used, and how your role fits into that.
- During the first read (whenever it happens), sit with your counterpart and ask if there's anything you can do to support them. Sometimes for a deaf actor it is helpful to have someone follow along in the script with a pencil and point to which line is being read. Then it's easier for the deaf actor to find their place when it's their line.
- Attend as much of the translation work as possible. It will be helpful to you to see how lines are being signed and to learn why certain signs were chosen.
- Use tablework as a time to discuss the play, answer major questions about given circumstances, debate your perspectives, come to agreements, build your character together, and in doing so, further build your connection together. Give feedback and be receptive to receiving feedback.
- Accept any mistakes you make, apologize, and work through them.
- During initial blocking, work with your counterpart to establish a cueing system for where you are in the lines. Such a system will help with keeping you both in sync. Cues may be physical movements, blocking moments, physical touch, etc.
- Throughout rehearsals, spend time becoming very familiar with how your counterpart is signing their lines. Just as you memorize your own lines, the more you know what they're signing, the better the two of you will stay on the same page.

Out of Rehearsal

Your time and investment during rehearsals are key to building a successful partnership with your counterpart that will enhance your character development. The next level of connection can come from time and investment outside of rehearsal. Building connections outside of work hours allows you to get to know each other as *people*. This is important in all casts but especially integrated casts. Bonding outside of the rehearsal room allows you to bring more understanding and chemistry into it. Find one-on-one opportunities to connect in social ways.

Scene Partner

The relationship between scene partners is different from that of counterparts. You are not portraying the same character. You have separate characters with separate motivations. However, in an integrated production, you may be using different languages. How such scene partners interact will depend on the vision of the directing team. That said, many of the ideas shared for counterparts can help when working with a scene partner:

- Your ability to connect as a person before an actor is critical. Bring kindness, flexibility, cultural humility, and a collegial mindset.
- Attend any and all cultural workshops or training sessions with a true intent to learn.
- If you have questions about deaf people, deaf culture, or ASL, ask a deaf person.
- Be attentive to your scene partner and give them the space to lead.
- When on your feet, allow a scene partner to completely finish signing their lines before you start speaking yours (even if their counterpart has finished speaking the lines).
- Throughout the process, put in the work to become familiar with your scene partners' lines. Knowing how lines look and what signs mean will only help ground you in scenes with them.
- Don't stand in front of a signing actor or an interpreter.
- Even if you don't know ASL, make a genuine effort to connect with your scene partner.

CHAPTER 5

Shaping the Performance

THE REHEARSAL PROCESS

Now that rehearsals have started, the director's focus is divided between working with the cast and ongoing production meetings with the designers. All the planning and preparation over the previous weeks and months starts to take shape. Costume designers now have actors to measure and fit. Scenic designers now have bodies to start interacting with their physical world. Stage managers have a cast of people to connect with and coordinate calls for. There's a sense of the full team moving the production forward together.

The First Rehearsal

For many productions, the first rehearsal is a prefatory one. The cast meets for the first time, the production concept is conveyed, designers give presentations on their work, and logistics are cleared up. Typically, a first read-through of the script occurs. These things are standard practice for many first rehearsals. For an integrated production, the first rehearsal should be structured a bit differently.

Deaf Culture and ASL Training

As with other parts of the process up to this point, we again recommend starting rehearsals with a workshop or training session led by a deaf person and geared toward teaching the basics of deaf culture, how to work with

© The Author(s), under exclusive license to Springer Nature
Switzerland AG 2024
A. Head, J. M. Bradbury, *Staging Deaf and Hearing Theatre Productions*, https://doi.org/10.1007/978-3-031-61446-0_5

deaf people and interpreters, and even foundational ASL. In fact, of all the settings for such a training session to occur, the first rehearsal may be the most important. This is especially true if your production is more to the right of the Deaf theatre/mainstream theatre spectrum and there are only one or two deaf actors in the cast. The other actors (as well as members of the stage management team) will gain so much from a training session to kick off the rehearsal process. It will help alleviate the initial awkwardness that can come with cultural and language differences. These training sessions can take an array of forms but should be led by a deaf consultant, a DASL, a deaf director, or in some cases, even a lead deaf actor. Remember, whoever leads the session(s) is doing extra work and should be compensated.

Teaching basic ASL to non-signing actors and stage managers can be extremely helpful. Of course, if there are actors signing onstage who have never signed before, they should certainly receive intensive training (ideally, they will have put in time learning ASL basics prior to rehearsals). However, providing ASL lessons to the full cast gives them a better way to connect with the deaf actors. Dedicating one hour, or one day, or one week to the study of ASL at the beginning of a rehearsal process will do wonders for the unity of the cast. Can a person learn an entire language in a week? Of course not. But enough survival signs can be absorbed in a few days to allow actors to communicate in ASL on a beginning level, and that's the first step. As stage managers are a critical part of the full team, encouraging or requiring them to join in these sessions will create further unity. While they are not acting onstage, they are the all-important link to the eventual backstage crew and how the show will run in performance. Directly or indirectly, they will be working with actors on a daily basis too. Remember that communication should be your production's top priority. What better way to promote communication than to provide language training? The way that you advertised auditions sent a clear signal about the values of your production. You can continue that work through how the rehearsal process begins.

First Read-Through

The first read-through can offer an excellent jumping off point for the cast. The director gets to see them all inhabiting their characters, together, for the first time. Actors get a sense of how their scene partners and/or counterparts approach a role. The entire group moves through the story together and can stop to discuss pertinent details along the way. Larger questions can be addressed. Viewpoints can be shared. Debates can be had. There's a feeling that you're viewing the text come to life for this specific group of people.

A downside for deaf actors is that, in some cases, they have not yet met with the DASL to work on translation. Yes, since receiving the role, they may have started a translation process on their own or started learning the ASL script. But remember, a speaking actor must read the script, interpret the lines in the context of each moment, receive what their scene partner is giving them, and respond appropriately. A deaf actor must do all of this, while also translating the lines into an *entirely different language*. Some actors are more comfortable with stage combat, some are more naturally skilled at dancing, and some are strong translators. The fact is that you probably don't know this person's ability to translate. As described in Chap. 2—"Artistic Challenges and Issues", the process is also different if you're working on a modern play compared to a Shakespearean play, which itself is vastly different than working on a musical. Depending on the timeline from casting to first rehearsal, deaf actors may not have had much time to work through the script on their own.

In addition to the translation itself, it's impossible to follow along in the script while others read *and* watch the interpreter at the same time. This is when it's helpful to have someone, perhaps a stage manager or counterpart, sit next to the deaf actor and use a pencil to follow along in the script. The actor can watch the interpreter and when it's time for their line, they can glance down at the paper, find the pencil, and know what line is next. We have two suggestions for the first read-through:

- Simply do not have a first read-through at the first rehearsal. This may actually be beneficial for all actors, signing or not. Consider holding on the first read-through until all of the tablework and translation have been completed with the cast. Then all actors can arrive at the read having talked through their characters and each scene with the directors. They are more informed on the vision and direction of their character in relation to the entire play. They simply know more and can produce a better read. For the deaf or other signing actors, the translation will be ready. Similar to tablework, they will have dissected each scene for language with the DASL, internalized the translation, and become better prepared to approach the read-through.

- If you are set on holding the first read-through at the first rehearsal, then our other suggestion is to give the deaf and other signing actors time to work with the DASL *prior* to the first rehearsal. With the ubiquity of Zoom and other video conferencing platforms, it's very easy for this work to happen before the cast comes together at rehearsals. For example, if you have months from casting to first rehearsal, this is plenty of time for the actors to work through the translation with the DASL and be ready for the read-through. Of course, this also means paying those actors for their time.

Either of these approaches builds in extra support so that everyone in the cast can remain on the same page. The last thing you want is to start rehearsals for your integrated production with the deaf team members feeling behind because you didn't set things up appropriately.

Cast Connections

For an integrated production, creating connections in the cast is supremely important. Yes, much of this depends on the actors' willingness to forge those bonds, but the director can build in opportunities for actors to foster relationships. The first rehearsal is the best place to begin establishing these opportunities. We suggest directors open rehearsals with some sort of group warm up activity. Establish a ritual to welcome actors to the room as people first and give them a chance to interact in an informal way. Acting demands dedication and focus and that is what rehearsal is all about. Give actors this chance to bond before the work of rehearsals begin. Your activity could be a simple game, a fun activity, a personal check-in, a moment to step into or out of character—there are many options. You could ask each actor to individually lead the welcoming ritual over the course of several rehearsals. You will figure out what works for your troupe. Once you have established this activity to open rehearsals, you can repeat it to close rehearsals. Ending with a quick check-in brings actors out of the characters and back to themselves. In these book-ending moments, actors see each other as people and gaps between them get a little bit smaller.

Interpreters at Rehearsals

One last consideration for the first rehearsal is interpreters. Now that rehearsals have started, it's important to check in with your interpreters too. Many of the ideas we've already shared for production meetings and auditions still apply here. Instead of recreating those lists, we'll add several new considerations that are more rehearsal-specific:

- Any room where there is a deaf artist working needs at least one assigned interpreter.
- If physically moving around the space, you may need to pause to allow the interpreter to get into a new position to be seen and/or heard.
- If you are behind the interpreter (meaning they can't see you), avoid speaking generally. For example, instead of saying "you, move that way" use the actor's name and define "that way." E.g., "Ana, please move stage left." Using blocking and stage direction terminology will help the interpreter appropriately convey your message.
- If you are teaching choreography or specific physical work, it's oftentimes easier to show with your body rather than explain with words. In this kind of work, be mindful of the interpreter's lag time. Remember that the interpreter may be as much as thirty seconds behind your words, which means the deaf person won't know to look at *you* right away. If you start showing something physically rather than verbally before the interpreter has finished, the deaf person will miss the first part of it.
- If working on a musical, include deaf actors and interpreters for music rehearsals. Incredibly important character and story information is conveyed through song. Deaf actors should be included in this work.
- When in doubt about something related to deaf culture, ASL, or interpreting needs, ask a deaf person.

One pitfall to be aware of when it comes to rehearsal interpreters is boundaries. Theatre as a creation process breaks down barriers and brings people together. Just as a cast of actors gets more comfortable with each other, it's easy for interpreters to become more comfortable with the people they work with. The interpreters are there with you every day, through all the hours, the obstacles, the breakthroughs. It's possible to start relying on them for other things, or asking their personal opinions, or adding to their duties. What once was a very clear-cut working relationship can become muddled and vague. It's essential that interpreters remain impartial and in role. They are there to ensure communication is happening. Respect that role and avoid deviating from it.

Translation and Tablework

These two topics are grouped together because they both need to happen before blocking can take place.

- We define *tablework* as: the period when the director and actors analyze and discuss topics of character and scenes throughout the entire play (oftentimes while sitting around a table). Different directors approach this work in various ways, but typically they share their vision for each character and allow actors to provide input on how they see their own characters. If working with counterparts, it's a time for those two actors to discuss the ways they see their shared character. Discussions may revolve around character relationships and backstories. Actors may read through each scene and dissect it line by line for meaning, subtext, character motivation, given circumstances, and context. Actors may be asked to think about the objectives of their characters, what obstacles are in their way, how they attempt to overcome them, and the running internal monologue of their character. Further ideas may be shared about what the design elements will look like and how these affect certain moments. When tablework is complete, there's a shared sense that the director and actors have come to a consensus about who these characters are and what each scene is about.
- We define *translation* as the period when the DASL and actors talk through and discuss how the lines of the play transform from English to ASL. This is a natural extension of the translation work a DASL has already done prior to the start of rehearsals. Similar to tablework, this process involves examining who the characters are and what happens in each scene. DASLs approach this work differently and how they lead translation may depend on the production and on the specific actors they're working with. In some professional productions, actors must strictly follow a video script. With this approach, the DASL will work with the actors to memorize the script. In other productions, the DASL may start from a fully translated video script that is modified as they work through it with the actors. Alternatively, the DASL may approach the script more organically, bringing a gloss

script and seeing how the actors would translate lines, then giving feedback on those translations. No matter the way, there is a dialogue between DASL and the actors about the best translation choices. When translation work is complete, the DASL and actors have come to a consensus about how the lines will be signed. Actors can then begin their process for memorizing their lines.

Much of tablework informs translation and much of translation can inform choices made in tablework. What's undeniable is that translation puts additional work on deaf actors. Hearing actors can read the script and start their work. Translation is an additional step that deaf team members must undertake first. If that fact is not acknowledged in your process, you may have hearing actors moving ahead while deaf actors are left behind. This is why we recommend not holding the first read-through until this work can be completed. Having translation and tablework happen concurrently with everyone present can be very beneficial. It forces the process to move more deliberately. Some directors want to quickly move through tablework and get actors up on their feet into blocking. That desire is understandable. When working in two languages, however, you must accept that the process will be different. The temptation to rush ahead must be disregarded. Tablework and translation, albeit slow-paced at times, lay a proper foundation for your integrated production. The benefits to holding concurrent tablework and translation sessions are many:

- Most importantly, it prevents deaf or signing actors from being left behind early in the process.
- Directors, DASLs, and actors are all present to join in major discussions.
- It allows tablework conversations and fresh ideas about characters and scenes to immediately impact translation work, and vice versa.
- The DASL is present to modify the translation as new character discoveries are made, rather than re-teaching new translations after actors have already learned a line a certain way.
- Non-signing actors are present for character discussions about why certain sign choices are made.
- Non-signing actors get a chance to see signs develop, at the same time learning what cues they're looking for and at what pace signing occurs.

- Scene partners and counterparts naturally bond over these discussions and discoveries, and their shared sense of a character is strengthened.

If it seems like a lot, it is! You're trying to accomplish many multiple things simultaneously and that's one more reason you simply cannot rush this work.

Prior to tablework and translation, the director and DASL need to agree on how the process will unfold. Who will take the lead? What questions will be asked? How much time *do* you have to dedicate to these sessions? What are the priority topics that need to be covered? Then, as the sessions progress, it's on the shoulders of the director to ensure conversations are happening equitably. It can be easy for one or two actors to steer, or even steamroll, a conversation. The director must engage with all actors around the table so their perspectives, insights, and thoughts can be shared equally. The same communication fundamentals you've applied to production meetings are necessary here.

- Maintain eye contact with deaf artists.
- Always take turns in conversation and avoid crosstalk.
- Implement a visible turn-taking system to signal who has the floor.
- Identify yourself before talking.
- If using pictures or documents, pause to allow everyone to see the materials before speaking.
- Remember that interpreting is not a word-for-word translation of a conversation and when someone has finished their point, the interpreter may not yet be finished interpreting it. Wait for the interpreter to finish before the next person takes the floor.
- Avoid visually blocking the interpreter.

Blocking

The blocking stage of rehearsals has arrived. You can put those tables away and get the actors up on their feet. Whether you are a director who approaches blocking in an organic way with the actors or you come in having pre-planned the majority of movements, there are specific things to keep in mind for integrated productions.

Focus is inherently a crucial feature of blocking. Directors decide where they want the audience to be looking in a given moment and will compose each stage picture to guide their eyes to that spot. Blocking for integrated productions should emphasize focus. Hearing audiences may look anywhere onstage and simultaneously listen to speaking actors. Deaf audiences need to be looking at the person who has the lines or they will miss those lines. Focus in this instance means several different things all at once.

- The audience should know who to look at.
- The signing actors should not be blocked from the audience.
- Onstage distractions should be limited. This includes movement by non-signing actors, especially if they are not near the signing actors. Deaf eyes are drawn to movement within their visual field. If a deaf actor is signing on one side of the stage and actors on the other side are throwing their hands up or performing some other kind of gestural reaction, for example, the deaf audience's focus on the signed lines will be broken.

Telling the Audience Where to Look

Several strategies can help guide the audience's eyes to the right place. Various approaches will work in different ways depending on your specific scene, cast, and venue, as well as how many actors are on the stage at a time. In general, scenes with fewer characters are easier to block for focus than scenes with many bodies onstage. Scenes with many actors can easily become challenging for audiences to know who to watch. The following tactics help pinpoint focus:

- Place signing actors in central locations closer to the audience. This naturally highlights actors by putting them in a clear, powerful, unobstructed stage position.
- Have other actors onstage look toward actors who are signing. Eye gaze functions linguistically in sign language as a form of pointing, so onstage eye gaze can direct the deaf audience where to look. This can be especially helpful in managing shifts from ensembles to individual actors.
- For important entrances or moments of action, onstage eye gaze signaling can again be used to guide the audience's focus to where you want it. Actors onstage can also point with their heads and bodies to further direct the audience's eyes.

- Position actors, especially signing actors, closer together onstage to limit the distance audience's eyes must travel back and forth to follow dialogue.
- Use subtle light cues to spotlight signing actors. This can be particularly effective when many actors are onstage.
- Have signing actors get attention before starting their lines. This is an important feature of deaf culture and ensures people are looking at you before you begin signing. In large group scenes, this tactic can be very useful and can be done by a slight hand wave, wiggling the fingers, raising one or both hands, raising a finger, or even just a slight pause. Anything that adds a few extra seconds for deaf audiences to refocus their attention will work. In musicals, it may be necessary to add or hold a note to create this extra time.
- Similar to asking a speaking actor to project to the entire house, a signing actor can project their lines by enlarging the sign box. Actors should sign from their backs, keeping the elbows up and using their full arms, rather than from the hands and wrists. Fingerspelling should be exceptionally clear, with the hand held out and away from the body. Exaggerating facial expressions can also help project signed lines. Projection is particularly important in large venues.

Sightline Obstructions

Depending on the timeline of your production, you may have more or less flexibility to make changes to the scenic elements once blocking begins. Hopefully conversations with other directors, the DASL, and the scenic designer have resulted in a set that provides a central open space and avoids sightline obstructions. Other tactics for avoiding sightline obstructions include:

- Utilize your scenic options, including specifically created areas, levels, and open spaces to position actors where they can best be seen.
- Remember that signing actors need to be seen by all audience members. During rehearsals, be sure to sit in many different areas of the house, including the extreme side seats, to ensure there are no issues in seeing the signing. This is an area where a DASL and/or a deaf consultant can give excellent feedback. While it is best practice to reserve a section of seating for deaf audiences that provides optimal sightlines, deaf patrons may not be able to secure seats in that area.

- Remember that signing actors also need to be seen by other actors onstage. Eye contact is crucial in deaf culture and so scene partners and counterparts need to see who's signing.
- Typically, a three-quarters body position allows signing actors to be seen by audiences and fellow actors at the same time. Their 'offstage shoulder' should always be open to the furthest side seats. Blocking in semi-circle formations is one way to keep actors onstage open to each other.

Limiting Onstage Distractions

This category is particularly important when blocking scenes with many actors onstage at the same time. The more people who enter the stage, such as during an ensemble number in a musical, the harder it becomes for the audience's eyes to take in everything at once. Directors should prioritize the action that needs to be seen and then limit other action happening around it. Here are several ideas to help with limiting distractions:

- Block important actions to happen in a specified order instead of simultaneously.
- Background characters should limit large or fast physical movements. Keep all background action subtle.
- Have background characters send their eye gaze to the prioritized characters or actions.
- Signing actors can move while delivering signed lines, but avoid major movements during important signed lines.
- Avoid entrances from other characters during signed lines as this new movement will immediately pull focus away from the signing actor.
- A tactic that works in specific situations is to have background characters freeze during particularly important signed lines.

Elements of Deaf Culture

Beyond focus, there are elements of deaf culture that will likely enter into blocking. This is an area where a deaf co-director, assistant director, DASL, and even deaf actors should take the lead. The way that a deaf person sets up a space will likely be different than the way a hearing person sets up a space and, depending on your play and characters, this form of spatial organization may become important. A deaf space prioritizes visibility, whereas hearing people may not initially consider how a visual orientation affects a setting. Other features such as eye contact, physical proximity, and attention-getting will likely also find their way into blocking. For a hearing director or co-director, you must remain open to the ideas of your deaf colleagues when it comes to how their culture is represented onstage.

Blocking for Dual Staging

How you have conceptualized dual staging for your integrated production will have a major impact on how you approach blocking. You may have one role that is being dual staged or your entire cast of characters might be dual staged. Each method of dual staging comes with its own set of parameters to be thinking about.

- **Double casting** (two actors, one deaf, one hearing, play the same role). When double-casting, you have to figure out the right balance between the two performers. There are many questions to answer: Who are they to each other onstage—what's their relationship? Do they acknowledge the other? How do you ensure that each performer gets an equal share of the role? Does their blocking mirror the other? Do they move together? Are they identical replicas or do they have separate movements? Do they interact with each other physically? Do they communicate lines together? To each other? Alternating lines? How can you block them so that they can see each other for cues? This is about finding the best balance for both actors and the director.
- **Shadowing** (pairing two actors for a role in which one actor is the primary focus for audiences). This approach provides more blocking freedom than double casting, especially for the primary actor. Several questions should be asked with this method: What is their relationship in the world of the play? Do they acknowledge each other? Does only one acknowledge the other? Where is the shadow actor positioned so that they can see the primary actor? If the shadow actor is voicing, can they see the primary actor when signing? If the shadow actor is signing, can they be seen clearly by the audience? What system of cues is established so the two can stay together during performance? The primary actor may naturally get more focus from the director, but it's important to keep the shadow actor involved in the process.

- **'Voice of'** (hearing character in the story is used onstage to voice for an entirely separate signing character). Many questions for double casting and shadowing are pertinent here. Who are these two characters to each other? What is their relationship, if any at all? Can the voicing actor clearly see the signing actor? How often does the signing actor need to see the 'voice of' actor? Do they recognize their connection or does it go unacknowledged? Does the 'voice of' share any blocking with the signing actor? Is it clear when the 'voice of' actor is playing their own character and when they are in the 'voice of' role? For the communication of lines, these two actors need to be in sync; however, the balance of their physical connection will need to be determined by the director and actors.
- **Disconnected persona** (a functional approach where accessibility for a character on stage is provided through another actor who is either unseen or unacknowledged). This method has one main challenge to address: sightlines. Is the disconnected persona in a place where they can clearly see everything happening onstage? Whether they are voicing or signing, they will need to see their counterpart at all times in order to maintain a close synchronization with them. There is less concern here about the character relationship to each other because they are disconnected. However, for synchronization purposes, they need to be able to check in with one another to know they are moving through the play together.
- **Interpreter-characters** (a hearing character's role is to interpret for a deaf character). The interpreter-character needs to maintain proximity to the character they're interpreting for, so again, sightlines are very important. Can they always be seen by their counterpart? Can they always be seen by the other characters onstage? Can they always be seen by the audience? When is this character interpreting versus 'being themselves'? What is their relationship to their counterpart? What is their relationship to the other characters? How can those relationships be shown physically in how and where they are positioned?
- **Simultaneous communication/SimCom** (an actor uses spoken English and sign language at the same time). As expressed in Chap. 2—"Dual Staging Models", this is a method we discourage you from relying on except in very limited and dramaturgically purposeful ways. However, if it is to be used in your production, be mindful of not asking the SimComming actor to do too much. They're attempt-

ing to communicate in two language modalities simultaneously and that alone takes a lot of brain power.
- **Signing-centered** (access to signed lines is provided by open captions without voice). This method removes the counterpart entirely and allows audiences to focus on deaf performers by withdrawing any voicing support. Though there are likely fewer bodies onstage that can present sightline issues, it is important to consider performers' proximity to captions and to avoid obstructing the captions from any seat in the audience.

Who Leads Blocking?

Just as with many areas of your integrated production, blocking includes the ideas and perspectives of multiple artists coming together. This is especially true if you are working with a co-director. If you're working with an assistant director or DASL, we encourage you to include them in the entire blocking process. It may be helpful for hearing and deaf directors to pre-block scenes together. Drawings of scenic designs can be used to sketch out how actors traverse the stage. Pre-blocking can be even more productive if you have a 3D scenic model to understand how physical bodies fit in that physical space. If you're working with co-directors, pre-blocking will save you a lot of time, confusion, and headache later when you have to work through difficult blocking moments with the actors. If you can enter rehearsals with some agreed upon ideas, the on-your-feet work will be much smoother. Of course, things may change in the moment as you work and you'll address these things when/if they arise.

If you are unable to pre-block then you should decide who is leading blocking during each rehearsal. For example, a hearing director may take the lead on blocking and the deaf assistant director and/or DASL will be there to observe and jump in as needed. The director can rough-block the scene, then run it, and the assistant director and/or DASL can make necessary adjustments. Once all parties have come to consensus on what works, the blocking can be recorded. Again, this may change as rehearsals progress, but it gives you a collective starting point. Consider allowing the deaf directing team members to lead the blocking for the signing scenes, as they will be more attuned to sightline and visual issues.

With either approach, blocking will start slowly. The first several scenes always seem to take more time to come together. As you work through them, you'll learn principles that can apply to later scenes.

Scene Work

By the time you get to scene work, hopefully your rehearsals are starting to flow with the ease of familiarity. Everyone now knows each other. Actors are building relationships. There's chemistry onstage. Rough blocking has been viewed and tweaked from multiple perspectives. Scenes are starting to connect to each other and a raw version of the play is coming together. There's an expectation of how the process will continue toward tech week. When rough blocking is complete, polish can be added through deeper scene work. Final questions will be answered, actors will take full control of their characters, and confidence will grow across the board.

Rehearsal Process: *Angels in America, Part 1: Millennium Approaches*

First Rehearsal
Millennium Approaches began with a very introductory first rehearsal. The director opted not to hold a first read-through for two reasons: (1) translation work with the actors had not yet occurred, (2) *Millennium Approaches* has twenty-one scripted characters and the directing team was layering on the concept of the Host of Guardian Angels—it was simply too complex to have a read-through on the very first day. As an educational institution, the actors were primarily students and so it was important to be mindful of balancing their workload in the production with their course workloads. This is one reason translation work with the actors prior to rehearsals could not happen.

Instead, the first rehearsal focused on general housekeeping and community building among the cast: introductions, design presentations, costume measurements, group bonding. Especially with students, some of whom were in their first semester of college, the director prioritized their coming together as a cast and building those relationships. Several students were brand new to deaf culture and had never worked with deaf people in the past. Due to this, the second rehearsal was led by the assistant director and focused on sensitivity training: fundamentals of deaf culture, working with deaf people and interpreters, and how deaf culture was infused in the production. Together, the first two rehearsals established a foundation of understanding and communication for the production.

Time was not spent on the script itself but instead on the team of people creating the production.

Translation and Tablework
One of the missteps during *Millennium Approaches* was not holding concurrent tablework and translation sessions. These two things did happen simultaneously but not together. Typically, tablework was happening with the director on one side of the rehearsal room, while translation was happening on the other side of the room with the assistant director/DASL. For example, the actors playing Harper and her Guardian Angel would participate in tablework with the actors playing Mr. Lies and his voice. At the same time, across the stage the actors playing Prior and Louis would be working through the translation of a scene. When those sessions ended, the actor playing Harper might move to translation but the Guardian Angel actor would be free to go. This meant only deaf or signing actors were called for translation when non-signing actors could be working on other parts of the play or have the night off. Immediately an imbalance was created. Yes, actors were able to bond through the shared tablework, but they missed out on further collaboration during translation work. This disconnected process also resulted in some actors learning a translation and then later needing to learn new translations when changes were made. This decision also led to a slight cast disconnect. Despite the effort that went into community building, actors noticed that those signing were generally called more often while their counterparts were excused. Their shared workload of co-playing the roles was not equal and at times tensions could be felt.

Blocking
Because of the large size of the cast and juggling student workloads, rough blocking began as translation work was still being completed. Some scenes or roles had not been fully translated with actors when blocking work on other scenes began. Ideally, one part of the process would have finished so as to start the next phase with everyone. Time constraints and scheduling conflicts with student actors meant needing to move forward as people were available.

Because of the staggered translation and blocking process, the approach to blocking included three steps:

- rough blocking/sketching broad movements of a scene with the director
- reviewing rough blocking with AD/DASL and incorporating feedback
- double-checking sightlines and finalizing blocking with director and AD/DASL

Of course, tweaks continued to be made along the way, but through this workflow, the majority of blocking was completed in a way that fit the director's vision while reserving specific space for the AD/DASL to make necessary adjustments.

As previously noted, the major exception to this rule was Scene 2.9—a nearly simultaneous split scene between Harper/Joe and Prior/Louis. Because of the extreme necessity for clear cuing and open sightlines, the AD/DASL took the lead on blocking the scene. The director was there to give input and feedback, but allowed the AD to visually organize the scene in a way that made sense to deaf actors and audiences.

The blocking process started slowly as the directing team needed to figure out how the various primary actors, counterparts, and scene partners existed in space onstage. Through multiple early blocking rehearsals, the team developed several principles that could be applied to future blocking sessions, which made that later work more efficient. Several of these principles included:

- Finding optimal positioning and proximity for Guardian Angels. This was a crucial element to solve because the Guardian Angels were ever-present onstage. After trying several options, it was decided that most speaking Guardian Angels should stand upstage at an angle off the left or right shoulder of the signing primary actor. This kept the speaking counterparts from creating any unintentional sightline obstructions, while also allowing them to see some of what the primary actor was signing. Because they did not have a full view of the signing, it was incredibly important for them to have strong familiarity with the ASL lines so they could still voice in appropriate synchronization from that upstage angle. In some cases, the speaking Guardian Angel needed to be moved downstage of the primary actor. When this choice was made, they sat on a lower step or the edge of the stage so as not to obstruct sightlines. They could then turn to see what was being signed. Once each character's Guardian

Angel had found their optimal position, they returned to this same position in each succeeding scene (such as Harper and Joe's apartment). Later scenes were blocked more efficiently because this problem had already been solved.

- Deciding when to use levels and who to stage at an elevated level. This principle relates back to finding optimal positions for Guardian Angels. The scenic designer had provided multiple levels to utilize, as well as four moveable 3 × 3 foot stage cubes. These cubes became very effective for signing Guardian Angels, who were also generally placed at an upstage angle from their speaking counterpart. The directors discovered that when both actors were on the same level, the primary actor caused sightline issues for the Guardian Angel. The AD/DASL suggested using the stage cubes to elevate the signing Guardian Angels and eliminate the sightline issues. Doing so kept these signing actors in clear sight of the audience, as well as each other, and also kept staging consistency with how speaking Guardian Angels were positioned in relation to signing primary actors. When in these positions, the signing Guardian Angels looked for physical movements and cue signals to maintain synchronization in the scenes.
- Establishing subtle movement patterns for Guardian Angels. These characters were tasked with achieving a delicate balance of being seen to provide accessibility but, as background characters, not distracting from the scenes happening near them. When a primary actor entered a scene, the directing team had to decide whether or not their Guardian Angel entered with them or was already onstage. Other similar situations also had to be addressed: what Guardian Angels should do when their counterpart did not have any lines; what they should do during split scenes when their counterpart was still alive and in the moment but not the focus of the current scene; how they should operate in location changes between scenes. Throughout early rehearsals, these decisions were made and then could be more easily implemented in later blocking work.

Scene Work

Once blocking was more or less established, the directing team turned attention to the finer details of scene work. By this time, all tablework, translation, and initial blocking was complete, and the director and AD/DASL were both available together. Scenes were approached in a variety of ways. At times, both directors worked on a scene together. At other times, the two split up and worked on separate scenes concurrently. What was important was that all scenes were being viewed through a deaf lens and a hearing lens multiple times from multiple angles to ensure the play was unfolding successfully for all of our audience members.

One aspect of scene work that was unique to this version of *Millennium Approaches* was the use of recorded characters in scenes. Examples such as when Mr. Lies surprises Harper, or when the Angel visits Prior, or when Ethel Rosenberg haunts Roy, were all situations where live actors onstage were working with 'frozen' actors on film. This meant the recorded characters had to be prepared earlier in rehearsals so that their 'final performance' could be captured on camera. The goal was for an onscreen Mr. Lies to still be talking *to* Harper in the room, not just looking straight ahead from the screen. These scenes took priority in early tablework, early blocking, and early scene work. They were prepared first because the recording had to take place weeks before opening night in order to give the projection designer time to incorporate them into the projection design. To get the desired look, first the scenes were physically blocked onstage. The actor playing Mr. Lies stood in the same place his projected self would later appear. Harper and her Guardian Angel were blocked around this projection surface. The screen was upstage of Harper and she was signing, so this posed an issue at first. It was discovered that if she stood stage right of the screen, instead of downstage, her body (and signing) would be open to the audience but it would look like Mr. Lies was still watching her. In rehearsal he *was* watching her, but his recording would be set and so it didn't matter if she later needed to cheat out more. Once the scene work was complete, the actors were recorded in these same exact positions on the actual set. The actor playing Mr. Lies stood in costume where he had been standing the whole time. The actor playing Harper did all of her usual blocking. The scene was recorded. Then, in post-production, the green screen was removed, the apartment projection was added, Mr. Lies was enlarged for audiences to see more easily, and effects were added to highlight his entrance and exit. Closer to tech week, once the physical screens were added to the arched entry-ways, the actor playing Harper could then rehearse the scene with her true scene partner—the recorded Mr. Lies. In working on this first scene, a system was developed that worked for all of the recorded characters and the same process and workflow was applied to those succeeding scenes with the ghosts of Prior's ancestors, Ethel Rosenberg, and the Angel.

Guidelines for Stage Managers and Front-of-House Staff

Throughout this book, we have stressed the responsibility of the director to ensure accessibility for deaf artists on the team as well as for deaf audiences. We recognize that this is not typically part of the director's role. However, it is part and parcel of producing integrated deaf and hearing theatre. This does not mean that directors have to do all of the legwork to make access happen. Stage managers are a key ally during the production process and can help promote and support accessibility throughout the entire rehearsal period and during performances, not only directly in production meetings and rehearsals but also in concrete ways backstage and behind the scenes. Similarly, front-of-house personnel can promote and support accessibility too. As we've reiterated, the deaf community is small and close knit. When a deaf actor gets a role, word of their performance will inevitably spread and deaf community members will show up to watch. When these patrons arrive, they expect and deserve to have high-quality access to the play in its entirety, not just the parts that are signed. We believe that when directors decide to undertake integrated theatre, they also take on the ethical responsibility to ensure deaf audiences get that access. That means directors should be advocating for and following up on accessibility backstage and front of house. Below, we offer some guidelines for both stage managers and box office staff. For front-of-house team members, these recommendations can be supplemented with the tip sheets developed by the Leadership Exchange in Arts and Disability Office of the John F. Kennedy Center for the Performing Arts.[1]

Guidelines for Stage Managers

Stage managers are a vital and influential part of the production team. They are one of the few team members who are with the production from the beginning to the end. While perhaps not in the room when the director is developing an initial concept, the stage manager will likely be present from that first production meeting all the way to strike. Throughout the rehearsal period, they are typically seen as the director's right-hand person. During tech week, they transition to becoming the leader charged with running the show and maintaining the director's vision after opening

---

[1] See Further Reading for links.

night. They're present at every performance and they're probably the last one to leave after strike.

High-Quality Communication

In many productions, the stage manager is a facilitator of communication—that is a main function of their role. Through meeting notes, reminder emails, quick hallway check-ins, rehearsal reports, run sheets, announcements, and more, they pass production-related information to the appropriate people to keep everyone from technical staff to actors to backstage crews to the directing team on the same page. In an integrated production, a stage manager is also a key team member for implementing the non-negotiable principle of ensuring that high-quality communication is happening day to day at every level of the production. These two kinds of communication are both important; however, they are distinct from one another. The first is primarily through written notes, emails, and summaries of things that have happened or things that need to still happen. The latter focuses on people interacting live in the moment, whether in meetings or rehearsals, and maintaining inclusivity and accessibility.

We've already made clear that what a director invests in will signal to other team members what is valued in that process. A director who seeks and follows the advice of deaf team members is promoting inclusivity. A director who takes time to schedule cultural sensitivity workshops or ASL workshops is telling designers and actors what is important to that production. In the same way, the words and actions of the stage manager establish a tone that others on the team will absorb. There are specific steps that stage managers can take to be that tone-setter and successfully promote this non-negotiable principle.

- Start learning ASL. From the moment you know you will be working on an integrated production, begin to learn basic ASL, especially signs related to theatre. This is important whether you are the head of stage managers or an assistant stage manager for several reasons. First, the stage manager interacts with people at each level of the production. Whether the team has a deaf scenic designer or two deaf actors or a deaf light board op, the stage manager will likely have multiple interactions with them. Being able to communicate directly helps form those critical bonds, which can then extend to connections formed outside of rehearsals. Second, in an integrated production, at least one actor will be signing onstage and there will likely be cues related to that person's lines and/or stage business. A stage manager needs to know what these signs look like and what they mean just as well as every acting scene partner does. Achieving a successfully called show will depend on your ability to know what all actors are signing. Third, depending on the size of the production and the number of deaf and hearing people working together, there may not be enough interpreters to cover all areas at all times. If an assistant stage manager is able to sign backstage, this will help both actors and crew members to complete important show tasks. Similarly, a stage manager in the booth who knows sign language can call cues when working with a deaf projection operator, for example. Fourth, a hearing stage manager who signs to deaf team members can influence other hearing team members, especially assistant stage managers and crew members, to also start picking up ASL. The stage manager is modeling the value of accessibility and inclusion in the production.

- Take care of the interpreters. The production interpreters are just as valuable as all other team members, and including them in certain communication channels will only assist them in doing their job. Fostering a strong connection with the interpreters is one important way the stage manager can help bolster the non-negotiable principle of high-quality communication. Include them in meeting and rehearsal reminders. Add them to the list of people receiving rehearsal reports, production meeting agendas, and rehearsal plans. Doing this helps them know what to expect when they arrive at rehearsal, which helps them do better work. If plans change, try to let them know as soon as possible. Make a 'cheat sheet' for the interpreters with the names, pronouns, roles, and photos of everyone on the production team. This is a tool that can be created and shared prior to the first production meeting. It can be updated when the cast is formed and again as crew members start attending more regularly. This cheat sheet is particularly useful in providing context for conversations, because the interpreters can connect the dots between name, pronouns, face, and role for everyone they're working with. Absent such a tool, they may go through the whole process without learning this information for some people. A cheat sheet is also supremely helpful if an interpreter is out and you have a substitute interpreter, or if you do not have the same interpreters throughout

the production. The new person likely does not know anything about the show. Having a guide can catch them up to speed as quickly as possible.
- Be an advocate. Because the stage manager is involved in most, if not all, meetings and rehearsals, they can see when high-quality communication is happening and when it's not. The stage manager is a witness to nearly everything happening throughout the production process. If people are not following the rules for good visual communication, such as turn taking, identifying themselves, or properly setting up a visual presentation, the stage manager can take steps to reinforce these rules, either by directly restating them, including them as reminders in reports, modeling appropriate behavior, or all of the above. If the stage manager notices that rehearsals will be split over multiple spaces and there aren't enough interpreters booked to cover the access needs, they can speak up. If they see that actors or crew members are not adhering to suggestions about how to best interact with deaf people, they can use their authority in the room to pull those people aside and point out what's happening.
- Know when and where interpreters are needed. Stage managers are responsible for a lot of scheduling, coordinating, and organizing. For an integrated production, they specifically need to be aware of the accessibility needs for the entire production team. Depending on the size of the show, that could be a massive task to undertake. In addition to meetings and rehearsals, stage managers need to know if interpreters are required for costume fittings, at a hang and focus, for paper tech, in intimacy rehearsals, during load in, and the many, many other things that happen in bringing a production to life. Accessibility needs to be happening in all areas of the production and the stage manager can ensure interpreters are properly booked and scheduled. When they see that needs are not being met, they can step in directly or pass that along to the directing team to evaluate how to address the issue.

Tech Week Timing

As tech week arrives, the stage manager is positioned to take the reins and begin calling the show. Tech week is a prime example of a time when production-related communication and high-quality accessible communication overlap. To get the most done during this period, you need both forms of communication happening together. Many different production parts are all moving at once as the show comes together. Lighting cues are written, sound levels are set, costume quick changes are worked through, scene changes are choreographed, final props are brought in, the last paint touch ups are applied. Things are constantly added, adjusted, and fixed. New team members join the growing collective. The days are long, tension can get high, sleep is at a premium. During this period, there can be an urge to rush forward quickly. So much needs to be accomplished as the days before opening night dwindle. Be cautious of this impulse and remind yourself that integrated productions cannot be rushed. When things become hurried, communication may get sacrificed. Though the stage manager knows the schedule and has the full to-do list in their mind, the actors and crew members may not know those things. Information still needs to be circulated among the group—perhaps now more critically than ever. One method of passing this information is through group announcements. Before any announcements, make sure everyone is in the room, that they can see the interpreters, and that the interpreters are ready. It does you no good to spread information or explain a rehearsal plan when not everyone is present, for you'll just have to repeat those things over and over, further delaying the process. Remember that you're working in two languages and that it just takes more time. This applies to anything shared prior to the start of rehearsal, during rehearsal when holds are called, and at the end of the day when things are wrapping up. Yes, there are many, many things to be done, and it's vitally important that everyone remains on the same page in getting to the finish line. Don't lose sight of the larger goals of the production in these high-stress moments near the end.

Guidelines for Front-of-House Staff

Seating
Seating is one of the most important areas for the directing team and box office staff to discuss early on. Blocking decisions can significantly impact the visibility of stage signing. As soon as directors decide to undertake an integrated production, they should meet with box office staff to discuss where deaf audiences will be seated. Box office staff should *never* assume that deaf audiences can sit anywhere in the theatre and still have a satisfactory view of the stage signing.

Typically, the first rows in the center of the house will offer the best sightlines. However, many factors come into play. These include how access is provided for spoken lines, the physical layout of the theatre itself, and even the rake. If interpreters are used, their placement needs to be taken into consideration. If they are placed to the side of the stage, then seating in the front rows of the section where the interpreters sit will allow deaf audiences to take in both interpreting and stage action. Similarly, if an open-captioning device is used, deaf audiences should be seated on the same side of the stage as the captioning device. Optimal sightlines will also be influenced by the theatre's physical space. If the front rows require audiences to look up, rather than straight ahead, then seating a few rows back from the stage may provide better sightlines than seating right in front of stage. This is where hiring a deaf consultant can be very helpful. The consultant can make recommendations about seating for deaf patrons based on all of the unique elements of the production, the access technology being used, and the physical site.

Once the optimal seating section is determined, directors should keep that seating in mind during blocking rehearsals. For example, if an actor will stand on one side of the stage to deliver signed lines, the actor's body should be oriented toward the deaf seating area. This will help ensure that deaf audiences have quality access to the onstage ASL. To ensure that sightlines will not be blocked or access mechanisms negatively impacted, DASLs should work with stage managers to monitor placement of props, set design elements, and accessibility mechanisms for non-signed lines. For example, if interpreters will be seated on stage or a captioning board will be placed on stage, that area can be marked off during rehearsals so that neither actors nor set elements encroach on it. Decisions like these need to be made very early in rehearsal to ensure access is built into the production, rather than added later as an afterthought.

These discussions are important to have even if no deaf actors are in the production. If a mainstream theatre will offer an interpreted or open-captioned performance during a production run, we encourage box office staff, directors, and stage managers to discuss how to best provide quality access. Nothing is more frustrating (and frequent) than arriving at an 'accessible' performance and finding that the placement of the access mechanism renders the show inaccessible. This type of experience will give the theatre company a bad reputation in the deaf community, reducing the number of deaf audiences who attend future shows.

Placement and Types of Access

As discussed in Chap. 2—"Dual Staging Models", not all forms of integrated theatre create full accessibility for deaf audiences. When spoken lines are not signed on stage, other methods of access must be used. These methods include placing interpreters on or near the stage, projecting open captions, providing open captioning via caption boards, or offering closed captioning via devices such as GalaPro. Each approach has advantages and disadvantages.

Regardless of the approach, successful use of access methods requires directors, stage managers, and front-of-house staff to avoid split visual attention. When visual attention is divided, deaf audiences are forced to frequently shift their gaze between the stage action and the access method, which results in lost information. Consider Fig. 5.1.

In a panel B or C setup, deaf audiences inevitably lose a bit of the story each time the dialogue shifts between a character speaking on stage and a character signing on stage. In a panel A setup, deaf audiences can easily take in the stage signing and the access for spoken lines without shifting their gaze. This setup is also optimal for an accessible performance with only speaking actors. Note also that in the panel A setup, the access mechanism is positioned close to center stage, rather than to the far left of the stage. We cannot stress enough the importance of interpreters and captioning being *within the same visual field* as the stage action for effective access. Position the interpreting or captioning in *as close proximity to the actors as possible* to eliminate loss of content due to having to look between stage signing and spoken line access. Many theatre companies make the mistake of splitting visual attention when providing access to deaf audiences, whether for integrated or accessible mainstream performances. This leads to a sub-par experience for deaf audiences and makes it unlikely they will return.

Theatre companies may wonder whether it's better to use interpreting or captioning. There is very little research to guide this decision. Both approaches have pros and cons. Some deaf people prefer interpreters, because they feel they get more of the emotional content that way. Other deaf people feel that interpreters take away from their experience of the production itself, because they have to watch the interpreters rather than the stage action. If the captioning is positioned effectively, they can take in both the stage action and captioning at the same time. Additionally, not all deaf people are fluent in ASL. Older theatre-goers may particularly benefit

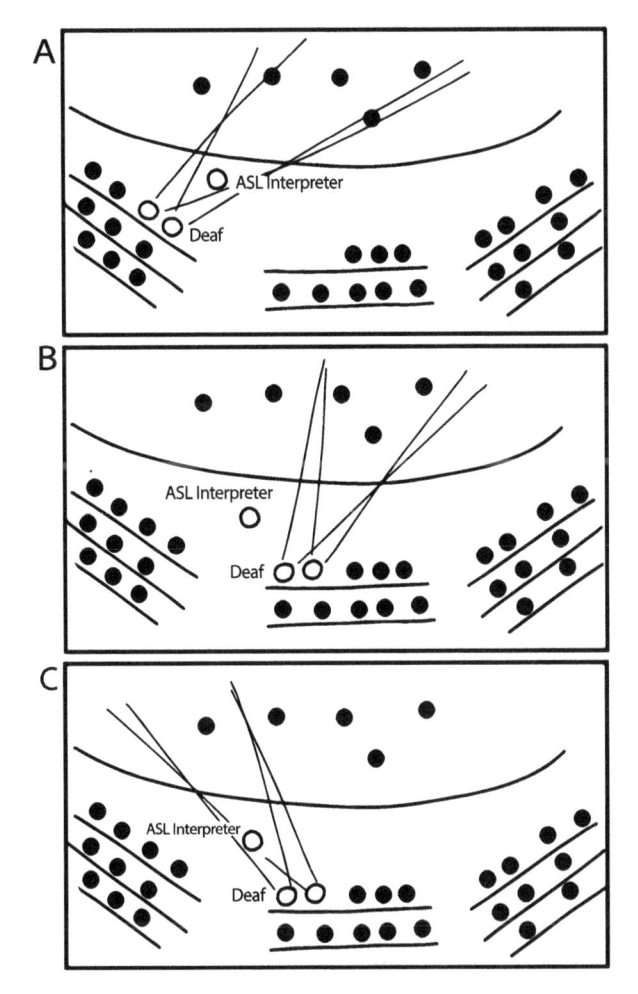

Fig. 5.1 Access mechanism placement—Dos and Don'ts. (Graphic: Brittany Castle)

from captioning over interpreting. The best approach is for a theatre to offer both captioning and interpreting to serve both types of audiences. If that is not possible, then the director and box office staff should consider who their primary deaf audience is for the show. Again, this is an area where having a deaf consultant involved can be very helpful.

Captioning can be either open or closed. Open captioning usually takes one of two forms. First, an LED sign is placed on the stage and an offstage captionist transmits a prepared script in sync with the dialogue. Second, as discussed in Chap. 3—"Guidelines for Designers", open captions can be integrated into the projection design. With closed captioning, deaf patrons utilize a device to view the captioning. These include tablets, handheld mobile devices, the audience member's own cell phone, and special glasses. The GalaPro system is becoming the most common technology for closed captioning in live theatre, although some theatre companies use the I-Caption system. This kind of captioning can be accessed via the patron's own mobile device or via a handheld device that scrolls a few lines of text at a time.

Positives with open captioning include:

- Others in the audience can benefit from the captioning.
- With correct placement of a caption board, deaf audiences have access to all of the stage business within their visual field without needing to check out equipment, download an app, or hold a mobile device.
- A caption board system can be purchased for around $6000, making it affordable for smaller theatre companies.
- If projected, captioning can become another way to express the production design.

Negatives with open captioning include:

- If the script is transmitted to the caption board using Wi-Fi, the Wi-Fi may be unreliable.
- The primary software used with caption boards is old, glitchy, and no longer supported by the company that made it.
- With caption boards, a captionist must be hired for each show, which tends to limit how many captioned shows a theatre company is able to provide.
- Deaf patrons typically need to sit in one section of the theatre to see the captioning board.
- Unless a deaf consultant is involved, the design and placement of projected captions may impede accessibility.
- As mentioned in Chap. 3—"Guidelines for Designers", scenic and lighting designs may undermine projected captioning unless the designers have worked from the beginning with this in mind.

Positives with closed captioning include:

- Deaf patrons aren't limited to one or two open-captioned show dates.
- Deaf patrons can sit anywhere in the theatre.
- Deaf patrons can move the device to follow where stage action is happening, thus avoiding split visual attention.

Negatives with closed captioning include:

- In order to view both the captioning and the action onstage, deaf patrons must hold the mobile device up near eye level for the entire show, which can be tiring and annoying.
- It may still be difficult to take in both the captioning and the stage action, resulting in split visual field.
- The small size of the font may make it difficult to read the captioning.
- Captioning devices depend on Wi-Fi, which may be unreliable in some theatres.
- Systems such as GalaPro are relatively expensive, and smaller theatres may not be able to afford them.
- It takes some time to prepare scripts. For Broadway shows, GalaPro captioning is usually not ready for use until four weeks after the show has officially opened. This limits deaf patron's choice of show dates. A show may also close before captioning is available.

Another issue with handheld closed-captioning devices is that both hearing actors and audience members may mistake the captioning device for a recording device. In 2022, an actor in a Broadway musical made headlines for scolding a deaf patron using the I-Caption system. Jill has been told multiple times by audience members to put away her cellphone while using closed-captioning devices during theatre performances.

There is very little research about deaf people's preferences for open vs. closed captioning. Based on anecdotal evidence and personal experience, we believe open captioning is preferred by most and that projected captions offer the best access. Thus, we advocate for open captions that are integrated into the projection and/or scenic design.

Ticketing

Once the optimal seating area has been established, tickets in this section should be reserved for deaf patrons. These tickets should be available at a low to mid-range price. Forcing deaf patrons to buy the most expensive seats in the theatre in order to have access is a form of price discrimination. For the same reason, if the number of accessible performances is limited, any ticket promotions offered for the production should be applied to the accessible performance. Doing this sends the message to deaf patrons that their presence is welcomed.

Scheduling

We encourage integrated productions to offer full access to every performance. Oftentimes, theatre companies cite high costs and don't offer captions or interpreters for more than one performance in the run of a play, thereby reducing accessibility. The accessible performance may also be scheduled on a day when ticket sales are low, such as a weekday evening or holiday evening, which limits the choices of deaf patrons. These issues also apply to accessible shows for mainstream theatre productions. Scheduling decisions like these send a negative message to deaf patrons. Instead, offer a choice of scheduling options. Again, projected captions that are integrated into the set and lighting design offer the most cost-effective option. Once created, they can be used on demand at any show.

Supporting Deaf Audiences

For deaf patrons, the accessibility experience begins well in advance of arriving at the theatre for the actual performance. The following elements send a message that is welcoming to deaf patrons:

- Information can easily be found on the website about which performances are captioned and/or interpreted.
- Box office staff have been trained to handle calls from relay services.
- Box office staff are knowledgeable about the accessibility options. For example, they know where the captioning box or interpreters will be located for a production.

- Box office staff have learned basic ASL and are comfortable communicating with deaf patrons.
- Lobby information is available in ASL.
- Ushers know sign language (volunteers can be recruited from the deaf community).

A Further Note on Reaching Deaf Audiences for Mainstream Productions

Much of what has been discussed in this section applies to productions that don't have any deaf artists involved. Almost all theatre companies offer one accessible performance per production run to comply with the legal requirements of the Americans with Disabilities Act. When deaf people don't turn out for captioned or interpreted performances, theatre companies may feel that financial resources devoted to accessibility have been wasted. There are several possible reasons why deaf audiences may not be showing up. First, aspects of the theatre's approach to accessibility (such as those mentioned in the previous section) may send the message that access is provided to satisfy a legal obligation rather than because of a genuine desire to serve deaf patrons. Second, deaf patrons may have had a prior negative experience at the theatre. For example, Jill will not go to any show at certain theatres due to where the captioning box is placed. Because the deaf community is small, 'word of hand' about a theatre's approach to accessibility will spread. Third, when only one show per performance run is accessible, it is more likely that deaf patrons will have conflicts. Finally, theatre companies may not be communicating effectively about their accessible offerings to potential deaf audiences.

If a mainstream theatre company wants to increase attendance by deaf audiences, they should first hire a deaf consultant to review their access practices to ensure these truly serve deaf audiences. A positive show experience will lead to positive 'word of hand.' Other strategies that can help theatre companies increase deaf attendance are as follows. First, cast deaf actors. As we have mentioned repeatedly, deaf audiences are highly motivated to see deaf performers onstage. Second, deaf people enjoy opportunities to socialize with each other. Hosting a pre-show happy hour or a post-show mingle can encourage deaf audiences to attend. Pre-show information sessions that are either interpreted or led by deaf individuals (such as the DASL or deaf consultant) and post-show talkbacks with deaf individuals involved in the show can also attract deaf audiences. If no deaf individuals are part of the show, local deaf theatre artists can be recruited to lead talkbacks and similar events. Third, offer multiple captioned or interpreted performances on various days and times. Fourth, marketing staff can build relationships with the deaf community by connecting with local organizations, schools, clubs, and individuals who have attended past performance. Instead of hoping deaf people will find out about interpreted and captioned performances from their website, companies should be reaching out to the community to spread the word. Many cities have deaf community Facebook groups where information can be shared. Local deaf schools and universities with Deaf Studies or ASL programs are also good places to send fliers or postcards. A deaf consultant can help with effective marketing strategies for the local community.

Throughout this chapter, we have stressed the importance of community building. Successful integrated theatre requires the ability to come together across culture and language barriers. Recognizing the importance of visual access for deaf people onstage, backstage, and in the audience is a key element of that success. Directors may not normally think much about their potential audience, preferring instead to focus on the artistic work in progress. But without consideration of the needs of the deaf audience, they will not achieve the definition of success that we have proposed for integrated theatre—'a production in which all artists feel included, supported, and able to achieve their best work, which then translates to a *powerful impact on audience members*.' Deaf audiences have seen plenty of integrated theatre that has a strong impact on hearing audiences, but gives them an unsatisfactory experience. They deserve better.

CHAPTER 6

Seeing the Performance

This section of the book is intended to put our four case study productions under the microscope to analyze what succeeded and what didn't from our perspective as deaf and hearing audience members. As we detail each production, we will be looking at accomplishments and missteps from the artistic angle as well as the accessibility angle. Any criticisms that we make are not intended to denigrate the effort, creativity, and talent of the artists who created the production. We know there are many elements, some of which may be out of the control of the people involved, that can impact a production. Our aim is to provide constructive critique, from both deaf and hearing lenses, to create opportunities for theatre makers to learn from other's work.

Spring Awakening

This production was not witnessed live by the writers, but was viewed at the Theatre on Film and Tape Archive, New York Public Library. The archived performance was recorded on December 8, 2015. Of course, viewing a recorded performance is not the same as viewing it live. As a patron in the audience, one is able to look wherever one likes, is affected by where one's seat is located, and is impacted by the responses of other patrons. In watching a recorded performance, one may not choose to look where one wants but instead is restricted to what the camera operators and editors have provided. This particular recording generally maintained a straight on camera angle. The camera was zoomed in on the performance to what we estimate was likely the equivalent of sitting several rows back from the stage edge. This ensured that we could clearly and easily see what the camera picked up. One benefit of viewing a recorded performance is being able to pause and think, take notes, even go back and rewatch. The analysis below has been supplemented with contemporary reviews from deaf audiences who attended the Broadway run.

Spring Awakening was undoubtedly an integrated production by our definition. A deaf and hearing creative team came together to produce the play bilingually in ASL and spoken English and the performance resonated to varying degrees with both hearing and deaf audiences. It clearly included several characteristics of integrated theatre:

- The production involves deaf and hearing artists working together toward a common goal.
- ASL, spoken English, and captions are purposefully incorporated into the telling of the story.
- There is a purposeful, story-driven explanation of how characters using different languages are able to interact and communicate.
- All deaf characters are played by deaf actors.

Because the production was originally created by Deaf West Theatre, we think it is likely that other integrated theatre characteristics were also met. We interviewed many individuals who were involved in *Spring Awakening* and none mentioned concerns about the following aspects:

- Inclusion supersedes accessibility, meaning all perspectives are included in the decision-making, not just given access to the information of decision-making.
- The production involves the bilingualism of ASL and English in the following settings: meetings, rehearsals, shops, fittings, onstage, and backstage, including an ASL translation of the script.
- The production involves a cultural exchange between deaf and hearing cultures that occurs in the following settings: meetings, rehearsals, shops, fittings, onstage, and backstage.

Spring Awakening was a commercial and critical success. During its Broadway stay at the Brooks Atkinson Theatre, the production was wildly popular with audiences, ran for 135 performances, and garnered multiple Tony and Drama Desk Award nominations. It was the most visible and well-known integrated production since Deaf West went to Broadway with *Big River* in 2003. It highlighted accessibility and inclusion in multiple ways, such as its integrated cast, featuring the first wheelchair-using actor in Broadway history, and hosting interpreted performances for DeafBlind patrons. In the cast of twenty-two actors, eight were deaf. Though this is not equal representation by numbers, one deaf actor was in a lead role (Wendla) and one was in a major supporting role (Moritz). Much of the story is devoted to the struggles of these two characters. Four other deaf actors played supporting roles (Adult Men, Adult Women, Martha, and Ernst) and two other deaf actors played featured roles (Thea, Otto) ensuring that nearly every scene included at least one deaf actor onstage. In all of these roles, the dual staging was created in such a way to spotlight the deaf performers. Offstage, the production team included three ASL Masters and one ASL Consultant as well as a deaf associate choreographer.

Dual Staging Models

Spring Awakening makes use of several dual staging models. Most prominent is the shadowing approach, used with the character of Wendla, played by Sandra Mae Frank, and Wendla's Voice, played by Katie Boeck. The musical opens with the two actors on either side of a mirror, mimicking each other's movements. They then each grab an object, Wendla a guitar and her Voice a dress, which they pass through the mirror to the other before starting the opening song, "Mama Who Bore Me." This moment immediately establishes a connection between the two and, in fact, sets them up as more of a double-cast character. However, throughout the play, Wendla very clearly becomes the primary character. Wendla's Voice is always nearby, and the two share several meaningful moments throughout the story. But whereas Wendla is always in the spotlight, her Voice is mostly kept to the periphery. The two are very much connected but they do not share focus, which is given to Wendla alone.

Another example is Moritz, played by Daniel Durant, and his Voice, played by Alex Boniello. Though their relationship is similar to that of Wendla and her Voice, they do not benefit from a similarly clear moment that establishes their connection. By the end of "The Bitch of Living," (the first song featuring Moritz) the audience is able to connect them together, but the absence of an initial moment of connection made their linkage less effective than Wendla's. Compared to Wendla's Voice, Mortiz's

Voice isn't as present with him throughout the play. However, they do share key moments onstage, most importantly when the Voice gives Moritz the weapon he uses to commit suicide.

While the program book for *Spring Awakening* identifies a 'voice of' character for most deaf actors, this seems a more functional designation rather than adhering to the 'voice of' approach as we've defined it. As already described, the Voices of Wendla and Moritz fit most closely with our definition of shadowing. For most other deaf actors, we see *Spring Awakening* using what we identify as the disconnected persona model, in which hearing actors provide voicing for a deaf actor for practical, rather than character-driven purposes. Several of the dual staging relationships seen onstage teeter between shadowing and disconnected persona, but ultimately land closer to the latter category. Examples include the supporting characters of Otto, Martha, Ernst, and Thea, played by Miles Barbee, Treshelle Edmond, Joshua Castille, and Amelia Hensley, respectively. All of these primary actors are deaf and their characters sign. Otto, Martha, and Ernst have Voices, played by Sean Grandillo, Kathryn Gallagher, and Daniel David Stewart, respectively, and their Voices are simultaneously musicians in the band. Moments shared between these primary actors and voice actors are minor; throughout most of the story there's little connection between the two. Thea has a unique circumstance in that her Voice is supplied by another character in the play, Melitta, played by Lauren Luiz. In scenes with the two of them, Melitta SimComs her own lines, and also speaks Thea's lines as they are signed. For the audience, this may add confusion because no other Voice in the play is supplied by a character in the same scene. As the only instance of the 'voice of' dual staging approach, it muddies Melitta's role in the story.

SimCom is used often in *Spring Awakening*. The primary character communicating this way is one of the protagonists, Melchior, played by Austin P. McKenzie. Nearly all of his lines are spoken and signed simultaneously. Additionally, SimCom is used almost entirely by Anna, Hänschen, Ilse, Georg, and Greta, played by Ali Stroker, Andy Mientus, Krysta Rodriguez, Alex Wyse, and Alexandra Winter, respectively. Playing Fräuline Knuppeldick and Frau Bergmann, Camryn Manheim almost entirely SimComs. Also, Herr Gabor, one of the five adult characters played by Patrick Page, used SimCom. While Manheim and McKenzie had prior knowledge of ASL, other hearing actors using SimCom did not (Paulson 2015).

Artistic Successes

From an artistic standpoint, the show had many triumphs that were evident even when being viewed through a video monitor in a library archive. It was captivating and compelling. One can only imagine how much more powerful it was live and in-person. First and foremost, deaf culture is woven through the production concept. Director Michael Arden explained in interviews that the world of the play was conceptualized as a small town in which an epidemic left many without hearing. The original play is set in Germany in the 1890s, a time in which deaf individuals were sterilized and deaf and hearing couples were forbidden to marry. Arden also invoked the impact of the Milan Conference of 1880, at which a mostly hearing group of deaf educators voted to uphold oralist over manualist educational philosophies (Theatermania 2014). As a direct impact of the Milan Conference, many schools for the deaf banned sign language. Students were punished for using it by having their hands slapped, tied behind their backs, and other corporeal measures. These historical contexts form a compelling backstory to the original play and are referenced when Herr Sonnenstich, the boys' schoolteacher, forbids his pupils to sign in class, verbally torments Moritz for his vocal pronunciation, and physically strikes Melchior with a pointer after he is caught signing to the other students. Such behaviors and incidents are well documented in deaf history. Various techniques that were used to teach speech to the deaf are also incorporated in this scene, including Herr Sonnenstich having the students feel and then copy the movement of his mouth and throat. Deaf culture is also present in other aspects of the storytelling, such as ways of getting one's attention. For example, Frau Bergmann bangs a chair on the floor to catch Wendla's eye. Hänschen taps on a piano to be noticed by Ernst, then touches Ernst's shoulder, and waves his hand—all attention-getting tactics done in the same scene. A separate example of deaf culture occurs during a scene when the schoolteachers speak to each other and the deaf pupils turn to the hearing students to interpret what is being said.

Though *Spring Awakening* utilized a variety of dual staging methods, and several dual staging relationships between actors/characters teeter between methods, the relationship between Wendla and her Voice is compelling. Their connection to the other is evident from the start of the play and is magnified later as they share important moments onstage. The production also used moments without voicing to artistic effect. First, Moritz and his father Herr Stiefel, played by Russell Harvard, have a scene about his failing out of school that is performed ASL without voice, but with captions. Later in the play, after his Voice hands him the gun, Moritz's last lines before killing himself are performed only in ASL.

From a design standpoint, the scenic elements were used effectively throughout. An unobstructed downstage center playing space is utilized frequently. Low, mobile furniture pieces such as tables, chairs, desks, and pianos easily roll on and off. Levels are used to great success in many scenes. Performers stand on the floor, on mobile furniture pieces, on moving staircases, and even on a giant staircase that is set upstage against the back wall. The scenery is minimalistic but strikingly effective. Lighting for the most part is also used extremely well throughout the musical. The main action and focal actor(s) remain in bright white light while the rest of the stage is often blanketed in dark shadows and subdued blues. Many times, lighting spotlights pick up the next actor to cue the audience where to look before new lines come in. Subtle background action and choreography often occurs in the shadowed areas. These darkened spaces are also where Voices are frequently stationed.

Overall, the ensemble was used creatively, particularly characters who are not featured in a given scene. Typically, they remain onstage, performing understated choreography, posing to create scenic pictures, sitting motionless in chairs, or watching as silent witnesses to the action that unfolds. One scene in which the ensemble choreography is particularly effective is when Wendla asks Melchior to strike her with a switch from a tree. A group of cross-legged observers slowly turn to watch him as he struggles with how to respond to her.

Last but certainly not least, there are many excellent performances, most notably from Sandra Mae Frank as Wendla, Daniel Durant as Moritz, Camryn Manheim as Frau Bergmann, Treshelle Edmond as Martha, and Russell Harvard as Herr Moritz. The final scenes and songs from "Whispering" through "Those You've Known" to the finale "The Song of Purple Summer" are indelibly impactful.

Artistic Critique

The points we discuss here do not erase the many accomplishments of the show. They are moments of storytelling that we as individuals did not feel were successful. Despite the many hours of ideation and labor that go into a production, some choices simply do not land with audience members.

Because theatre evokes unique responses from each patron, the thoughts shared here only are the perspectives of two people.

Director Michael Arden's invoking the Milan Conference is pointed and powerful, and Herr Sonnenstich's audist behavior to his deaf pupils is searing to watch. However, Headmaster Knochenbruch, who is deaf, signs and has a disconnected persona speaking for him, while Associate Headmaster Fraulein Knuppeldick SimComs all of her lines. We wondered why school leaders would use ASL when conducting school business while pupils are severely punished for signing in class. The approach to bilingual accessibility and the dramaturgical concept seem to be in conflict here. Again, this is not to disparage the work of those actors, nor the ideas of the director himself, but this disconnect could not be overlooked in our viewing of the musical.

The other major disconnect for us is related to Thea and her Voice. The Voicing convention is embedded into the concept of the show. In every instance except one, a nearby Voice is clearly connected to a primary character but left unacknowledged by the other characters onstage. As an example, Wendla's Voice is always present but is treated as invisible by others in the scene. Thea's voice was supplied by the actor playing Melitta. However, Melitta was *also* a character in the scene, meaning the actor playing Melitta SimCommed her own lines and then also voiced for Thea. Because the Voice was not a shadow actor or a disconnected persona, it first appeared that Melitta was speaking for Thea. This did not make sense to us because all the characters in the scene knew ASL and there would be no need for Melitta to interpret. Likely, it was a pragmatic choice to have the actor doing double duty with lines. This isn't a bad choice in and of itself, but it goes against the convention that has already been established for other Voices. Thea and Melitta are the only acting pair that uses the 'voice of' approach. The lack of consistency, even minor, created a moment of confusion, taking us out of the experience by causing us to question why this exception to the rule was made.

Accessibility Successes

In addition to the overall artistic successes of the production, we saw two main examples of accessibility success. First, the signing of the deaf actors was excellent. Their ASL was true stage ASL. Just as speaking actors must project their voices, signing actors must project their signs and that was done to the highest degree by this group of actors. Signing onstage requires larger signing, bigger facial expressions, and more purposeful and deliberate movements for the sake of clarity. Sandra Mae Frank, Daniel Durant, and Russell Harvard were all superb in their performances.

Second, many of the smaller scenes with only a handful of characters were well-staged and well-lit to maximize accessibility. Scenes with Wendla and Frau Bergmann, or Wendla and Melchior, or Melchior and Moritz stand out because they were much clearer compared to the busy group numbers. With fewer bodies onstage, the audience knew exactly who to focus on and could see everything happening in a scene. Additionally, as mentioned earlier, levels were used creatively in various scenes. For example, ladders allowed the ensemble to gather in configurations other than a straight line, but kept their signing in close proximity to each other. Lighting and scenery amplified the signing by providing clear space, levels, and additional light.

Accessibility Critique

Despite the artistic and accessibility successes of *Spring Awakening*, there were some accessibility failures that hampered the experience for us. The principal critique is that SimCom was relied on too heavily. While we appreciate the actors' hard work in delivering their lines simultaneously in two languages, it's a very difficult task to accomplish well. It was a lot to ask of them to do this throughout the entirety of the performance. Oftentimes the nuance of ASL was sacrificed, or the signing felt stilted. Facial expressions convey a lot of meaning in ASL and a speaking actor will use their face to emphasize what they are saying, not what they are signing. Some actors pulled off this feat better than others. We were not alone in finding this to be a poor accessibility choice. *Spring Awakening* was frequently and consistently critiqued by deaf audiences for its use of SimCom (see, for example, Epstein and Needham 2015). From a storytelling standpoint there were also moments when SimCom did not make sense. Why is Wendla's mother using SimCom with her and not just signing? Why is Melchior using SimCom with his deaf mother and Moritz when they are alone? The deaf actors were given Voice counterparts, so couldn't the speaking actors have been given signing counterparts too? This decision seemed to make signing clarity a second priority. Hearing audiences received spoken language no matter what, but deaf audiences got some clear ASL and some ASL that was less than clear because the actor was using SimCom.

Additionally, though captions were used in the production, they were (as far as we could see in the recording) not consistent. First, multiple caption locations existed throughout the play: two projection surfaces on the back wall, one for the stage level and one for the second level; a blackboard in the school room scene; written on placards during "Totally Fucked." These different locations created a situation where audiences were unsure where to look to see captions. Second, captions appeared in some scenes, but not all scenes, creating a situation where audiences could be confused because they expected to see captions where none existed. At times, the captions seemed to be used for the hearing audience members rather than deaf, as in Act 1, Scene 3 when Moritz's signing is captioned but the talking between the hearing schoolboys is not.

The song "Mirror Blue Night" had two lighting effects that were not friendly to the signing. First, Melchior is illuminated by up-light when the song begins, throwing shadows across his body and making his ASL incredibly difficult to decipher. Second, the scene included a darkened stage with multiple performers wearing gloves with light-up fingertips. Though it was apparent some signing was happening, it was not possible to make out what they were signing. This artistic choice was also heavily criticized by deaf audiences who saw the show in person.

Finally, costumes did not always contrast with the actors' skin color. Many wore drab grays and light browns, or white. Although visually distracting patterns were mostly avoided, one scene had actors in black and white striped shirts.

ASL Midsummer Night's Dream

This production was also not witnessed live by the writers but viewed via recorded performance on YouTube. The beginning of the streaming video states that the recording was made for archival purposes, "with the intention to capture and create an official record of the unique sign language crafted by Howie [Seago] and the company for this production." Then, as part of its 2021 season, Sound Theatre Company streamed the production online. The digital offering was a single-camera recording of the May 4, 2018 performance at 12th Avenue Arts—Mainstage, a 125-seat black box-type theatre in Seattle, Washington. As with *Spring Awakening*, it was not the same viewing experience to see the performance on a computer instead of live and in-person. However, Sound Theatre Company generously gave us unlimited access to the recording, so that we were able to watch and rewatch.

ASL Midsummer Night's Dream meets our criteria for being an integrated production. To begin with, it was co-directed by a deaf and hearing team. A quick glance at the program makes it clear that deaf culture and ASL were woven into and throughout the entire production process, with phrases such as "in partnership with Deaf Spotlight," "an ASL-mainstream production," and "all shows bilingual in ASL and Spoken English" jumping out. The first page of the program offers notes from Howie Seago, the Deaf co-director and highlights his deaf perspective on the play. It explains the partnership between Sound Theatre and Deaf Spotlight, "a non-profit organization serving the Deaf community, fostering artistic and cultural and experience in a variety of areas including cinema, literature, visual arts, and performing arts" that strives "to inspire, encourage, and showcase creative works of, by, and for Deaf people in the Pacific Northwest through events that celebrate Deaf culture and American Sign Language." Page four of the program extends a heartfelt thanks to the many ASL interpreters who worked on the production.

ASL Midsummer Night's Dream very clearly includes several common characteristics of integrated theatre:

- The production involves deaf and hearing artists working together toward a common goal.
- Inclusion supersedes accessibility, meaning all perspectives are included in the decision-making, not just given access to the information of decision-making.
- The production integrates ASL and English bilingualism in the following settings: meetings, rehearsals, shops, fittings, onstage, and backstage, including an ASL translation of the script.
- The production involves a cultural exchange between deaf and hearing cultures that occurs in the following settings: meetings, rehearsals, shops, fittings, onstage, and backstage.
- ASL and spoken English, and captions are purposefully incorporated into the telling of the story. (The recording on YouTube was captioned, but the live production was not.)

A deaf and hearing creative team came together to produce the play bilingually in ASL and spoken English and the performance resonated to varying degrees with both hearing and deaf audiences. When the recording begins, a note from the co-directors states, "This production was created, quite literally, to center the experience of Deaf artists and Deaf audiences. The 19-person cast includes 10 actors who are Deaf and 9 actors who are hearing. Every line of Shakespeare's text is both signed and spoken. The center seats of the theater were reserved for Deaf/HoH audience members to assure them an optimal view of the play." From start to finish, from the directing team, to the concept, to the casting of characters, to the experience of the audience, this play intentionally put the spotlight on accessibility and inclusion. More than half of the cast was deaf and every major character except two (Oberon and Titania) signed almost exclusively throughout the play. Sound Theatre Company also created a separate YouTube video that introduced all characters with their name signs.

In all of the roles, the dual staging was created in such a way to highlight the deaf performers, and every scene included at least one deaf actor on stage. Offstage, the production team included a deaf co-director, an ASL Master and two ASL Coaches, as well as a deaf assistant scenic designer and assistant stage manager. The production ran for four weeks of performances in 2018, was available on-demand in 2021, and won a local 2018 Gregory People's Choice Award for Outstanding Production of a Play. Ryan Schlecht was also nominated for Outstanding Supporting Actor in a Play for his portrayal of Nick Bottom. The Gregory Awards are given to theatre companies and theatre makers in the Puget Sound region for artistic excellence.

Dual Staging Models

ASL Midsummer Night's Dream relies most heavily on the 'voice of' approach, albeit one that doesn't neatly fit into our definition. For example, Puck, played by Michelle Mary Schaefer, is voiced by a lesser fairy, Moth, played by Jason Treviño. Puck and Moth are separate characters who occasionally share moments of interaction onstage. Moth also supplies a voice for Puck's lines—all of which are signed. At the same time, however, Moth *also* voices for Lysander, played by Kai Winchester. The primary difference is that, unlike Puck, Lysander does not interact with Moth. As far as we can tell Moth is the only character voicing for both Puck and Lysander. In our definition of the 'voice of' approach, one distinct character provides a voice for one separate signing character, and the two share a sense of unity due to their established onstage connection. The specific use of this approach in *ASL Midsummer* breaks our mold by assigning Moth to be the 'voice of' for two separate characters. However, due to an obviously stronger onstage bond with Puck, Moth seems to function more as a disconnected persona with Lysander. Their lack of contact and interaction displays a markedly different level of connection compared to Moth and Puck. This is tricky though, as Moth is onstage and clearly voicing for Lysander, making it hard to fit their relationship into any of the three variations of disconnected persona that we've detailed. Thus, in the case of Moth in particular, a hybrid approach to dual staging was taken. Most other characters sign for themselves and their voices are provided using the 'voice of' approach. There are a few instances when characters speak lines, primarily Oberon, played by Michael D. Blum, and another character signs for accessibility purposes. Oberon is connected to an invented character named First Fairy, played by Guthrie Nutter. The relationship between these two characters shares some similarities with the shadowing approach, but also verges on a 'voice of' or in this case 'hands of' counterpart. There are also several instances in which SimCom is used.

Artistic Successes

Though viewing the performance on a screen was not ideal, the performance itself was engaging and entertaining throughout. Above all, the translation was masterful. Co-director Howie Seago and Amelia Hensley worked together as DASLs. Seago created the initial translation draft and then worked with Hensley and the actors to finalize it. As discussed in Chap. 2—"Artistic Challenges and Issues", Shakespeare in sign language presents unique challenges because of the highly poetic language. Translation approaches can range from close adherence to the original text to a freer conceptual alignment. The translation for *ASL Midsummer Night's Dream* fell on the free side of the continuum. The artistic qualities of sign language were skillfully leveraged to create powerful visual images that made the textual meaning clear. One prominent example is how Nick Bottom used techniques such as personification and transformational signs to great comedic effect. For instance, the lines "I will aggravate my voice so that I will roar you as gently as any sucking dove, as any nightingale" are shown with a two-handed lion roar quickly diminishing to a bird tweeting plaintively. In a separate example, two-person signing was used creatively in several scenes. In Act 1, Scene 1, Lysander's lines "How chance the roses there do fade so fast" are signed with a flower drooping into Hermia's palm. Hermia's response, "Belike for want of rain, which I could well beteem them from the tempest of my eyes," is signed showing Hermia's tears dripping onto the top of Lysander's hand. Then, Hermia's hand becomes a new flower pushing up through Lysander's hand.

Deaf culture and experience are also firmly built into the play. DEER is used on occasion by characters to get each other's attention. This is a common attention getting technique in deaf culture. When someone signs DEER, everyone copies the sign as they see it. Because the sign for DEER requires both hands to be on the head, further conversation is halted. As another example, during Act 2, Scene 1, Demetrius (Kyle Seago), who is played as a hearing character, and Helena (Brittany Rupik), who is played as a deaf character, are arguing in sign language. As Demetrius' anger escalates, he verbally shouts at her, "Do I entice you? Do I speak you fair?" Helena's response is to point her finger at her ear and shake her head. Coupled with Demetrius grabbing her shoulders, this moment of speech without sign shows the violence of audism.

The scenery was expertly designed to emphasize visual openness and limit physical pieces becoming sightline barriers. The set itself was a series of connected wooden platforms rising at different elevations across the stage. This offered several prominent playing spaces: an open space on the center stage floor, an elevated platform stage left, another elevated platform stage right, and a slightly higher platform upstage of these two. The upstage platform was wide enough that it alone could easily hold half a dozen or more characters at a time. Each platform had stairs, making them available to enter on multiple sides. Gauzy white silks draped around the offstage and upstage sides of the platforms. These were used later in the play to create Titania's sleeping chamber on the upstage left platform. The platforms and the silks comprised the scenery. The company did not utilize any furniture or moving pieces. Instead, the blocking rotated around the stage to create the sense of movement through the play. Designing the scenery this way ensured that the onstage signing would always be the focus of attention.

As with *Spring Awakening*, several actors gave truly standout performances. Ryan Schlecht as Nick Bottom was phenomenal, as proven by his Gregory Award nomination, and made one wish the Rude Mechanicals featured more in the story. Guthrie Nutter, Kai Winchester, and Jacob Merz (Peter Quince) also did outstanding work onstage.

Characters such as Oberon and Puck used magic in effective and humorous ways throughout the play. These moments reminded the audience that much of the play, especially scenes in the forest, takes place in the fantastical world of fairies. Lighting and sound were simultaneously utilized to raise moments of magic by covering the stage in vibrant hues and enveloping audiences in the twangs of an electric guitar.

The play is bookended with short scenes that depict the world of the fairies. In the opening scene, Puck calls on the lesser fairies of Moth, Peaseblossom (Jessica Kiely), Mustardseed (Corey Spruill), and First Fairy, and takes them through a series of movement sequences using primarily gestural and visual storytelling. These foreshadow the themes in the play and eventually introduce Oberon and Titania (Kathy Hsieh). When the opening moment concludes, the fairies scatter as Duke Theseus and Hippolyta, portrayed by Michael J. Schweiger and Carolyn Marie Monroe respectively, enter. The play ends with this same cohort of fairies performing another group movement sequence that uses Shakespeare's final lines of the play shared simultaneously by the entire group in ASL. This group moment transitions into Puck's ending lines and then finally one more group line in ASL before the lights go out. These moments not only emphasize the role of the fairies in the play but also create space for visual storytelling and deaf perspectives within Shakespeare's text. They frame all of *ASL Midsummer Night's Dream* as a play within a play, elevating deaf art and visual communication over written and spoken art.

Artistic Critique

Again, the points we discuss here do not erase the many accomplishments of the show. They are moments of storytelling that we did not feel were successful. And again, these are the reflections of only two people seeing the play.

This specific world of *A Midsummer Night's Dream* is a world in which almost everyone knows sign language. Nearly all the characters sign for themselves. This is true of the Duke, Hippolyta, and Egeus, played by Thawin Choulaphan, the four young lovers, the Rude Mechanicals, and all the fairies except Oberon (who does use a few signs, but primarily only speaks his lines). However, there are several moments when the dramatic concept is incongruent. First, Hippolyta's fluency is inconsistent. In Act 1, Scene 1, she is visibly new to ASL. She SimComs her lines but struggles with the signing, prompting Theseus to show her the appropriate signs. But in Act 4, Scene 1, when Theseus, Hippolyta, and Egeus find the young lovers asleep in the forest, Hippolyta signs easily without speaking and Titania voices for her. Then, in the final scene, at the performance of

Pyramus and Thisbe, Hippolyta again signs while Titania voices the lines. Are we supposed to believe that her signing has magically improved in four days? It isn't clear if that's the story being told.

In general, counterparts are established and consistent throughout the play. However, with a few characters, the actor who is voicing for them changes mid-play, which is unsettling and distracting. As an audience, once we've become familiar with two connected actors onstage, it throws us for a loop when their connection is broken. The primary approach to dual staging taken in this play is 'voice of.' As already described, the role of Moth served several purposes, including 1) performing as a distinct character, 2) serving as the voice of Puck, and 3) serving as the voice of Lysander. We take no issue with these specific examples. However, with the Rude Mechanicals, counterparts are not so clear-cut. For example, when the audience first meets Nick Bottom, he is voiced by Francis Flute, played by Nick Rempel. Later in the play, Mustardseed takes over voicing for Nick Bottom. This change might seem minor but it's jarring and points to one of the drawbacks of the disconnected persona variation we dubbed 'voicing by committee.' As discussed in Chap. 2—"Dual Staging Models", using multiple actors to provide voicing for a single character can be perceived negatively by hearing audiences and end up undermining the performance of the primary deaf actor. Again, though *Midsummer's* use of dual staging leans closer to 'voice of,' the use of multiple voices for a singular character doesn't land well. This comment is magnified for Tom Snout, who does triple duty. The actor playing him, Catherine Kettrick, voices for both Robin Starveling (also played by Thawin Choulaphan) and Peter Quince, *and* SimComs Tom's own lines. Francis Flute, who SimComs most of his lines, is later voiced by Peaseblossom when he plays Thisbe—but only for *some* of the play within a play, not all of it. Again, it is jarring when someone who has been communicating a character's lines unexpectedly switches. Because the lesser fairies have already been established as voices in some scenes, why not simply keep that convention going and have them also voice for characters in other scenes? Yes, it gives those actors much more work to do, but for the audience it also keeps those character connections clean and easy to follow.

Another point of critique is the mouthing of contemporary English words by deaf actors throughout the play. As mentioned in Chap. 2—"Artistic Challenges and Issues", mouthing is an under-theorized area of artistic sign language. For us, the mouthing of contemporary English words felt in conflict with the spoken lines. We feel it would have been more coherent to have the characters use ASL mouth morphemes, in keeping with the elevated ASL register, or to have the characters mouth sixteenth-century words, in keeping with the spoken English register.

Finally, in one scene, the deaf actors positioned on the upstage platform performed while silk hangings were being waved behind them. This movement might have been meant to represent the "whistling wind" referred to in the lines. However, the visual distraction made it difficult to focus on the signing.

Accessibility Successes

In addition to the overall artistic successes of the production, there are multiple instances of accessibility success that we want to highlight. First, this play was made with deaf audiences in mind. Nearly every major character in the play signs their lines. The only exceptions are Oberon (whose counterpart in Guthrie Nutter is masterful and entertaining) and Titania (who speaks with Oberon but later signs with Bottom). The voicing actors are always blocked to avoid sightline issues for other actors or audience members. This is a true triumph of deaf performance, ASL, and deaf culture on the stage.

Not to be understated, the hard work done between counterparts was obvious. It's not always easy to find synchronization between spoken English and ASL, particularly when performing Shakespeare's verse; however, all the counterparts onstage were clearly connected and aligned with each other. Oberon and First Fairy, Moth and Lysander, and Peaseblossom and Hermia, played by Elizabeth Ayers Gibson, were all standouts in this way.

Although the live production was not captioned, the streaming version was. In the video, creative captioning was used effectively to provide access to the production's use of music and sound design. For example, in the opening scenes, the following captioning appeared: "slow music with a background of crickets; twangs of electric guitar and a pulsing drone." This was a great effort to give deaf audiences more information about the sound design in the production.

Finally, some of the costumes were well done and utilized smart contrasts with the actors' skin colors. These include Puck's dark green top and Theseus' purple tunic. The latter made clever use of patterns by keeping a solid panel in the middle of the signing box.

Accessibility Critique

Though few, there were some accessibility critiques we want to point out about the performance. First, as mentioned with *Spring Awakening*, the use of SimCom was at times problematic. Though SimCom was not used much, the actors who were tasked with SimComming were not up to the challenge. Moments with Francis Flute and the Rude Mechanicals were lost to deaf audience members, especially during *Pyramus and Thisbe*. To a lesser degree, Titania was asked to SimCom a few times when an easier decision would be to have Peaseblossom speak or sign for her. Once or twice, the lesser fairies used SimCom and in each of these instances, though brief, their lines were not equally communicated. Second, disappointingly, captions were not used during the live performance.

The Music Man

This production was experienced live by one of the writers in July 2022. Both writers later viewed an archival recording of the production at Olney Theatre Center. The single-camera recording was taken on June 29, 2022, the first public performance after multiple COVID-19-related performance cancellations, at the Roberts Mainstage on Olney's campus, a 429-seat proscenium theatre.

The Music Man meets our criteria for an integrated production. Like *ASL Midsummer Night's Dream*, it was led by a co-directing team with one Deaf director, Sandra Mae Frank, and one hearing director, Michael Baron. The sixteen-person cast had equal representation onstage between deaf and hearing artists. The cast also included several swing actors who were not seen onstage unless called upon to stand in for a role. The creative team included Deaf artists Michelle Banks as director of artistic sign language and Ethan Sinnott as scenic designer. In the program, the note from the artistic director explains the production concept of River City being a sister city to Martha's Vineyard in the nineteenth and early twentieth centuries, where deaf and hearing people lived in a bilingual community. The program includes a page explaining why producing this version of *The Music Man* was important to Olney Theatre Center and a page explaining the history of Martha's Vineyard. As noted by Jason Loewith in the introduction to the archival recording, fourteen ASL interpreters worked on the production.

The Music Man includes several of the common characteristics of integrated theatre:

- The production involves deaf and hearing artists working together toward a common goal.
- Inclusion supersedes accessibility, meaning all perspectives are included in the decision-making, not just given access to the information of decision-making.
- The production integrates the bilingualism of ASL and English in the following settings: meetings, rehearsals, shops, fittings, onstage, and backstage, including an ASL translation of the script.
- The production involves a cultural exchange between deaf and hearing cultures that occurs in the following settings: meetings, rehearsals, shops, fittings, onstage, and backstage.
- ASL, spoken English, and captions are all purposefully incorporated into the telling of the story.

The production was undoubtedly a success. A deaf and hearing creative team came together to produce the play bilingually in ASL and spoken English and the performance resonated to varying degrees with both hearing and deaf audiences. It was led by a co-directing team and had an almost equal balance between deaf and hearing actors (seven to nine, not including the swings). The production featured deaf actors in lead, supporting, and ensemble roles. These included James Caverly as Harold Hill, Mervin Primeaux-O'Bryant as Maud Dunlop/Constable Locke, Gregor Lopez as Olin Britt, Andrew Morrill as Mayor George Shinn, Amelia Hensley as Eulalie Shinn, Nicki Runge as Mrs. Paroo/Mrs. Squires, Christopher Tester as Winthrop Paroo/Oliver Hix, Anjel Piñero as Zaneeta Shinn, and Michael Anthony Spady as a swing. *The Music Man* used ASL, spoken English, and open captions throughout the entire story, including multiple scenes that were acted only in ASL with captions. The production concept centered deaf characters in the story. In every scene except one, at least one deaf actor was on the stage and ASL was used in the scene. The production ran for approximately five weeks of performances—despite several COVID-19-related cancellations—and was nominated for nine Helen Hayes Awards in 2023. Helen Hayes Awards are given to theatre companies and theatre makers around the Washington, DC area for artistic excellence. The production won three awards: Outstanding Lead Performance in a Musical for James Caverly, Outstanding

Directing in a Musical for Sandra Mae Frank and Michael Baron, and Outstanding Ensemble in a Musical.

Dual Staging Models

The Music Man made use of several dual staging models. The disconnected persona is used frequently throughout for characters such as Harold Hill and others played by deaf actors. The production slides a bit into 'voice of' territory as the actor playing Marcellus Washburn often voices for Harold. However, the two are not consistently connected enough to signify a true 'voice of' pairing because Harold has multiple scenes without Marcellus voicing his lines. There were also multiple instances of an already-established character becoming an interpreter-character. For example, at the Fourth of July celebration, deaf Mayor George Shinn gives a speech and several hearing townspeople, including Ewart Dunlop and Jacey Squires, played by Dylan Toms and Jay Frisby respectively, step in to interpret. These characters are already written into the story and in that moment, were each tasked with interpreting for the rest of the characters (and the audience).

SimCom is also used often in *The Music Man*. In many scenes between Marian Paroo, a CODA in the production, played by Adelina Mitchell, and her deaf mother, played by Deaf actor Nicki Runge, Marian SimComs her lines. This is done for the audience's benefit because her mother can understand her via ASL and doesn't need her to voice her words. In another example, many hearing members of River City, Iowa SimCom their lines when speaking to Harold. Again, this is for the benefit of hearing members of the audience because Harold can understand these people without them speaking. The access barrier introduced for deaf audiences by the use of SimCom was alleviated by presence of open captioning throughout the production. If what was being expressed was unclear, they could look to the captions for clarification.

Artistic Successes

In viewing this production both live and as a recording, multiple artistic achievements were apparent to us. As the backbone of the production, the concept of River City being akin to Martha's Vineyard was a strong artistic choice. The real-life communities on Martha's Vineyard existed at the same time *The Music Man* takes place. This coexistence of deaf and hearing people was highlighted by making not only Mayor George Shinn (an elected official) but also his wife Eulalie and his daughter Zaneeta deaf. Furthermore, Marian, the prominent town librarian, was a CODA with a deaf brother as well. Maud and Ewart Dunlop gave one example of a deaf and hearing married couple. Oliver and Alma Hix, played by Heather Marie Beck, gave another. Winthrop Paroo and the young Amaryllis, portrayed by Sarah Anne Sillers, gave a potential third, while Zaneeta Shinn and Tommy Djilas, played by Matthew August, offered the possibility of a fourth. The town was truly a blending of these different cultures into one single community.

As with the other productions we've looked at, deaf culture was referenced throughout the story. For example, when the mayor gives a speech, hearing townsperson Ewart Dunlop steps in to interpret. Dunlop struggles and the mayor replaces him with another interpreter, Jacey Squires. But the mayor is no happier with Squires' interpretation and replaces him with a third interpreter. Finally, the mayor is satisfied enough to go forward with his speech. This scene is humorous for both deaf and hearing audiences, and also incorporates deaf culture because many deaf people share the frustrating experience of working with unqualified interpreters. Deaf culture is present in another key moment near the end of the story, when Harold decides to come clean to Marian. He signs I CAN'T LIE, then removes his hearing aids and tucks them into his coat pocket. Harold sharing who he really is with Marian encompasses admitting his deafness, rather than trying to pass as hearing. This character development resonates with deaf individuals, especially those who are raised oral and gradually come to embrace their deafness.

Given the predominantly hearing audience base at Olney Theatre Center, performing scenes in ASL with only captioning for the sign-impaired was a major risk taken by the artistic team. Multiple conversations and scenes took place solely in ASL, either between two deaf characters or between a deaf character and a hearing character who was signing. For example, Harold and Vishal Vaidya's Marcellus Washburn signed to each other. There were no voices added to their conversations. This forced hearing audience members who didn't know ASL to watch and read instead of listen. It also made sense in the Martha Vineyard's–style world of the play. This risk paid off, as shown by critical and audience responses.

From an acting perspective, and as evidenced by the multiple Helen Hayes nominations and awards for acting, many actors gave strong performances. Beyond Caverly as Harold Hill, Andrew Morrill (Mayor Shinn) and Amelia Hensley (Eulalie Shinn) added so much in their supporting roles. Vishal Vaidya as Marcellus had great chemistry with Caverly and added a solid singing voice to his songs. Adelina Mitchell and her stellar voice created a mature, grounded, invested Marian. Even ensemble members Florrie Bagel (Ethel Toffelmier) and Heather Beck (Alma Hix) enriched the production in their moments onstage.[1] In addition to the acting performances in general, multiple moments throughout the play were truly impactful. One example comes very near the end of the play. Together, Harold and Marian sing "Till There Was You" and in the final verse, they sign it without voice. Harold is clearly guilt-ridden by his actions and torn by his feelings for Marian and the life he's lived up to now. She is clearly opening herself up to him, even knowing his past. They've won each other over and it's a magical scene onstage. To successfully bring the audience to this lovely moment and land it, the actors had to build an engaging arc throughout the story, and they were successful in that.

From a design perspective, Ethan Sinnott's scenic design highlighted open spaces across the stage. It included a short, circular center stage platform that could be accessed by a ramp on the downstage side and a separate ramp on the upstage side. This large, main playing area was kept open throughout the entire story. Small, mobile furniture pieces easily rolled on and off to establish new locations. Elements flew in to add to scenes, for example train tracks in the opening scene or musical instruments when the Wells Fargo Wagon arrived at the end of Act One. A decorative trellis hugged the proscenium arch and offered one captioning position. A secondary captioning screen was flown in upstage at various times. These pieces add visual interest to the design while keeping the stage visually unobstructed.

Artistic Critique

Again, the points we discuss here do not erase the many accomplishments of the production and the artists. And again, these are the observations and reflections of only two people seeing the musical. One area that stands out most to us as audience members is that despite situating the story in a Martha's Vineyard–style town and utilizing the various storytelling

---

[1] Florrie Bagel replaced Adelina Mitchell as Marian mid-way through the production run.

benefits of that choice, the concept had moments that pulled us out of the story at times. It seemed like many instances of using ASL or spoken English were done for accessibility reasons for the audience rather than logically making sense in the play itself. Yes, accessibility for the audience is a clear priority. It also needs to be done in a way that supports the storytelling. For example, when Harold and Marcellus are reacquainted, their entire scene is performed only in ASL. As already noted, we applaud this artistic choice. However, directly before Marcellus enters, Harold meets two other characters and these two people SimCom to him. Why do they use SimCom but Marcellus doesn't? Then, immediately after this encounter, Harold bursts into song with, "Ya Got Trouble" and Marcellus seamlessly adds his voice to support Harold's signing. There is no noticeable acknowledgment between the two that Marcellus is doing this, he just does it. In the world of the play, who is he singing for? All the hearing characters we meet can sign to some degree. From the audience's perspective, is he still Marcellus, or is he now shadowing as Harold? In all of Harold's songs except one, this is the way the two perform. The outlier is "The Sadder But Wiser Girl," when Harold has another actor stand in to sing for Marcellus—likely because Marcellus has his own part of the song to sing. The muddiness here could easily be solved by having Harold indicate that Marcellus should step in to sing his songs with him. In only one song, "Marian the Librarian," does Harold make such an indication for Marcellus to sing the song. However, this particular song is an odd choice for doing so because Marian is a CODA and can understand Harold without Marcellus.

Continuing with the lack of clarity regarding SimCom, throughout the play, Marian generally SimComs to her deaf mother, but not to other deaf characters such as her brother Winthrop or Harold (both of whom at times are in the same scene with Mrs. Paroo). Why does Marian do this? These communication choices are unclear. To complicate matters, in some of her songs, Marian sings while her mother signs upstage of her. Much like Harold and Marcellus, there is no acknowledgment of this shared song between them. Her mother just appears. At other times, Marian SimComs songs. Why are the songs approached in these different ways? To us as audience members, it creates questions that pull us out of the story.

Finally, in many group scenes with multiple townspeople, the deaf characters don't have a connected voice. Instead, the hearing characters SimCom their lines. To reiterate, all the characters we meet know ASL, so why does the SimCom happen? These inconsistencies are jarring for audience members and seem like choices made to support the audience without supporting the story. In other moments, the choice to use signing without voice succeeded so well that we are perplexed as to why that same decision wasn't made in these scenes. The artistic team very well might have had conversations about these choices and justifications for why they work in the play. However, the audience isn't privy to these conversations and justifications, and without them, the choices don't make sense while watching the play.

Accessibility Successes

In addition to the overall artistic success of the production already discussed, there are multiple examples of accessibility success. To start, the stage signing was amazingly clear. Caverly, Hensley, and Morrill are some of the top deaf actors working today. It was a joy to watch them take the spotlight in this production. Additionally, the translation was well-done. *The Music Man* contains a lot of early twentieth-century slang and some songs with nonsensical words, such as "Shipoopi." Director of artistic sign language Michelle Banks had a big job with the translation, musicality, and sign coaching. This is one of those shows where a team would have been ideal, making Banks' work even more impressive. To add to this, the stage signing was always visible. It was never obstructed by blocking, props, scenery, or poor lighting. As a contrast to *Spring Awakening* and *ASL Midsummer Night's Dream*, open captions were utilized onstage throughout, at times in multiple locations. This was a success. However, the way captions were handled was not consistent, which we discuss in the next section. Lastly, the level of integration in this production was very high. Several of the people we interviewed were involved in the show and they all had positive things to say about the process.

Accessibility Critique

Though few in number, there were some accessibility issues we want to pinpoint.

They can broadly be grouped in two categories, one related to the clarity of stage signing and the second related to design aspects. In the former category, three things stood out. First, *The Music Man* contains many fast-paced songs with quick transitions between the major characters and the ensemble. Some deaf patrons, including Jill, struggled to keep up with these transitions. Second, as noted with other productions, the times when characters use SimCom are generally not successful. On an artistic level, they don't always make sense in the story. Also, anytime a person SimComs, their primary language is the dominant one. This means in these scenes, songs, and situations, the ASL was diluted. It's clear the actors who were asked to SimCom put a lot of work into their use of ASL. It's just an incredibly challenging thing to do. The presence of open captions throughout supported equal access for deaf audiences. However, we would have preferred to have seen just ASL used, instead of SimCom. Third, multiple hearing actors used only ASL for certain scenes and conversations. These actors were clearly new to ASL. Despite how hard they worked, there was an artificial quality to some of their signing. Because they are learning a new language, they lack the prosody of fluent signers. Perhaps if a team of DASLs had been hired, the actors might have gotten more intensive coaching that would have improved the quality of their stage signing. Again, the open captioning prevented this from negatively affecting access for deaf audiences.

For the latter category, the two main areas were apparent. First, the costumes were clearly done by a hearing designer. Costumes were not deaf-friendly at all. Because this play took place in the 1910s, many of the color choices were beiges, tans, browns, light pinks—which did not contrast with the skin tones of many of the actors. Mostly skin-colored costumes made the signing even harder to see, especially for audience members farther away. Additionally, plaids and patterns were used on many of the suit jackets and dresses worn by the actors. Second, there were two caption areas and one was flown in and out at various points. Why was the secondary screen added when there were already captions on the trellis? Why have two captioning screens for some scenes but not for others? It was very distracting each time the second caption area was flown in and out. To add to this, the captions, especially in ASL-only scenes, were not always correct. It was clear the person running the captions didn't know ASL and was often behind, ahead, or skipping around on the captions.

Angels in America, Part 1: Millennium Approaches

We have already discussed this production extensively, as Andy was the director and drew on his experience with this show throughout Chaps. 2, 3, 4 and 5. This section briefly summarizes the points made previously and provides Jill's perspective as a deaf audience member. Jill saw the show multiple times throughout the performance weekend of November 19–21, 2021, as well as later viewing an edited recording of the production. Results from an audience survey are also discussed. *Millennium Approaches* was performed at the 449-seat Panara Theatre on the campus of Rochester Institute of Technology.

Millennium Approaches meets our criteria for being an integrated production, having a hearing director and a deaf assistant director/director of artistic sign language. The lighting designer identified as hard of hearing, but other design team members were hearing. The script was translated by a team of four deaf theatre artists with cultural competency in the backgrounds of the main characters. Of the twenty-one actors in the cast, nine were deaf and twelve were hearing. The student stage manager was deaf, as were multiple members of the shop and run crews. Multiple hearing actors and stage crew members were CODAs and/or ASL interpreting majors able to communicate easily with their deaf team members. Others in the cast and crew had never worked with deaf people or integrated theatre before.

Millennium Approaches very clearly demonstrates several common characteristics of integrated theatre:

- The production involves deaf and hearing artists working together toward a common goal.
- Inclusion supersedes accessibility, meaning all perspectives are included in the decision-making, not just given access to the information of decision-making.
- The production integrates ASL and English bilingualism in the following settings: meetings, rehearsals, shops, fittings, onstage, and backstage, including an ASL translation of the script.
- The production involves a cultural exchange between deaf and hearing cultures that occurs in the following settings: meetings, rehearsals, shops, fittings, onstage, and backstage.
- ASL, spoken English, and captions are purposefully incorporated into the telling of the story.
- There is a purposeful, story-driven explanation of how characters using different languages are able to interact and communicate.
- All deaf characters are played by deaf actors.

The production was successful from multiple perspectives. *Millennium Approaches* was selected as one of six invited productions to the Kennedy Center American College Theatre Festival for Region 2. It went on to receive a Kennedy Center Citizen Artist Award at the 2022 KCACTF National Award Ceremony, as well as special recognition in lighting, sound, and projection design, stage management, and assistant directing. The performance resonated to varying degrees with both deaf and hearing audiences. NTID Performing Arts administers an audience survey for its performances and thirty-seven attendees responded for *Millennium Approaches*. However, only eight respondents were deaf. Thirty-one respondents rated the production excellent, while six rated it good. No average or poor responses were recorded, which is an outstanding achievement for a production with no theatre majors involved.

Dual Staging Models

As discussed in Chap. 3—"Pre-audition Period", the shadowing model was primarily used to provide effective access in both ASL and spoken English via the Guardian Angel characters. Open captions were also used throughout.

Artistic Successes

As with the other productions we've looked at, *Millennium Approaches* offered multiple areas of artistic success. Though it was not as widely seen by audiences as *Spring Awakening*, *ASL Midsummer Night's Dream*, and *The Music Man*, surveys provided data on the experience and perspective of additional audience members beyond the writers of this book. In these surveys, various patrons mentioned how the shadowing approach added depth and nuance to the staging. Numerous comments were also made about the passionate acting in both ASL and spoken English, and how the two languages blended together onstage. Many of the hearing audience members remarked that the captioning enhanced their experience, supporting the idea that accessibility benefits everyone. Comments included: "It added another way to understand the performance"; "One actor in particular talked too fast to understand"; "The ideas in the show were so poetic and deep that it was helpful to have the content in written form to better process"; and "As someone who can lose focus really easily, captions were helpful to keep me paying attention and knowing what was going on."

Looking at the production from a big-picture view, its concept envisioned a network of relationships between major characters with logical explanations for which characters were deaf, which hearing characters knew sign, and which hearing characters did not. Although these explanations were not communicated to the audience in the program book, the language modality choices made sense as the play unfolded. Though deaf culture was not a major thematic focus of the story, it was present throughout the performance, such as the flashing light for the telephone call and how couples like Harper and Joe interacted with each other. Finally, *Millennium Approaches* presented a rare opportunity to see a play of major significance in the dramatic canon of the United States done in ASL.

Artistic Critique

As we've mentioned with the other case studies, the critiques presented here do not take away from the success of the production nor from the hard work of the production team and the actors. That said, a few audience surveys mentioned that the captioning did not always align with speaking/signing and that this was distracting. These comments reinforce our view on integrating production teams as much as possible, as well as offering ASL classes to hearing members of the cast and crew. We've mentioned that ASL and English are distinct languages, and so there will inevitably be times when the two languages, and therefore the captions, do not perfectly align. This is a natural part of an integrated production. However, it's a different thing altogether, as well as being very evident for both deaf and hearing audiences alike, when the captions become unintentionally out of sync with the performers.

In addition to this, there were occasional issues with the blocking. One audience respondent commented, "Sometimes it was hard to see the signing actors because they had their back in my direction." Jill also found the blocking confusing in Act 2, Scene 4, when Joe and Roy, played by Leon Marcus and Wil Clancy respectively, are conversing at a bar. In this scene, the Guardian Angel actors, Ryker D'Angelo and Sam Bowerman, were seated downstage of the primary actors (rather than the typical upstage positions) and were stationed on the opposite side of their counterpart (compared to mostly being blocked on the same side of the stage as their counterpart in other scenes). Due to this break in the established blocking principles, Jill thought the Guardian Angels were signing for the person they were closest to in proximity. Therefore, the beginning of the scene didn't make sense until she matched up the counterparts correctly.

Accessibility Successes

From an accessibility standpoint, use of the shadowing approach ensured that patrons had equal language access throughout the full production. In fact, all survey respondents agreed that the story was communicated in a way that they could clearly understand. Twenty-six comments specifically mentioned the dual staging model and accessibility positively. As many students at NTID come from mainstream educational backgrounds and are learning sign language, the use of open captioning throughout the play ensured accessibility for everyone in the audience. One respondent commented, "I am not fluent in signing yet and the captions helped me pick up on segments I could not hear clearly." Some of the actors were also not yet fluent in ASL or not experienced in acting in ASL. Captioning supplemented the experience of their performance by deaf patrons fluent in ASL. One respondent commented that the captions were especially helpful when the actors' fingerspelling was not clear.

Accessibility Critique

Despite accessibility successes, *Millennium Approaches* had areas calling for critique as well. One audience survey mentioned the need to "have a deaf eye to ensure ASL users are able to follow the conversation in ASL instead of watching the captions." The show did have a deaf assistant director and director of artistic sign language. Although a student, the AD/DASL had professional experience working in the theatre and enrolled at RIT after several years in the industry. However, in addition being a full-time student, this person was taking on the role of DASL for only the second time. While Andy signs proficiently, he does not have native-level ASL skills. As a hearing person, he also does not have the lived experience of someone who relies on visual language for communication. Thus, as the director, he was not able to support the AD/DASL in this area. This is an example of how bringing in a deaf consultant can be very beneficial. Because the AD/DASL and director were both deeply immersed in the show, bringing in a fresh pair of deaf eyes could have helped identify aspects that might be problematic for deaf audiences.

Several design choices also fell short in providing an equal experience for audience members. First, costuming was sometimes an issue for the signing actors. The Guardian Angels wore dark gray t-shirts, which provided decent contrast. But black would have been better. Some costumes for other actors included light colors on top, such as tan jackets, light blue pajamas, white/light blue hospital gowns, light gray t-shirts, etc. Some of these choices could have easily been fixed, for example, a dark cardigan over the nurse's uniform instead of a yellow one. Second, Jill found that the purple lighting used during the shared hallucination/dream sequence with Harper and Prior (Act 1, Scene 7) negatively impacted the visibility of the stage signing.

Finally, at a run time of three and a half hours, *Millennium Approaches* puts a lot of strain on deaf eyes. It is tiring to focus on signing for long periods of time. Because this relates to the script itself, it's not something that could have been changed for this particular production. However, it is important that directors are aware of this challenge with lengthy productions.

REFERENCES

Epstein, Kayla, and Alex Needham. 2015. Spring Awakening on Broadway: Deaf Viewers Give Their Perspective. *The Guardian*, October 29, 2013.

Paulson, Michael. 2015. Lights, Gestures, Action! How to Stage a Broadway Musical with Deaf Actors. *The New York Times*, October 2, 2015.

Theatermania. 2014. Michael Arden Reinvents *Spring Awakening* with American Sign Language. September 10, 2014. Accessed November 15, 2023. www.theatermania.com

CHAPTER 7

Conclusion

Lessons Learned

This final section of the book is intended to summarize major points that we've made along the way. First, we return to our three non-negotiable principles.

1. If the play calls for a character to be deaf, it must be played by a deaf actor. No hearing person should portray a deaf person onstage, period.
2. When a deaf actor is cast, the leaders of that production must immediately plan to make the rehearsal process inclusive for that actor *and* plan to make performances inclusive for deaf audiences.
3. From the start of a production, high-quality communication must be an imperative. In all aspects of an integrated production there should be 'equality of communication' between all deaf and hearing people on the creative team—no matter their role.

These principles serve as the foundational guidance for your production. So much of what has been covered in this book derives from these three points.

For those leading the integrated production, whether you are producers, directors, artistic directors, or stage managers, invest in deaf talent by giving them first, the opportunity, and second, the support, to succeed. If you hire a deaf actor, hire a director of artistic sign language to focus on how sign language will be utilized in the story and how deaf culture will be represented on the stage. Then hire a deaf consultant to focus on helping create and maintain an accessible and inclusive working environment during the production process. Once these deaf team members are on board, seek their input. Ask their opinions, offer them space to provide feedback, give credence to their ideas, and respect their advice. The way in which production leaders collaborate with deaf peers will reverberate to everyone else working on the show.

Just as importantly, have a budget line to hire ongoing professional interpreters with theatre experience. These team members should be consistently booked to provide accessibility between signing and speaking artists throughout the production—at every meeting, rehearsal, and performance where they are needed. Remember to respect the boundaries of their role. They are communication facilitators. That is their purpose for being in the room. They are not there to provide expertise on deaf people or sign language.

Demonstrate the values of your production at every opportunity. Following the non-negotiable principles, partnering with deaf colleagues, and bringing in appropriate interpreters are major actions that exhibit your production's values, but they are not the only steps you can take. Keep in mind how accessible meetings should be run. Be cognizant of how you highlight inclusivity in announcing your casting call. Rethink the way you organize auditions and callbacks to include deaf perspectives. Examine your plan for the first rehearsals to keep everyone starting on the same page. Review marketing and publicity materials with your integrated audience in mind. In all of this, carry an *open heart* and *open mind*. Of everything we've covered, those two things may be your best tools to forging a successfully integrated production.

Post Mortem

The final piece of advice we have is to hold a post mortem after your production closes. The goal of the post mortem is to look at your process, gather feedback from various perspectives throughout the process, and develop new approaches for future productions. Depending on your theatre company, this might not be an easily achievable event as directors, designers, and actors may have moved on to new gigs in other locations. An idea to combat this challenge is to include the obligation to attend a post mortem in your contracts. A post mortem meeting can take many different forms and perhaps it should. Although one large meeting with everyone who worked on the production may get the most people in the room at the same time, there will be topics of conversation that only apply to select members of the team. If possible, multiple, specifically targeted post mortems may work better—for example, a post mortem with the production leadership team, a second with the design team and directors, a third with the performers. This approach allows more in-depth conversation related to that specific area of the production. In the case of an integrated production, we recommend a post mortem with the deaf artists specifically. If your production team includes only one or two deaf artists, it may be more comfortable to hold a meeting with everyone in that area so as not to put those artists on the spot. For example, if you have two deaf actors, include them with the entire cast, but use time to specifically ask for their opinions related to the production's accessibility. Because the post mortem is intended to see where a production succeeded or struggled from the artist's point of view, incorporating the perspective of deaf team members is critical for your company. We suggest a simple, three question approach to a post mortem.

1. What went well on this production that we should keep doing?
2. What did not go well on this production and how could we make that better?
3. What are new ideas that we could incorporate into our process?

In a meeting with the actors, these three questions can be applied to various topics moving chronologically throughout the production process. Start with the audition announcement, and ask #1, #2, #3. Then move to auditions and callbacks, and ask #1, #2, #3. Then move to the first rehearsal, and ask #1, #2, #3. Repeat this process for each step the actors were involved in.

For all post mortems, we advocate for having the meeting(s) led by someone invested in the success of the company, but not directly involved in that specific production. By having more distance from the production, the facilitator can bring an unbiased approach to the meeting and lead from a neutral standpoint. They can ask follow-up questions or dig for deeper information without having any feelings associated with the topic under discussion. We also advocate for scheduling the meeting(s) for a designated amount of time and for creating an agenda with specific topics of conversation. If given too much time, or unspecified discussion goals, the post mortem can easily leave you without the results you'd hoped for. Finally, we advocate for multiple people taking notes during the session(s).

Once all post mortems have occurred, these notes can be collated and distributed to those in the company planning or working on future productions. Action items can be created and carried into the next production process.

All too often, a production ends, people go their separate ways, and nothing further is discussed about *how the production unfolded*. Yes, having an enjoyable and moving final product onstage is important. At the same time, knowing where your integrated production succeeded and failed from multiple perspectives gives you concrete areas to work on in the next one.

Final Words

Doing this kind of work is hard. It's difficult to get it 'right.' Unfortunately, *right* isn't a one-size-fits-all word. You're never going to get it right for everyone. The perfect production doesn't exist. Where your production may succeed in one area, it may fall short or fail completely in others. Where your audiences are happy, perhaps your artists aren't. There are many perspectives to consider and many ways to evaluate the success of a show. We said from the start, putting up a theatrical production is a complicated process. If it wasn't apparent before reading this book, staging an integrated deaf and hearing production adds multiple layers of complexity to the work. In spite of those layers, people all over the country (and world) are challenging themselves, their companies, and their audiences to offer work that is more inclusive and more accessible, not only to deaf artists and audiences but to artists and audiences of many marginalized groups. If you're considering producing a play or musical that will integrate deaf and hearing artists, we hope that reading this book has given you tools to guide your way. We acknowledge that, if this is uncharted territory for you or your company, there is likely an element of fear to it. Remember that deaf artists are hungry for opportunities to collaborate, to work, to create art. If you go into this work with a sense of cultural humility and respect for Deaf theatre as a cultural expression, you are well on your way to an equitable, successful, and rewarding experience.

Appendix A: Excerpts from Interviews

We felt it was important, in a guide book such as this, to include the perspectives of many different people who've worked on integrated productions. The insights of the thirty-plus people we interviewed have informed the previous chapters. However, the interviews contain rich discussions which make important contributions to the history, theory, and practice of Deaf and integrated theatre. The interviews also tended to flow freely and in whatever direction the conversation went. Some of the thoughts, opinions, and experiences that we thought needed to be included in the book didn't fit neatly into previous chapters. In Appendix A, we have excerpted quotes from interviews conducted in late 2022 and early 2023. They have been lightly edited.[1]

Integrated Theatre

One of the most important questions we asked our interviewees was to define integrated theatre and, based on that answer, to define success for integrated productions. We also asked what their dream integrated production would look like. We received a wide range of answers. These differing perspectives are important in advancing the general understanding of what deaf and hearing integrated theatre looks like and how we can

---

[1] Most interviews were conducted in ASL and transcribed into written English. Interviewees had the opportunity to review and correct the transcripts.

© The Author(s), under exclusive license to Springer Nature Switzerland AG 2024
A. Head, J. M. Bradbury, *Staging Deaf and Hearing Theatre Productions*, https://doi.org/10.1007/978-3-031-61446-0

critically evaluate it. We also asked our interviewees what they see as the benefits of integration. Our first version of the question was, "Why is it important for productions to integrate deaf and hearing artists?" As we conducted more interviews, and depending on the interview itself, the question evolved to include sub-questions about the benefits for deaf and hearing people, the benefits for artists and audiences alike, and the possibility for this kind of work to open minds in various communities. Below are snippets of how various artists answered these questions.

Definitions of Integration

Tyrone Giordano, Deaf Actor and DASL

We really have to have a dialogue and identify what the center means in integrated theatre, to ask where is the integration leaning toward? Is the integration towards us, or are we integrating towards them, or is it both of us toward each other? That's an important question. In my experience, I notice the typical model of a hearing-led and hearing-funded model inviting a deaf actor or creative to come in with some involvement slants heavily more towards a hearing center, because that's who their audiences are. They may be wanting to bring in more deaf patrons, but this is usually a one-off and not a deep commit. Usually in these productions, deaf collaborators must spend time and energy advocating for the deaf perspective. Sometimes these deaf collaborators are given the power to make or veto decisions. Sometimes we're lucky enough that there's more than one deaf person involved to help balance things and provide more than a single representative deaf perspective. On the other end, you have a stronger deaf-centered integration like with Deaf West Theatre. Back when they ran a theatre on Lankershim Boulevard in North Hollywood, a small, 66-seat theatre that featured mostly Deaf West productions, they tried some experiments. The access equation was flipped, with ASL front and center and hearing people were given "accommodations" to access the ASL through spoken English in various ways (via headphones, or voice interpretation in the back of the house, etc.). There were varying degrees of success, and it was discovered that the most positive response by hearing audiences was to put the voiced element onstage right with the deaf actors. Still, that desire to reach hearing audiences had an influence on the experience and outcome. That became clear to me after I joined Deaf West with the original *Big River* at the Lankershim theatre in 2001, which was so successful it experienced three new iterations and spawned a second company over the next four years. I noticed that as *Big River* accessed larger venues (the Mark Taper Forum in downtown Los Angeles, the American Airlines Theatre on Broadway, and a national tour with a stop in Japan at all the big touring houses, and a second company at the Ford Theatre in Washington, DC) that audiences were overwhelmingly hearing, so to me, it felt that the voicing was just as or more important than the ASL in this case. I knew this because we could have been waving our hands nonsensically in musical fashion, and hearing people would still have loved our performances. It was clear to me the center of integration shifted between hearing and deaf people in appealing to a broader audience and in the interest of increased ticket sales. I began wondering if the center of this production was determined more by who was in the audience, than in any original intent or effort by the creators of and artists in a show. We were fortunate with each iteration to go deeper into the ASL, improving on the translation with each successive show and venue, and testing new tweaks to our signing and acting on different nights. So that's the question: What does integrated theatre mean? It depends on who you ask, I think. There's a range, or spectrum, of different forms of this integration. Thinking about an example of a fully integrated center, it's really tough to say because there is a tendency to favor one element over another. There are challenges going parallel in two languages with different modalities, grammatical structures, and even how much time they take for each line, and also set to music. The slant towards the hearing center, in the case of *Big River*, was that the music and libretto had to appeal to hearing audiences in the attempt to recoup production costs, and deaf people and ASL worked to claim space within that. In theory, I can imagine what a fully integrated center might look like, but in execution, I haven't seen that challenge met yet. Maybe true integration is a place where either everybody or nobody will be satisfied.

Christopher Robinson, Hearing Theatrical Interpreter
How we in our American deaf/hearing ASL community, how we use that word *integrated*, I think leads to some errors. I have a frame of thinking in relation to anti-ableism, with that term *integrated*. That changes the meaning. I don't think that integration provides equity or equal experiences. I believe, by definition, that any time we mix any element and

proportions or different sizes, you make something new. Each thing is not maintained in its original feature. When you mix things, they influence each other. That's the science. Therefore, my definition of integrated, for me, not the dictionary definition, for me, it means a fluid ability to respond to change. Closer to, let's say, some of the older interpretations of integration in the civil rights era. Back when I was, maybe thirteen or fourteen, I was watching a movie with my cousins about race in New York, and the male identity, and all that. My uncle came into the room and said, "You know that the civil rights protest period was the worst time for me as a Black male." We all sat there confused because he was a Black male. How could he say that? Our notions of Dr. King and the movement caused some cognitive dissonance in us, at the least. He told us that he wasn't within the inner circle of the political discussion, legal discussion, legislative or Congressional process. He was just a blue-collar worker in the DuPont oil business. There used to be signs everywhere in front of restaurants that said, 'Whites only,' 'Blacks only.' When the civil rights law passed, these signs were banned, so they were taken down, right? From there on, he couldn't feel confident and safe because he didn't know which places he could enter safely. He was hyperconscious and unsure. It was an awful way to live. I understand the value of *rights*, but he still was hyperconscious because before the laws passed, he had warnings in the form of signage that made it clear where he could go and be safe. That's the same thing with *integration* in theatre. Often, we use that word in different spaces, but it's not really integration, it's not equal. We use the term and we performatively make people aware of the signage that says, "ASL interpreted shows" with the interpreting icon, which gives people the impression that they will receive equal access, and enjoy it as equally as hearing people. And it's not true. So that's why I said it's not equitable or equal, so we have to be careful how we use that term. It's a hearing-dominated system. Now, that means theatre space, by definition, is not made for deaf people or visual people. Some argue with this saying, "Hey, there's a screen and a proscenium." The stage is higher and easier for people to see. Hmm. Let's discuss that. The term *auditorium* already shows that it's ear-focused—*audio*—which is designed for optimal hearing abilities, not sightlines. You can go to major theatres, like Broadway tours, and buy tickets for obstructed views but you can't buy tickets for obstructed sounds. You can sit anywhere and hear perfectly while not seeing the stage. They charge people less for that. So, by definition, that's one example of inequality. I could go into that more. [Interviewer follow-up: Do you use a different word? What would you call it?] I don't think we should come up with a new term. I think we should clarify or expand on what we already have. It's *theatre*. Period. We often automatically default to a vision of a Broadway musical or a straight play—that's by default. It's already rooted in ableism. The infrastructure of it obstructs access. If we can include all people, that's successful theatre. To come up with a new term, I think that would cause additional problems, like my uncle said. Integration is a "nice word." But we have not yet experienced that. So, remove the structural barriers, the programming barriers, and you'll have theatre. If we change the word, we give a false sense of equity.

Alexa Scott-Flaherty, Hearing Director
The parts that feel crucial about that term *integrated* are that we feel like we are actually in the same world, in two or more languages. That we're fully inhabiting that world together. As opposed to a feeling of it's one person's world, but someone else is getting access into it. There's not a feeling that someone has to work to join something that belongs to somebody else. There's a world that we're all in, even if we have different entries into it, or are seeing slightly different things, which is always, in my mind, the experience of live performance anyway. All of the different players being together in the same world in some form of an equal experience and everyone who is in the audience is feeling that same thing. That they are automatically in the whole of the performance. That they don't—they're not getting a special way in. The whole performance already is their way in, if that makes sense. As opposed to feeling like this performance is designed for a particular community, but I'm going to make sure someone else has access to it. Instead, everyone who's there to see the performance, the whole of the performance is available to them.

How Do You Define Success for Integrated Productions?

Aaron Kelstone, Deaf Actor, Director, and Playwright
Where performers, hearing or deaf, work together in a way that the audience, also hearing or deaf, none of them has a feeling of not being able to fully achieve or understand what's going on. That's the ultimate, perfect scenario. I don't think many productions are able to get there for a variety

of reasons. Money, resources, time. But that's probably the best goal, where actors, directors, and audience members all can enjoy. I often talk about [as a metaphor] sometimes I watch something, I take off my glasses and I can watch it. That's a perfect experience as an audience member. Or do I have to squint or struggle to figure out what's happening. That's my definition. Am I watching with squinted eyes, or am I comfortably watching? That's how I consider a production to be successful or a failure.

Joseph Santini, Deaf Theatre-goer and Playwright
I'd love to see a production where every performer had a character arc and changed. One of my biggest criticisms of Marvel's *Eternals* is that it has a very common problem—the deaf characters don't really change or have problems. So, a successful production is one that treats all its characters as characters. A successful production is also where each audience member has been fully engaged throughout. The engagement doesn't have to be the same for each member, everyone takes away their own perspective from performances, but it has to be there.

What Has Been Your Best Experience of an Integrated Show?

Amelia Hensley, Deaf Actor
I'd say *Oedipus* [Deaf West, 2022] because we also had DeafBlind people involved. We had a workshop on how to work with them, what to say, what not to say or do. We brought in a consultant. The hearing director also was incredibly good about checking in with us, making sure we all were okay. She'd ask what our boundaries were, making sure we knew what it meant to have both deaf and hearing people. It was very educational at the very start. I felt really recognized, and she was very open. "What does not work for you? Why not? That's not how deaf people would do it? Okay, show me how deaf people would do it." She was very open, and that was really impressive. She listened to what we could do to improve the experience for both audiences, not just hearing audiences.

Aaron Kelstone, Deaf Actor, Director, and Playwright
In 1990, 1991, the National Theatre of the Deaf [NTD] worked with Pilobolus [dance company] and that was really very much focused on movement. And that led to the production of *Ophelia* later [1992]. That

was a beautiful production because of how physical the play was. It was well-choreographed and blocked. And the signing was very clear, very well-done. It was the classic style at the time of NTD. The hearing actors were shadowing the deaf actors and it was very well-blocked. I could see the deaf actors perform and I didn't feel like my eyes had to guess where to look. Everything was in the same frame. It wasn't exactly shadowing, but quite close to it. It wasn't distracting, and we could follow it with logical movement. It was beautifully done.

Joseph Santini, Deaf Theatre-goer and Playwright
I still remember seeing Peter Novak's *Twelfth Night in ASL* in Philadelphia. The translation took two years to make and every step was taken to ensure that the production was integrated, accessible, and meaningful. I was twenty at the time and powerfully impacted by the use of language.

Why Is It Important for Productions to Integrate Deaf and Hearing Artists?

James Caverly, Deaf Actor, Director, DASL, and Playwright
I need a job! How else—I want to work! [LAUGHS] I think bringing to the table that. Yeah, deaf artists, or deaf people, have a place at the table. They have a place in society. We are here. We're not going anywhere. We have stories to tell, we have lots of anger, frustration, joy, and a lot of stories we want to share with people out there that they need to know. It's valuable for you to digest and change your practices because the theatre is a place where revolution happens—where change happens. So, the theatre is a place where people go to be uncomfortable, and deaf people are already uncomfortable for a lot of hearing people. Why can't you use us to bring on stage and shake things up? The primary thing for me is always thinking about the big picture: what does this represent? What I want the audience to feel, to experience from watching the play, whatever I create. That's always the primary thing for me.

Aimee Chou, Deaf Actor, Director, and Playwright
Really, it's a two-way street. It benefits me as a deaf artist because it provides me with more opportunities to network. Networking is critical. So many of my projects are when people reach out to me and they say, "Oh,

I saw you on stage and would like to cast you for another project." I mean, it's great working in a deaf silo sometimes because you know it's accessible and you don't have to explain yourself, you don't have to explain culture, or all of that. You don't have to teach anyone. But at the same time, I like working in deaf and hearing integrated productions because it opens worlds for me. On the other hand, benefits for hearing producers, right now, in the theatre world, we are trying to dismantle traditional theatre structures. We're trying to provide room for other voices, especially from marginalized communities. We're trying to bring them in and show more of their stories. We have an amazing language, we have an amazing culture, and we are so generous with sharing or showing our stories. It's also important to acknowledge the cultural value that we bring to the stage. Often, right now, people are feeling pressure that they have to provide this and that. It's transactional, but they're also thinking about the cost of interpreters and how expensive it is. People often forget that deaf culture is itself valuable. You're not going to find that in the mainstream. If you work for that, it opens up the possibilities for production of stories.

Tyrone Giordano, Deaf Actor and DASL
Hearing people love to talk about how their lives are forever changed because of the experience of working with deaf in theatre. But that change isn't significant if, having said as much, they go about their careers with continued or greater success thanks to us, and don't advocate for us. As an example, I've seen a number of these hearing folks posting videos on their social accounts that aren't captioned. It's mind-boggling to see. But this kind of contact with hearing artists, it's impactful, so that means more of the foundational work of advocacy needs to be done by us, where people have direct contact, and through interacting with us their minds and perspectives are changed. It's important work, for sure, but hearing people need to take on some of the burden of advocacy in their own lives afterwards, and not leave it to us. For me, advocacy work is nice, but what I really want is to put more focus on creating art, to be exposed to a variety of skilled actors and creatives at the top level. I'm fortunate that in my career, I've worked with a number of amazing actors, both hearing and deaf, and I've always learned from them. Us deaf people, we've got the opportunity to work with each other, which is great, but we also need to create art on increasingly higher and more challenging levels. For me, it's not about deaf or hearing, it's about aspiration and inspiration, about

being in contact with greatness, being in contact with professionals who are at the top of their art and craft. The National Theatre of the Deaf and Deaf West have historically invited some top actors as part of their troupes, and their contact with deaf actors has been valuable. We deaf artists need more cross-pollination and exposure to different artists as we work to define our own art. And on the other side, hearing people need more of that exposure if only to realize that deaf people can hold their own with them and are good artists.

Hayden Orr, Deaf Actor and DASL, RIT/NTID Student
There are some benefits to what we call integrated theatre. I think it really puts the spotlight on more deaf artists and provides more opportunities, all that, yes. But one thing that is unfortunate—maybe I'm wrong, but I've noticed that with more integrated productions, Deaf theatre is going away. There haven't been many deaf productions by deaf people for deaf people in a long time. It's going away and being replaced by more and more deaf artists trying to satisfy hearing audiences. I think it's important to spotlight deaf people for hearing people, but it's also important to hold onto our culture, our language, our heritage, and our shared experience of discrimination. Throw all that away just to accommodate hearing people? No. I think it's good to have integrated productions, yes, because it gives deaf actors the experience of what professional theatre is like. Many of us don't know what it's like. What the training is, the memorization, the roles, and so forth. I work with deaf actors who often will ask me to help them rehearse. No, it's their responsibility. So that experience and learning is incorporated for them, then they can bring that skill set to revive Deaf theatre. And plus, hearing actors working with deaf people can see that we're skilled. Then in future productions, it'll become easier. People suffering now will not have to suffer in the future. I think that's important.

Malik Paris, Deaf Actor and Director
One benefit of working together with a hearing person is that it's nice to have a colleague who works differently. They can learn how to work through the challenges of communication barriers. They have to really open up and cross those barriers. You get to learn each other's body language and all those aspects to improve, or rather, to become a better actor. To increase confidence, and not feel so nervous, "I'm not sure how I can do this, I can't follow this." I think it's good to work together, express ourselves, and share our work to create a better outcome. There's a double

language benefit, and for the actors and the audience equally. We'll all enjoy it more. There's increased understanding and empathy as we open our minds and hearts. And we can feel as if we are welcomed without barriers, because a play should be a safe space. It's supposed to be that way, and everyone's supposed to be willing to open their minds and hearts as we interact. That way we can learn from each other's experiences, learn new things, be open to new ideas, and even throw in ideas to help each other. That'll help them realize that, "Oh! We do have similarities" that they didn't realize they had.

Serena Rush, Deaf Actor and Director, RIT/NTID Student
I think there are lots of benefits for both the experience of working on a production but also as an audience member. From that perspective, it's easier to explain. First is bringing awareness about the deaf community and culture. Even though I already know the culture and community, I went to see *The Music Man*, to use that as an example. I saw a lot of hearing audience members learning as they went through the show. "Oh, interesting! Oh, that's how…" like how deaf people often will put their hands on their heads to say "Everyone, quiet." Just, little nuances, learning little new things. But also, for deaf audience members, it lets us see our representation on stage. I feel like, "Yes, I can connect to that. That's me, that's my life. That's what I experience every day."

Alexa Scott-Flaherty, Hearing Director
First of all, this idea that we have, and I think we're working on it in the American theatre, but this idea that if you have enough time or if you have enough resources then you will give people the gift of some kind of inclusion or access, right? And I think that we have got to end that, you know? In general, in every way, in terms of just how people approach storytelling. I also think it's a giant mistake to pretend theatre is a mainly auditory experience. Because theatre is also a gestural landscape, a visual landscape, a landscape of movement, of, you know, emotion, emotionality, storytelling. And I actually had a person who I worked with for directing, who said, you should be able to look at a stage and turn off any sound. And everyone should be able to get the story, or you're not doing it right. So, I just think it's fascinating that we have this idea that it's access to hearing it, that makes the play a play. I've had this experience when I've watched things that sometimes, especially when you're doing the integrated theatre, I'll watch a scene where people are signing and it will be so *alive*. It

will be so present, so full, you know, and then it will switch to, like, the two actors who are talking to each other in spoken English, and you lose all of this storytelling. And so, I think that, for me, the fullness of storytelling is like a huge aspect of what I think is added working with deaf artists. How to communicate a story visually, in terms of just bringing the entire world to life. And I think that layer is just something that hearing artists can learn from, the full commitment of your whole body and your whole self in the communication. That fullness of storytelling is just a huge piece. And then the other piece is, of course, the diversity of perspective, of ways of looking at the whole world. I think it benefits from having as many different perspectives as you can get, in the working process, too, as well.

Visions for the Future

A second question that we asked during many interviews was: "As the theatre community moves forward, what do you hope to see in terms of accessibility and inclusion?" The question could be answered from an artist's perspective, the audience's perspective, or both.

James Caverly, Deaf Actor, Director, DASL, and Playwright

I think you've probably heard this many times, but we need more deaf writers. Many of these conversations come up over and over. Deaf writers, and we also need more opportunities to show their work out there. Another probably tough part of the theatre industry is that the turnover rate is high. Very high in that industry. It happens all the time. For example, I know of one theatre company that used to have a steady stream of deaf audiences. Over several years, they built a solid foundation to bring in deaf actors and deaf audiences. Then, overnight, *boom*. They swapped the artistic director out with a new one who had a different vision. Everything was dropped. New people came in as replacements, and then deaf people just…went away. I don't think it's the only theatre where that happened. I think it happened with other companies that had a strong deaf base and had people coming in—and then it just stopped. They lost their connections, or changed their strategies where they didn't have money to provide interpreters for accessible performances anymore. It could happen. So, break the mold, meaning people who are involved with the theatre industry, people who are being replaced, they should have at least some kind of cultural sensitivity or awareness and acknowledge the surrounding community. What is lacking? Whose voices are not being told? And work to bring in these people to become involved. And I think through these discoveries, the mold can be broken with different ideas. We can bring these up and create more ideas and more connections. A new ground-breaking play comes up, a new ground-breaking play is written, and then it succeeds from there.

Brian Cheslik, Deaf Actor, Director, DASL, and Theatrical Interpreter

I hope to see more deaf-integrated shows, that's for sure. I hope to see more theatres become more willing to provide interpreters and captions. I often prefer to read the captions but I still like to have interpreters to fall back on and I'm always curious to see their interpretation of the content even though I already know the show. I want to see more and more of that. I am done with hearing that money or budget is an issue. There are things the theatres can do, things cities can set up for funding and for access. Accessibility is a tax write-off. Theatre companies can use that. I'm just done with the excuses. There needs to be changes. I want to see more and more opportunities for deaf people. Yes, more are emerging but it's like a slow drip. I want to see an outpouring of support.

Victoria Covell, Deaf Actor and Dancer, RIT/NTID Student

I want people to keep in mind that accessibility and inclusivity are not one size fits all. It's important that every production is ready to accommodate anyone who auditions or is part of the production. So, if you feel there's something that isn't working or not up to expectations, then expect changes throughout the production. Be willing to be open minded and approach something if it should be changed. As always, be willing to accommodate anything that arises and don't be restrictive.

Luane Davis Haggerty, Hearing Actor and Director

I'd like to see new work develop. That, again, is all baby steps and—it makes me frustrated, but I'm willing to have that frustration because the end goal: new deaf playwrights, new perspectives on theatre as an art. New characters and life experiences being expressed or shared. If I keep my faith in the end goal, I'll accept some failures, but keep on trying to have people come together in that shared space where theatre overlaps culture. All cultures have theatre. So, if we could find that magic spot where your vision and your culture overlap with mine and theirs and with the audience, that would be cool. That'd be amazing, that's worth the time. Worth the struggle.

Tyrone Giordano, Deaf Actor and DASL

I don't really dream of the future of integrated theatre other than like how it's important to have a DASL or co-director so that artists can just be artists and have more opportunities to explore their craft outside of advocating for themselves. I don't dream as much about that kind of effort towards integration with the accompanying advocacy work. Instead, I dream more about having a separate Deaf theatre that is more pure, strongly deaf-centered with a deaf core. It is my belief that expanding that will influence or move the needle and affect what integrated theatre that includes deaf people or sign language looks like out there.

Amelia Hensley, Deaf Actor

On a day I want to see a show with captions, I don't get told "Sorry, it's only on specific dates." I wish I could go see plays anytime. They all should have live captioning ready just in case. You know? Secure a good financial grant for interpreting costs. I feel that's really important, because it means the AD could breathe during the production and appreciate and hire deaf actors more instead of worrying about losing money or needing financing.

Cath Kiwitt, Hearing Theatrical Interpreter

I hope to see more deaf and hard of hearing people in positions of power. I mean, it's a good start to have the DASL there, but from the very beginning, so they can build a show that isn't an afterthought. "Oh, I forgot to add that." So having a consultant there from the beginning. Or bring in a deaf director, or do a deaf play. Why not? So, again, just like other industries, if you have deaf people in positions of power, even if not at the very top but still in the top five, then that will make the show itself more integrated.

Hayden Orr, Deaf Actor and DASL, RIT/NTID Student

I feel many deaf people who succeed as actors are gambling—they're lucky to get jobs, but many fail. Many because they don't have the resources that hearing people have. They don't have that training. I'm fortunate, extremely fortunate, to have gone to art school and learned and trained under teachers in classes that were phenomenal in helping me navigate the world, along with professional training. Many young deaf actors I work with have no idea of that. So, I try my best to help them, yes, but I'm just one guy. I don't have the time to set up and teach them how to do all that. I want to think that's important. Like, I know NTD set up a summer program. I think that's really essential for training deaf people because if deaf people become excellent and know how to operate in the professional world—because the theatre world is awful. It's very competitive and tough. So, if you have people who can endure that, then wow, they can do more. Then hearing people will say, "Hey, come on, we'll accommodate you." However, again, I notice I'm putting it all on deaf people. No, hearing people have issues too, and they don't always have access to resources or things like that. So yes. Training is essential.

Malik Paris, Deaf Actor and Director

I want to see a different, shifting perspective—something different than just traditional theatre. Something different, like experimental theatre, maybe, or a new level of signing, raising the bar for that, and having more integration. Or even DeafBlind involvement, having them be more integrated into the deaf community. I hope that could be a goal. And of course, more BIPOC actors. Bring them in and expand that. I want to see more visibility of Black cast and crew, producers. That'd be nice, to have Black producers be more visible all over the United States. I'd also love to see more integration in young children's theatre or educational productions for youth. Hearing K-12 students would benefit greatly from our deaf experiences and cultures.

THE INTERPRETER ROLE

In addition to interviewing a wide range of theatre artists and theatregoers, we also interviewed several hearing interpreters, all with backgrounds in theatre. Throughout the book, we've emphasized that the interpreter plays a critical role on integrated production teams. The snippets below provide insight into the specific perspective interpreters bring to the process.

From an Interpreter's Perspective, What Do You Want People in Theatre to Know About Your Role?

Cath Kiwitt, Hearing Theatrical Interpreter
One, that the interpreters are part of the team. Which means the interpreter must be there throughout the process. You can't just bring them in at random times during rehearsals. That's not going to work out. It won't. Second, for me, as a production interpreter, the director or whoever I'm talking to has to understand my job, understand what I'm doing, understand why interpreters are important, understand why or how—well, basically understand the interpreting process and that it's not just facilitating the languages between actors.

Christopher Robinson, Hearing Theatrical Interpreter
I want them to expect to use me less throughout the process. That idea has many complicated parts, but that's the theme of what I want hearing people in the production process to know. Use me less and less. Develop alternate ways to communicate and get the work done, instead of relying on me as an interpreter. It doesn't mean eliminating the interpreter. I mean, have an interpreter available there, as a second or third resource, just not as a primary or default resource. If you use the interpreter less, you are doing better art, doing a better job creating. On day one, you might use the interpreter often. By day ten, if you're using interpreters less and less, that means you're making a more equitable environment, especially for actors who rely on underlying energy and chemistry. On stage, I'm not there, and if you rely on me, you build a relationship with me, but I'm not on stage with the deaf actor. So less me, means more interaction with each other. That's one point. Also, I want them to expect to hear my voice. I want hearing people to feel, when I speak, that it doesn't mean something is wrong. If I speak up for clarification, it doesn't mean something is wrong or the deaf person isn't understanding. As a human, I can't hear what you said, that's all. It doesn't mean an emergency, that I'm stupid or anyone is, or that I'm a bad interpreter. Often people in the room don't hear everything and disassociate or tune out or whatever,

thinking, "Oh, that person is just talking nonstop," so they don't bother to listen. I bother to listen; I bother to collect all the information. Some people are quiet or passive, so the person who is speaking never notices when people are tuned out or not listening, but when I speak up, they become startled. Don't be startled. Expect to hear me. That's it. Sometimes, of course, I'll check in and say, "Yes, yes," or "I'm on that, thank you." It's not an interruption, just normal discourse.

Lindsey Snyder, Hearing Theatrical Interpreter, Actor, and Director
Interpreters are an important part of the production team. Not, "Oh, the interpreter's attached to that deaf person." We need to have access to the team at the beginning of the production planning. This means conversations with producers, directors, theatre people, administration, and then meeting with the deaf people involved in advance. Knowing how to work together, everyone works differently. Any theatre production has prep time and that's part of it.

From the Interpreter Perspective, What Do You Want to See Going Forward in the Theatrical Community?

Lindsey Snyder, Hearing Theatrical Interpreter, Actor, and Director
Right now, performing arts interpreters, *whew!* There's a lack of education for interpreters. I just tweeted this. [LAUGHS] I'm mad. There's a lack of education in performance for interpreters—no, the arts in general—for interpreters that is problematic. Interpreter training programs don't value the arts, so that means interpreters are clueless about what to do or how—how to negotiate their roles. Yes, you must be flexible, but not take over. Don't assume you know what diversity means. How can anyone advocate if there's no instruction, no knowledge? Sorry, I'm on my soapbox. I think having background knowledge is valuable and open conversations with everyone involved. And knowing how to set clear boundaries. When it's appropriate to accept that job, and when it's not appropriate. I'm just constantly shocked and disappointed with people who should know better. But I realize, oh, we're not teaching, interpreter training programs are not teaching this. Another thing, interpreting for designers. Set design and lighting design have specialized vocabulary and you need the right interpreter for that.

What Are a Few of the Unique Challenges Related to Interpreting for Musical Theatre?

Cath Kiwitt, Hearing Theatrical Interpreter
Dancing! Interpreting for choreography is the worst. The worst! Because directors have their own language and I'm not a dancer, even though I work with a lot of musicals. I'm still, "What are you talking about? In English, please!" For one production, it was nice because the associate choreographer was deaf. And the choreographer was a great guy. He'd say things and I'd be like [to the associate choreographer], "What does that mean for you?" The choreographer loved to talk, but it was better to show the deaf people, rather than explaining. Just show it. That's really—I mean, for pure interpreting, in the sense of interpreting, dance is hard. Music is, too. Again, with that same production, they brought deaf actors into the music rehearsals because the musical director gave really important information about what the characters were trying to say during songs or the implicit meanings within songs. I found that interesting because not a lot of people think to include deaf people for music rehearsals.

MISCELLANEOUS QUESTIONS

This final section contains an assortment of interview questions and answers. Many of these topics have been touched on throughout the book. The statements we share below express powerful perspectives that both reinforce ideas already shared in previous chapters and highlight the individual viewpoints of each artist's background and lived experience.

How Have Approaches to Integrating Deaf and Hearing Theatre Evolved Over Your Career?

Aaron Kelstone, Deaf Actor, Director, and Playwright
In the earlier works, directors, either deaf or hearing, made decisions on who to focus on: the hearing actors or the deaf actors? Suppose they focused on deaf actors, then that meant the hearing actors became 'voices'—readers outside of the play, rather than part of it. If the focus was on hearing actors, that meant the hearing actors were in the play, but sometimes it meant, back then, that deaf characters or actors would be more lost, separated physically because of the shifting focus. Or the deaf

actors had to translate the work and adapt it to fit the hearing way because hearing people spoke faster. They'd have to sign faster or something, because there was no relationship between the deaf and hearing people. And then in later years, I saw, for example, Shanny Mow began to promote what he called 'lobster time.' He'd have both hearing and deaf come together and work together to sign and speak in sync, slowly, so that each could sign or voice smoothly and more naturally. He called that lobster time. I've seen that changing, moving from picking one over the other, to more working together and blending. More recently, I think it's more trying different ways to integrate both and respect both. But I still think—part of the challenge is there's never been any training for how to perform in sign language. Hearing actors have vocal work as part of their training. There's a lot of focus on accents, vocal expression, and heavy training on fluency in speaking lines in English during the play. For deaf people, the actors tend to sign in their natural communication style. You don't get what I call performance sign language. Today no one thinks about or studies how sign language should be performed on stage. So deaf actors tend to sign how they customarily do, even though they're in character; they still sign their daily way of signing. That ties into musicals. Hearing actors take courses in singing and acting at the same time. That's one area right now that is very weak: there's no formal study and no formal technique development, no formal teaching or formal development of sign language for performances. That's some of the changes I've seen. There are some things still lacking.

What Does Equity Look Like in Integrated Theatre?

Christopher Robinson, Hearing Theatrical Interpreter
I have an easy answer and I have a complicated one. The easy answer is *time*. That's it. Now, what do I mean by that? Sometimes everything fits me, but not for you [POINTS TO JILL]. Not for you [POINTS TO ANDY]. But over time, later, it doesn't fit me, and will fit you or you. The next day it will fit you and fit me, but not Andy. It goes back to the word I used, *fluid*. In our academic spaces, in society, and in western thought, we often visualize equity as meaning something that we can hold or that is tangible. No. Equity is fluid like weather, like there's spring, summer, fall, and then winter. Everything changes. Sometimes it will last and sometimes it doesn't, so you have another chance for something to grow again. In relation to the stage, if there is one deaf woman and one hearing woman,

and the others are hearing men—where's the disparity? Or you have five women and one man. Or you have hearing people of color and the fifth one is white and then the deaf person is white. Or you have two white and four people of color. What is the goal of equity? Sometimes you don't have good representation of women but you have good representation of people of color. You might not have full representation of transgender people, but you have full representation of Asian people in the cast. It changes. Often, we think, "Oh, that play doesn't have good representation" and criticize it, but if you enlarge your view a bit, it changes. Look at the entire season of that theatre company and you might see that there are diverse people involved. Maybe an Asian person is the director of *My Fair Lady*, and that person isn't the director of another play related to the eastern or Asian identity. But the representation is there. Sometimes it isn't in front of the stage; you may have to look at the production staff to find it. Sometimes we assume that what we see is equity and if you don't see it, then it's inequity. But that's not always the case. That's part of my answer. So, time is the most helpful part of it, not just what you can see or measure now, but over time.

What's One Thing You'd Tell a Hearing Director Who Wants to Do Integrated Deaf and Hearing Theatre for the First Time?

Michael Arden, Hearing Actor and Director
Make sure that the theatre company has taken into account all the budgetary needs for the show. It does not, it should never be spoken about, in that doing a deaf show costs twice as much. Every show costs more money, and the expense is just something that you have to figure out. And that you should commit to doing the show knowing that a budget needs to be created that's honest, that isn't going to frustrate the theatre or someone later in the process and cause a problem. Also, as a hearing director, stop talking and figure out with the deaf artists what stories they want to tell and are hoping to tell by being involved in the project, and trying to honor those, at least figure out what those are, and tell those stories. Hearing audiences, hearing artists don't even understand what being a deaf person is like, what life is like. And so having those conversations about what does it mean to do the show with the people in the room at that moment, and celebrating who they are as opposed to bringing on expectations of previous productions, what the show previously required. It's what's freeing about the whole process.

Cath Kiwitt, Hearing Theatrical Interpreter
Stop being nervous about deaf people! I get it. Most hearing people have never met deaf people in their lives, but stop. Stop making a big deal out of it. Get on with the work. If you have open minds and hearts, and you have interpreters, get on with the work. Include everyone equally. Trust their expertise.

As a DASL, What Do You Think Is the Most Important Thing to Keep in Mind When Working on an Integrated Production?

James Caverly, Deaf Actor, Director, DASL, and Playwright
A DASL is there to support the director's vision. As a director, you're there and everyone is looking at you. They have to follow what you say, right? While the DASL role is, I think, more of a strongly collaborative process than what a director does because the DASL works with a variety of people who might or might not view the DASL as an equal. They think that a DASL is there to work with an actor, deaf or hearing, if the actor says, "Oh yes, I need your help." While others view the DASL almost like a vocal coach. There to help but isn't needed as much. But the key there is to always have people's involvement and figure out how to work collaboratively and at the same time, figure out how their voices can be heard more and viewed and respected. It's definitely different when you're a DASL working with a hearing director compared to a deaf director. The way you're treated is different. A deaf director will really listen and go back and forth with the DASL in conversation on things like certain lines for translation, while a hearing director really doesn't know anything [about ASL], so most of the decisions have to come from the DASL. A lot of decisions have to be made by the DASL about what will work and what won't work for the show. When I worked on a show with a hearing director, I had to make decisions about whether to use regional signs, what the translation style was and whether it should be contemporary or old signs. And you know, a lot of decisions were based on *me* only, and I couldn't check in with the hearing director because the hearing director wouldn't have the right answers or didn't know. So, I had to make the decisions myself and then follow through on my decisions. And at the same time, I had to jump into conversations with the director anytime there was a group meeting. I had to make sure that I wasn't off-base or that I was getting new information that I should incorporate into the show. DASL is

relatively new in this field. It's new in the industry where, we're like…what are the types of training you have to have to become a DASL? There's no training. I've been, as a DASL, thrown in the fire, you know. I come in and say, "Okay, let's try to do this." I learn things as I go along.

Tyrone Giordano, Deaf Actor and DASL
You cannot expect the lone deaf person acting in a production to be just an artist. They're going to end up advocating for themselves and their needs as a deaf person, the needs of the deaf community, and also their own needs as an artist. It's a lot for just one person. You have to try to reduce the burden of that advocacy work. One way lead creatives can do this is to have another deaf person in that advocacy role, perhaps as a DASL, or even better, as a co-director. It's a must. A co-director or DASL will see things the hearing director cannot and have the power and capital to advocate for things that the actor might be hesitant or fearful of as to not burn any goodwill. When artists are able to unload that burden of advocacy, they can elevate their artistic capacity and tackle any artistic challenges and be better collaborators and contributors to the whole production. And the co-director or DASL must be granted that increased responsibility and power and not just be in a representative auxiliary role. The responsibility and influence of this advocate role on a production becomes more akin to how a dramaturg, assistant director, or director can impact a production. From the moment you decide to have a deaf character, actor, or sign language in a production, someone should be there in that advocate role, from pre-production all the way up through rehearsals. That person ideally would have access to the design team, including costumes and lighting, to everything in the creative and design phases of a production, which could affect how a deaf character or sign language presents, and how any potential deaf audiences might experience the production. The role of the DASL is an especially interesting one to me. I've been the DASL for a good number of productions, and my work on each was unique, with varying degrees of power, access, and effectiveness. I worked with actors, interpreters, creatives, writers, designers, audience members, and sometimes a combination of these. My responsibility in each was always multifaceted, where I could function as a creative, a director, a writer, an accessibility provider, a counselor, a mediator, a coach, and so on, depending on the needs of the situation. I think the most important thing is that a person in the DASL role has the acknowledgment and respect of the production head as a director of sorts, as that person is directing a part of the show that people will see.

Ultimately, the director of the show has the final say as it is their production, which is where a deaf co-director role would have more power to realize a vision or shared vision with a hearing one than a DASL might. And no offense to hearing people, but they can't be trusted with that responsibility when it comes to deaf culture or ASL. They can't. Unless they're immersed in deaf culture, know ASL, and have more than one deaf friend! [Interviewer comment: Even in that situation, I think that you still need the deaf eye because hearing people can't turn off their ears.] Exactly. That lived experience is crucial. Right now, I'm at the point where I advocate for any production that wants to bring a deaf person or have sign language in that production to bring in a DASL or co-director and integrate that person as an essential part of your team on the same level as your head designer, lead designer, set designer, lighting designer, costume designer. The same level, or higher. That's my opinion.

If a Director Undertakes Integrated Theatre, Does the Director Have an Ethical Responsibility to Ensure Access for Deaf Audiences?

Christopher Robinson, Hearing Theatrical Interpreter
Yes. That's it. Case closed. The director has an ethical responsibility. Why? Any director worth their salt is creating art with actual human people in the room. You're liable for people on the stage, people in production, you're responsible for their access to create a story, you're responsible for the whole human. Often, we start with the label of responsibility for deaf audiences, responsibility for deaf or disabled production staff, responsibility for deaf or disabled actors or talent. "Ugh, here we go, again." That creates more segregation. Without a person with a disability there, without a person who is deaf in the room, put that aside—a 'hearing' production, we care about how…any action on the stage will impact the audience. Unfortunately, or fortunately, it's for money. If a show doesn't sell, you're not bringing the money in. If people don't think that story is interesting, they don't buy the ticket. That's one reason. It's not *my* reason, but it's one reason the director thinks, "If I put something on stage that human people will hate, they won't buy the tickets, and the show itself will close." So, my basic answer is, yes, the director has an ethical and moral responsibility to not do damage to other humans on stage and that value applies to people in the audience watching.

Lindsey Snyder, Hearing Theatrical Interpreter, Actor, and Director
Any director should advocate for access, period. If you want ASL, you're responsible to advocate for your audience, that's a definite one hundred percent. But I think if you use the word "ethical," people will feel unsure or uncomfortable. Because the arts and ethics have a long, dramatic history. So maybe it's the form of the question. Phrase the responsibility like—"If you have signing in your show and a deaf person is integrated into your show, what does it look like when your deaf audience shows up?" Yeah? "You know they're coming, so how are you ready for them as artists?"

What Do You Think Is the Best Thing a Designer Can Do to Help Support or Build or Create an Inclusive Design Process?

Erin Auble, Hearing Scenic Designer
I have to be open to adaptations. Sometimes my initial set design doesn't fit the goal. It doesn't fit the actors. It doesn't fit the audience that we're hoping to bring in for the show. Sometimes I have to recognize that we all might like this but we need to put that aside and try the next idea. That flexibility, especially with educational theatre, it's important. You have to have open dialogue. I can't design it on my own and give it to them and say, "That's it." No, you have to negotiate it with the design team. I have a crew, too. If the set is blocking the crew from seeing what's happening, it's important to figure out how to resolve it. You have to be ready to problem-solve. As well, we have a deaf crew on stage, so part of the design is how the deaf crew can function. One production I had to change the design a bit because there was a deaf student with Usher Syndrome who needed to leave the stage in the dark. It wasn't safe, so I had to modify the design to give the student a clear, accessible path.

Sacha Glasser, Hard of Hearing Lighting Designer
You need to be willing to change. You may have ideas of what the best lighting is, such as a really dark scene, but maybe that's not possible because of access. So, you can't be stuck in one way. Make the design work. Be willing to adapt and learn, because again, the challenges may be for the designer who has never worked with that before. Adapt to the design to fit accessibility needs. It's a big thing when you work with an integrated production. You must be willing to be aware and figure out if

there's a better idea when something doesn't work a specific way. How do you keep the idea but change it to be accessible?

Describe a Production You've Worked on That You Found to be Particularly Inclusive During the Audition, Rehearsal, and/or Performance Periods

Michael Arden, Hearing Actor and Director
I think I'll speak to that in terms of being an actor. I've been lucky enough to voice, I've worked as an actor where I signed and voiced for myself, I have also played an interpreter onstage for a deaf actor, I have also shared a role with a deaf actor onstage. I really loved having those three different relationships, and they're all very different. But when I was sharing a role, we really had to make sure that we were having the same interior thoughts that weren't expressed through language, as well as understanding the meaning of the language and signs that were chosen to convey that language to the audience. So, we had to really be in tune, both in timing and in comprehension. And I absolutely loved working with that actor. It was when we were doing *Pippin* at the Mark Taper Forum, Ty Giordano and I were sharing the role and it was exciting to get to let our individual performances grow through an understanding of what the other was doing that we weren't necessarily able to—wouldn't have been able to understand upon first viewing or first speaking. So, it was a real sharing of both information and impulse. And trying to—grappling sometimes with what we believe the character was doing. So, you know. Sometimes there were arguments, good, nice arguments, but arguments nonetheless, that led us to a sort of better understanding of what the character was going through. And I love that process.

What Are the Best Strategies You've Witnessed for Making Plays Accessible to Both Deaf and Hearing Audiences?

James Caverly, Deaf Actor, Director, DASL, and Playwright
Well, the key question is accessibility for who? If you're talking about deaf access, that's fine, or for hearing people, or for DeafBlind, or you have low vision, you have Deaf-plus, and the list goes on. It's crazy the amount of "access" we often overlook, but I think what is valuable learning here is that I think once you accept the fact that you will not always be one

hundred percent accessible, you accept the fact that you will have some flaws, but you are willing to work through the flaws instead of deliberately ignoring them. You identify it and you acknowledge your mistake. If an audience member, deaf, hearing or DeafBlind, says something, don't defend yourself. Put your defenses down and accept that, yes, there's a mistake here, sorry. There's always room for improvement, and that comes with accepting your mistakes.

Is There Anything We Haven't Asked You That You Want to Mention?

James Caverly, Deaf Actor, Director, DASL, and Playwright
I don't like any kind of conversation about the cost of access, the cost of bringing in interpreters or that kind of conversation. I understand it's a very real thing. It's something that theatre companies have to deal with. It's a real thing, the cost of access, and I completely understand that. But as a deaf person, you know, going to a doctor's appointment and being told that they can't afford an interpreter, or any public event and they say they don't have a budget for interpreters, or all that. That comes up often, and then to go to a space where I have a career and I want to be *in* that career. But then you say, "Oh, it's costly to have interpreters." What you are basically telling me is that you don't want to bother having me there. Because I'm too expensive? That's demoralizing to me as a deaf person, as a deaf actor, or rather as a theatre-maker. Theatre companies have said that time after time. My art is irrelevant because of the cost of access? It hurts. I think, really, the best thing for theatre companies is to try not to put the burden of financial costs on the deaf person. Absorb this information and hold it within yourself. Talk with your peers, but don't put it upon the deaf actor. They're trying to do their work the best they can without feeling like they're a burden. That affects their consciousness when they're doing a show.

Brian Cheslik, Deaf Actor, Director, DASL and Theatrical Interpreter
I was just asked to be part of a ZACH Theatre board meeting. It was a big board meeting with everyone around the table. Several Broadway producers were on the board, people with money. My co-director was like, "Thank you all for approving this huge interpreter budget. I know it's a really expensive decision." I said, "Yes, I echo that," and I told them, "You

guys don't understand. We deaf people don't get this opportunity often." I explained how I was turned down for a lead role. The director wanted me in the role. But then he chatted with the interpreter coordinator and found out the cost, the cost of providing access for me, and then all of a sudden, there's another person who didn't have to sign. I said, "It is very humbling as a deaf actor for my value to be based on this director, and the price the directors put on interpreters. Thank you for being willing to give us a time to shine, provide us with this opportunity to collaborate and present this story." Many of them started crying because they had never thought that people would turn me down because of the cost of interpreters. That didn't seem fair. If they don't hear it, they don't know what's happening. So, it is very important for everyone within the theatre world, within the deaf world, to speak out and not hold things in. We deaf artists shouldn't have to bow to other people. We need to fight for our place to prove our worth. That's important.

Christopher Robinson, Hearing Theatrical Interpreter
This is really sticky to say as a hearing person but I am in conversation with deaf artists about this. Right now, the big question that we must address is how much time do deaf people want to invest in 'integrated' access? How much time do they want to invest in making art for and by deaf people? These are two different things. This is my bias—right now, we are investing a lot into making access happen. We are bleeding resources in deaf people, bleeding resources in deaf art, in deaf talent. We can take them out of the community to invest in and make interpreted theatre. That builds and grows the hearing industry. I'm thinking this parallels what is happening to African land. Slavery, colonialism, taking things from them and now we wonder why we have so many poor countries. It's the same idea. We're taking resources to create access, but what is the impact on the environment, the weather, the forest? What's the impact? It's the same with deaf artists, who are like trees that we've deforested to build houses. Now the birds and animals have no home. The birds and animals are a metaphor for young people, the young ideas of deaf people that are just completely—deaf history, deaf art, from generations before. New young ideas can't grow because they'll die in the sun. So that's a conflict. That's a discussion that needs to be in the book. Environmental changes, climate changes, and the whole -isms discussion on racism, sexism, ableism—it's negative. Talking about how we can adapt to survive, and sustainability. That. That's what I want in the book.

Appendix B: Full Interviews

Michelle Banks

Michelle Banks is an award-winning actor, director, playwright, and director of artistic sign language. She founded Onyx Theatre in New York City, the first Deaf theatre company for people of color in the United States. Banks' original work includes *Reflections of a Black Deaf Woman*, which has been performed throughout the country. She co-founded and serves as artistic director for the Washington, DC-based Visionaries of the Creative Arts (VOCA), which supports the growth of deaf artists of color. For VOCA, Banks has directed *ISM* (2021), *A Raisin in the Sun* (2023), and the Helen Hayes–recommended *ISM II* (2023). She was DASL for the Broadway revival of *for colored girls who have considered suicide / when the rainbow is enuf* (2022) and for Olney Theatre's *The Music Man* (2022).

Jill: How would you define integrated theatre? What does it look like?

Michelle: Well, based on my experience, integrated theatre includes hearing and deaf on the creative team. We have the same common goal in terms of producing this play. Both hearing and deaf people are really understanding their roles in this production and we have accessibility for both, communication, understanding, and empathy on the job.

Jill: If the show only has one or two deaf with the rest of the cast being hearing, is that integrated theatre?

Michelle: Well, at least one is still considered integrated because they included that person, even though it might not seem that way because there are only one or two. There should be a certain number that balances out, but that doesn't always happen. It really depends on the production company, which is typically run by hearing people. What are they looking for? What do they want from the deaf community? To be on the creative team, acting, or what? But I'd call that integrated theatre because there are one or two. I would say yes, at least they've included someone.

Andy: If a hearing director wants to include deaf actors, maybe one or maybe several, or if the director wants to use ASL during the show, does that mean the director has responsibility for making sure the whole show is accessible to the full audience?

Michelle: Yes. Definitely. One hundred percent. And the producer. Not just the director, but the producer, too.

Jill: In your experience, do hearing directors accept or agree about that or do they feel, "No, that's not my job"?

Michelle: My experience so far has been that hearing directors are very accepting of their jobs and responsibilities to make sure that, as an actor or as a DASL, I have access to communication and interacting with others to get all the information I need to do my job. For example, as a DASL, if the hearing director wants me to use a certain sign for a deaf or hearing actor, the director will talk with me, with an interpreter present, and explain. They'll discuss and consider it and they'll always ask me what I think. That's what I love about my experience with directors. They always ask, "What do you think, Michelle? Do you think this will work?" It's not just, "It's my way." No, they do ask for my opinion and my input, so I appreciate that when I work with hearing people who value my opinion, my input.

Jill: There's a lot of ambiguity about the DASL role because it's a relatively new term. In the past, it was called sign master or ASL coach and now it has evolved. In your opinion, what responsibilities does the DASL role include?

Michelle: That term was focused more specifically on signing while DASL is more broad and doesn't focus only on signing. The DASL also focuses on interacting with people who use signs, to make sure that their signs deliver the message clearly. The DASL also engages in intensive assessment and translation of the script from English to ASL. And it's not just the script. It's also the character, how the character will be presented as a signer. How I show my signing, different ways and styles, um…where I'm from or my culture. What the character's culture is. It's more of looking at that really deeply. It's also working on the ASL gloss, creating a gloss, making sure the translation is perfect, and putting all that information into what is almost like a bible. Any time this production is done again, that bible could be used again as a guide for ASL translations. I think the DASL is more of looking at the production from an artistic perspective, rather than specifically at the ASL translation. It's the big picture, what it looks like on stage overall. That's similar to the director envisioning what it'll look like on stage with the actors, costumes, lighting, sounds—that's the same with DASL, but focusing on the signing, clothing colors and choices, etc.

Jill: What do you think the DASL's role is related to visual access for the production design, like the costumes, set, or even lighting? Does the role include advocating for access for the audience?

Michelle: Yes. Not only working with the director, but also with other creative team members. The designers, there sometimes may be a bit of a struggle because they create the design, but I have to remind them, "Hey, this may be too dark for deaf people." It's not just the clothing, but sometimes they want the lighting to be dimmed, but then you can't see the signing, so I have to remind them about keeping it a bit brighter. "But but but…" they'll usually say. I do understand the director's vision, but how do we see deaf actors signing? I mean, be open-minded and find different ways to come up with a solution. Even if you want to keep that look, find a way to make it clear enough to see. So, we really have to work and go back and forth a bit and then we work it out. But usually they'll agree and say, "Sure, sure," and it works well because they trust my expertise, my experience, and my knowledge, so they trust me.

Andy: So, for the integrated production itself, what does success look like to you?

Michelle: Ha. That's a hard question. [BLOWS A RASPBERRY] What does that look like? It varies. It really depends on the producer and their vision of what integration looks like for them and for the audience. So, my experience with that is to give workshops to those hearing people who haven't experienced working with deaf artists and how to communicate. The first thing is to have a workshop to explain about deaf culture, the ASL community, and how to communicate and use interpreters. Some people have absolutely no idea how to use interpreters or how to talk directly to deaf actors, saying, "Tell her—" No, no, speak directly to me. Having a workshop first, getting everything established, and then going from there. Kinda like having an introduction during the pre-meetings, and then going from there. For those who want to acquire ASL to communicate, I think the production company should offer ASL classes for them before production or even during production. Maybe send ASL videos to learn—that's what I did with *The Music Man* and *for colored girls*. Some will take that class, others won't. It's their choice; you can't force them. All you can do is offer them the opportunity and that's it, my job is done. It's up to them, their choice to take it or say, "Nah." It's up to them. I hope I answered the question. I'm thinking out loud. Getting through the rehearsal process, I hope that the director will have some kind of warm-up activities to increase trust and to increase the comfort in interacting with deaf and hearing actors.

Andy: What about other kinds of success, success for actors or for the audience? What makes it successful for them?

Michelle: For the audience, having a talkback to discuss the production. Bring deaf people in, interpreters, have access to captions, access to GalaPro. What's successful for audiences is to have access in captions, ASL interpreters, signing onstage. The audience can then make choices and watch what they want. With *The Music Man*, we had captions and signing all the way. So, the audience had the options to read captions, watch the signers, or all of it. They really enjoyed that and they said we needed more of that. So that was successful for the audience. For actors, making sure they have access to interpreters during rehearsals, during production, during meetings. Making sure they have interpreters all the way through and they're with the actors at all times. So that deaf person has the same access to everything like the hearing person.

Jill: I'm curious about *The Music Man* and *for colored girls*, how do they fit with your definition of success?

Michelle: Both productions had strong points and weak points in terms of inclusion and access. *for colored girls* was Black led by Black women. Most of the creative team were women of color. *The Music Man*, the diversity was so-so. The creative team was all white, except me, the only Black one. But *The Music Man* team was more knowledgeable. They understood because they had worked with deaf actors in the past and knew all about providing accessibility. They were really pros with bringing in access, with six interpreters who rotated and moved around. They had that budget, so great. With *for colored girls*, it was on Broadway, and it was completely different because *The Music Man* was at a nonprofit theatre, while *for colored girls* was at a for-profit. So, the producer with *for colored girls* was more worried about money and we had to get by with interpreters. They'd sometimes ask if we could work with only two interpreters. I'd say, "Ehhhh." I understand that it was a budgetary issue and I'd try to be flexible and work with them. I would say, "Fine, but you'll have to ask the other deaf people, not just me." With *for colored girls*, I had to educate them about how to work with deaf people. But with *The Music Man*, I didn't have to do anything. All was good. Half of the cast was deaf. There were more deaf people there, so they were more progressive. With *for colored girls*, it was just three of us out of, let's say, 20. So we really had to educate them, but toward the end, they finally began to understand and had breakthroughs in their thinking. It was a learning experience for them, really. So sometimes you have to really fight your battles to teach, to create teaching moments to make them realize that they have to do this and that, and what they can or can't do, what they should or shouldn't do.

Jill: Both *for colored girls* and *The Music Man* involved music. What are some of the unique challenges for DASLs in regard to music or musical theatre?

Michelle: *The Music Man* was tough, whew. The entire show had music. There was dialogue, but it was all music. There was only me—one person. I didn't have a team. We brought in an intern near the end to focus on the dialogue while I focused on the music, doing translations. I also asked the actors to help, too; it wasn't just me telling them, "This is how you do it, my way." No, I wanted their ideas. "Show me, show me." And if I liked it, or something didn't make sense, I'd modify it a bit. So, I think it's really important to have teamwork. It required teamwork from the actors and the intern who worked with me to make my work successful. With *for colored girls*, not as much was required—I could have had another person working with me, but it wasn't the same amount of work like with *The Music Man*. I could handle that, but with *The Music Man*, oh my goodness. I thought to myself, "How am I gonna do this?" I felt like I was drowning. But thank God I worked through it. Based on that experience, from now on, I will, any time I work with music, I will demand a team or I won't take the job. Yeah.

Jill: Because it's not just the words, but the music, rhythm, cueing. It's all so much, right?

Michelle: Yes.

Jill: I'm curious about "Shipoopi." I loved the translation but how did you approach that? How?!

Michelle: I had to really figure out what the hell that word meant. It was just a word with no real meaning. "Oh, okay. Ahh." But then the actors played with their ideas and I liked a sign they came up with. The choreographer, her name was Karma Camp. We worked together great. I love her. She would say, "What do you think of this?" I wanted to make sure her choreography and the signs aligned, and I'd look and say, "Beautiful!" One actor, Christopher [Tester], developed his own translations. I would approve it; I looked at his work and modified a few things to make them clearer and more specific. It was good. Joey [Caverly] and Chris did their own translations, which really helped me. I didn't have to translate all of it. I allowed them to translate and gave them room to learn their lines. They learned how to become the character as they signed. I gave them the opportunity to do that, then just told them to show me, then I watched to see if it worked well. Sometimes I'd ask the director what a word meant, because I really didn't know some of them, and then after the director explained, I'd be like, "Ohhhh," and play with the signs and visualize them, then convert them into signs. But I still wanted the actors' involvement, so I'd have them show me and we'd find the right choices that aligned perfectly with the rhythm and expressions. Yeah.

Andy: In your experience so far, what are the best examples of integrated productions you've worked on?

Michelle: I think *The Music Man* was my—well—both [*The Music Man* and *for colored girls*] were good, I mean, both presented positive experiences for me in working on the productions and seeing that integration of both deaf and hearing. However, the more progressive one would be *The Music Man*. That's my best example because it presented the best of what integrated theatre should look like. Because of the process we went through and it was such a good, positive experience. We had more deaf people in the cast and on the creative team, with an increased number of interpreters. And the hearing creative team members were more open-minded and understanding. So, I feel that's the best example of what integrated theatre should look like.

Jill: Other shows you've seen that you felt were really good?

Michelle: *Spring Awakening*. I saw it on Broadway. It was a nice integration, but what happened behind the scenes, I don't know. But how they used signing and speaking together in a musical, I think it was a good example, a positive example. I liked the way they put it together. What else? Oh, *ISM*, my show. [SMILES] Because the cast was deaf and hearing, and they were both on the stage at the same time, and the hearing performers would speak and let the audience see and hear the message at the same time. They could see deaf people signing and hear the voicing, and it'd match for them. So, I think that's one of the best works I've done, directing *ISM*. People want more of that, some people said interpreters voiced perfectly, wow, good voice, champ. So, it worked well. I think the reason is—during the parts where deaf people had monologues, we wanted to give the deaf BIPOC people a space to tell their stories. They [the interpreters] wanted to back off and allow the actors to tell their stories with voicing in sync. That was my intention, so for the opening and closing, both hearing and deaf interacted onstage. But then when it was time for the monologues, the hearing people backed off and watched.

Jill: In regards to strategies for plays becoming accessible for deaf and hearing audiences, there are many different strategies like sitting off to the stage, being onstage side by side, it could be the 'voice of' or having an ensemble of actors voicing for—captions, no voice and just captions. What do you think is the best strategy for access? Or is it dependent on the show itself?

Michelle: Yes, it depends on the show itself. I mean, what are the director and producer looking for, what is their vision? It varies. For example, I'll be doing *A Raisin in the Sun* next summer, 2023, and I have to figure out what to do with the interpreters. I have to figure out how to best use hearing people to voice for deaf people. Onstage? In the background? Or…I'm still trying to figure out the best strategy for accessibility. I haven't decided yet because I want to try something different this time. But I think for my upcoming production, I might want it to have subtitles all the way. Because I'm thinking that one of the characters is a CODA, so maybe no speaking. Maybe signing, or maybe there's a hearing character with the CODA, so they have that conversation, similar to *The Music Man*, where spoken conversations in everyday environments were shown in captions. We have to come up with a creative way of how we want to represent our vision and how we want to represent what the play is about. So, it really varies. They [the interpreters] could sit, they could become the background, they could be up above the stage, there could be no speaking or no signing. It really varies.

Andy: For auditions and rehearsals, do you have examples of situations you felt were very accessible or inclusive, or were *not* accessible or inclusive? Depending on your role.

Michelle: I haven't been involved with auditions as DASL that much, but at rehearsals, I've always had interpreters. As an actor, if I audition, there's always an interpreter there. Interestingly, if you audition virtually or submit self-made tapes, they tend to ask me to have a person speaking for me next to me. But I don't have that person to speak for me. I feel they should, if it's a deaf person, to have a back-and-forth with someone else.

If that person is deaf, how would they speak? I feel they depend on sound, and that's not accessible. They should accept that the person is not hearing and figure out, imagine that the person is talking while watching me sign the lines. They haven't had that visualization yet. That's something to be taught to the casting director, or director. They depend on hearing so much. I notice now that Hollywood often does that and I want to reduce or minimize that. I feel that isn't accessible. But when it comes to auditioning, as an actor, they just want me to sign back and forth with the casting director or interpreter, I feel that's accessible. But sometimes I feel the interpreter's role is on the fence. They should stay in their role as interpreter, so they shouldn't do readings. The casting director or someone else should read, not the interpreter. So, I have to negotiate that.

Jill: Does the interpreter know how to evaluate? If the casting director, or director, are hearing and don't know sign, how do they evaluate your audition?

Michelle: If the interpreter is asked to read, that shouldn't happen. They should be interpreting and not being involved. Use the casting director or bring someone from your casting team to read with me. That's it. The interpreter just voices for me, and signs to me what the other person reads. "Oh, okay." Sometimes the casting director has no idea how to use interpreters, how to interact with deaf actors even though the role description says it's for a deaf actor.

Jill: That's a reason for a DASL to be involved with the audition, right, because who can evaluate their skills as a deaf actor?

Michelle: True, true. That's interesting you brought that up because I don't know if it's ever happened where an audition involved a DASL? For me, with *The Music Man*, the director sent me videos to watch, so yes, that was different. But for hearing productions out there, they usually don't bring in a DASL to the room to evaluate the ASL, no.

Jill: But also, *The Music Man* had a Deaf co-director, Sandra, who was involved with casting, right?

Michelle: Yes, yes. She would ask me, "What do you think of the signing, yes or no? Have you worked with this person before?" She did ask for my opinion, so that was nice.

Jill: Another person we interviewed said there's a bit of an imbalance in auditions because hearing people have scripts in their language, while deaf people have to translate the script. So, I'm curious if you've ever experienced an audition where an ASL script was provided for actors?

Michelle: Interesting. No. I've never experienced that. I'm trying to remember. With VOCA, I just give scripts in English for auditions. But the idea of translating the script into ASL, would that help? But honestly, honestly, as an actor, you should be able to read and write in English. You gotta learn how to read, period. In the theatre world, everyone is hearing. But an ASL-translated script during auditions, that's a good idea. Some deaf people will say, "No, I prefer an English script. Why did you give me the ASL version?" Some won't understand the ASL translation. That could be a win-win.

Jill: In your opinion, why is it important to have integrated deaf and hearing theatre? Artistically important, philosophically important? Why should hearing people do that?

Michelle: Because they need to do that. [LAUGHS]

Jill: But why?

Michelle: Because they work with people. You can't always work with the same group of people all the time. You have to learn to broaden horizons and include people other than yourselves who aren't the same. Now in the entertainment business, the theatre, they emphasize inclusion, but what does inclusion mean? What does diversity mean? Equity, what does that mean? They talk about it but no action is taken. So for them, they have to say, "Oh, we're diverse. We support equity and inclusion. That's what we do." Really? What about deaf? "Oops." Black? "Oops." Their talk is no good. You have to really walk the talk. That means for them to say, "Oh, okay," and broaden a bit and include other people who are deaf, hard of hearing, BIPOC, whatever. Women, gay, LGBTQ, whatever. DeafBlind, whatever, but I think for hearing people, they have to be open-minded and understand the importance of integrated theatre. They'll gain in the number of audience members, too, because deaf people like to go see theatre, but don't feel they're represented. If you bring someone in to represent a community, more will see that show. I think it's time for them [hearing theatre makers] to understand that. It's the same for Hollywood, which is run by white males at the top, but bringing in more female and BIPOC directors, it's time for that. Integrated theatre, I think that makes it more, I don't know what the word is...I think it's important to have that visualization of working with diverse people and seeing that range for integrated theatre.

Jill: From an artist's perspective, how do you think hearing directors and actors can benefit from working with deaf actors? Artistic skills?

Michelle: The benefits of learning culture, ASL, and how to better work with people who are different. Becoming more empathetic, more open-minded. I think they would understand themselves better. I think the more they analyze themselves, they become better people because they're interacting with deaf people. They'll say, "Ohhhh." From my perspective, from my experience, a lot of the time when they work with deaf people for the first time, they learn so much from deaf people, and they become better persons who are more motivated and want to work more with deaf people. They want to work with different people and have inclusive learning in the community. So, I think that's what benefits them, and it benefits them to really do more projects, which leads to more opportunities for working together.

Andy: For the theatre community moving forward, what do you hope to see in terms of accessibility and inclusion?

Michelle: More integrated deaf and hearing productions like *The Music Man*. More of that. I think [hearing theatre makers] should be open to receiving ideas from deaf artists like us, and listening and trusting that we know what we're doing. They worry, "How do we communicate?" Be open and listen and understand. We deaf people need to be more patient in breaking down barriers, but we will finally break through slowly and surely. It's already happening. It's just the process of bringing in hearing people who are willing to work with us and learn more about us, who we are, and how they can really align with us. So, yes, I see more integrated theatre in the future.

Jill: From a director's perspective, what do you think is the most important thing to do to build an inclusive cast, and for the production process?

Michelle: Well, that would be to be open-minded. You have to have talented people, and really, to be able to interact with diverse people with different ethnic backgrounds. And your vision has to be bigger than you. It's not about me; it's about them, not me. That's how I work, that's how I operate. I will invite people from different cultures and backgrounds, and have them come in to see what they can offer, through auditions, dialogue, and seeing if they're willing to try this or that. I did that with *ISM*. It was the same idea. My vision, okay, I want different people to audition and to see if they can try this and talk about this, and then find people based on their experiences and cultures. I have that respect for them. In my experience with Onyx, I set it up when I was really young. I had just graduated from college, State University of New York—Purchase. It was an awkward phase for me. I'm not sure I really had any experience—well, in school, I did produce and direct my senior project, yes, but in the real world, professionally. I was really overwhelmed. I learned from that experience and it gave me the wisdom I needed. I took a break and then I came back here to DC and founded VOCA. My experience with Onyx helped me understand what I could do better this time with people's support, and to have a better vision of how to work with people, communicate better, how to bring people in to be involved. To include them in this space. I realized it's not about me. It's about them. Okay, what do they want? They have stories to tell, fine. How do I use them in good ways? It's important that energies must vibe and align. And that's it. If it's not aligned, then avoid that.

Jill: As a director, Andy is always curious about specific strategies for helping people to bond, especially deaf, hearing, or people from different backgrounds. Do you have activities early in the rehearsal process to help people develop working relationships?

Michelle: Yes, I have warm-up activities that have to do with trust, mirror exercises, games of truth or lies, physical touching exercises, one person speaking positively about another person or asking something they don't know about that person. One on one exercises and group exercises, and that's where they start to learn more about each other, get to know each other as an ensemble. And then during the rehearsal process, I make sure they have their moments to breathe. I will have an actor or two take the lead for an activity so they can really interact on their own, rather than depending on me to lead. I encourage them to get to know each other through these activities by having one of them lead and empower them to create some kind of game, to share.

JOSHUA CASTILLE

Joshua Castille is an award-winning actor, director, playwright, and director of artistic sign language. While a student at Gallaudet University, he joined the original cast of Deaf West's *Spring Awakening* and remained with the show through its Broadway run. For A Contemporary Theatre in Seattle, Castille had starring roles in *Tribes* (2017); *The Hunchback of Notre Dame* (2018), for which he received a Gregory Award for Outstanding Actor in a Musical; and *Romeo + Juliet* (2019). Most recently, Castille appeared in Deaf West's *Fidelio* with the LA Philharmonic (2023) and directed *Peter and the Starcatcher* at the Janesville Performing Arts Center in Wisconsin.

Andy: How would you define integrated theatre? What's considered integrated and what's not?

Joshua: I thought we would start with an easier question than that one, but I guess we're going to start with that one. Just dive in! [ALL CHUCKLE] Fine. It's funny because I started a conversation about "Deaf theatre" and "theatre for the deaf"—I mean, Deaf theatre, and theatre including deaf people. Where I feel like *integrated* has many different interpretations. It could be like *Romeo + Juliet*, my production that Jill just saw, which just had me and Howie [Seago] who were deaf. We had some characters who showed up and signed a bit but didn't really communicate with everyone. That's where I feel it's theatre including deaf people, while I feel like *The Music Man* in Maryland was Deaf theatre. But one aspect of Deaf theatre that isn't full deaf is shadowing. That interpreting and acting, that pairing is what I've always felt was inclusive for both audiences. And I feel like that usually is more successful if there's a deaf director behind that because you can keep deaf audiences interested while having hearing audiences interested by the signing itself.

I'm not sure that we've seen a successful production of true integration. I think that *Spring Awakening* was not a perfect production. Myself, who was part of that process and then watching the Lincoln Center film, I think it was closer than I expected. The reason I say that is because Michael Arden did something that I'm calling creative justification for the voicing, by having our voice actor become our inner innocence, our virginity, our naivety, and then once that moment in the show breaks that, they left. I felt like that became more of a creative solution rather than integration like in *The Music Man*, which again—all due respect to them, I love them, they're my friends, but I'm talking about this academically. That was just "hearing people for your access, we have a deaf person for your access." It didn't feel like the story was motivated or access-driven. I think we're in a time where we're analyzing story-driven versus access-driven and access in theatre. So, when you bring up integration, my first response is that that word has so many different meanings. Integrated like me and Howie in *Romeo + Juliet* where we were normal everyday people and had everyday characters who helped us communicate with our peers, or you're talking about, like, *The Music Man*, where we had this ideal world of deaf people signing while hearing people come up with microphones behind them, or are we talking about *Spring Awakening*, where we have creativity. Three different forms.

I don't feel like any of these is right or wrong. I just want to know what your goal or intention is. If you want to reach a hearing audience, then that's your approach, or if it's a deaf audience, then that's your approach.

I think for me as an artist myself, my goal is not either. My goal is, because I'm an actor first, I think in the given circumstances and if I was actually that character, in that situation, how would I navigate the world? I think that itself gives a real feeling, the art or capturing of reality, possibilities, and what these are. And for me, I'm constantly looking for integration in what we see in the real world. If we are at a deaf school and the story is about that, fine, leave it. If there are many deaf people and just one hearing person, that's fine, leave it. But if we're in a hearing college with one deaf person, I'm not interested in adding more deaf characters for the sake of my eyes, *whoo*, seeing more deaf actors on stage. No. Is that the story or is this the story, in my opinion? Integration is an approach that we choose for the purpose of the story in my work. I feel like I want the story first, not access first, not the ideals first. The story first. What is this story and how do I approach this? I do get into some tense conversations with my deaf peers because they feel rejected, right, but I'm like, okay we reject hearing audiences too if it means that for the story. Which way do we go? I recognize that's something I have to keep unpacking and exploring. I'm not making conclusions yet, but that's where I stand right now in terms of integration.

Jill: Integration itself is a practice, not a style? It's most successful when it serves the story first. Is that fair?

Joshua: Yes. I would agree with that.

Andy: If a director, a hearing director, wants to cast a deaf actor or use ASL during the show, do you think that director has the responsibility of making sure the whole show is accessible to the deaf audience?

Joshua: This—you really are putting me on the hot seat today. I will start off by saying that I know not every piece of work is for me. I know that some Black people will make art that's not for me to understand. I feel sometimes hearing people make art that's not for deaf people, period, and I feel like that's fine if you don't emphasize or exploit the situation like saying, "Look at us! We have signing! We have deaf characters!" If you start promoting the deaf thing, then that's where you have the responsibility. Generally, personally, I feel that yes, every show should be accessible, period. Period. They should have captioning, interpreters, and they should, should, should. It comes down to your principles as a businessperson. If you want to capitalize on deaf audiences' money, then you're gonna give them access, period. But if you have a deaf character in there—that's why sometimes I as a deaf actor will say, "This show isn't really accessible to deaf people." So, I share it on social media and point out that I'm the only deaf person and there isn't captioning. When I tell people, some will be disappointed, but I'm telling them so they don't waste their money. You know where this motherfucker stands by not giving you access. I'm obviously stuck in this position, so it's on them. So ideally, yes, but if you're not capitalizing on it—like in *The Prom*, there was one moment where they had signing. If they don't use that signing in any of their promos, nothing at all, that's fine. That's okay. That's good. We're not thinking, "Oh, deaf people are involved! I want to watch!" But if you're spotlighting this, and then half of the show isn't accessible, come on! No. That's my opinion.

Jill: I'm curious. I know you directed a show recently and they chose you not because you're a deaf director, but because you're a director.

Joshua: That's what they said, yes.

Jill: When you directed that show, did you feel it necessary to think about access because deaf people knew you were directing and would want to come?

Joshua: I did. I did think about that, and I brought that up in the production meeting, and it seemed that their budget thinking was not aligned with that. I was told that I would have this and that, then I showed up at the production meeting and things were being taken back. So that was a lesson learned for me. So that's part of why I did not market the show or tell the world it would happen. I just said I was directing, but they wanted to spotlight it and interview and do promotional marketing. I said no because the show isn't captioned. They said, "We'll have GalaPro." And I said, "No, not until I see you have it. I don't want you to spotlight me." I think they got a little angry with me on that, but again, you can't bring me in and say we have a deaf director when I did nothing about deaf people in that show. Nothing, not one deaf person was in that show, no signing, nothing. Nothing, so why would we have to mention I'm deaf? Why do we have to spotlight that? You know?

Jill: I'm sure that impacted your relationship with them. And then will they invite you to direct again? Probably not because of that, so that could have an impact on your career.

Joshua: They did invite me and I said no and they really got mad about that because I said, "You promised captioning and you didn't deliver, so why should I believe that?" Also, I felt a bit disempowered as a deaf director because hearing people would talk over me and I'd be like, "Hey, I'm like the minimum level of deafness and you can't even handle communicating. Good luck." I'm not interested in continuing that relationship if you're going to hurt my community. I don't mind being the guinea pig, I don't mind going in and being fed up, I don't mind if you talk in front of me without an interpreter. That's fine, we can learn together, but if there is no improvement, no change, then see ya later, I'm not interested in this. I'm not interested in continuing to create a space. So that's where I feel, yes, I have privilege as a hard of hearing person, but I'm using that privilege to test the room and encourage, or discourage, involvement. So, I can—already now if people ask me about that company, I say, no, don't get involved with them, no. No. I think that's why they're upset, more because they knew I'd do that. They're like, ugh, but I'm like, no, I'm not telling more deaf people to be involved in a harmful environment. No.

Andy: You've already mentioned *Spring Awakening*. One of our questions is what your best experience with an integrated production has been, so could you expand on *Spring Awakening* or mention other productions you've worked on?

Joshua: I've never been a fan of feeling special or different, that's something that I always...I feel like I'm a normal person. I can do these things. I just can't hear or I communicate differently. So, when Jules Dameron suggested that I refer deaffriendly.com to consult for a theatre company before I got there, maybe that'd help with my workload as an actor. I felt that's—"You're asking them to hire sensitivity trainers. I'm not sensitive, I'm fine. So, what's that for?" *The Hunchback of Notre Dame* hired deaffriendly.com and had them give a workshop—Guthrie Nutter gave a workshop about deaf culture, about me—superficial information on my background and so on. That experience working in that room—wow. I was able to focus on my art and I didn't have to advocate as much. I was fighting for the story, yes, because the director sometimes made choices that didn't really make my character strong or I felt this was a strange moment where the focus should have been elsewhere instead of, "Oh, deaf people sign." I also didn't have to explain to them how to call my attention by tapping my shoulder, nothing like that. They all knew the basic alphabet to fingerspell, they all understood my hearing level, they all understood what an interpreter was, how to look at me instead of the interpreter. They all knew not to say, "Tell him..." None of that. That introduction process really allowed me to do my job, so after that, I felt, yes, we should have deaf awareness training or something that allows hearing people to ask the dumb questions before I even arrive so I'm not burdened with teaching and advocating. That's where I really realized that. That being said, I feel like *Hunchback* was the best creative process.

Romeo + Juliet was also amazing because I worked with Howie Seago who is an older Deaf actor who has a lot of experience in this industry, so really our relationship made the experience more integrated for me because that was the story, actually. I was supposed to feel rejected by everyone aside from the one I connected with. And I felt it was a bit of Method acting in a way where I only had Howie to talk with. We connected because we were the only deaf characters, so I felt that really fed the story, that connection and the real ensemble energy. When people came to see the play, they saw clearly how two people could come up and the room changed completely the moment Howie and I talked to each other. They have that moment of realization: "These two people love and cherish each other," and then the room changes again with Romeo and Juliet because they can't communicate in their languages. They have to gesture, and I liked these moments of real integration, as opposed to hand-holding throughout to make a perfect experience.

Jill: This leads to the next question about accessibility for audiences, especially with integrated deaf and hearing shows, but we could talk about any show providing access to the audience. There are many different strategies. For example, *Romeo + Juliet* had interpreters, and offered captions, too. It had some characters who were hearing characters learning sign and they would come onstage and sign for you or Howie. Other characters would come and voice for you and for Howie. But there are other shows that use shadows, double casting, or interpreters at the front of the stage, captioning, open captioning, and all these different strategies or models. So, what, for you, is effective?

Joshua: Again, it's about the questions for the creator to consider. I always start with first, what are your vision and rules for access within the acting world and access for out there [the audience]. So, like, Benvolio who interpreted for me, Romeo, and his work just happened to benefit all of the others. When speaking for Romeo, he gave the other characters access, not the audience. So that is more creative in my opinion. When we have me, a deaf person, giving a soliloquy to the audience, that now becomes me giving access to the audience. So, I think we have a clear distinction and creative rules between these two. That's the first thing you have to figure out.

Andy: For the soliloquy, how did the director approach that?

Joshua: In our production, we had the parents come onstage. The parents talked because John Langs, his vision was that parents need to listen to the kids better, so they need to really understand the kids' feelings instead of saying, "No, I'm the parent. I'm right." His idea was to have all the actors in the audience, not on the stage but actually in the audience. Every time they spoke for Romeo and they weren't in the scene, they'd stay in the audience, speaking. It was very abstract and he added scenes where they were prologues...he said—it was strange, the monologues were when we switched scenes. For example, we had fences, three giant fences and actors would come and move the fencing as they spoke. The monologues helped transition the scenes, so he had clear rules. So even though it wasn't like exact rules, but the audience could feel a clear distinction between the two. I think that's where I started to feel that theatres don't think about the difference. Are we giving access within this world or that world? That's my first one. The second would be that I encourage people to think within the given circumstances. So now we're talking about *Romeo + Juliet* again, I know, but we're talking about having Romeo signing half of the play, and then Juliet is a big part of the play, too, but most of the second act is just her. And I'm not there, so she's speaking, so the deaf audience will think, "Where's Romeo?" If we look at Juliet's scenes and the setup, we see she's in her room like a caged bird. So, within that scene, what if we put guards on each side of Juliet's room to help with that feeling of being caged, suffocated, and have the guards interpret the speaking. So, they're there holding their guns and signing. They're not [GETS UP AND DUCKS BELOW CAMERA, THEN SUDDENLY POPS INTO SCREEN] JUST RANDOMLY POPPING UP and the audiences think "Who are you? Why are you here? You're not even part of this world, and now you're in a black outfit? What's that?" No. I really enjoy this idea because we already start the show with the guards walking around the theatre with guns in hand, and the people are uncomfortable. That energy, that vibe sets the tone for the whole show. So, I feel like once you have that tone, keep it, and have the access be part of that tone.

Jill: How do you balance that creative reasoning or motivation to fit with the story with accessibility? Creative reasoning and motivation can sometimes conflict with access. For example, I went to see Russell Harvard in *King Lear*. I felt like I wasted my money big-time because of how access was provided. First, Michael Arden is not a fluent signer. Second, his character is an advisor. He provides access for Russell only, not for the audience. Often, he stood in a place where I couldn't see his signing. Russell could see him, but the audience couldn't. I couldn't see what was happening. I had GalaPro in my hand and I was trying to look back and forth between that and the signing. I was completely lost, and it was a very, very frustrating experience for me. So that's an example where creative reasoning failed to provide access for the audience.

Joshua: Yeah. I don't see that as a creative reasoning failure. I see that as they didn't ask the question of what is accessible for the audience and the actor. I feel like they just went forward without answering these two questions. If you start to answer these two questions, you'll start to see the gap in these two areas. The audience knows what's going on but how does this actor know what's going on? Oh, yeah, we need to add that, so you have to fill in for both sides, not just one. So, it feels like they didn't say, "Is this for the audience, for this world? If for this world, and it's not clear to the audience, how do we give access to the audience?" Like *Richard III* in Central Park recently, Monique Holt was signing her speech and actors walked in front of her. Everyone in the audience who was deaf had to lean over to see her, so I literally screamed to the interpreters, "Sign for us!" and the interpreter said, "Oh!" and signed so we could understand. I was right there, and they thought, "Oh!" But we couldn't see. So that's where you have to figure out that balance, that journey, and I always say hearing theatres have how many years on us? You know? They've had since the Greek and Roman times to figure it out. If I stand here, you can hear me better, or is it over there? We're just *now* finally looking at that [for signing], so I'm excited, yeah. If it doesn't work, okay, what's next? How can we fix that? These questions you're asking, I think, are helping with the journey.

Andy: Why do you think it's important for productions to integrate deaf and hearing artists? Why is that kind of work important? Why is it worth pursuing?

Joshua: Michael Arden, I'm very happy to work with him. He's an amazing artist. I feel that each artist I work with has a great sentence. I want to give credit to Michael, who said, "No matter what you do, if you put humans in a room, at some point they will make a circle and tell a story." And I found that fascinating. Telling a story to learn, to share an experience, to pass along a culture, to remember the past. Even though we have technology, we're at the point where theatre is still a way for people to have this difficult conversation that is hard to have. For example, I can't discuss privilege with my family right now. I can't, they're too sensitive about it. They cannot have conversations without taking it personally. but we can sit together and watch *Zootopia* and discuss animal privilege. That art helps us to have those tough conversations. That art helps us, allows us to have the vocabulary for what separates me from them. I think integrating deaf and hearing people allows us to see the different ways of life without exposing our own ignorance or our own misconceptions of those types of people. So, when I answer that question, I don't think it just applies to deaf people. I think it applies to queer people, Black people, trans people, women, men, etc. Theatre is a place to capture the human experience or to communicate a concept that allows us to further understand the human experience. So, when you say why, what's the benefit, I say if you can't figure that answer, then you shouldn't be doing theatre in the first place.

Jill: But we want to know *your* answer.

Joshua: That is my answer! To capture and document the human experience. I think learning from perspectives that you don't have. We're going, it's like, my BIPOC friends during the Black Lives Matter movement talked about bumping into people in the store. White people often don't realize Black people are there, but Black people are hypervigilant about not bumping into white people. And I'm like, really? I realized it's true. Oftentimes, I'll go into an aisle and see a Black person and they will always move immediately. So now I'm trying to approach and move before they move, like, we're equal but that's something subconscious that we as a class have done for years. Occupying this space, we don't think about things like that. That's something—"Oh." So, perspectives I never would have gotten unless a BIPOC person told me. So, we as deaf people have that, you know—you hearing people don't look at each other when you talk. I told that to one of my friends. "You know that you talk away from each other's faces? Why? Why don't you look at each other and connect?" He was taken aback. Deaf people have perspectives and experiences in their approach to life so allow us to come in and tell that story and we'll all learn from each other. That's the benefit of deaf people in theatre.

Jill: From an artistic perspective, what do you think hearing people can learn from working with deaf actors, directors, or DASLs, in relation to the craft of acting?

Joshua: I will say our biggest benefit is space-holding. We deaf people know how to go in a space and communicate concepts around us and all that. Hearing people struggle with that because they rely heavily on words. I feel like deaf people have that skill in our language to communicate big concepts through space. Jules and I just gave a workshop through Deaf West for the general public on ASL and Deaf theatre, and we talked about how we physically show that the present is in our immediate area, past is back there, and future is over there. Some hearing actors were like, "Yeah I could lean forward as I speak for tomorrow and lean back for yesterday." That's already built into them; they don't have to sign. It's just including the parameters of language that already make it visually clear. I do think hearing people have a lot to learn from us in terms of visual communication, other than overacting or using exaggerated facial expressions. It's about space and how we use it and communicate ideas.

Jill: In the theatre community moving forward, in the future, what do you hope to see in relation to integrated content, and accessibility for deaf and hard of hearing artists?

Joshua: I'm currently with the ACT Core Company, a group of forty artists in the Seattle area. Some have moved away but most did shows at the ACT. That company is intended for actors to hold theatres accountable, and that's part of it, but also to have resources in artists who support each other, writing, giving each other workshops, developing, pushing each other. John Langs, the artistic director of that company, wants it to be ensemble-led, meaning the team is leading it. My hope is that more theatres like that have deaf people involved, so we can really learn from each other and interact. I'm just going to be blunt and say that I feel like, myself included, we're not qualified for the big-level projects. I remember *Fidelio* with Amelia, Russell, Gabe [Silva], me, Indi Robinson, and Gregor Lopes. We had Colin Analco, we had Natasha Ofili, we had DJ Kurs. It was a really great powerhouse in the community but we all were not qualified for that job. I say that because we couldn't read the opera score, we didn't understand the background. That gave us the benefit of bringing a fresh perspective to the opera, for sure, yes, but I know that we spent more time trying to understand the music than the story. I feel like I find myself constantly in the room where I wish we had more information to bring to the job other than I'm new, so prove it to me. "Oh, I have to prove why musical theatre works with deaf people." Prove, prove, but I want us to see us as a deaf community to get to a place where we actually bring our perspective rather than spending the whole process trying to understand your world. So, is it our fault that we're not qualified? No, and yes. We could argue all day, but ultimately, I do hope theatres consider giving more deaf people training and support in that way. I've been looking forward to ACT Core Company because we're talking about writing labs, and I said I love the idea of writing labs but many deaf people don't write. Some do; actually, many do write, but others have anxiety. I feel like we've already eliminated entire crowds of ASL, visual vernacular, and performance artists who could bring something to this space. How do we open it up rather than calling it a writing lab? Maybe call it a creative lab, so disabled artists who do not write or speak, maybe they could perform their stories. But then again, they have to have a script, so how do we create that document? The conversation could start there. I feel like we should have more diversity, more disabilities, and deaf people all in these spaces, and allow them to listen and change and learn from each other.

Jill: Is there a production you were involved in whatever role, where the process from the initial steps to the very end, such as from audition to the actual performance, where you felt fully included and it was very inclusive all the way? And why?

Joshua: I own a production company with Jules Dameron. We did some projects and Jules is definitely better at casting. He's really good at that. Jules and I have been in our own productions. We've also done projects where others picked the actors, and *whoo*, it's a big difference. It's really tough. Tough because we knew they would not listen or respect us as artists, or sometimes it's not about talent, it's about, "Can you listen and respect a deaf person's perspective because we're not equal, we're lower in your perspective?" If I have an actor in the room who doesn't respect me as a human, how can I do my job? How do I do my job? Third, throughout the process, we also were kind of assistant directors for a project. They sent us videos; we watched and chose who we felt were ideal. That made the process of filming easier because we knew their signing styles, so they told us, "This character is from Brooklyn, and this character is hearing who just learned sign." Jules and I already knew we'd need to cast someone who signed faster for the Brooklyn one. So, we knew what signing style to pick. They did go ahead and cast one actor without us knowing. When we arrived and saw that the actor was deaf but was supposed to play a hearing person who signed, we already knew right there that this deaf person wasn't able to code-switch. That doesn't mean any deaf person can't do that, no. It's just it was this one person specifically, but we didn't vet or screen that person, so we said to them, "You know, this isn't going to work." They were surprised. I told them we could go ahead, but the signing style wouldn't fit. I did try to work with that actor, but that person didn't have the ability to code-switch. They also cast a hearing person who claimed to know sign, but that person wasn't at all fluent. They didn't have us screen these, so now we had to find someone else. We ended up having a deaf person in that role. Having the deaf person in the casting process, which will save thirty to forty percent of the trouble in the process. Every time they pick someone without discussing with deaf people or leaving out deaf person's perspective...this always happens, with Deaf West shows, different projects, all of them. I just keep seeing this waste of time and confusion, breakdowns because the hearing person does not understand what this deaf environment is about and deaf people try to share but the information is not being received. It creates frustration and is a waste of time. As a writer, again if you do not respect me as a deaf person then this isn't going to work. You do not see me as someone who has merit, someone who has experience. I worked at my high school, a small school. My classmate clearly did not respect me and kept changing my script, saying, "Oh, that's not what happens. Hearing people won't do this." But they do! If you really do not respect deaf people or you feel like deaf people are just a bit lower-class but say, "But it's important we practice affirmative action to include them," then it's done. The project is tainted, period.

Jill: As an actor, have you ever shown up at an audition where there's a DASL in the room?

Joshua: No! I have yet to see that in the room. Not ever. It's always been just hearing people. But again, that doesn't mean they didn't film the audition and send the tape to the DASL. I know for *Romeo + Juliet*, they sent me an audition and I gave them my eye as a deaf consultant. That deaf eye. I tell them my insights based on what I see. "This person signs more English-like, while this person signs more poetic ASL." I'm not saying yes or no, I just tell them input based on what I see. They cast however they want and I share things like if this person can be trained to express more in ASL format. The director has the power to make that decision. As an actor in the room, I do feel like I prefer a reader who can sign or a director who comes in with a clear vision of like, "I know the reader is hearing but can you show me what it'd look like if you tried to date her?" We did that with *Tribes*, my first *Tribes* audition. I didn't get the role but they did have an interpreter. The director said about the reader, "I know she doesn't sign, she's taking classes, but I know that the script says she knows sign. Can you just act as if she doesn't know sign and see what the scene looks like?" And it did change the scene for sure, but that ability to own up to the fact where the director said, "I know I'm not bringing everything on my end of the table..." That made me feel more trusting and comfortable as a deaf artist rather than telling them, "This isn't what it says," worrying and being blown off. No, the director owned up to it and asked if I preferred an interpreter in that role or to go ahead with the reader. That kind of dynamic in owning up, you know what you don't know, always makes me as an actor feel okay, I'm working with my given circumstances, and it's not just random "You're not signing to me but I have to pretend..."

Jill: How do you think a director makes casting decisions if no DASL is present to provide feedback about signing quality?

Joshua: Beats me. Some rooms I've been in, they like me because of the video they saw, some directors like me because I challenge them in the room and say, "This doesn't make sense," "Why?" "Because we never do that, let's talk about it." Some like my looks, some just like my energy in the room. Some just think I was good and got me...I don't know. Fuck if I know! I'm trying to figure that out.

Andy: What's one thing that a director can do to create 1) inclusion in the cast, and 2) an inclusive production process? So, if a new director comes up to you and asks for advice, what's one thing you would say to that director?

Joshua: The director is the head of the room, head of the room, and how the director approaches any misconception—if the director doesn't sign, that influences the room tone. So, I would recommend the director signs as much as possible in the room. If you, even if you fingerspell just the first letter of each word, other actors will pick up on that and sign to the deaf people. But if you speak all the way, the actors will follow that via the interpreters. How you act influences everything else in the entire room. You're the standard. If you show how deaf people can provide benefits, actors will appreciate it, but if you just do whatever and go along without saying anything, they'll also go ahead without anything. So that's my advice.

Jill: What are specific activities you use to try and create collaboration between deaf and hearing actors?

Joshua: I tend to play games where everyone stands in the middle, then I say, "Those who have kids go over there, and those who don't, go to the other side. Okay, come back. Who likes *Harry Potter*? Go over there. Who likes *Lord of the Rings*, go over there." I do this repeatedly so they already have topics to talk about, and can converse with each other. The ice is broken immediately. See? You all have commonalities. What do you have to talk about? Those kinds of questions on a daily basis. I try to do that. I also just directed at RIT. Every day I assigned the actors to go to each cast member and ask a personal question. Just one. "Do you have pets?" The more you ask, the more hearing people will feel comfortable about interacting with deaf people. They're afraid, so I feel like, as a director, having hearing people ask deaf people and deaf people ask hearing people, that gives them more opportunities to see each other as humans. It's ensemble-building, really, I think.

Andy: You've worked in musical theatre. What are some of the specific challenges in musical theatre that don't come up in non-musical space?

Joshua: Mostly it's choreography and signing, finding that balance between dancing and signing. Sometimes, most of the time they don't put any dance in. No. I'm like, we can have some dancing, some movement, find that balance between signing and movement without visual noise. Then I'd say the musical process. I was very lucky with E.J. Cardona who did my voice [in *Hunchback*]. He really, really, *really* watched me and my acting choices. He'd stop me and say, "We have to do that song again. Josh is playing this very hurt. I'm playing this very angry. And I need to change my approach." And we'd do the song again. I think the challenge is finding a voice actor who really knows to physically watch, and make choices that they think should be in the role. The voice actor needs to really look at the deaf person. And I think that started because the first time I met with E.J., I told him we're sharing the role together. We have to share the role. It's not me doing the role and you're doing things for me. We're sharing so if you don't feel right about something, you have to tell me. We can fight and have two different characters but by us being on the same page, we can align and we can see if he wants to try something that's different than what I was envisioning, and that's okay. It's important that I'm aware, rather than me not knowing and looking like a fool on stage. I don't want that. So, make sure the voice actor and actor know they're working together. The deaf actor has to be the leader. If not, it'll fall apart.

Jill: Can you talk a little about your *Spring Awakening* experience? That kind of musical compared to working on *Fidelio*? What were the challenges? Was it similar or different?

Joshua: Oh, very different. First of all, *Spring Awakening* was in English, so I could easily pick up cues from lipreading. *Fidelio* was in German, and I could not decipher a thing. And operas are known for parking and barking. There's no choreography. No checkpoints, nothing. So, in *Fidelio*, a week before tech week, I had to go up to the director and say, "We're behind!" He said, "I know, you all don't know your lines." I said, "No, we know our lines, we just don't know where we are." He was like, "But look at the conductor." But all I see are hands moving in the same four-count rhythm over and over. How is that any different from the past ten minutes I've watched? I said, "How do you know?" The director said, "Well, sometimes I hear beats." Right, but I don't see it! I don't see that. I just see the same movements over and over again. Musical theatre tends to have more movement. When someone does a certain gesture, I know to sign this, and if they do that gesture, I know to use that line. While in *Fidelio*, there were no cues. It was all mouthing in German. I would just sign, hoping I did it right. So that's where we need to have a discussion about increasing lightingcues for operas, more lighting cues, or if we have a qualified ASL director who could read music and could design signs to fit the tempo. We could then sign using a one, two, three, four rhythm. Again, that's a technical aspect we haven't ever done, so how? That was our biggest concern, the checkpoints in ten minutes. Standing and singing about your husband versus a dancing number where deaf actors have clear blockingcues that help us know what part of the song we are in and what's coming up next.

Patrick Graybill

Patrick Graybill is a renowned actor, poet, DASL, and storyteller. While attending Gallaudet University, he studied under Robert Panara and performed with the Frederick Hughes Memorial Theatre. After earning his master's degree in education, he joined the National Theatre of the Deaf (NTD) in 1969. Graybill toured with NTD for ten years and also headed NTD's summer Professional School Program from 1971 to 1984. After leaving NTD, Graybill taught, directed, and performed at NTID for twenty-three years. While at NTD he continued his work in professional theatre, including Deaf West's *The Gin Game* (1991), and also performing his original poetry around the country. Now in his eighties, he remains active in the performing arts, appearing in NTID productions in 2022 and 2023, and serving as DASL for local interpreted shows.

Jill: How do you define success for an integrated deaf and hearing production?

Pat: Having fun. Doing a show and not simply putting up with it or doing it for an audience or—no. It should be like playtime in the sandbox. If the team has a wonderful time doing that show, that's successful.

Jill: Would your perspective change if you're thinking about the director, actor, or DASL, or the audience?

Pat: I've been in so many plays that were integrated, like with NTD. As an actor, I learned so much from them [the hearing actors] while rehearsing. In the early days, I never felt comfortable as an actor on stage because I didn't trust the voice actors. I finally felt comfortable when I started to trust the process. I realized I can act without worrying about voice actors being able to follow me.

Jill: How did that trust develop, through experience, because the director set up an environment that created that, or where did that trust come from?

Pat: From day one, the director, voice actors, and the deaf actors were all on the same page. In the past, I would rehearse on my own and then have my voice actor join me two or three weeks later, no. Not like that. It has to start from day one, where we all come to agreement on the same level, and then go from there.

Andy: I'm curious how a DASL can help support that trust-building?

Pat: I'm happy when the DASL starts several months before rehearsals, working with the director, to have a shared thought process. The DASL has to support the director sometimes; sometimes actors will come up to me and it's not exactly what we want. Maybe their signing skills aren't so great, or they have psychological struggles. A DASL has to be flexible and adjust. It's important to have the DASL there from the very beginning. Sometimes in my past years, they'd call me in during the third or fourth week of rehearsal, which made it seem as if I was doing a band-aid job trying to fix things. No, that's not how it works. The DASL, voice actors, deaf actors, I mean hearing actors, all of them have to work together. So, the DASL has to be ready. The DASL should be prepared when rehearsal starts.

Andy: Can you share the best example of an integrated production you've worked on and explain why that production was successful.

Pat: I directed *One Flew Over the Cuckoo's Nest*, in my second or third year as a teacher at NTID (1980). That was really integrated. Nurse Ratched, she was a hearing woman who worked in an art gallery. She came and auditioned. She looked so perfect for the role but didn't know sign, so I came up with an interpreter-nurse [character] who could interpret with her—I remember it clearly. I had just finished being part of NTD and I had never directed. I trained as an actor, but never as a director. So, with that production, I came in as the director. There were some struggles. Maybe two or three weeks into rehearsals, the head of the theatre department called me into the office and said, "Where are the sound effects?" I was puzzled. I said, "I don't care." He said "No, no, hearing people won't come to the show! We need money!" Ohhh. So, I brought in a co-director, and we had some struggles because that person didn't come in on day one. They arrived in the middle of the process. So, there were some struggles. The co-director did help me, yes, with hearing actors on stage. But on opening night, I thought the show wasn't ready. I sat in the very back of the theatre and let it go, just let things unfold. I was astonished. *Magic* happened. The lighting designer, the costume designer, the actors themselves, they were free to do things on their own without me interfering. I needed to let the actors have relationships with each other. Really, *One Flew Over the Cuckoo's Nest* was a successful show. But I wish I had a dramaturg. I was the DASL for that show, and that was really risky because it was hard to focus on directing and then be the DASL. That wasn't a good idea. They should be separate roles so the director can focus on the work and the DASL can watch and provide support.

Jill: So, you said in *One Flew Over the Cuckoo's Nest*, it was like magic, why? Why was it successful?

Pat: The cast had fun. They worked cooperatively. My struggle during that process was with my co-director, who came during the third or fourth week. But the cast had fun. Even though the leading man, he knew nothing about acting but he looked right for the role. I feel that college productions are supposed to let anyone come in regardless of talent. They're there to learn. So, we need a good team of directors, designers, and DASL to work with them and teach them, and go from there. That was a four or five-week process, whew. I wanted the whole year!

Jill: I wanted to ask you, because Patrick, your entire career has been filled with integrated productions. You started with NTD, which was the first time deaf and hearing integrated productions happened all the way up until now. You were involved in Andy's production of *Angels in America*. How have you seen deaf and hearing integrated productions evolve over your career?

Pat: I came into NTD in its third year, so I didn't see the beginning. The artistic director had expertise from Broadway, but didn't know deaf people, no. He often hired different directors who came in and they made mistakes. For example, one time we did *My Third Eye*. In "Sideshow," the second segment of the show, which had five segments, he brought in a famous director, Joe Chaikin, who came from Open Theater back in the 1960s. It was a sort of revolutionary acting group. On his first day, he asked what we were angry about in terms of hearing people. We were caught off-guard. A hearing person was asking us deaf people this? That's a private world, our private world. So, things were a bit tense for a few days. One hard of hearing actor told him, "It's not your business. You don't know us." He walked out on that job. Ahh! The artistic director then hired one of our troupe members as the director, and we became comfortable with her. We then developed and created that show. But NTD, after its third, fourth, fifth, or sixth year, began to let go of the idea of "hearing and seeing" words at the same time. I had to sign closer to English because the voice actors didn't know sign. They were skilled actors, no question, but we had to sign in time with their pacing. I think David Hays, the artistic director, realized this mistake after I left NTD. More ASL was allowed in, but it was a slow process. The first few years, the A.G. Bell society was angry with us and interfered with us a lot because we dared to sign in public. It was a rough start, indeed. I left NTD after 10 years and saw things slowly changing. What I'm really puzzled about today is that more and more integrated theatres are focusing on musicals. It makes money. I'd feel a bit uncomfortable if I were in one because I'd have to follow the rhythm in singing and all that. Younger actors are more flexible. Sandra Mae Frank is very deaf like me, but her family taught her how to read musical notes and she picked that up. That's really impressive. Russell Harvard is impressive, too. I must admit it's better than *Big River*, which was done at the Mark Taper theatre. I didn't like that myself. *Spring Awakening* was all right—

Jill: Why didn't you like *Big River*?

Pat: Because I couldn't follow it and the signing was visually distracting. I feel the director himself must be trained using the deaf eye while directing. If someone finishes signing, the direction that person's head turns will help me know who to look at next. Sometimes the director is incompetent. It's what I call audio-addicted. Music, music, music. It looks good with sound, but not to the eye. In the early years of NTID with Jerry Cushman, he was himself a dancer. He was so mean as a director. It was so terrible. But he had a talented eye for movement, which made it easy for me to follow the show. [With *Big River*], it was hard to follow everything visually.

Jill: *Spring Awakening* was better?

Pat: Yes. Deaf actors need to be confident doing musicals. They have to be comfortable in their own skin, acting and enjoying it. If that happens, it'll work. *Spring Awakening* showed—there was unity among the cast. I enjoyed it, in comparison to *Big River*. It was an improvement, but not perfect, no. I saw Deaf West's *Arrival and Departure* [2018] which wasn't a musical, but the ensemble was dazzling. It was clear. Deanna Bray was so good. I want to see more of her. She's more focused on ASL teaching, unfortunately. Troy Kotsur was in it, too. The theatre only had seventy-five seats. It was a small stage where Phyllis Frelich and I did *The Gin Game*, the same stage. I think for deaf people, I'd like the theatre to have two hundred and fifty seats, that's it. Not any bigger because then that makes it harder to see the show. I prefer smaller.

Jill: I'm curious, did you see *Equus* with Lewis Merkin?

Pat: No, I didn't.

Jill: That was an early integrated deaf and hearing production

Pat: Lewis was influenced by *Children of a Lesser God*. That's another early integrated show, but I heard that behind the scenes that the hearing and deaf actors were at odds. Because the hearing actors didn't really want to work with the deaf actors. They'd often arrive and not say hello to the deaf actors, so it was tense.

Andy: Can you describe one or two productions you worked on that you felt very included during auditions, rehearsals, and performances. One or two examples where it was very inclusive.

Pat: Honestly, I never auditioned at NTD.

Andy: Really?

Pat: David Hays and the director decided who would do what role. We were always surprised; we never auditioned. But maybe our summer school training during class, uh, art classes, dancing classes, and creative writing classes. Anyway, I never auditioned. Imagine that, I never auditioned! [LAUGHS] Maybe one or two times I auditioned; one was for a movie and one for a TV show, but I was not cast. I wasn't cast.

Andy: Those two auditions, were they inclusive?

Pat: Luckily, the directors knew what to do with the interpreters. I didn't feel left out of the loop. I came in and the audition was for five or ten minutes. I was comfortable, yes. If the director didn't expect a deaf person to audition, it'd be a different story. They expected deaf actors to show up at the audition.

Andy: What about the rehearsals and performances? Any that were very inclusive?

Pat: During my NTD days, I always felt included because it was all day from 9 a.m. to say, 4 p.m., with lunch or coffee or short breaks, but it was always all day. At NTID I did *Moliere* with Matthew Moore. Jerome Cushman directed—that wasn't fun. I prefer a director who is patient. I'm off the point, but I wish I had worked with Alexandria [Wailes]. She knows acting skills, but she's also a DASL and also an acting coach. My experience as an actor at NTID while teaching—it was fun. *The Importance of*

Being Earnest had a small cast and a good director. It was fun working together. I was the DASL then.

Jill: When you were at NTD as an actor, did you have interpreters? Did the hearing actors have interpreters? Or were they expected to pick up signing?

Pat: NTD was lucky to have a CODA living in that town who interpreted for us. When we did *On the Harmfulness of Tobacco* by Chekhov, David Hays told me, "You will rehearse with a voice actor behind you and an interpreter," who was that CODA. She was a sweet woman. The rehearsal process, I did it alone. David Hays didn't know ASL, so he just told me, "I want you to rehearse without any other actor interrupting. I want you to do it on your own using the signs you use in the dining room." I didn't understand. Dining room? At that time, we signed English on stage. Use what I use in the dining room? I was confused. So, I rehearsed on my own, and the director often *slept* during rehearsal. The one who kept me entertained was the interpreter, who was attentive and excited. The voice actor, I was nervous because he was a skilled actor, a Shakespearean actor who didn't know sign. If I skipped a line, what would we do? I was fretful about that, and it was a struggle. So yes, we had interpreters. Looking back, NTD used that CODA, and a CODA from Syracuse, New York, and Linda Lamitola, among a few others. Yes, during rehearsals.

Jill: It seems like you emphasize that hearing actors should know enough sign to follow, such as if you skip lines. Or trust, that's part of that, and hearing people must learn to understand signs, yes. Maybe that's one strategy for inclusiveness.

Pat: Definitely. One nice thing about Andy casting several interpreters or interpreting students, that really helps. They know signs and can follow. I remember [for *Angels in America* at NTID]—certain hearing actors didn't know sign, or never signed onstage. I watched deaf actors interpreting and I was impressed, really. It was hard to follow the fast speaking, especially in the scene where they picked up the phones so many times. I was worried about my deaf friends coming to see the show. Afterwards, they told me they really enjoyed the play because of the captions, and the signing was wonderful. They really loved that play.

Jill: I think that leads to a question about how plays can become accessible for audiences, deaf, hard of hearing, and hearing audiences. What strategies help integrated plays become accessible?

Pat: It's challenging. The director needs to know how to work with the lighting designer. Don't make the show so dark. You can still use mood lighting, but not completely dark. For music, I'm clueless, but the director can work with the music director. I think some hard of hearing students love sound effects. We have to think of these, but I don't want to rely on captioning. Captioning is the last choice for me. If I'm stuck and don't understand, I'll look at the captions and become a book reader, missing the show. [CHUCKLES]

Andy: So why do you think it's important to have integrated deaf and hearing productions?

Pat: I've always complained that I don't want that [integrated theatre]. But see what happened with *CODA*? Deaf people got jobs and were integrated. Hearing people learned about deaf talent. It's important, yes, and that means deaf people can learn how to design sets, design lighting, serve as DASL. Many young adults are used to seeing deaf classmates in mainstreamed schools in their upbringings and know deaf people—they're willing to work with deaf people. Eventually, it'll become something that isn't what I'll object to. It'll look normal. Normal. Hearing or deaf people can audition; it's fine either way, they'll be cast. I still want to have a separate theatre for deaf space. Something that allows hearing people to see what we're like in our own world. It'll become like a patchwork quilt that can be beautiful if you do it well. NTD was founded because so many deaf people went to vocational rehabilitation and when asked what they wanted to do in the future, they said "I want to act." It wasn't possible, but is possible now. They're equal to hearing people.

Jill: Anything we didn't discuss you feel is important to talk about on the topic of integrated deaf and hearing theatre?

Pat: Yes. Not necessarily related to integrated productions, but I'm concerned that in colleges, teaching stage signing is not offered. I think it's time because most of us grew up at deaf schools practicing clearly signing on stage. Serena [Rush] for example, the student who was recognized by the Kennedy Center American College Theatre Festival, she attended deaf and hearing schools. She signs so beautifully. I want more students like her. We need a class that teaches how to sign on stage. In the movies and TV, it's different. Offer signing classes. Hearing people could join if they know how to sign.

Jill: Why is her signing beautiful?

Pat: Maybe I can say she's like me. It's clear, truly. Her fingerspelling is clear. Her internal acting is very collaborative with other actors and clear. I look forward to seeing her work in the future. She'll become a classical actor, yes.

Monique Holt

Monique Holt is an actor, director, playwright, director of artistic sign language, and theatrical interpreter. She is one of most accomplished deaf people in professional theatre, having worked as an actor and DASL with Oregon Shakespeare Festival, Chicago Shakespeare Theatre, and numerous other well-known theatre companies. She can be seen as the Duchess of York in The Public's *Richard III* (2022), featured in PBS's Great Performances. Her original work includes *Please UNTranslate Me* and *Not Another Deaf Story*. She holds an MFA in Theatre from Towson University and is an assistant professor in the Theatre and Dance program at Gallaudet University.

Jill: You've had many years of experience in integrated deaf and hearing theatre. What does success look like? How do you define it?

Monique: I've only had one best experience. Then the rest of my career, I never saw that again. *Our Town* by Thornton Wilder. The artistic director at the time was with Milwaukee Repertory Theater: MRT, and his name was John Dillon. He was the assistant to one director (Colleen Dewhurst) way back when for an NTD production. He wanted to do the show Martha's Vineyard–style, where hearing and deaf families blended. So, when he cast, there were five of us who were deaf, and the rest were hearing. An artistic director from NTD was also involved, Will Rhys. So, there were six of us who could sign fluently, while the rest didn't. We had a stage manager, and only one interpreter. Just one. The director, John Dillon, or JD, decided to announce to the entire company—not just the cast, but the entire company, including the crew and stage manager and everyone else, that we would offer from 9 to 10 a.m. daily a crash course in ASL. *All* of the company members participated. That was amazing. So, the five of us deaf actors took turns teaching ASL. It was basic ASL that we taught. Okay. Then the rest of the day we had an interpreter, and the actors and crew would watch and pick up a few things from the interpreter that we didn't teach, and then they'd check in with us to be corrected. By the second week, they all signed fluently. Yes, sometimes there were awkward situations, but they really tried their best. They weren't intimidated. They jumped in and learned to sign their lines, and we all worked together. The Webb family was deaf and the Gibbs family was hearing (historically accurate). The Gibbs father was a doctor while the Webb father was a printer. And it was just really seamless and beautiful. And in the second year, we toured Russia and there were two boys who played my brother—we had kid A and kid B, because they were underage. Their parents didn't allow them to travel to Russia because of school schedule conflicts, so I was like, what do we do? We contacted a Russian company to reach out to deaf schools there to see if they could find a deaf Russian boy to play my brother. I had to learn a little RSL [Russian Sign Language] myself so it worked out. We taught each other RSL and ASL, and it went well. But we did have three interpreters, one spoken Russian to spoken English, one spoken English to ASL, and one spoken Russian to RSL. It was an incredibly slow process, but it was something we just went with on our own. The signs were easier to work with, but for the hearing people, it wasn't as easy to speak. But that was one of the most integrated hearing-deaf productions I've ever seen and I haven't seen again since then.

Andy: What year was that?

Monique: 1992.

Jill: That's a unique experience, the whole company learning.

Monique: That one really beautiful model. I think we need to do more of that often, mostly if you really want the show to be integrated.

Jill: So, what's your definition of integrated theatre?

Monique: First, again, I really think it's on the director. What is the vision? If you really want the hearing actors to sign, that becomes another element of the story—pushing the signs and needing hearing people because we have hearing characters. If it's back and forth, then that's integrated. That's how I see it, so to speak, to be integrated, but if, as another example, it's like NTD or Sunshine Too, then that's definitely integrated.

Jill: In your experience, if you have many hearing characters with one deaf person, what do you call that? Mainstreamed?

Monique: Good question. Tokenism. Oregon Shakespeare Festival hired me as a DASL in 2013 when Howie Seago played the lead in *Cymbeline*. I really had to fight and fight for time slots, fight for actor's time to work one-on-one. Oh my gosh. It was really tough. I was really—I think I established high standards. I have high expectations. I really pushed them. I think they were rooted in their habits and old ways. Oh, it's like a last-minute remedy, we can fix that, no worries. I said, "No! You need to have everything in place and the schedule all set. I need the actors. I know you need the actors, but when can I have time? You want him to sign, you have to give me time." It was a battle. But he said, "It's not in the Equity handbook." Hmm. And we had to do the video signing, and then help the actors understand when they weren't signing right. "Well, we can't do that because it's not in the handbook." So, I talked with a deaf actor who was very active in the union and I asked and told them to help me. I'm union, but I wasn't there in New York to add a new bill. So, we finally made it happen. It's on page eighty-eight, the right to use video for sign translation purposes.

Jill: If we could go back to the definition of integrated theatre—do you have a specific number of actors you feel is needed, or should the play itself have a deaf theme like Martha's Vineyard or a similar theme to be "integrated" theatre? How exactly would you define it?

Monique: I don't know if you need more than one deaf person or one kind of group, like foreign speakers. I'm not sure. One is hard. But if you have a group…if you want to be integrated, we need to be thoughtful of how to present the show. It doesn't have to be related to their foreignness or otherness or deafness, no, that's not the point. The point is the story. How does that convey the story? And from the actor's perspective, can they work together? And the director, artistic and creative team that are producing this integrated experience. Again, I'm just one view, but other views may be different from mine. But in my view, I'm arguing about the word *inclusion*. Intersectional…I hate inclusion because it's like, "Oh, shit, we have to bring in an interpreter for that person." It's not, "Because we need one. SHE needs one." Wrong. We should be thinking, "You don't speak, okay, we don't sign, so we both need an interpreter brought in to facilitate." That's intersectional thinking. Inclusive is more of, "Oh, ugh, this [deaf] person needs this…" And they feel the financial burden. But integration is an artistic exchange, yay! "How can we make this work?" That's intersectionality.

Andy: Your first example of *Our Town* was fantastic. But we're curious about your dream integrated production. In an ideal world, what does that look like?

Monique: I'm not sure if this would fit, but one time New York Deaf Theatre [NYDT] asked me to direct something, anything, my choice, my decision. I decided on *Titus [Andronicus]*. Maybe it was a good idea, maybe a bad idea. I don't know. I felt that Shakespeare wasn't as popular, so I thought that was an opportunity. I think that was my dream play. All we did was VGC: Visual Gestural Communication, nothing in ASL, nothing in spoken language. NYDT suggested that we partner with the Broken Box Mime Company, based in New York. I said, "Okay, sure." What we did was give a workshop to their hearing company and our deaf company actors, two groups. They gave us a workshop on mime techniques, and then we did one on VGC techniques. The first half of the day, our actors picked up mime quickly. Of course, deaf people like visual stuff. Then we did the VGC workshop. [The hearing actors] couldn't do it because it requires two people or two groups to work together for a conversation. They could do abstract stuff, but they couldn't hold actual conversations. The guy who led the workshop on their end, he said he learned so much in our workshop. It's not hard if you have an open heart and open mind to listen with your eyes. Many people have no listening or heart-listening skills. They want me to tell them what to do but they don't want to listen or don't have time. That's not integrated. I realize that a lot of deaf people are afraid, hearing people are afraid of Shakespeare. So, I had to edit and summarize each scene. And I said, "Okay, this situation or story, you know the lines, right," but we wanted to focus on the story. We went back and forth on how to do things. So, I set up the story in a circus setting with three rings. In the center was the emperor, and then on the left was Titus, and on the right was the Goth. And the emperor was the master or ringmaster of the two conflicts. So, we did shadow play with lighting, and we did a finger mime film. All of the actors were involved with using their hands in the black and white film, using only their hands. All of them. Then the Aaron character mimed and manipulated people. He then became a puppeteer to fool people. The audience was shocked they could understand *Titus*. That was the point. Yes, it was bloody. The rape, we showed it using shadow play and you could see what was happening. And you could understand now why Titus went berserk. So, with all that, both the hearing and deaf audiences saw and experienced the same show.

Jill: So interesting, both your examples, *Our Town* and *Titus*, both had what? Deaf and hearing equality on stage.

Monique: Yes.

Jill: So, they brought their art and work together without communication barriers.

Monique: Yes. Yes.

Jill: The next question is about how plays can become accessible for deaf audiences. You talked about *Titus* becoming visual, and deaf people could easily understand it because of the visual communication. What are other examples or strategies?

Monique: Provide a pre-show or post-show dialogue. Include wine and cheese and crackers. Then we can talk about the basic stories that you'll see in this play. We share name signs, names, and all that. What the climate is, what the situation and conflict are. We don't tell the ending, but share this information so they're prepared and can go into the show and understand. Here's an example. The Shakespeare Theatre Company did *Old Times* by Harold Pinter. My job was to bring in deaf people to see the show. But we didn't have a pre-show discussion, none of that. We didn't plan anything. People came to the show and I was introducing the name signs because it was an interpreted show. After the show, people kept asking me in the lobby and we had so much dialogue. We were there so long we had to leave the lobby at closing. People really wanted to understand the psychology, schizophrenia, all that. I think it's really important we have that place for a pre-, or post-discussion. It's nice to have a fluent signer explaining things and answering questions before seeing the play. Having that discussion with a first party rather than a third party. It then becomes even more accessible.

Jill: What about more traditional access strategies like captioning, interpreters. You know how interpreters can really fail sometimes, captions can, too, or they can work wonderfully. In your opinion, what makes it successful in terms of access?

Monique: Involving the community. Often, [hearing theatre companies] don't involve the community. They make the decisions for them. That's really a big failure. We have to have people who are deaf and invest in that company also. It's a two-way street. Involve and motivate them, see what works or doesn't work, and communicate this to the team so the team can know and figure out how to resolve it. We forget that often the mayor's office for deaf and hard of hearing people has resources that they can use for better captioning, or report when a software app doesn't work. Again, it's not really—they just want shortcuts, that's the problem. They want a fast remedy. No, it takes time to try different things, test things out, and then send out surveys. People don't want to deal with surveys or with deaf people's feedback. "Here it is, we're done, we're good." The federal requirements, they get that money and say, "Okay, it's checked off my list. Done."

Jill: True.

Monique: So—yeah, you see that, too?

Jill: In my experience, yeah.

Monique: Like with *Tribes*, they had the language on the walls. It was really lovely. One show had nothing to do with deaf people, but The Living Room—no, no. [THINKS] I think it was Woolly Mammoth. They did a show, and I can't remember the name of the show, but it had nothing to do with deaf people. But I think they spoke English and Spanish. I could see that foreign languages had the same challenges and issues, but again, they used walls instead of placing the captions on the far end of the stage, making audience members have to move their eyes far away from the stage and missing things on stage. It was the same with, uh, *Color Party*? Marlee Matlin wrote a play for the Kennedy Center, *Purple Party* something. Sorry, I can't remember the name, but it was cool how they put the captions in different places. Again, the director—that's another issue. Sometimes the director doesn't want anything, like access, interfering, or ruining vision or their aesthetic of stage. It's an ego thing.

Andy: This question, you can answer from different perspectives, such as an actor, director, DASL, whatever you want. Thinking about a production that was very inclusive, what strategies were used during auditions, rehearsals, and performances? Specific things that a director or actor did that helped the production be inclusive and accessible.

Monique: I haven't seen that happen with auditions. Often, they don't include the DASL in the auditions. That has to happen way, way sooner in the process. Really, it should happen in the pre-production because it really helps handle logistics. Oh, what kind of deaf people are you envisioning? Are they SEE [Signed Exact English] signers, ASL, or minimal language? Are they hard of hearing, deaf-like, or they are deaf but behave hard of hearing? Speaking, don't sign, all that. That's why it's really important to have that individual involved in the preliminary production meeting. For example, recently I got an email from a theatre in Florida. They're doing *Silent Sky*. It's a beautiful story, really. Lauren Gunderson said one character was hard of hearing. I said, "Oh, okay." I read it and I saw nothing about that character that was hard of hearing. So, we had a video meeting and chatted. I said there was nothing. She said, "What do you mean?" I said, "Oh, hard of hearing people have mannerisms and behaviors." She asked like what, and I said, "Missing when people speak from behind them and not responding, being startled when tapped, and so forth." They have nothing to sign, but they have these mannerisms. Or they'll dominate conversations, which is common among hard of hearing people—

Jill: Or doing the fake nod thing!

Monique: Yes, yes, that! Exactly. She was astonished. I said, "You want hard of hearing, but there's nothing. I encourage you to contact hard-of-hearing organizations in Florida, maybe like late-deafened adults or any of these." She said, "Ohhhh." Even A.G. Bell. It's a huge organization. Audiology centers. I'm sure they have people who come together to talk. She said, "Oh, wow, great suggestion!" I'm glad she's doing that now before they started auditioning. They're doing it this January. Anyway, that's an example that we need to think about. Do we need interpreters? What kind of interpreters? They [hearing theatre companies] often try to hire them one day before, or one week before. No, you have to do that way sooner in the process. Often interpreters are already booked two to three months prior. I have to put up with that again and again, and then I end up doing all the work myself. I have to call around and beg people. Even call in a few favors from friends. It's not fun for deaf actors, really. Or for the DASL. During rehearsals, having interpreters set in place, like OSF [Oregon Shakespeare Festival] tends to have two or rather three—the third is a standby for if one of the two gets sick or has scheduling issues, which is nice. Again, we need to educate directors, stage managers, and hearing actors to not stand in front of interpreters. It happens and they block me. I'm like, come on! Or when we have breaks, and then the stage manager speaks and they don't think about the deaf actors. Maybe we're in the bathroom or in another room during breaks and don't see the stage manager. Then later they tell me and I'm like, "Oh, I had no idea," and maybe the schedule has changed. So, I have to remind them to make sure an interpreter is there next to them the next time; don't expect the interpreters to independently notify us themselves. Sometimes deaf actors don't know and we have to train them on how to advocate for themselves. That's not the theatre's job. I don't know. That's a responsibility, but then again, it's important to train them so they'll know. It's the same with scheduling if—recently I was involved with *Richard III* for the New York Shakespeare Festival. I was the Duchess of York. For example. We had another [deaf actor]—who was the understudy for me, but also played in the ensemble, in different roles. And then we had a DASL. So, who was the interpreter for whom? Which one of us? The understudy had a lot of sword-fighting scenes, while I was with the primary actors going over the lines, but that understudy needed an interpreter for safety issues. The DASL is teaching signs, too. They're all important duties, so we needed six interpreters—or three could rotate because we sometimes came together. One time—oh, not one time, but in that show, the director thought an ensemble member could become an "interpreter." On the actor's resume, it said they signed ASL. Nope. They learned ASL maybe 10 years ago and hadn't used it since then. And the director didn't ask if they could sign until after that. "Oh, shit!" We literally had to hire another actor who could sign but this was already in the third week of rehearsals. Luckily, they had a lot of money, but what if they didn't? That's why it's important to have a preliminary meeting so we can figure out the logistics of what we need, how to plan it, etc. After—during the show, it was interesting, because we needed access for cues. Lighting, or would we need interpreters? It's nice to have interpreters for conversations with other actors, which is part of networking, but it's not required. If it's low-budget, we would have to do it ourselves, but if the budget is there, okay, we need two interpreters—one for one wing and another for the other wing, or emergencies. They can be on standby, ready to work. We still needed them while setting up the lighting cues because the hearing actors needed that, too.

Jill: You've directed many plays, and I'm sure some were deaf and hearing integrated. So, what specific thing did you do during rehearsals to help create a cohesive or good collaborative group and inclusiveness for both?

Monique: I establish rituals. Like I'll say, "My name is Monique, and now I'm (character's name)." And we go around the room. Then it's the same after rehearsal, but we reverse the process, and I say, "I'm back to Monique again." So, we all laugh and sometimes we can vent, not too much, but a bit like, "Today, I didn't feel very good," or "How do you feel?" "I'm great because I got a role for another play." And we go around the room and we encourage signing and being more verbal, then going to focus on the character. That's really very helpful.

Jill: Why is that helpful?

Monique: First, we need to recognize we are people first. That makes us more human. And we're still doing theatre exercises, knowing that we're now in this space. Not at home, not at work. We're here, so the mindset shifts to the stage. It's the same for both deaf and hearing people. They're equals. So after, sometimes we'll go out to have drinks or coffee or whatever. It really helps them to say, "Oh, okay, what do we need to work on?" Sometimes we're so focused on the lines and scenes that we don't have time to chat about the play itself. So, when we go out, we can remove that pressure. That's really helpful, also. Some people do leave right after, so we feel they're not interested in us or the theatre. They're just punching in and out. Okay. That says a lot about that person. It doesn't happen often, but it's happened once or twice. It's important to have that feeling of unity. Oftentimes I'll try to get them to talk or say, "I've noticed my character isn't this way," and then we go around. Sometimes the director has to be open-minded. If you don't feel right about something, I ask, "What's your interpretation? What do you see? Tell me." As the director, I have to listen to their view, and maybe we can try it and show me what they have in mind. If it's great, I'll accept it and we can keep it. If it doesn't work, I won't let it happen and they have to accept my vision. But now they know I'm open to negotiations. It's all about negotiation and what you bring to the table. It's unfortunate if you have limited time because I don't give too much space for negotiation then. But when you have three or four weeks, then yeah, because it's important they feel they own the show and the character.

Jill: What are some unique challenges working with musicals and deaf and hearing integration?

Monique: I addressed that recently in Canada. I wrote an opera piece and it wasn't opera at all. [LAUGHS] Okay, but really, basically, you have to have breathing techniques, even a workshop because breathing can help you control the beats. The speed. The mood. Storytelling. It's interesting because hearing actors tend to speak and then inhale and keep speaking while deaf people can just keep signing and forget to breathe. And then they speed up and I have to tell them to slow down. So it's really important that deaf actors take breathing classes, or workshops, to help. This applies to all, though. It doesn't matter which genre, but it helps open up emotionally. It's an opportunity to feel or for the rhythm of music itself. I do that. The second is to understand what the songs are really about. I often will sign and not understand what the song is about, what the metaphors or abstract information are. I just sign what the text says. The third is translation. How much translation do we do, or how much do we keep it similar? Is it locked in? But play with the classifiers and show the rhymes, similar, with Shakespeare's sonnets. Using handshapes or whatever. Fourth, performing. Really, if a person memorizes the songs, it's a lot easier. Some hearing people will memorize the songs by rote because they can hear it repeatedly, but deaf people can't, so they have to sign it and repeat it by rote. So, I did *Cloud Nine*. I love that play, *Cloud Nine*, and it had a major song. I wanted to build muscle memory in signing and moving, the choreography, in all directions, like a conductor. After they incorporated that, then I was ready to play with different speeds. Once they could do that, then I showed them the speeds to do certain songs. They got it. That's how I worked, in sequence. I couldn't skip these steps.

Jill: In watching musical theatre, the transitions between the main characters and the ensemble can be a struggle for me. How can that be handled successfully?

Monique: There are techniques like eye gaze. It's really helpful for audiences to know where to look. That's one technique. That's why musicals that use that are very successful. Or you can use your hand to present something, in a flourishing style. That way you know it's coming. The lighting designer helping with maybe turning up the light brighter by two or three percent. When that happens, my eyes can't help but look at something that's becoming brighter, or even color shifts. Changes in the rhythm of signing, signing slower but larger. It has to be really sharp. That creates a clear distinction when you flip.

Jill: Why do you think it's important to do integrated deaf and hearing theatre. What are the benefits?

Monique: Some of the benefits are for community strengthening, working together. It's an opportunity for them to experience how to work with others, teaching each other. I feel there's always something they can teach each other. And if the money is there, sure!

Jill: Artistically, what do you think it can bring to the table?

Monique: It's really about how we'll always have "others" no matter where or what kind. And it's showing the humanity of interaction. And for example, interestingly, when you see Shakespeare, you see that hearing people often will have frills on their costumes, fancy costumes with patterns. Deaf actors can have that, but it's different. People will look at that and ask why. Oh, it's visually distracting or noisy to have the fringes. It's interesting, I think. Like how they set up sign codes. Hearing actors have their codes, and deaf actors have their own. And…having different goals for integrated theatre. Yeah. One time, I was working with Damon Rodriguez, who works a lot in Portland, Oregon. He's a big name in the west. So, he wasn't expecting to have a deaf actor—me—in his show *Romeo and Juliet*. So, I played the mother of Romeo. Okay. He said, "What can I do with you?" I said, "Don't worry, we'll do VGC. I won't use ASL. It wouldn't make sense because I'm the only deaf person in the show, so I'll use VGC and make it reasonable." He said, "Okaaaaay." He was skeptical. So I thought, we did the prologue where the mayor is explaining the two deaths to the town and all that. I used VGC and he could understand me easily, which surprised him. I told him that it was VGC. Oh, okay. He said he wanted everyone to use VGC, and I agreed. It's interesting because the audience really enjoyed that moment. Now they're softened up, and now they watch a deaf mother who has love, is able to communicate. They learned from it. If it was in ASL, it'd have been a barrier of a different language they couldn't understand. That's something we can teach, gesture. Tell hearing people who forget that they can use their hands.

Andy: If a director came up to you and asked, what's the most important thing I can do in my production process, what would your advice be?

Monique: How would I answer that question, hmm. If a hearing person, a director, came up to me and asked how I'd make it a successful process?

Andy: Yeah, one piece of advice to them, what would you say?

Monique: I can't just have one!

Andy: Nope, just one!

Monique: Oh, wow. Find a fucking good interpreter.

[ALL LAUGH]

Monique: Yeah. No bad interpreters. Bad interpreters, bad idea. Deaf people are fed up and will leave if you don't have that. If you're doing *Children of a Lesser God*, *Tribes*, you have to have good interpreters, then we can negotiate. Bad interpreters, you can't negotiate. That barrier is there already.

Jill: What do you hope to see in terms of integrated theatre in the future?

Monique: We need to support each other, go see my shows and I go to see yours. Often, we don't do that. That's not showing community. I don't know. It's all for the self.

Andy: Is there anything that we did not ask yet that you'd like to discuss?

Monique: Translation. That's a big thing. We—NYDT is developing a technique. Maybe NTID, I heard, is doing a similar thing. We developed a "viscript" or a visual script. Meaning people aren't writing scripts; they're signing videos as a visual script. The script shares signed stories about what is happening, the character name signs, stage directors, and dialogues. All of that is filmed and then edited in order. We experimented—we did a recent workshop with actors who weren't part of this collaboration. It was their first time seeing the viscript, and they were amazed. If they had read the script struggling with translation and thinking about how to do everything, what the character's goal was, etc., it'd have taken them one or two weeks, and time would have flown away. But with viscript, it took them one day. They already memorized everything. Maybe later we will try to develop a software program so it becomes friendlier. So, we can easily copy and paste the signs. We want to do that.

CROM SAUNDERS

Crom Saunders is a Deaf actor, performer, director of artistic sign language, and educator. Stage appearances include Feste in *Twelfth Night in ASL* (2006). He has performed at improv events across the country, as well as on the ASL Comedy Tour circuit. His own one-man show, *Cromania!*, has toured nationally and internationally. Saunders has interpreted dozens of plays, from children's theatre to Broadway musicals. As a DASL, he focuses on Shakespeare and has worked with interpreters and deaf actors at Oregon Shakespeare Festival and Chicago Shakespeare. He is currently an associate professor and acting director of Deaf Studies at Columbia College, Chicago.

Andy: How do you define the word *integrated* as it relates to a theatrical production?

Crom: For a production that has deaf, hard of hearing, and hearing people involved together, I think it's important that all the roles be equal. Regardless of who has the role. Onstage, behind the scenes, off stage, on set, whatever, because what happens often is that communication tends to be superficial with deaf people involved. But a lot of things happening in production are organic. Meaning people throw out ideas, discuss why not. That part is often missed. Group discussions, input, there is not always an equal opportunity for deaf people to be involved. So integrated, that means there is equal opportunity for communication, consideration of input, questions or whatever, any ideas are considered, and not just being informed what they need to do by the director, etc.

Jill: Do you think that if the show has one deaf person, is that integrated?

Crom: It depends on how it's done. It starts really any time you have a deaf person present, accommodations must be made all around for everyone involved. It's a start. There are different degrees of integration, I would say.

Jill: And in your opinion should integrated theatre have deaf culture involved, infused in the show themes?

Crom: Interesting question, because again, I think it depends on the production goals. You know, there is a difference between inclusion of deaf characters or the deaf perspective, whatever, or incidental—you are deaf, not affiliated to the story, just one of the group members. The first part, yes; the second part, it depends. I think the second part would mean people one hundred percent should be aware of how to interact with the person, not necessarily just for the audience, but lead by example. With the first part, you want to teach the audience.

Andy: Suppose the director wants to select a cast that is deaf, even if only one deaf actor, or use ASL during the show. Do you think the director has the responsibility of making sure the whole show is accessible to the audience?

Crom: Definitely. The director's vision is what directs the show. The show itself, for whom? The audience, right? You have to know your audience and make sure you fit the goal. The goal is to shock, give them a story, or educate them. It should be equally accessible for all. The director, I agree, is responsible. It's part of their responsibility for the show.

Jill: In your experience, do hearing directors realize their responsibility?

Crom: It varies. I mean, there's a whole spectrum. There are some that are really open and want to listen and see what they can do and absorb the information well. The others are like, "This is how it will be." That's it.

Jill: Sometimes roles in professional theatre are strictly defined about who does what. The director does this. The house manager does that. In that situation, it can be a little difficult for directors to influence the audience's access. Right?

Crom: Yes. For what it's worth, I've noticed a trend lately. Again, my personal experience. I think I have had more opportunities recently to work with directors who are open to integrating different perspectives. In my experience, those directors who are open-minded to integrated theatre and producing work that is integrated get more grant money. Their theatres accomplished more during the pandemic. They survived better compared to other theatres. Their audience tends to be more diverse.

Andy: In an ideal world, what's your vision of what an integrated production would look like?

Jill: Money is not important. All the money in the world is available. What would you do?

Crom: Ideal. Yes. I wasn't thinking of money, but it would be nice to have a budget so there are no worries. I think really, when you talk about money, I think about numbers. The number of people involved in a stage production is an important tool. DASL is one, but why limit the production to just one expert? You can have a team. Often, we see set designers as well. You have teams that build a set, teams that build something else. ASL experts, DASL, a dialect coach if needed, actors, mentors, etc., all just for supporting people on stage. That kind of thing is ideal. You could even have a deaf culture consultant who would be separate from an ASL consultant because there's a lot involved. One will advise the cast and director, the other applies [the advice].

Jill: In the dream world, what else would you include in integrated shows?

Crom: For me personally, the concept of engaging deaf people—again it does not necessarily mean showcasing deaf people, just including them. You know, including them as part of the play, the artist pool, I like that. For example, in a production of *Equus*, a long time ago, I had the role of the doctor and there was no discussion of the fact that I was deaf, but the other actors would do things like tap me. There was stuff that made sense. I signed to them and they talked to me and the show went on. We all could understand each other in that world. It was my favorite production and the director felt that she could retire after that. She felt like it was a wrap. It was ideal and perfect. When you have talent that is not spotlighted, you know, you are not doing like, "Oh, look at this [deaf] actor. This is so cool, there are skills that match this show." Because you bring something to the table. That's my favorite.

Jill: So that ideal, have you experienced it? Either as someone involved or as an audience member?

Crom: Yes. *Equus* was my example. It was pretty close to that ideal. Some things could be improved but I liked how the director established that, just that we just spoke different languages but understood each other in that "world." I saw Josh Castille in *The Hunchback of Notre Dame*. The character is supposed to have a hearing loss, yes, but still, it was perfect how it all was integrated. They selected a well-chosen actor. He fit the role.

Jill: In *The Hunchback of Notre Dame*, how was integration handled? There was one deaf character, right?

Crom: Another character signed sometimes too. You know, actors learned from him, or knew—like the dad, Frollo, he raised him, which means he [Frollo] could communicate with him superficially. But it was all within the context of the story, of him growing up, part deaf-blind, so that part of his upbringing, who he was, how he identified and his identity. But it wasn't spotlighted the whole time, you know. The signing itself was not the point. Of course, Josh signs beautifully, the songs were really cool, but that wasn't the point. The point was the delivery of his character, in his own language. The show wasn't marketed as having a deaf actor in it, but rather as 'this is our version of the story.'

Andy: Jill and I are curious what kind of specific things are happening in the room to make it successful? The director wants everyone to work together collaboratively but it doesn't always happen that way. In a perfect situation, how would that happen? What specific things need to happen for you?

Crom: Again, it is my personal bias, partially because of how I direct shows. As a director, I am very organic. I let the actors develop a lot of the show because really, we cast them for that reason, to represent the people. If they are comfortable in their skin, meaning they are immersed in the role, then they will really bring their character to life. I have noticed that I prefer that process, too, for how to engage and integrate any person on the stage, how to integrate different people with different backgrounds and experiences. The director really needs to open their minds and ask what the actors can do for the show. Rather than "you will do this." I have seen that. It tends to not turn out as well. There are a few directors here in Chicago who have done a lot of work with deaf actors, but they tend to be very strict and tell them how things will occur on stage. It always feels very artificial. It feels very standardized and forced, not natural. I think a lot of discussion needs to happen during rehearsals, during blocking, and everything to really see what happens as things go along, naturally. I feel like sometimes the director does not even say, "Oh, that works! Keep it." They just say nothing. But if the actor feels good, they will keep doing it. I think that discussion needs to happen. But also there should be that freedom, throughout the entire production, to see where things go. Workshopping it as you go along.

Jill: Let's talk about audience accessibility. There are many different approaches like open captions, GalaPro, the gooseneck captioning devices, interpreters sitting off to the side, standing next to actors, double casting, 'voice of' characters. In your experience, which is the most effective and why?

Crom: In terms of accessibility for a regular production, not integrated, I do tend to prefer captions because it gives me an opportunity to see and analyze what's happening on stage. But with integrated theatre, it really works when there is a double cast. This can be a voice actor together with a deaf actor on stage. Or it can be a voice over, with actors to side or off stage, allowing the audience to really watch the signing and for those who don't know signs to watch and still be able to listen. It's really accessible for both. I like it, too, when it's more interactive, like a lot of Deaf West's work. Not all of it, but a lot of it tends to be interactive. I think my favorite is *A Streetcar Named Desire*. The first time I saw Troy [Kotsur] onstage, I remember, I was just in awe. They had replicated the set design of New

Orleans, old-style French Quarter and the balconies and all the voice actors were on the balconies. They were drinking tea, looking down, and voicing. And all the sign actors performed on the stage. It was really cool. The hearing actors were still involved, but you could even forget they were there. It wasn't visually distracting. It was really clever. It was not disembodied voicing. But it also wasn't voice actors shadowing the deaf actors. That can be distracting, sometimes.

Jill: What are some strategies that are not effective when providing access for integrated plays?

Crom: Sometimes, it's really a designer's choice, which means it can impact the audience in understanding what's going on. For example, in *Spring Awakening*, there's one song where the actors wore gloves. It was too dark and it was awful. Those of us who were deaf in the audience were looking at each other, including me, were looking at each other in confusion. We couldn't understand what was happening at all. Only the people who could hear could appreciate that part, because they could hear the singing. But for us watching the signing, we were totally lost. I also remember a while back, I saw the National Theatre of the Deaf's *Curious and Curiouser*, their version of *Alice in Wonderland*. It had many amazing choices. But one thing they had was a puppet. It was hard to understand because we could only see the hands signing. No facial expressions. The design can really impact the show. Another example. Related to modes of accessibility, sometimes the caption setup splits the audience's attention so they have to look back and forth between the captions and the action on stage. Sometimes they just don't work. Maybe there's a Wi-Fi disconnect. Captioning is not always as reliable compared to live interpreters. If there are live interpreters, I prefer them to be onstage, integrated with, maybe a little dressed up to match the characters, but look like they're part of the production and not random. Not like two black birds in a field of flowers. A lot depends on the setup rather than the accessibility mode.

Andy: Why is it important for deaf and hearing artists to work together, what's the benefit for the deaf artists? What's the benefit for the hearing artists?

Crom: The craft—learning from each other. Theatre has so much to offer anyone that wants to be a part of it. Anyone can learn from working with colleagues. It's a craft. Also, any time people have the opportunity to work across cultures, work with people from different backgrounds, disability, life experiences, so much learning happens. During the workshops, during the rehearsals, so much learning is happening. One thing I enjoy as a DASL is doing research. Not just the research I do for the story itself, not just how to sign a specific thing but why sign it a particular way. I enjoy that. Often you dive into a rabbit hole learning the history. I think it benefits hearing people to learn more about interaction with the deaf world, but also deaf people benefit. Theatre has a long history. That established theatre world has not always been accessible to deaf people, and now they're learning, "Oh, this is how this is done." Learning what they can incorporate or adapt in a deaf-friendly production. I also notice people who really invest in working with deaf actors, often they can maintain contact with the deaf community, become more fluent in signing, working with deaf people again regularly, and vice versa.

Jill: What do you hope to see happening in the theatre community in the next five to ten years in terms of accessibility?

Crom: I hope to see more deaf people behind the scenes. More directors, more writers, not necessarily writing or directing deaf-centered stories either, because obviously they are deaf, but just have a deaf person direct whatever. Why limit themselves to their community only? If you do good work, you should be able to do good work anywhere. Writing, directing, tech work even. I would like to see more of that happen overall.

Andy: Changing subjects here: from a DASL's perspective, what is the most important thing to consider when working in an integrated production?

Crom: I think this answer fits people who work as DASLs but also people who work with DASLs. *Learn what a DASL is.* That role is still very unclear. Many people don't know what a DASL does. I have seen people approach this very well, very professionally, with all the responsibilities that I believe should be included in the role. While others just basically show up and give thumbs up to the actors' signing. Being a DASL is more than just being a sign consultant. It's more than that. It's really equal to the dramaturg role. But it also involves consulting on linguistic elements. Those two areas can't be separated. It's a lot of work and that also means their pay should be equivalent to the amount of work involved. The DASL should be aware going into the job that it's a big-time commitment. It's a lot. And sometimes they will face people saying that they're fine, they don't need a DASL. The DASL needs to say, "No, no, no. I am here for this work and I will do this work with you."

Jill: Can you expand on what you see as the DASL's role?

Crom: As a DASL, I prepare myself, before even meeting with interpreters or actors. I learn what the story is about, what the background is.

Then, I always call for a meeting with the director and stage manager. I ask them many questions about their vision. Because the language choices I make will change to match their vision. Again, it's very similar to dramaturgy work. I think it would be amazing to see more DASLs have training as dramaturgs or have degrees in dramaturgy. I think that's something to keep in mind for the development of this field. Then when I actually start working with signers, often I will analyze and discuss the story and the background with them. I work with them on the translation, but I also explain why I want to see specific translation choices that match the production background, the director's vision, or whatever. I help them remember that it's not just signing, not just the audience seeing what is said. Their signing has to match the character and the role. They have to become the character, that's very important. One of my favorite experiences was working with an MFA student at the University of Illinois in Urbana-Champaign, UIUC. The student was in Shakespeare's *TitusAndronicus*. He played Titus.

Jill: Andrew [Morrill]?

Crom: Yes. I worked with him as his DASL. One time he told me, "You are really so specific about every little thing." I said, "Yes, because your role needs to be believable. You want people to watch and say, 'Oh, yeah. That makes sense, that's Titus.' Not, 'Oh, it's a deaf actor doing this role,' but really being in the role." Seeing him as Titus, period. That made me ask myself, "Am I really that anal?" Maybe I am. But that's because I take this job seriously, really. It should require a lot of time. It's not just polishing the signing. I think a lot of DASLs are under that misconception, because they're told that's the job. Currently there's no formal training for DASLs. There are a few workshops here and there but that's it. I know Monique [Holt] wants to set up some kind of round table discussion about DASLs in general and what their role is.

Jill: In your opinion, is the DASL also responsible for thinking about the audience's accessibility?

Crom: Yes and no. In the same way interpreters will sometimes speak up and say, you know, the lights will not work for this part because it's too dark. They can point out logistics. But should the job description include that? Not necessarily. Sometimes that is part of DASL's work. For example, if an actor walks in front of a signing actor, and you can't see the signing. But being responsible for deciding where the deaf audience should sit, and things like that, not so much. They can give input, but include that as part of the job description? I don't think so.

Jill: Not necessarily responsible, but advising? For example, where to put the captioning devices. I asked Alexandria [Wailes] the same question and she was a hard no, there should be an accessibility consultant. Keep that role separate from the DASL role.

Crom: I think that's better, yes. I mean there should be room for input from everyone. The DASL should be able to offer suggestions, but again, it's not their job.

Jill: What about set design? Lighting design, costume design? Should DASLs be involved with pre-production meetings to advise and provide input and feedback on visual accessibility?

Crom: That's a great question, and I don't really have a lot of experience myself with that. I have provided feedback about costumes and how they can impact the ability to see the stage sign clearly. It couldn't hurt. It really couldn't hurt. But again, when the DASL's role has been clarified and people can offer more experienced training in that field, then we will see that role expand. The role could include being part of pre-production, yes. I think it's worth considering.

Jill: As a DASL, have you ever experienced being called in with the director and being involved with general auditions?

Crom: No, but I have experienced screening interpreters for interpreted shows with the interpreter coordinator. It's kind of similar, because you have to "audition" and sign the song, or a passage from Shakespeare, or whatever for the screening. And then I sit with the interpreter coordinator and discuss why this interpreter is a good fit for that story, for this part, and not for this. For actors, no. All my DASL work has been with actors who have already been cast.

Jill: Do you think DASLs should be involved, giving advice about actors, deaf actors, their signing, and skills during the audition?

Crom: I think no. As a director myself, I think directors make the ultimate decision who to select, for better or worse. The DASL could, again, provide input on signing skill. Also, like Andy said, an integrated show could have ASL in it. That doesn't always mean the actor is deaf. Maybe in that situation, the actors will be taught ASL. In that case, casting is not necessarily about their fluency, but more about their acting ability and their ability to portray the role. I think no. Feedback, maybe, but responsibility? No.

Jill: Suppose a deaf actor shows up who doesn't speak, just signs. How does the director judge and evaluate their acting ability? Based on what?

Crom: Good question. They should have an interpreter for the audition. Period. They should have one. But that means it's on the interpreter to expand and explain too. That's not so great.

Jill: Is that appropriate? What are the boundaries? The interpreter has the power to judge and if the interpreters themselves aren't that great, that would impact how the hearing director, who doesn't know sign language, perceives the deaf person's acting ability.

Crom: Right, exactly. I agree with that. I've experienced that in an acting class before. The teacher really relied heavily on the interpreter, not on my work. That's a good area for discussion. It's a very gray area, obviously. But again, the DASLs can give input on various things, but the vision is on the director. It becomes more of an assistant director that way. Is that the role of the DASL to become assistant director? I think no. If there's a team, then yes. The DASL team—one focuses on the language, one focuses on the logistics, one could focus on supporting and working closely with the director on the integration. Having a team will solve a lot of these questions. Who does what, who'll be responsible for what, who will shoulder the responsibility, etc.

Jill: My last follow-up question has to do with translation. There are a range of different approaches, from actors translating lines themselves with consultation from the DASL all the way to the script translation is done in advance and given to the actors as 'frozen'—meaning they can't make changes to it. In this range of approaches, where is your preference and comfort zone?

Crom: Again, productions vary. Sometimes actors have more freedom to translate because it makes sense for that production. The size of their role, their work up to that point, their experience with DASLs. Sometimes, it makes more sense for the script to be translated and given to them. I had one experience where it was kind of half and half. I worked with Dr. Peter Novak on his San Francisco production of *Twelfth Night in ASL*. The Philadelphia production was the original one, from his dissertation work. He did the production again in San Francisco and I participated in that, the same role as Peter Cook in the Philadelphia version. Feste. The script was already translated, and it was just given to me. At the same time, Peter Cook was the only one out of the whole cast who created his own translations. Peter Novak said, "I don't want you to sign Peter's translation. You are not Peter." I said, "Thank you, I don't want to be in Peter's shoes. They're big shoes to fill." I translated the lines myself. We did not have a DASL until the last week [of rehearsals]. Adrian Blue. Which meant the translation work that I had rehearsed, he revised, so for me that required a lot of mental changes and memorizing the lines again. His advice was good. The advantage of having pre-translated work is being able to focus on the character. You already have the translation and you can focus on the character in depth. But at the same time, it does not always feel natural. It may not fit me. I might never sign those lines in that particular way, in any of my own interpretations of the character. But directors have their own vision. Other times I've translated, but it might not be the best fit if I don't have feedback. I think it's really important, again, to have that loop, that feedback loop. The DASL can translate some of the lines in the script in advance or work with the actor's translations, but there should be an ongoing interchange, rather than all or nothing. Not, "Here you go. You follow this, period." Not, "It's all yours. I'll just sit back and watch. Looks clear enough." I think the better approach would be some of both.

Jill: But hearing actors don't have the ability to modify the words at all. Right? Do deaf people have a little bit of an advantage here?

Crom: True. At the same time, I have to disagree with that a little. They can't change the words necessarily, but they can change their delivery. The way the words are spoken, the cadence, the accent. They can change those. That's where their expertise is. I have also seen—my first-ever theatre experience, not as an actor, as an interpreter. I was interpreting the show for my good friend's production. I was interpreting for him. I was attending rehearsals, watching them. One actor almost never performed his character the same way twice. This made the director agitated because the show was already open. It was already too late to be making changes in rehearsal. Changes needed to stop. But this guy, the lines were all the same, but one night he was more serious, another night happier. It was very interesting and also frustrating. I had to figure out how I was going to interpret him the night I was interpreting. I had to watch him from my peripheral vision to see what he was doing. So, there is some flexibility there. But deaf people have more of an advantage of really creating the language.

Andy: Some DASLs prefer to use gloss scripts and some prefer videos of the signing. What are your thoughts about the two different styles?

Crom: I don't like any kind of discussion about ASL that isn't in ASL. You know. For example, in linguistics classes, the teacher is discussing ASL by speaking [not signing]. Why? It doesn't make sense to talk about the linguistics of ASL without using ASL. Similar concept. I rehearse in ASL, learn the lines in ASL. I prefer to record myself; I prefer that. It just feels more natural, more organic. And honestly, muscle memory, you know, the more you sign the lines in ASL, the more you build that muscle memory. And of changes to the signs based on feedback. Then when it's time to actually sign on stage, you know, you may make small changes as you perform, but it's still a natural and fluid expression. I think a gloss is really open to interpretation too. I might sign what I read one way, but another person has a different vision. But if we discuss in ASL, then we can agree on the same vision.

Andy: If you record yourself, do you notice actors copying your way of signing, getting into character the same way you do? Have you ever experienced that happening?

Crom: Probably, but again, I work with that knowing that I can explain why they should not mimic what I'm doing. Make sure they use their own facial expressions and so forth. Tell them things they can change to help fit their interpretation of the character. For example, with *Titus Andronicus*, the actor, Andrew, his family or Titus's family, all sign. They should all sign in their own individual ways. I videotaped the translation and taught them the lines, but I met with them after they memorized the lines to provide feedback, made changes to their expressions. It happens, yes, but hopefully, the DASL will have an opportunity to work on that and correct whatever is needed to make sure it's really their own signing rather than just rote-copying. But I have noticed it happening, yes.

Jill: Can you talk about some of the unique challenges working as a DASL for musical theatre?

Crom: I have worked as a DASL with interpreters who are interpreting musicals. I haven't worked with deaf actors for musicals. I want to make that distinction. Many interpreters want to match the music exactly with the signing, rhythm, but sometimes that really can throw off the translation. They try to make the lyrics look cool, cute. They are "dancing" and signing, not really interpreting. At the same time, you don't want to throw out the musicality. It is a song. It's supposed to have rhythm. So how do we meld both? That's the challenge. And the other part, I cannot always hear everything in the music. How some words are sung, I can't always hear that. I have to rely on the interpreters and their input. Right there, it's already a skewed perspective. That isn't necessarily bad. I just can't always take their word for it. But I have to work off that. It's a challenge.

Andy: During the rehearsal process, how can the DASL contribute to creating an inclusive environment for the whole group of actors?

Crom: One thing that can be really effective is to have the opportunity to talk with the director during rehearsals. If I can sit at the director's table during rehearsals, I can observe the rehearsals. I can ask the director to pause so I can give feedback to the actors, or ask the director to take notes on my feedback. Then when we discuss notes, my feedback is part of that. Directors should always make sure they have notes from the DASL. For the overall rehearsal. Not necessarily just the signers. For example, sometimes, I have to let the hearing actors know to look at the deaf actors when they are signing. How else are their characters going to know what the deaf characters are saying? That kind of thing. Notes in general from the DASL, incorporated with the director's notes. That way you get a sense that the DASL and the director's authority are the same. So, it's not like DASL is way below the director. No, they are on the same level as the director and stage manager. They have the authority to provide feedback, and recommendations on what to do. Sometimes during rehearsal, I am shut down [as DASL]. I have to take notes and give them to the actors individually or email everyone later. But it's really effective—it's really effective if communication happens at the same time when we're sitting at the table together with the director. I can nudge the director or even the stage manager. I can nudge them while watching rehearsals to bring something to their attention. Then later, we can have an intensive discussion about those things.

Jill: As a DASL, do you have any activities you like to use to develop relationships between deaf actors and hearing actors?

Crom: Well, what I do most of the time, to be honest, is create social opportunities. Let them have an opportunity to interact and learn to communicate on their own as themselves, not as characters. So that means interacting. So, I've hosted social gatherings, invited the cast to mingle. After the rehearsals, we go and socialize. I encourage that. But like icebreaker games, or warm-up activities, I don't really do that myself. I mean, I could, but I have never really done that. I just tend to encourage individual interactions in the group. Now I'm thinking maybe I should. [LAUGHS]

Andy: Do you have examples of when the process was not inclusive or accessible? And looking back, how would you resolve any issues?

Crom: A couple of examples. As an actor in a production, I was the only deaf actor in one show. No one else in the cast signed. I was actually a last-minute replacement for another actor who just couldn't sign. He really struggled, at which point they decided that perhaps they should have a deaf actor. I had only three weeks for rehearsal, that's all. I was mostly on my own, translating, but I noticed that some of the interactions between characters were not realistic because the actors were used to working with hearing people or those who could hear a little. I let the director know this, but the director did not really listen and kept saying, "This is how I want to do this." Because it didn't look real, it was not believable. I kind of half-followed what the director wanted, but during the show sometimes I would just ignore what the director wanted and do my own thing. Just so it was more believable. For example, a person comes in, there is loud banging and I'm supposed to be completely unaware of that. But everyone is looking in the direction of the banging. So, I would lightly glance instead of really turning my head fast or acting like I totally missed it. I acknowledged what was happening. For me, intuitively, I'm a deaf character, so I have to make it work somehow. The director had no idea. I had no interpreter either. Really, it was a lot of lipreading, getting by, my first-ever experience working in a community theatre and it was interesting. From that experience, I learned what I want to have when I work in a show. One other time that didn't work, when I saw a show where the interpreters shadowed the actors. But the way it was staged, the way it was done, it felt like the interpreter was more prominent than the deaf actor. It looked like the deaf actor was secondary to the interpreter. It felt like it was too much acting on the part of the interpreter, too much presence. I don't know if the show had a DASL. I saw the show, I didn't work on it. I wondered if there was actually a DASL or not; if the DASL really understood their role to support the deaf actor's role; or if the DASL just overlooked the problem. It just felt really off. It felt the spotlight was on the wrong person. It felt very ableist or audist.

Jill: Is there anything we haven't asked that we should be asking?

Crom: What can we do to really make the DASL role a profession? Really, it seems like DASL has never been seen as a profession, but it is. It should be. It's a field. What can we do to develop tools for that? How can we create more DASLs who really understand the role and have expertise to go into the field? What needs to be done? Training programs? Degrees? Workshops? I think it's important we think about that. Actively think about it.

Howie Seago

Howie Seago is an award-winning actor, director, and playwright. He began his professional career as co-founder, associate producer, writer, director, and actor for Rainbow's End, an Emmy award winning PBS series for deaf children, then joined the National Theatre of the Deaf. He broke into mainstream theatre with Peter Sellars' *Ajax* (1987), for which he received a Helen Hayes for Outstanding Actor. Seago is also the first Deaf actor to appear in an integrated Shakespeare production (La Jolla Playhouse 1989) and to perform at Oregon Shakespeare Festival, with roles in *Hamlet*, *Cymbeline*, *To Kill a Mockingbird*, *Into the Woods*, and more. His film credits include the Oscar-nominated *Beyond Silence* (1998) and *Wonderstruck* (2017). Seago has also directed for film, television, and the stage. In 2018, Seago received the Gregory A. Falls Sustained Achievement Award in recognition of his contributions to theatre in the Puget Sound region. Most recently, he co-directed *ASL Midsummer Night's Dream* (2018) and directed *Autocorrect Thinks I'm Dead* (2023) for Sound Theatre Company.

Andy: From a director's perspective, how would you define success for an integrated production?

Howie: If they enjoy putting on or doing the play and feel that it's a success and both sides are satisfied. And second, clarity. I find that many plays that have deaf people, I don't understand the signing. For example, NTD used to use "artsy fartsy" signs that I couldn't understand. I didn't understand at all! I remember one show, I performed, then I left the stage and my brother came on, and I couldn't understand my brother! [LAUGHS] The signing was too stylish. So, it's very, very important that the play is clear to both deaf or hearing audiences. And that the play is openly available to deaf people any time. That means a lot. And fully accessible. Even though the whole play isn't in ASL. For example, there's a scene with hearing actors and no signing, but there's an interpreter. That's still a sign of success for me.

Jill: Are you thinking of a specific production?

Howie: I'm thinking of the example of Josh Castille. He was in *The Hunchback of Notre Dame*. His performance was, wow! But not the entire cast signed, no. Sometimes they'd sign as a choral response where the whole cast would sign, but you had to have an interpreter for other parts that Josh's character wasn't involved in. But the demand for interpreted characters was so great because of Josh drawing in the deaf community. So that's a sign of success for me. And that was an integrated show, yes, but he was the only deaf actor. Is that truly an integrated production? I don't know. No, mainstreamed. Where it's one person, I wouldn't call that integrated theatre, no.

Now that you brought up that question, hmmm, how do you define integrated theatre as opposed to mainstreamed. These are different. With me as the only actor, not on stage the entire play, that's not fully accessible to deaf audiences. Integrated means the entire play is accessible. There may be some hearing characters who don't sign but they are signed by other deaf or hearing actors who sign for them on stage. So that show stands on its own with the interpreting built in. Mainstreamed means there is an "interpreter" who signs for a character or other characters and voices or copies for him, but the rest of the cast doesn't sign. No language access. I've done so many of these. It does get lonely often when I'm the only deaf person. But I have had a good life, I mean, career life. I'm lucky.

Jill: Any other productions that you've been involved in or seen that you feel met your definition of success?

Howie: I'd say *To Kill a Mockingbird*. That was so intense and had interesting layers of racism—specifically against Black people—and deaf people incorporated into the show. The overlap of the deaf point of view and Black point of view, and the white woman—the daughter's—point of view, and all of these worked well. It was so good that it looked like it was written that way. That really included deaf culture. I played a mean drunk man, the father Bob Ewell, and I forced my daughter to interpret for me in court. Our sign language was not standard. We used home signs. We decided that my character had gone to a deaf school in another city but couldn't survive more than one year. They threw me out. My character only learned ASL for one year of signing, so my skills were really limited. I made up home signs with my daughter. Carol Padden [a well-known sign language linguist] was really impressed with that. It was really innovative, and all of it was really redneck sign language. [LAUGHS] For example, for HOUSE, I used [SHOWS SIGN RESEMBLING ROOF], and then I used this [TAPS CHEEK] to mean Black. We came up with things like that. Then my daughter was forced to interpret in court, she had to interpret my lies which she knew weren't true. So, it was really filled with powerful layers. During the court scene, I sat at the front in the audience who were looking at the stage. I had to act through my back. So, they couldn't see my face but could see my back. I was completely worn out after every performance. It was so intense. That was the best production because I had full access during rehearsals. One problem I have in mainstreamed and also integrated shows is having no interpreters during breaks. The interpreters need breaks, too. So, my hearing colleagues, some of them will continue having in-depth discussions full of wisdom during breaks, and I can't be part of that. That was one common issue throughout all of the productions. And also, after the show, many will go to the bar to unwind, and I couldn't because of no interpreter. I tried to sit with some of them one-on-one and chat, but then when someone else came into the conversation, I was automatically left out. Socially, that's one problem. So, yeah. It comes with the territory.

Skin of Our Teeth (2007) was also very good. I get goosebumps as I remember. It was very good, and it was directed by Bart Sher. Bart was very sensitive and made sure that I had my needs met. Bart really took advantage of ASL at intervals throughout the show. At the end, there are a few philosophical quotes, and he decided to have me sign them, which was atypical. He had me sign them and it really added another layer of, let's call it, language, emotion, and human nature, to it. Bernard Bragg saw and he was so flabbergasted. He had never seen anything like that before involving only one deaf actor.

Andy: Can you describe a production you've worked on that you found to be particularly inclusive during the audition, rehearsal, and performance?

Howie: I'm thinking of the recent *ASL Midsummer Night's Dream* that I co-directed at Sound Theatre Company. Of course, we had interpreters there in the audition for hearing people, and for deaf people. My co-director was hearing. I ran the auditions mostly by myself. At the rehearsals, it was the same thing. We had a good team of interpreters, two interpreters. We knew we had a lot of work, so we brought in more interpreters in groups. Interpreters are one of the most important parts of integrated shows. We tried to make sure we had teams of several interpreters so we wouldn't depend on one interpreter, because we don't pay much. It's community theatre, so to speak, or rather, one level above community theatre, so we couldn't afford to pay well. Many people were willing to interpret, but for that many nights? It can get to be really long hours, so we had an interpreter coordinator figuring out how much people were willing to contribute. That was wonderful, having a person responsible for that. I didn't have to think about or worry about it. That one person also knew a lot of people and it worked out really well. Bless that person.

Jill: What are some of the best strategies you've seen for making plays accessible to deaf and hearing audiences?

Howie: With *ASL Midsummer Night's Dream*, I made sure we had language accessibility, that every sign was complemented by voice and every voice was covered by signs. And that's one thing I noticed; my deaf eye was different from the hearing director's. The hearing director would have a hearing person or someone come in and if something was happening over there on the opposite side of the stage, I would have to turn my head to look, so I took over most, if not all, of that responsibility to make sure it was all covered so we could guide deaf people into where to look at. So, I had that deaf eye for watching the stage. Actors or characters would exit one way and there'd be something happening in that vicinity, so if someone else came in, it'd be natural to look over there. So that glance helped guide you into where to look.

Sometimes with lighting, when a person exits and the next actor is on the opposite side, you'll see a light fading in, which naturally guides you to look there as the exiting person's light fades out. That's one technical aspect.

Andy: What does your dream integrated theatre production look like?

Howie: One ideal is that all of the cast be deaf so that their signing skills are on par or at least similar. When you have a hearing actor learning signs during rehearsal and then going on stage, you can always tell because it's a bit of an eyesore. The person doesn't sign perfectly. Just like in *Spring Awakening*, so many hearing people signed but I couldn't understand, and many friends told me they couldn't understand what was said. I told them I didn't, either, and I was in the play. [LAUGHS] My best would be to have all deaf, or deaf and hearing people who are already fluent in signing. Having a deaf director, of course. The DASL is deaf, of course. Lighting, it's important to have a deaf person controlling or designing the lighting, because I know what we need to help, like I said, draw the eye. While I'm dreaming for the moon, deaf writers, too. Deaf writers, directors, all deaf. But not all deaf people are equally talented, just like hearing people, so if I had to pick, some positions I would want—I mean, hearing people can have a lot to contribute in terms of skills. Like lighting, if that person has better lighting skills than a deaf person, I'd go with them because they'd know how to make it better. Sometimes it's better to have a hearing director who is really skilled and who knows how to visualize a dream, is very creative, and have a deaf person serve as an assistant or co-director. But that hearing person must respect that deaf person. If the deaf person says something, that hearing person will *listen* to the deaf person. The director makes his own decisions, but at least listens. That's what I had with *ASL Midsummer Night's Dream*. Teresa Thuman was the co-director. I would give my input. It was received well. My point is that sometimes we need that hearing talent that we may not have available in the deaf community—yet.

Jill: What's the best example of an integrated production you've been involved in or seen, and why?

Howie: Maybe just because I saw it more recently, but *The Hunchback of Notre Dame* with Josh Castille. It was so professional, so grand, and then it also became very private, very intimate through the lighting and it became smaller until it was just one person. Josh's translations were really sublime. He signed, for the word *sanctuary*, he signed—I didn't catch the English word at first but I understood the sign [DEMONSTRATES] because it meant that the people were down there and the world was alive, but then he had his own safe place up here. When I finally understood, the hair on my arms and neck stood up because it was just such a beautiful sign. I'm sure there were other signs that were wonderful, too. There were some things about that play that didn't quite work for me, but from the story's perspective, it was impressive. The acting. Josh had a wonderful voicer who really fit him [E.J. Cardona]. That guy signed well; it was impressive. I'm not sure if he was a CODA himself or his parents or something, but he signed fluently and clearly while singing. That's hard to do, you know. I was impressed. He contributed to the performance and didn't take away from it like most hearing people would. It was so—the deaf community came out eight times. There were eight interpreted performances, and the deaf community came out. They really enjoyed seeing one of our own up there in a big-time theatre. There was respect by hearing people, too. Amazing. It came together well.

Andy: What are some of the unique challenges of directing integrated musicals?

Howie: The quality of the signs by hearing actors singing and signing at the same time is not the greatest. Most of the time it's not the greatest. In my experience, I've heard of some ego problems between hearing and deaf actors; the hearing person wants more attention and thinks the spotlight shouldn't be on the deaf person. That's the fault of the director not making it clear. I remember my first experience in…oh, what was it? Not the first, no, a play by Peter Sellars. He picked a singer he knew was very humble, and was a wonderful team player, to sing with me. So that person respected me. We were equals, or he was a bit under me. That's what Josh had with that guy in his show, it was obvious that they had equal standing and that they liked each other, they respected each other. It really showed through in the performance. *Into the Woods* at OSF, I played the Big Bad

Wolf, and my voice was a nice guy whose attitude and personality was great, but I was limited by what they did with us. We were just left to rehearse with each other. The whole experience was less than perfect. We ended up looking like we were performing apart from each other. He was physically under me, but like my alter ego, or that's what it was supposed to be. But signing—I was very, very ASL, but it was not where we really matched signing for word, sign for word, no. Two free-flowing actors going at the same time. Later, we moved the show to Los Angeles, and one woman from Deaf West Theatre who was experienced with musicals came to see my show. She asked, "Did you know you two aren't in sync?" I said of course I knew that, we were two separate characters. She made a face, and I thought that was interesting. [SHRUGS]

Jill: Do you think it's desirable for the English and the ASL lines to align all the time?

Howie: Really, it's impossible, impossible to match, but you can meet, touch, interact. You can take advantage of ASL to highlight the English words and when you can match, *whoo*, it has a greater impact.

Jill: You mentioned *Spring Awakening*. I didn't realize you were in the show.

Howie: Yes, in Los Angeles. When they moved from the small theatre to the Wallis. The original actors left, so I took over, and then they moved to Broadway. They got another actor. I heard a rumor that it was a bigger name and he was younger and had a bigger, uh, online following. I don't bother with Instagram, all that, doing selfies. [LAUGHS] Baring my chest on camera. So, they replaced several actors there.

Jill: Can you talk about some of the challenges Deaf West faced in doing *Spring Awakening* as an integrated musical?

Howie: That's a hard question for me to answer because I came in later. So, I didn't see their challenges. They already worked out their challenges by the time I got there. One that perplexed me a bit was when they signed in black light. They had lights on their fingertips. They had that beautiful singing still on and hearing people could see and hear, but the deaf people, nope. That was a problem for me because you're making the deaf audience disconnect. It's pretty to look at, but it's like cotton candy. It's all fluff, and then you go back to the story. But they had really creative techniques, wow. And when the deaf character and her alter ego or voice came and signed using mirrors and then they walked together—wow! That is what I mean, sometimes hearing people, just because they have more experiences and more opportunities, they can contribute a lot to dramatic ideas. Deaf people haven't had that opportunity yet to experiment or practice or develop, so sometimes we need hearing people sometimes.

Andy: What is the best thing you think a director can do to build an inclusive cast and production process?

Howie: Two things. Meet with deaf actors first. Get to know each other so there is a connection. Often you do not have that. I often didn't, couldn't make connections with the director beyond superficial conversations. I see other actors having long, deep discussions. I've tried doing that myself with interpreters, but it's still very brief. It's natural for hearing people to have that, connecting more. They feel awkward with deaf people, and I think that's natural. I'd say it's rare, but no—not many directors have that empathy to make a deaf person comfortable. I remember one woman who ran OSF invited me to her home, and her husband was part of the performance, too. So, I really enjoyed it, with an interpreter. We talked and talked, and after that, I felt comfortable approaching her with anything I wanted to talk about. And, I'm not sure who's the best person but maybe the DASL can provide awareness, deaf awareness tips, to hearing people on how to interact, don't be afraid, go ahead and write, gesture, communicate. You'd be surprised how many hearing actors are afraid to gesture. Come on! They're actors! The DASL could explain. But again, you have to be careful. What are the boundaries for DASLs and their jobs? It's good for me as a deaf actor to explain some things or tips that will help me do my job. For example, if you're ahead of me voicing and I'm not finished signing—this happened a few times. In one rehearsal at OSF, I was reading my lines. I looked up and they're done voicing. The director said, "Let's try that again. This time you watch Howie." The voicer was red-faced. It was funny.

Jill: Why do you think it's important for productions to integrate deaf and hearing artists?

Howie: Why not! [LAUGHS] I read that question and scratched my head. For us, the deaf community, it helps me with deaf awareness being spread to the hearing community but—my question is when will we stop being that and become something deeper than just saying "Oh, we work with hearing people so we can spread deaf awareness." Move beyond that. We do that because we're the best at what we do. This is happening at Deaf West Theatre. They're doing things, all for artistic sake, not for deaf awareness like they used to. That's been happening the past few years, integration for art's sake, and it has resulted in better shows or different kinds of artistic shows. Different interpretations. How to make play more physical. Hearing people listen but do they really look and see what's happening onstage? Bring their own lived experiences into the characters like I did with Bob Ewell in *To Kill a Mockingbird*. I brought in my deaf experience, wow. So, we can add a deeper, or another, level of human nature. There's one moment when I'm trying to attack the Black man in the courtroom and I'm yelling the "n" word at him. The director wanted that and it's in the script, but I felt guilty about using it. I felt like every time I yelled, it was my anger at hearing people for looking at deaf people in a negative way. Bob was mad because people didn't think highly of him. He was a misfit, an outcast, so my feelings as a deaf person in the hearing world over time—I really brought that in and exploded towards him. So, I think people really picked up on that.

Jill: Did you sign the n-word or speak it?

Howie: Speak. They're holding my arms and I speak.

Jill: There's a lot to analyze about when and why deaf characters use their voice on stage. And about what they can and can't hear. Especially related to music.

Howie: Yeah. That irritates me a bit now. "Oh! Deaf hears or speaks! Oh!" Ugh. "Deaf person plays the piano, oh!" Ahem. Passé. I remember when I yelled in the play, the purpose was to get attention or something. I think yelling in anger or something is natural. The musical part of that annoys me. The ear, the guitar, that kind of thing, blah. Hearing people everywhere do not see that, so it's new for them. But it's old for us oldtimers. The first play I did at OSF was one where I played the tavern host or owner. I was cleaning the bar top when a woman came in saying she wanted Falstaff. I knew Falstaff was upstairs in a room with a woman. So, she comes in, and I had two beer stein mugs and banged them together—no, it was a metal pitcher and a stein, and banged them. And then he came down and I pointed to the woman. I called him with that bang, not yelling. If I had yelled, it'd have taken away from the moment. It's an important moment when I call him to come from playing around with a woman, so *bang*. And instead of yelling "FALSTAFF!" They'd laugh. No. So that's one technique we used.

Andy: As the theatre community moves forward, what do you hope to see in terms of accessibility and inclusion?

Howie: More deaf writers. In-depth plays. Right now, we're just scratching the tip of the iceberg. I want more depth. It'll take a while to get that level of profound writing for the stage. Movies and television, too. It's challenging. I'd like to see that. More deaf directors, deaf actors.

That's coming, we don't need to worry about that. There's a tidal wave of young deaf actors coming, but we need directors and more writers. We probably also need businesspeople who know how to find money to produce our own shows. Hearing people find money to sponsor Deaf West and other theatres that involve deaf people. It would be nice to have several rich deaf people who have contacts or money. For example, Deaf West Theatre should be comfortable financially and they're not. DJ Kurs is doing a really good job, wow. He's a brilliant thinker. They should be comfortable based on their success to date. They've accomplished *Big River, Spring Awakening*, but money is still an issue. We need that too.

ETHAN SINNOTT

Ethan Sinnott is an actor, director, and set designer working in the DC metropolitan area. He has designed for Mosaic Theater Company, Theater Alliance, Rorschach Theatre, Faction of Fools, Constellation Theatre Company, and Washington Shakespeare Company. He designed the set for Olney Theatre's Helen Hayes–winning *The Music Man*. Sinnott is a professor and director of the Theatre and Dance Program at Gallaudet University. He holds an MFA in theatre—scene design from Boston University.

Andy: How would you define integrated theatre?

Ethan: The word integrated is loaded with many triggers. "Integrated" is basically my mainstreamed experience. I was mainstreamed as the only deaf kid all the way, so integrated feels like…anytime an integrated production is announced, it almost never captures exactly what the goals are with its integrated production. Are its goals lofty and well-articulated, or an exercise in tokenism? Will it involve deaf and hearing creatives as co-equal partners creating work for their intended audiences? Or not? There are a lot of variables involved. Really, to have an integrated production, what are its aims? To show that hearing and deaf people can work together? Been there, done that. Or is it to make stories that represent parts of life from all over, where deaf and hearing characters coexist and have a common language? That's the beauty of what *The Music Man* represented to me. It was a new type of experience for me compared to what I've typically experienced as a Deaf set designer in the past. Integration more often than not comes across as an attempt to shoehorn diametrically different cultural-linguistic identity groups together, when, ultimately, it should be a perfectly and proactively planned scenario, where everyone knows and understands their roles, where there are a set of well-articulated goals supported by those involved in such a production, and there are no power dynamics at play.

For me, that's the requirement for an actual production, from the beginning where ideas are shared freely, with deaf-proposed ideas being equally valid as hearing ideas, and collectively, unconditionally collaborative all the way through to the end. Power dynamics have to go. It's based on the ability to speak, based on the ability to sign, and based on the ability to do both. I don't speak well. I grew up deaf. I was born deaf, and I have a deaf voice. Of course, I'm aware of that, and I think that has hurt my career over time. I have worked with hearing theatre companies in the past where the collaboration usually was, 1) their first time working with a deaf designer, with interpreters brought in and all that, with struggles to communicate in their absence. The onus was almost always on me to speak instead of being on them to learn more sign language and meet me halfway. And 2) limited to that one time. Read into that what you will.

Ironically, I didn't really feel all that connected to myself or my deaf identity until I arrived at Gallaudet back in 2005. Before that, I was in this weird limbo and struggled to occupy that space between two identities and worlds. I struggled and I didn't feel like I really belonged anywhere until I arrived here. Do I feel like I belong at Gallaudet? Not necessarily, but I found a belonging within myself. And, now, I know clearly what I'm willing to put up with and what I'm not anymore.

Back to the idea of an integrated theatre production and deaf/hearing groups. Viewing this issue through a mainstream frame (in terms of the theatre industry at large), we have relatively few deaf people involved in the technical and theatre-making aspects of productions, whether it's a design discipline, directing, dramaturgy, technical direction, and so on. That's something I had at the forefront of my mind when I came to Gallaudet. We have an obligation to make our (usually deaf) students recognize that they have voices, they have artists in them, they have career options available to them within the industry going beyond performance. In the room, usually, it's just me or my colleague Annie Wiegand in rooms full of these hearing people who have never met deaf people before or have had very limited interactions thus far. There are very few. I'm one of three deaf set designers in the country. One is in New York City. He's still early-career, and like myself, he doesn't speak well enough to pass for "hearing." The other one grew up oral with no real connection to the deaf community. Then there's me. Annie is the only lighting designer who is

Deaf. For costume designers, I can think of two or three costume designers off the top of my head, but they haven't had many career opportunities come up for them. So, often, when that kind of integrated production concept comes up, the real challenge is making sure there's equal representation in the room. It can't be one deaf person and all hearing people with an interpreter.

Plus, the interpreters obtained by different theatre companies can be wildly inconsistent. Some come in with theatre backgrounds making them well-suited to handle design and production meetings, which makes things go easier for me and helps me focus on just being a scenic designer, while others who come in unversed to theatre as a process and are often lost due to their lack of familiarity with the terminology, which not only makes my job harder, they become my handicap. And the room (consisting of hearing theatre creatives, techies, administrators) doesn't know or realize that, they're not able to pick up on it—they've never worked with deaf people before and—they think, because of how these interpreters voice-translate for me, that is how I articulate my thoughts. It makes me very self-conscious. So, it has gotten to the point where I have made it a practice to type my comments or thoughts beforehand and pass it out before the meeting. It's more work, but by doing this prior to my presentation to show them the final design, it becomes a fail-safe method against the interpreter's misunderstanding or mistranslation.

Lack of interpreters in the room is also a problem. If you know I'm deaf and you have a production meeting and say, "Oh, I'm sorry, we couldn't find an interpreter," or say it's because of the cost, or ask me to help find an interpreter. No, that's not my job. I just want to be a set designer, not a deaf advocate and set designer. It's exhausting. Serving in a dual role is exhausting. There are boundaries. To bring in an interpreter is full-on the theatre company's responsibility, and they should know better. They know that I'm deaf, and shouldn't wait until the last minute.

Jill: From a designer's perspective, how would you define success in integrated theatre?

Ethan: There are a lot of variables to what makes integrated theatre work, I think the biggest, most immediate issue is the lack of representation on the creative control side of things. Not the acting, not the writers, but who makes or who produces? Having deaf people in these roles would go a long way toward assuring creative and producing equality and equity in the room. Until that happens, power dynamics in the room will always favor hearing people. I have worked with a good number of hearing directors who have never worked with deaf people before, and re-teamed a few times with an even smaller number of such directors. They may have been well-meaning, but they never made the effort to learn some foundational sign language, to meet me halfway, other than through ASL interpreters. That makes me wonder about their interest in understanding the deaf perspective, or their desire to do so.

Right now, it's unrealistic to expect an equal number of deaf and hearing people in the room. But I think it's realistic to try and make every effort to bring in as many deaf people as possible. If a show is produced by a hearing company that has never worked with the deaf community before or is enthusiastic about bringing in deaf people, the production manager has to make every good-faith effort to have deaf people in key roles, build up their numbers to the point where not only these deaf people can establish a support system through which they can connect and compare stories, but also to establish and maintain the precedent of deaf people collaborating with hearing counterparts on design/production teams, so that the historical absence of deaf people in the room no longer influences hearing attitudes about deaf people in professional theatre settings, as if we aren't capable of being theatre makers. I can't tell you how many times I've been frustrated by my efforts to interact with lighting designers who are hearing, and they're not interested in conversing with me or are just too busy or distracted, or maybe they find it awkward to discuss ideas. That leads to the point where I question if I'm crossing boundaries or not. How the hell do I know? Bring in as many deaf people into the room as you can. If you can't get an equal number of deaf and hearing team members, then try to get as close as possible. Put a deaf person in a position where creative decisions are made. It'd be nice to have another deaf person, someone at that level of a co-director, fellow designer, stage manager, etc., in the room, so that I don't have to be the only Deaf person in there coming in with my Deaf-informed perspectives on aesthetics, stagings, visual compositions, the like.

Successful integration means I don't have my ideas or thoughts minimized. It's one thing to have heated discussions. In the industry, there are always going to be a lot of strong personalities in the room. You have a lot of creative collaborators with their convictions and opinions, and that's okay. But I will not tolerate my views or my ideas being minimized based on the fact that I'm Deaf. That's happened. It wasn't intentional, I don't think. I think it's more about the comfort of the primary modality of communication in the room—spoken, speaking—and it probably is more comfortable and easier for them to just keep going, maintain their free flow rather than to spend time trying to adjust how they communicate. Whenever there's a Deaf person, like me, and hearing people are around, the mainstream theatre automatically becomes a space for cross-cultural or cross-linguistic communication. I'm used to that because of having been mainstreamed, but hearing people are not. It's new to them. I'm not there to be a teacher. I'd prefer not to be. I'm not there to help them feel better about themselves. All I want to do is create works of theatre as simply and straightforwardly as possible. At the same time, I have to remember that, like it or not, I am representing the deaf community in making in-roads within the industry. I can say that my diplomacy has improved over the years in terms of being much more mindful of how I am reacting in the moment and its potential long-term impacts on not just for me but for other deaf people trying to break into the field. If I argue or say, "Fucking hearing assholes," then they don't hire me back, and based off that, they probably will be less inclined to hire other deaf people. Andy, no offense when I say that; I'm speaking in general, not targeting you. But it's a tricky balance.

Andy: No offense taken. Can you expand on Deaf gain in set design?

Ethan: As a set designer, I find myself wanting to bring Deaf gain, the deaf perspective into design. My design has been influenced by my experiences watching theatre growing up. I got bored watching set designs where the environment didn't change at all. Whether it was the unit itself or a single, static set, when that visually stayed the same while the actors moved. Hearing people have sound design and effects that function like a thread throughout the production to keep them engaged. They have sounds at the beginning through the middle to the end. I want a similar set environment that visually shifts, shifts, shifts with the play's narrative and trajectory. It may be more work involved, and more money involved. It can be a pain in the ass from the hearing theatres' perspective. But experimenting with in-performance visual adjustments and transformations, for a deaf audience watching, is parallel to a layered and well-executed sound design carrying hearing audiences through a production happening on an inert set, keeping them engaged. I always want to experience and be stimulated by theatre that is conscious of being experienced and watched by audiences whose main processing sense is sight, not sound. This requires productions to commit to visual storytelling through an actively changing set, instead of asking audiences to tolerate one set or stage image all the way from start to finish.

The set space needs to have a series of clearly defined focal points that make it easy to view onstage signing. There needs to be balance or contrast between what we see being signed and the environment. I look at it like a range. That range really depends on the size of the space where the production is taking place. The distance between the audience and the actors is key in influencing design. I went to the premiere of *Spring Awakening* in Los Angeles in 2014. It was in a small space and it was really cool. But nobody thought about the angle of the seats in that space: the tiered seating rows were set up at a shockingly slight incline, and for the deaf person sitting in the back row, this added another obstacle to the theatre-going experience. That obstacle? Rows of heads obstructing stage ASL, particularly when the action shifted downstage. If an actor kneeled or fell way downstage, it seems to the deaf person in the back row that the actor has been swallowed up into the sea of heads, and if his/her/their fellow actor is visible signing to that actor in continuous dialogue, good luck following that scene. Deaf people shouldn't need to have to expend that much effort within what should be a straightforward theatre-going experience. Decisions made about the seating layout could have given more consideration and sensitivity to sightlines for deaf patrons in less-than-ideal seating locations. What could have been done was give these rows a steeper angle, analogous to a medical theater setup, intimate enough to sit close to the stage but from a taller vantage point, which eliminates the aggravation of other people's heads being in one's sightline from house to stage. But there was a lot of interference with signing on stage. If the cast was downstage, everyone in the middle rows would sit up taller to get a better view, forcing the row behind them to react similarly, and so on, a ripple effect that stopped at the back row. Then I watched *Spring Awakening* again on Broadway, and that was a different experience. It was at a much larger venue, the increased distance from the stage was noticeable, and the average reaction I got from other deaf laypeople who went to this production as well, is that it was difficult for them to connect with this particular staging at times. It was hard to keep up because the focal points weren't as clearly established, which is a necessity in larger and traditional proscenium stages and theatre houses. The original staging did not change all that much for the Broadway stage. What may work well in smaller, more intimate spaces does not necessarily translate successfully to larger spaces, with the deciding factor being house-to-stage sightline distance. Deaf actors can't overcome that regardless of their skill. What worked for the original and more intimate space was lost in this level-up to Broadway from a Deaf theatre-going standpoint, because of the "giveth and taketh" range of distance: the closer to the stage, the less effort it takes for deaf audiences to follow stage action and signed dialogue, and they become relaxed enough to emotionally, psychologically invest themselves into the play being presented before them. As far as I'm concerned, if I were designing for a large space with a huge audience and deaf actors are involved, I would likely opt for stage minimalism, without any busyness, clutter, or visual distractions. That type of set design has to be a clear composition putting deaf actors in positions to ensure they have maximum dramatic/theatrical impact. How? You can transform and shift the set, avoid certain aesthetics such busy patterns or the incorporation of scenic elements as unintended visual clutter that competes with actors for attention/focus. But for smaller black box theatres, due to their intimate nature, I think there's a lot more freedom to experiment with aesthetics long considered traditional taboos in Deaf theatre.

That was the exact reason why the Gallaudet theatre program shifted to its black box as its main venue, along with practical reasons stemming from budget cuts. We don't have a lot of resources, so we're trying to achieve the feeling of a complete production in a smaller space rather than with an audience. Plus, with a closer proximity, there is less pressure on actors to sign bigger. They can sign in a more natural style. The space becomes our canvas to play with what we want or can do, and create focal points. Contrast that, for example, with the "duck row" associated in the old days of mostly amateur and community Deaf theatre for group scenes—that would be when deaf actors line up in a horizontal row engaging in group dialogue that requires one actor in this line to bend forward or lean to the side to respond to another actor, and this behavior is repeated throughout, characterized by ping-pong signing back and forth. That was a popular feature of the Deaf theatre productions I took in when I was younger. Then, I often thought a lot about deaf stage blocking and what it would look like if one challenged longtime practices, tendencies, and traditions. I was curious about potential compositional and dramatic impacts resulting from shifts away from downstage center as a default setting to, say, downstage left, or upstage right. I have always been intrigued by the artistic possibilities of sculptural three-dimensionality within Deaf theatre stage blocking approaches without (1) losing deaf audiences who may have become accustomed to Deaf theatre being produced in more conventional and traditional ways, or (2) unintentionally generating gaps in information (during the theatre-going experience). So, we play with what is possible in terms of deaf actors communicating and interacting on stage as their characters. Playing with the idea of the three-fourths rule where it's not fully frontal, but three-fourths signing, and even signing with your back turned to the audience. We play with that, too. It seems to contradict with the natural gravitations of Deaf theatre conventions, but this depends on context and how it's used. Art starts to stagnate once novelty wears off with time. It's inevitable and cyclical.

I'll give you an example. In 2008, during my first, no, my second year at Gallaudet, I directed *The Oresteia*. It had never been staged in ASL before and I could see why. For modern audiences, the script can come off as off-putting, with little in the way of action and more with stationary rhetoric. Take the chorus. Instead of having all the signers in one place signing synchronously, or close to it, I gave each person their own lines in succession. This created a visual rhythm that the audience really responded strongly to. It was great. In the last act, the Furies represented the chorus, representing the early evolutionary human struggle to communicate and articulate. With the successive rotations of lines and words as continual relays within choral odes being this new feature, there was less pressure on actors to stay synchronized, and it became this exciting generator of opportunities to experiment with choreography, turn-taking, visual movements, coordination and cohesiveness, all in a quest to develop a rhythm and flow parallel to the original choruses amplified by the exceptional acoustics of their original venues. That's one approach to adapting ancient Greek theatre to deaf frames, if you want to shift away from the typical chorus singing all at the same time. It's not always coordinated. You can always tell if someone is off.

Multiple levels in the set helps define the focus upstage, too. For example, in my set design for *A Midsummer Night's Dream*, I wanted to create a sense of ... a constructivist approach to the forest because typically a production of *MSND* has a set design representing Athens and then the forest. But the problem is that the forest design is typically static. You have three groups of people who are running around into the forest—how can they not be aware of each other if the trees stay the same? So, my set design involved pieces that actors could move themselves to create more configurations, and placements. That helped the audience arrive at that feeling of being lost in the night with no sense of direction. And the terrain was represented through groups of grades; horizontal grades, stage right and stage left. A series of intersecting ramps that actors walked down, slid down, jumped off. There were two ramps, plus three lights in downstage that went on at different times. And the vom. That was the second time—no, no, I started using the vom in the audience back in 2015. We made a vom where actors went off-stage. That's not something you see often in Deaf theatre productions, where an actor goes into the audience and the audience feels like a real part of the story, of the experience. I started using voms, and that influence also helped consciously choose actor positions, what we could do. For *MSND*, you'll remember when Puck started to sign, we had moments where actors signed with their backs to the audience, depending on the lines. If it was a short command that could be quickly caught, yes. But if it were a longer line, no, we avoided that and found repositioned ways.

Shadows are a big metaphor in *A Midsummer Night's Dream*. I think for many deaf people, their worst fear is not the darkness, but that we can't see in the dark. If, for example, you're in a house you've lived in for a while, and it suddenly goes dark, we know our way around, right? But in a new, strange, foreign place that we're not familiar with and it suddenly goes dark, it becomes scary. That's an element that comes up in my other shows, like Hamlet and the father. Jill, remember that? There was no face in the video [projected on stage]. Audiences couldn't read the facial expressions. So, in *A Midsummer Night's Dream*, I threw out the idea of a typical forest, and used more of a shadow realm in which viewers catch glimpses throughout from small flashes of light. The only time we see the full environment is when we're back in Athens at the beginning and ending. Because it's well lit, Athens represents safety, familiarity, and comfort. But between those scenes, it's a scary environment for any deaf person. They're thinking, "Where am I going? What's next that I can't see?"

Jill: Can you talk about the set design for *Julius Caesar* [2015, Ethan also directed]. How did you incorporate a deaf perspective in that?

Ethan: It was a circular set. I don't think that had ever been used in a Gallaudet production before, that circular, arena-style set. The new seating system we designed for the Black Box Theatre happened to work well with *Julius Caesar*. The themes of the play fit with things that come up in the deaf community, like power struggles. That's a human thing, but it's magnified in the deaf community due to the simple fact that it's Gallaudet. Gallaudet is small, and it's in DC, and it's an old university. When people come to work there, they feel territorial. They'll do whatever it takes to stay there. It's not by accident that I mixed in a bit of Gallaudet and Roman architecture in the set design. Some people noticed that I pulled some styles from Chapel Hall and College Hall. The setting is the nineteenth century and was intentionally customized to be recognized by people from Gallaudet. I wanted them to see it and analyze themselves. They are participants in this kind of power struggle and the concept of crab theory applies. Many people have good intentions that get lost in the whole mess. *Julius Caesar* was my way of processing the 2006 protests. That was my first or second year at Gallaudet as faculty, and I always remember how it was messy and not coordinated...just like the events in *Julius Caesar*, taking place in a vacuum.

Also, the blocking. I really wanted to get further and further away from what I usually saw growing up. That generational shift. The blocking of deaf actors used to be more standard and we had to get out of that rut. Being stuck there didn't challenge audiences or make audiences respond. "Just give them what they're used to seeing." If you do that, you're not doing your job—that's my perspective. *Julius Caesar* was a way to play with a group scene in a way that felt realistic instead of being a duck-row scene. I've seen a group scene where the actors all stood in a long line or even two rows deep, tapping each other's shoulders to converse. Because clarity of signing was a priority. I prefer to have one hundred percent authenticity and seventy-five percent clarity, rather than one hundred percent clarity and less authenticity.

I'm trying to create worlds in which the target is not necessarily deaf audiences. Of course, they are included. I'm more targeting hearing audiences to bring them to the deaf perspective or the deaf way of seeing the same thing. Hearing people filter through a particular sense, which is hearing. We filter through our eyes and that influences how we orient ourselves, our stream of consciousness, our life experiences. I try to bring some of that into set design, which succeeds more at Gallaudet because it's easier to communicate with my colleagues, peers, actors, with the communication access. With hearing collaborations or co-producers, that's more of a challenge.

Back to focal points, *The Music Man*—the first thing that had to go was the expectation that this production—as far as its set design was concerned—had to pay homage to the golden age of musicals featuring set designs as jam-packed spectacles. *The Music Man* is the type of musical that feels like a temptation for scenic designers to go wild, pack in as much as they can, as if to push the limits of the stage one better than their predecessors. Those types of sets may be intended to impress and wow, but from a visual standpoint, they compete with the actors for my attention, focus, and interest. For hearing audiences, it's not an issue because they can see and hear what's going on. But this was neither an ideal or smart approach to a well-loved musical featuring deaf and hearing actors in a setting imagined as close to a utopian community, where deaf and hearing peoples are able to coexist without communication struggles and understand each other. In the world of that production, they have a system; hearing people are accustomed to signing and learn to sign, and everyone interacts. There's some kind of harmony there. So, for that to work, I pushed the idea of getting rid of all the visual noise and just focusing on keeping things simple and minimalist. Start with the geography of the Midwest. It is so flat and open. So, the set was flat and open, too. Plus, some time ago, there was an attempt to set up a signing town in Laurent, South Dakota. It failed, but the idea is, why establish it there, geographically? Because it is a big, open space. I also emphasized the need for visual flow because if you want to sell the audience on the idea of the deaf and hearing communities living in harmony in 1912, the first question is: how did they adapt to each other? What did that space look like? Not just on stage, but what were their daily experiences like? What makes sense is an open space, a house with an open plan. Not necessarily Deaf space or new architecture built for deaf people, no. What if they had to adapt existing American architecture? There were a lot of Victorian houses, like the Painted Ladies and they were fancy and ornate. How would such a community adapt its space to support the communication needs of individuals and of the community? Having a town square? Making it more circular? Because corners represent blind spots for me as a Deaf person. In real life, I am wary of sharp angles regardless of where I may be. I don't know what's around there. There's always something there. Will someone come in front of me? A car? I'm always careful around corners because I can't see what's around the corner. But if the corner is arched, then that solves the problem because I can see around it.

This principle can be applied to a community. There aren't a lot of community spaces defined by soft boundaries where everything is visible and the communication distance varies. So, suppose we show that on the set itself. We could make the set a geographically rolling area with an outside ramp that could slope down gradually. We could use wheels to move things up and down, and open with the musical orchestra there. The plan was for a caption board but you see it only on the border. Of course, the issue of hearing people having to crane their necks to look at the captions came up during the meeting. I tested it out myself and thought it was fine. My first response was, learn how to adapt, just like deaf people always do.

We have to deal with interpreters being off to the side and looking back and forth, missing everything. It's time for the mainstream industry to think about access as part of universal design in the world of theatre as opposed to finishing all the details and thinking, "Oh, shit, where do I put the interpreter? The captions?"

So, the design was a combination of Victorian styles, but it included different windows where deaf and hearing people could see what was happening both inside and outside. When Harold Hill arrives, everyone immediately knew, as opposed to a regular town that slowly finds out that there's a new guy around. And we know that the window serves as a metaphor for the soul. We know that the window creates a nice combination of people who comprise the community as opposed to physical appearances. From there, it was easy to figure out what to do with other scenes that needed clear delineation from each other in terms of experience. Wells Fargo, the library, the gym. I took a minimalist way of showing that this is how life happens in this community. In the gym, I imagined hanging banners showing all the championships. In the library, the idea of reverse or negative space where you create an outline of the library building but using a border of books. So, when you see the library, you know it's a physical building, but it's not literally one—kind of oxymoronic. For Wells Fargo, there was a lot of discussion about that. We didn't want to eat up time and have Harold come in to hand out the trumpets. That'd be time-consuming, and with a deaf audience, momentum is key, especially visual momentum. Even in terms of scene changes, shifts, overlaps—it's not linear. We have to keep it moving through all the overlaps and transitions quickly, so there aren't a lot of pauses. Keep it going. The scene when the instruments arrive on Wells Fargo took up a lot of that. We ended up deciding, what if it's an abstract representation combined with the vastness of space in that design? We had trumpets, trombones, drums, and different flutes all hanging on hooks. When Harold pointed, it all dropped down. That was a nice dramatic effect.

The same principle with "Shipoopi"—audiences had mixed reactions to it. Some thought it was cool, while others completely misunderstood and didn't see the point. But if you think about language, spoken and signed, what's the third rail? Visual. Visual language. Textual or pictorial forms of the language itself. The cartoon style was intended to reinforce the silliness of the word "Shipoopi." It sounds funny, like something that would be said in comics, and it hews close to the random gibberish, nonsensical words (or sounds) that have come up (and, in some cases, used regularly) within deaf and hearing communities. That connection was a reason why we had all the various cut-outs of the word "Shipoopi" in cartoon-style fonts drop down.

Andy: In your opinion, what was your best design? What design really fit your visualization while also fitting the director's visualization?

Ethan: There's one production I'm very proud of, *TitusAndronicus*, with the company Faction of Fools. That production had two deaf actors, one Gallaudet senior, and three students working backstage. That set required that we start with white and later blood splatters everywhere. The blood was messy by the end, and then we had to clean it up and restart. Time for reset was limited, and there was a lot of experimenting involved.

That's from an artistic standpoint. But from my standpoint, the creative process, with Deaf gain involved, and a hearing director's involvement, did I feel satisfied... hmm ...I don't think I've ever experienced that. The only times I felt really good about the outcome have been at Gallaudet. I had control over the world I created, because I designed the set and it was easy to explain to the actors what was happening. And the environment is deaf—with minimal hearing people involved, other than in minor roles. In my experience, I've always lost. I've always lost in artistic creative discussions. Whenever I suggest this or that, they're always resistant and say no, that costs money. I'm thinking of one production, *Native Son* by Richard Wright. About a Black man going through multiple racist systems in America—legal, justice, economic, all at once. The production concept was a metaphor for the system. I had tentacles sticking all over the actor to show that as a Black man, he is stuck and cannot escape. He was trapped. And there were LED snake lights shining, representing eyes looking at him, profiling him. Racial profiling him like when he walks the streets or drives, white people would say, "Why is a Black person in our area?" and be suspicious. But it was apparently too ambitious and not budget-friendly. Okay, I can live with budgetary decisions. We had to pare it down. That set design ended up being a very minimal representation of what could have happened. The original design was exciting, but it didn't happen.

Jill: You've done lots of work with hearing theatre companies in DC. I've seen pictures and you've done some really beautiful, amazing sets. With any of those experiences, even though it wasn't for an integrated production, did it feel inclusive for you as a deaf set designer?

Ethan: Often when I work with a new director I've never worked with before, it's the same outcome. At the end of opening night, they say,

"Nice work, beautiful process," but then I never hear from them again. The exceptions were Greg Morrison (aka Psalm 24), Kathryn Chase-Bryer, and some of my old mates at Faction of Fools. But others, it's always one time. I always wonder if it's because they're a small company and can't afford the interpreter costs. Interpreters, on average, are paid more per hour than we are paid as designers. I typically get paid a flat fee. A show in DC, I might make maybe $2000 to $5000. I'm not doing this for profit. I'm doing this to scratch my creative itch. But I'm getting paid for my work at a lower value than interpreters are being paid for their work. Tech meetings, hourly rates add up. And then the company ends up paying interpreters more than they pay me. That comes up, so I wonder if the company thinks, "Ugh, I don't want to go through this again because it's too much." There needs to be an endowment or funding to help pay for interpreters. Or help give theatre companies incentives for investing in deaf talent again. I'd like to do design work or behind the scenes work with an interpreter there without having to worry about the cost impacting the organizational budget.

Jill: The problem is that they don't plan for access, they end up including that as an afterthought. If every year, they figured out this as part of their budget, built it into their budget...but they don't do that.

Ethan: Right. With *The Music Man*, it was good to see Olney make the effort to be proactive about interpreters. It wasn't perfect, but it was more than other theatre companies have done in the past. They took that bar and raised it, not to the highest level possible. But they raised it to what was possible for a deaf and hearing co-production.

Andy: When you work with a hearing director, what's one thing they could do to improve the working process? In relation to accessibility or inclusivity.

Ethan: Learn some fucking basic signs. I'm not asking them to become fluent. Meet me halfway. Try to make it easier by learning fingerspelling or recurring signs. Learn other ways to communicate. Maybe not signing if you're not comfortable. Be comfortable with other ways outside of always speaking. I can't become a great speaker. The first thing is: do you have time and interest to do that? It may be challenging, but the gesture counts a lot. At least try. You speak, I don't. Could we try to do some other communication methods than just speaking or having interpreters? I'd like to see directors make good-faith efforts to pick up some signs. You don't have to be completely fluent in ASL. Show me you care enough to talk with me and make me feel like I'm part of the process and someone to bring in.

Another thing the director could do is... this is actually the stage manager's responsibility, but there are many situations where discussions take place and I'm trying to jump in. But there is no turn-taking, and so much cross-talk, so when I try to say something, I get spoken over and can't get a word in. And I'm left out. So, I have to take charge of the conversation and say I go first, and take turns. Hearing people in general take these things for granted. They're used to doing things their way and are not willing to step out of their comfort zone. If they're more willing to do that, then I think we'd see a lot more co-production between deaf and hearing people.

Jill: We know you don't have a lot of power in the room as a set designer but is there anything you feel you could do in this role to help create an inclusive theatre experience?

Ethan: During my time with Mosaic Theater, I pushed the idea of incorporating captions in the show before we get to the technical aspects. Because I think that's part of the language in the world of theatre. *Native Son*, that was their second show where they included subtitles. The first was *Hooded: Being Black For Dummies* the year before. I did that set design as well. After that, every production automatically had captions. Deaf people have professional commitments and to tell them, "You can only come one night when interpreters are available," and they can't go because of conflicts, fuck that. We have lives. Respect that we have lives. So having subtitles on demand is what Mosaic did pre-pandemic. Even if deaf people decide to go at the last minute, they can still view the play with captions that can be turned on or off. That's a proactive approach to accessibility. And I think the next step will be how to incorporate interpreters into the set design. I've tried to encourage that, but there is strong resistance. To have the set design incorporate space for interpreters within the world of theatre, rather than set off away from the stage. When Faction of Fools did *Merchant of Venice* at Gallaudet, I was part of planning conversations. I didn't do the set design, but I did suggest that the set design have a canal with gondolas. Interpreters were seated in the gondola, built into the world as things unfolded. They were in the sightline of deaf patrons rather than having patrons look back and forth between the stage and the interpreters. They weren't set to the side, but built in to the point where they weren't distracting viewers from the play. I think that's the next frontier: interpreter access somewhere in the set design.

I'd like to see more deaf people experiment with in the round productions. It can be done, but it depends on what's being offered. Not heavy dialogue in ASL, but if you did something in the world of visual gesture theatre rather than voice, narrative storytelling through physical action, bodies communicating, that would seem to be a smart play for theatres in the round, venues not typically associated with Deaf theatre.

Jill: What do you hope to see in the future in terms of integrated deaf and hearing theatre?

Ethan: I haven't had the space to really think that far ahead. But if that future was to happen, we would need regular, consistent exposure to theatre for K-12 students at deaf schools and those who are mainstreamed. Lots of them are out there. I was mainstreamed—in my high school, I was the only deaf person mainstreamed out of 2500 students, and it wasn't fun. I hated high school. What about those kids? I'm not the only one; there are many in the same situation. I remember I wanted to be involved with theatre in high school, but I always felt intimidated by the flyers saying, "Come prepared to sing or play piano" every year. I thought maybe one year, they'd drop that idea and do something else. I wanted to see if I could try and convince them, where a deaf person could provide something different, a new layer to a redundant character. But no, it was always music. So, I was uncomfortable. I didn't get involved in high school theatre until my senior year, when we had a one act play festival. I used that opportunity to create a 15-minute silent version of *Hamlet* using visual gestures. One of my teachers mentioned that the audience couldn't keep quiet throughout the festival, but when my show came on, with no sound, every person was silent and focused because the lack of audio forced them to watch using a way of experiencing theatre they were not accustomed to.

Jill: You got into theatre at RIT?

Ethan: More into it, yeah. My senior year, that festival, plus I was in the NTID production of *Grapes of Wrath* in 1992. I played the Joad kid, Winfield. It was cool, sitting in that jalopy with the family driving west. It was a good cast, and one of my most important mentors during college was Jerome Cushman. He was definitely not for everyone—a force of nature, an acquired taste—but we really connected and understood each other. He really encouraged and supported me, and I loved him for it. He helped me understand that being deaf didn't necessarily have to be a barrier to my pursuit of the arts, imagination, and passion. He directed *Grapes of Wrath*, and then my freshman year, he was the director of *The Miser*. I had a leading role, Cleante. That was my first leading role. From there, I completely fell down that theatre rabbit hole. The Rochester Shakespeare Players—it first started in 1994. They opened with *Twelfth Night*, and I remember stopping by Peter Scribner's office. I was maybe twenty years old. I had seen an article about Peter setting up a Rochester Shakespearean theatre company and given my love for Shakespeare, I wanted to be involved. So, I stopped by Peter's office and point-blank asked, "Is there anything wrong with me auditioning as a deaf person? Do you have a problem with that?" [LAUGHS] Peter was gracious, though. "Yeah, that's fine, not a problem, please audition," he said. I don't think he had any choice. So, I auditioned and was cast as the Captain in *Twelfth Night*. That led to roles as Caliban in *The Tempest* and Hotspur in *Henry IV: Part I*. That was a very forward-thinking and personally rewarding involvement which felt ahead of its time, and due to that, I knew it could be done and replicated elsewhere. My precedent had been set.

I've held onto that moving forward. If it happened once, it can happen again and become a thing, a norm. Incorporating deaf people as equal creative artist partners in theatre productions. That's my priority and hope, to see that becoming the norm. I often struggle with advocating— do I speak up or say nothing? Will that have consequences later? I've become more mindful of what could happen as a result of the decision at that moment. Do I say something or shut up? When is a good or bad time? To have to educate peers and all of that exhausting work. It'd be nice to have all that thrown out so that I can be part of the show, whether to design or act or direct, and be on equal footing from start to finish. That's why I was attracted to *The Music Man*, because the idea of River City in that production was that the deaf and hearing communities lived in harmony and understood each other even if they had their own modalities of communication. They knew how to communicate with each other, coexist, and interact. With *The Music Man*, I felt the most optimistic ever. We're not there yet, but I'm optimistic.

Alexandria Wailes

Alexandria Wailes is a Deaf actor, director, choreographer, and DASL. Her work on Broadway includes Lady in Purple in *for colored girls who have considered suicide / when the rainbow is enuf* (2022); DASL for *King Lear* (2019); DASL for *Children of a Lesser God* (2018); associate choreographer for *Spring Awakening* (2016); and Ensemble and ASL Captain for *Big River* (2003). She is a Tony Honoree for Ensemble in *Big River*. Notable recent work off Broadway includes Jocasta and co-DASL for Deaf West's *Oedipus* (2022); and DASL for *CODA* (2021). She has worked in theatres throughout the United States, as well as in television, films, music videos, and more. In 2020, she received an Obie Citation for Sustained Excellence as an Artist and Advocate.

Jill: How would you define deaf and hearing integrated theatre? What are the key characteristics?

Alexandria: Integrated theatre, from my perspective, is about bilingualism, and also cultural exchange. These are the biggest aspects. Of course, there are more detailed aspects, but it depends on who's in the group and the different communities that come together. I find that for every integrated theatre production, it is really very informed by the production and the people at the top. Hearing people, deaf people—their knowledge of ASL, culture, history, and all that—how does that influence trickle down? Awareness of what it takes for a successful integrated production, meaning the creative process. Who's in the room? Who's behind the creative table? The qualifications of interpreters are part of that process, too. All of that comes together for integrated theatre. Yeah, that's the simple answer. It really depends on the production and what the show is. Because if it's a musical, that would look different from if it were a straight play or dance. I've had experience in different areas, so it really depends on which we're discussing.

Jill: If a show has one deaf person but everyone else is hearing, is that integrated theatre? Is it still possible to have that cultural exchange if there's only one deaf actor

Alexandria: Yes, it is absolutely possible. I've actually seen that in different shows where I was the DASL. I've seen, it's interesting how all it takes is one person. If the cast is all hearing with one deaf person, that space has already shifted because how do they communicate? That means they need a DASL. They need awareness, cultural sensitivity workshops, learning how to communicate and best practices. They'll need all that even if there's only one deaf person. Also, for the director, it depends on if the director has previous knowledge about ASL and deaf culture. If not, then if the director has an open mind and heart, and is willing to work with and learn, do their work away from the actor, then great. Sometimes that doesn't happen. Sometimes the deaf actor will feel burdened about having to teach them, so it's important to have a DASL. Even if there's only one deaf actor, you should always have a DASL because it's always good to have someone on the creative side of the table there to look at the overall vision rather than having actors direct each other or give each other notes. No. Put it on the person behind the scenes, so the actor can focus on the play—their lines, character development, relationships between characters.

Jill: What does a successful integrated production look like?

Alexandria: Success is at different levels. It depends on the hat I'm wearing. If I'm the producer, that means money and ticket sales. If I'm the director or artist, success means, "Is this work influencing people's thinking? Are people provoked in the way that art can cause thinking?" The pros and cons aren't the point, but are they at least thinking or reorienting their world? That's an artist's perspective. As an actor, I feel successful if I'm able to put my all forward as an actor and I'm not hindered by communication misunderstandings or breakdowns because of a lack of access in terms of interpreters, signing, awareness on the part of the backstage crew, sensitivity, and communication overall. Success looks different in different areas. Overall, if actors feel satisfied and supported, and if the director and the creative team feel supported, and if everyone else feels the same way, and we were all able to give our best, that's success to me.

Jill: In your experience, whether as an actor, or DASL, or audience member, what's a production that's come closest to that definition?

Alexandria: That is a hard question. Let me think...we're talking about feeling pretty good, and that means to me that the production has a high value. Second, it means access from within, meaning if there are multiple languages within the production, everyone feels good about the access. Everyone feels confident, comfortable, safe, and supported. Thirdly, the creative vision is good. If all those can be checked off equally, then the production meets my definition of success. But usually, those three areas aren't equally successful. There's variation in meeting that ideal. I will say that I am definitely tough. Because my expectations are high, you know. I'm blunt. I mean, from experience, from what I've seen and experienced, I don't feel it's okay to give some leeway and accept whatever results. No, we can do better. Come on! It shouldn't be something we're struggling with at all. Unfortunately, I have plenty of that experience rather than feeling supported and, *ahhh*, no tension around access, no cloud hanging over us. I've never had that, and I'm waiting for that.

Jill: When hearing directors are working with deaf actors, what are their responsibilities—maybe not on the level of logistics but on the level of ethics, to ensure access for a deaf audience. If they want to cast deaf actors, if they want to include ASL in their shows, then do they become responsible for that commitment to access for the audience?

Alexandria: Two things. Before I answer that, I want to go back to the previous question and say—I'm trying not to be too vague—but there's one show I did over fifteen years ago that did get close to my definition of success. However, I will say that where I was at in my career back then is different compared to now. So maybe at that time, I thought, wow, this is cool, but later I said, "Hey, wait a minute!" [LAUGHS] But fifteen years ago, there was one show that came close, it felt very close to where I could say, yes, that felt good overall. But since then, ehh. Now, the second question, this question, about being responsible. I think the director should be open minded enough to bring in a DASL. And also communicate with the theatre company in regard to what they have and their resources. The process of identifying the right DASL can really take time and once identified, they can work with the theatre to consider possible accommodations as far as what needs to be done for deaf audience access, because the director already has a lot to manage. So yes, the director is responsible for bringing in the deaf actor, but I think the director's responsibility should focus more on the vision of the show. Supporting the actors. Access for the audience, I feel yes, it is part of the director's responsibility. However, the director should bring in people who have more experience in that area. So it's more of a collaboration rather than just taking that on completely. If the director focuses exclusively on the audience, it's likely the director will forget the rest of the stage.

Jill: At the same time, I've often seen hearing directors say, "Oh, I want to work with deaf people and ASL in my show," but they don't realize that if the deaf community sees someone deaf on stage, they'll come in droves. So then, who is in place to serve as an advocate for access? Not that directors themselves have to make those access decisions. But I feel the director has some responsibility to say, "Hey, we need to make sure that the community can access this."

Alexandria: I would say that the responsibility could be more on the artistic director of the theatre company because it's the company's reputation. The director does one show, but the theatre company has a reputation and so it's for the artistic director to say, "Fine, okay, we need to work together side by side to figure out how we can identify the right people," and then build it out right there earlier in the process. Don't wait until the tech week or wait until the preview, no. Do that planning way earlier.

Jill: I know that in the professional theatre world, roles can be very established and that attention to access can disappear because it doesn't really fit within any one person's role as a significant responsibility. What needs to change to move from a traditional perspective on responsibilities to make sure that we have equal access not only on stage, but backstage and in the front of the house, for the audience?

Alexandria: I think a large part of that is, number one, always, *always* have a budget line for access, always. Have it ready. You never know. You just want to have that cushion for unexpected circumstances, so if you have that ready, then you can add if needed. I notice that [access] budgets tend to start at zero, and then money is an issue and it becomes burdensome on the actors and director. If the theatre company has a budget for access, which can translate to how the website looks when you purchase tickets, or at the front of the house of the theatre itself, or backstage, all that—they need to have that already in their heads, knowing it's there and being aware. It doesn't always have to be a detailed line-item budget, but have something set aside for that. That's important. I also wonder—honestly, my current thinking is for the different colleges and universities have theatre majors focused on the stage and best practices and all that, should have more courses related to universal design and how to modify established, rigid architecture. Because that's part of the challenge especially in New York City where a lot of buildings are really old or historical landmarks. So, modifications to these buildings would take forever, or be too expensive, or too costly to take it out and rebuild. That's a huge challenge. I think that's part of the bigger picture. As much as the director may dream, if the architecture isn't friendly for the general community, then what do you do? Blame the director? No. It goes deeper than that. But how do you improve that? That's a question for ongoing conversation and analysis. I think it's important to have passion, desire, and creative thinking. The budget line is really important, especially for nonprofits or for producers who want to be open to bringing in more people. They need to have that budget ready and know who to reach out to for funding or find the money. And for colleges and universities to really consider what it means to shift into the real world that already has a lot of limitations. And how do we go beyond that for new development? What do those areas and spaces look like? How does one think about that? What would be needed for lighting, sound, space, backstage, you know, communication, and all that. I think that's exciting, but someone has to start it.

Jill: What have you seen as good strategies that work for providing access to deaf and hard of hearing audiences? What strategies have failed?

Alexandria: I think it works when the production or theatre company creates, on that website, a crystal-clear note about accessibility on the calendar. It should be explicitly there, not where I have to look for this information in menu within menu within menu. That's a barrier. It needs to be clear where accessibility information lives on that website. If it's an interpreted performance, be clear on the calendar where and when. Also allow me to click to see where the interpreters will be located within the house of the space. This information often isn't shared, so people don't know where to sit, and then they have to chase down that information. I also think it is successful to have videos in ASL on the website and to provide different types of access for deaf and hard of hearing people. Also emphasize if the show is ASL-interpreted, open-captioned, or captioned via devices. Have all of that clearly stated on the website. In terms of arriving at the theatre, I've seen companies who already know to have dry erase boards ready for communication with patrons. I've seen some theatre companies put up signage on the bathroom stall doors or even on the mirror showing basic signs or name signs. You can learn from that as you wash your hands. Videos in the lobby showing signs, interviews, with captions. Any supplemental information available. And then when you go into the theatre, it helps if the ushers know basic signs like COME, SIT, or RESTROOMS THAT WAY. What makes it successful is the showing of effort and commitment, having open minds and hearts. That makes the experience completely different compared to having to struggle and being frustrated. By the time you sit, you already have so much negativity and your show has already been ruined in those ten minutes since arrival. You then have to put that away and focus on the show. So, the experience begins from the ticket purchase all the way through and that really has an impact on the show experience itself.

Jill: What about different strategies for providing access in theatre like open captioning, devices, shadow interpreting. What do you feel about any of these strategies? Is one more successful than others, or does it depend on the show?

Alexandria: It really depends on the show itself. Ideally, all people on stage will already have signing fluency, the acting would be outstanding, and the director's vision would be perfect. That'd be ideal. As for shadow interpreting, I'm personally not fond of that because from both an actor's and audience member's perspective, I feel like the interpreter supports the actor, so whatever the actor's decisions or choices, the interpreter has to follow, so what's their value? They're the shadow, so that feels a bit off-putting. So, when I'm watching, I am not totally fond of a lot of bodies duplicating the same character or the storytelling for the sake of access, so that doesn't always work for me. However, it does depend on the production and how thought through the concept was/is. Generally, I prefer that all people on stage are fluent in signing and can really interact. ASL interpreted shows are fine. They're cool when it is done extremely well. Open captioning is cool. Devices are cool. It's fine. I do get frustrated with devices because typically their reliability depends on where you sit in the audience because of the WiFi signal. Sometimes it disconnects, and when it goes out, what do you do? Or it doesn't really work. So that's the only device and if it goes off, your experience becomes so-so. Interpreters and open captioning are more consistent. So, it depends on the show, really. I also would encourage more design, set design where the captions are creatively projected within the show. Where my eyes can easily flow around the stage. I can absorb everything without having to look away or looking down at my device. You know, that ability to see everything at once. That's more equitable for more people. Even if they don't need or do need captions, it's great to have that built in.

Jill: What about the 'voice of' approach. I'm curious about *Oedipus* that recently happened. That wasn't really shadowing, but more of 'voice of.' Do you prefer that or do you have thoughts about that approach?

Alexandria: For that approach with *Oedipus*, we let the deaf actors and the deaf characters lead that choice. We would tell the voice character "Come here [and voice for me]" or "No [don't voice for me]." WE made that decision. So that empowered us. All the choices about voicing were deliberate. I told the voice actor that when we [as characters] are in the public space, great. But when we have a private conversation, they don't need to know this, so 'turn your voice off.' Then we'd talk privately. So that was very empowering. It was not shadowing, where the voice actor is always following and speaking the lines. That feels a bit awkward and forced, rather than the voice actor consciously supporting what's happening in the scene.

Jill: I thought it was very powerful when Ashlea [Hayes] at one point was like, "Go away, I don't want you to interpret for me." Right?

Alexandria: Right, right.

Jill: Going back to our discussion about success and what that looks like. What would your dream integrated show look like? If money were not an issue and you could have anything?

Alexandria: I think it really depends on what the show is. Ideally, everyone, new or experienced, would come in with a deeper understanding of, support for, and appreciation of being culturally sensitive. I feel that training is important for everyone as a human. But in theatre storytelling, I'm noticing more, especially post-pandemic, that a lot of people are going back to the pre-pandemic habit of ignoring, disregarding people's feelings, not respecting boundaries, or disrespecting people. Wait a minute. No. We need to do better as theatre makers and artists in how we tell stories. I think from the accessibility perspective of the creative process, do we have outstanding interpreters? No discussion there. There should be no getting by and trying to do what we can. No. How is that fair? How is it? Tell me how it is fair that someone who's been doing this for twenty-five, thirty years and is constantly trying to negotiate barriers, and then have someone who doesn't know theatre come in and do a half-assed job of interpreting? Who is missing things, misunderstanding things, and causing communication breakdowns? I need to focus on my art and my creativity, but instead I have to focus on trying to work with the interpreter. So, my artistic work gets neglected. That's not fair. So, my vision would be to surround ourselves with people who understand what it takes to make good art, to have the appropriate DASL team. Not just one person who takes on the responsibility for all of the work. Have a good, strong team of people who can share the vision and work collaboratively, support the director, choreographer, and others, and support that process. Have a strong accessibility team, which would be separate from the DASL team. Accessibility from the audience's perspective is different from the actual production, where people involved have different experiences. There needs to be a stronger delineation of roles to identify what's missing, the gaps, and how we can fill those gaps. That will, I think, get to the point where we can really focus on generating more inclusive art. And that could lead to higher levels of achievement. I think we've been lucky; we've been able to make exciting art when we are really just squeaking by with resources. But I'm curious what it'd look like if we didn't have to constantly fight or work on things that should not even be an issue. I should not have to worry about the quality of interpreters. I should not have to deal with actors venting about their access or communication struggles, you know? We should have that space where we can focus on our identified roles, and really be able to do our jobs as actors and humans.

Jill: Has there been a production where you felt really included during the audition, rehearsal, or performance?

Alexandria: Every production has a few great aspects, a few ehhh. Not good, at all. They need to improve. I try not to dwell on what didn't work, but how do we get better? You know? I've worked on several productions where there was a large group of artists who were hearing and deaf, but one interpreter for all of us. Really?! That's just ridiculous, especially if the interpreter works with both the creative part and the actors. Whoa. That's out there. So, I will say that I feel it comes from a history and traditions dating back to the 1960s, 1970s, 1980s, where the cultural mindset was different compared to where we are now. We've learned from that era. It worked at that time, but that doesn't mean we can still use that method as an ideal one, no. Because that one interpreter is human, too, and they need breaks. They need, you know, to live their lives and get paid, you know? So that's really, whoo. That's really my recurring issue, interpreters. Unfortunately, I've worked on productions where we had two interpreters and one wasn't the greatest while the other was outstanding. I pity the interpreter who has to take on more pressure and work because the team isn't so great, you know? That means the artists are compromising to put up with the interpreters. Why?! Why are we doing that? It's not right. It's not right. So, when the director advocates and names it and calls it out, that personally gives me a lot of respect and appreciation because they notice and want to change things. Sometimes they can't because that train's already long gone, whether it's because there's no budget or too many factors happening and overlapping. It's not so cut and dried. Life happens, so again, have the budget to begin with. If you know that the show will be bilingual, that means we automatically will need interpreters and all these things. It shouldn't be a question of "uh, can we do this?" You gotta figure it out earlier, with the right people, and make sure they're paid for their time and energy.

Jill: How often have you as an actor shown up at auditions and had a DASL present. Or you as DASL, how often are you involved with auditions?

Alexandria: As an actor, auditioning with a DASL, never. That's bold. I haven't had that. I imagine if it's an all-deaf production, I'd be a bit, "hmmm." But often it seems the assumption is that you don't need a DASL because everyone knows sign language. I have to swallow that. I disagree, but okay. And then later on, they say, "Oh yeah..." There is tremendous value in having DASLs as part of the creative team. As a DASL, I've been—I've sat in on one or two auditions, not that many, and noticed it makes a difference. It does make a difference when I'm invited to be part of the creative side panel. Actually, for one show I wasn't the DASL. However, I worked on the show and the director wanted me to sit in to help filter out who really signed fluently and who didn't, or what their range was, to provide a better understanding of the actors. But that director already had worked with deaf actors, so that director's inherent knowledge was already there, which made a difference.

Jill: It puzzles me because how can a hearing director audition deaf actors? What are they evaluating? They have no knowledge of sign language. Is it the interpreter's voicing, or—

Alexandria: Often, they ask the interpreter for their opinion.

Jill: Wow.

Alexandria: Yes! So, the interpreter is a communication facilitator, not an artist, yet they are making the decision based on...yeah.

Jill: That's a bit of a problem, sometimes, you know?

Alexandria: Yeah, sometimes! [LAUGHS] I will say that the last show I worked on, the director again knew and understood the value of having a DASL, the value of having deaf people behind the creative table. She showed me a list and asked me, "Do you know who these people are?" We shared their levels of competency and if we didn't know who they were, we could ask if the actors wouldn't mind sending videos for us to look at. That was included in the director's experience. But if a director doesn't know anything, they tend to rely on interpreters for whether the audition is any good. Oh my God. Interpreters can have too much power and influence.

Jill: Can you give examples of shows where, in the rehearsal process, the director had specific strategies or activities that helped create an inclusive environment for you as an actor?

Alexandria: One director on a recent show, at the start of every rehearsal, had us sit in a circle and do group warmups together. Just to check in, a group check-in. And then at the end of the rehearsal, we'd do that again—a check-out, if you will, just to get a feel for each other. That was really beneficial because it reminded us that we were all in this together. That isn't a deaf or hearing thing, just a way for the company to be together. It was really beneficial for all of us. That's something I thought was very useful.

Jill: What about as DASL? Any activities you've done to help build an inclusive environment for deaf and hearing actors in rehearsal?

Alexandria: It really depends on the production, first, and on the level of competency. How much time we have, you know, we try as DASLs to create a space for integrated activities. Like having one on one time between the hearing and deaf actors, and giving them five minutes of creativity using a prompt, just throwing something at them for that scene.

Let them figure it out together without my involvement, then they come and share what they came up with, talk about their discoveries. Because really, often an actor's discovery is sometimes better than the director telling them what to do or finding that sign. If a sign doesn't feel right, then let's try something else, and how can we adapt? I'm very collaborative in the process, especially with those who are already fluent in signing or enjoy that part of the process. I support them because I want them to feel ownership of the language. At the same time, as DASL, I will remind people that I'm the one on the outside looking in. I will tell them what looks okay, and what doesn't. I understand a sign may feel good and feel right, but if it doesn't read well from back in the audience, we have to change it. Sorry, you know. I still maintain open dialogue and try to respect their wishes and dreams as artists, but at the same time, I'm doing my job. There's an art in the work I do as DASL, too.

Jill: Many don't quite agree on the DASL role job description. In your opinion, what does the DASL job involve?

Alexandria: Funny you say that because I'm actually working with two other people who work as DASLs. We are in the process of creating a more collective group of DASLs, almost like IDC, Intimacy Directors and Coordinators. They started with just a few people coming to an agreement on common core values and listing them. How each person works might be different, but they always follow these core values. They spread the word, and then #metoo happened, and demand for their work increased greatly and they had to expand that community. I feel like with DASLs, we kind of have that happening, with the demand for more ASL on TV, in film, and on stage. That's expanding, so we definitely need more collaboration. My personal perspective is that a DASL is many things. First, ideally, the DASL would be involved in the audition process, and second, pre-production, and then during the production, and then fourth, post-production. I'll come back to that later. The most important thing is for the DASL to meet with the director to have a conversation to learn the director's vision. Talk and find out what the director wants or needs, and then explain to the director what a DASL can contribute to this process. Once that discussion takes place, during the audition, both the director and DASL can keep this information at the back of their heads and discuss the auditions. The director has the final decision, of course, but this helps the director learn how to process things and what the rehearsal will look like. The DASL does many things. If you ask one DASL to do the job, it's a lot of work, but if you have a team, for example, two or three DASLs for a cast of ten, let's say. And of that ten, eight can sign and two can't. That's fine. That means the DASL team will be part of each individual's vision of how all the characters communicate with each other, what the levels or ranges—class, gender, relationships, all that information does enter the assessment of sign choices, region [the character is from], ages, and all that. So that work is of a dramaturg in a way, where the assessment takes place in collaboration with directors and actors. Then you work as you go, developing what that looks like, because the first day of rehearsal and the first preview will look very different. You have to start somewhere, so you use that time to work, translate, incorporate movements into the body. Then during rehearsals with other actors, see if it works or not, and make modifications, look at sightlines from the house, consider the use of the space on stage. Also, how to support the changes as more discoveries about characters are made and the director adds more, and have ongoing conversations with the creatives and with the work itself. Everything in real time, so that means a lot of time, energy, and commitment. It's not just one time for three hours each week and then you take off. No. You have to be there every day, you know. It's that type of work. I also think that it's also useful for the team to have some kind of 'book' for the translation process, documenting that. It could be video or on paper, but have something because that will become beneficial once the show is established, especially if an actor has to be replaced. You'll have this information ready, and for the understudy, too. If you can't be there and someone has to come in your place, that person can watch or use this document for reference and understand what has already been visualized. My perspective is that DASL work is like choreography work, like the director, like the costume designer, all these roles. Would actors be allowed to throw on costumes on their own or change lighting on their own, or do choreography without the creative team? No, absolutely not for many shows. The DASL's work really maintains the integrity of the production overall, and really supports the actors, the vision, and their own work, too. It involves a lot of research, collaboration, development, and all that. And then when the understudies show up at rehearsal, the DASL can support them to make sure everything is clearly understood. If there are concerns or issues, to help resolve them. Because the stage manager often doesn't know sign language. So how do they know if a line is being signed correctly? Some may ask, "Why don't we rely on the interpreters?" No. That's not their job as interpreters to be making decisions or corrections on the sign language that the DASL and production already has in place. It's more artistic. As an actor, your modification may be fine, but make sure you use this agreed upon sign because if/when you replace that actor, you are going on stage into an established environment where other actors are already used to specific signs. If you go in and use different signs, the other actors will be confused or thrown off. The DASL is about giving a lot of support and allowing actors to be themselves and bring their own delivery, but at the same time, maintaining the look, essence, and sense of spirit of the production.

Jill: Do you think a DASL is also responsible for feedback about the costumes, if something is deaf-friendly, lighting, or other parts of the design? What about audience accessibility, is that part of the DASL role?

Alexandria: From my experience, I think there is more value in having a separate ASL team focus on the access, because the DASLs are in the production's headspace and typically become too close to everything. They need to disconnect to focus on that. And that's my priority. I'd be happy to collaborate with the access team for interpreting or accessibility, but I sort of like to give that over to them. Their experience as audience members will be different, so what the vision is can be communicated with the access team to determine the best seating. I could certainly provide some input because of my perspective, but they know better. I'd just agree or suggest modifications, then go for it. I've seen DASLs in charge of access for the community plus access within the production world of the story. Whoo! They're two different things. They can co-exist, sure, but they're very different things. What the needs are, the requirements of both areas. And then I've seen the DASL who gets involved too much and abandons the production. Ehh, just go back to the production and focus on the show. You have to let go if you're not satisfied with the access part. You know? For example, in my experience, I've seen DASLs wanting to work with the ASL interpreters for the interpreted shows, and I've also been asked to do that. I always say I would rather not. I can support the ASL team for interpreters, but for me to be completely responsible and focus on and work with interpreters, whoa. No time. I'll hit my threshold, and then I feel that what you experience—already being in that world of the show, it'll look different to the audience. I can give some names or help clarify or make sure it's not confusing. I want the ASL interpreting team to be empowered to figure out what works best from their perspective watching the show. What makes sense for the audiences' perspective in the facilitation of storytelling? It's a really interesting and diverse perspective.

Jill: Can you tell me about the unique challenges in working with integrated musicals. That could come from the DASL or actor perspective, whatever perspective you want.

Alexandria: For a musical with that kind of integration, you always need more time, more time because usually the hearing people—not always, but usually—already have knowledge and expertise in musical theatre, and they know and understand how that space works. Often, although not always, it's deaf artists' first time doing a musical, so they're really learning a lot. The hearing artists still have a lot to learn, like how to sign while singing, kind of like rubbing your stomach while patting your head at the same time. They are learning a lot too, but it's different from what the deaf actors are learning. So that means we need more time, which we almost never have. How do we economize on our time, figure out the most efficient way to support and move the production, push it along? That's a big one. I think also translation, any musical or direct play, the translation process is quite challenging because for a musical, you already have the benefit of the rhythm in place, the feelings, and you can live and analyze within these parameters, yes, but also is the musicality of the signing choice and concept clear? All that. Who is signing? It's really challenging. These are the two big ones for me, from my experience, yes. And of course, usually in a musical, I've worked with only one interpreter for the entire group. Really?! That's a lot. I mean, that interpreter really was exceptional, yes—it was a must—but wow, whew. I definitely would want three interpreters so they can rotate and have two always on, while the third goes do other things or other tasks, or even just eat. Because on a musical, and plays too, the creatives are never off. During lunches and breaks, we're still meeting, still talking, so we need an interpreter all the time. So, if there's only one interpreter, that person is gonna have to eat while interpreting and won't have time to really process anything. It's the same for actors who want to talk to each other but if one doesn't know sign language, the interpreter can go work through the lunch break and be with them.

Jill: If you were working with a hearing director for the first time who wants to do integrated deaf and hearing theatre, what's the most important thing you'd tell them?

Alexandria: I would say it's a different culture. We are culturally different. Period. And you really have to have lots more patience than you're used to because of language—you have two languages being used. You have interpreters mediating conversation, which means there's inherent interpreter lag time. You'll have to be more patient. You have to really learn what's different between the cultures and what's similar. Learn to put aside your own fears or uncertainties. Learn how to empower deaf people, too, in the process. And empower your hearing actors who have never worked with deaf actors before. Or even those who have worked with deaf people before—make sure everyone feels equitable. That's among the first things I'd say to someone who hasn't worked with deaf people before. I'd teach and emphasize patience, patience, and patience. Lots more of that. And the cultural and community differences, and how to empower the room to make it better for all.

Jill: What do you think are key cultural differences, the top three differences between deaf and hearing?

Alexandria: How we take in the world. For sighted deaf people, lighting and visual cueing. And a lot of built in cues involving touch, too. Often in hearing spaces, people will speak and then move on immediately, and I'll be like, "Yo! Where are we?" I'm lost because I'm looking at people a second too late. I might look at something, take a sip of my coffee, then I look up and they've already jumped to the next topic. Hearing people are not accustomed to making sure everyone is comprehending everything. Another example: flashing lights for everyone, not just deaf people, to collectively get attention. If a hearing actor is next to me, don't just look at them and move forward. Use the hearing actor to support me. They can tap me on the shoulder and direct my attention to whoever is speaking. These are little things but they're so deeply rooted in that hearing world, that space that they forget how much they depend upon their ears and forget that they can use other senses, too. So, I have to say, "Come on." That's the biggest difference I've noticed, that the lack of experience and awareness influences everything. *Everything.* Sightlines from different parts of the room. Where you are. Even the simple idea of taking notes. Hearing people can write and listen at the same time, while for deaf people, we have to wait for them to write, and then they look back at us. Lots of pauses, lots more. Hearing people are accustomed to working through information they're being constantly fed, and they can look anywhere. But for sighted deaf people, we have to look. If I look away but you keep talking, I'll miss everything you just said. We need to say, "Hey, hold on, how do I empower people in the room?" Suppose a hearing director notices I'm looking down as I write, that person could say, "Wait, wait" and then "Okay, go ahead" when I'm done. Sometimes they're so into the moment and forget things like that. Just like for Protactile theatre—how you make sure things are clear, support communication access, and then move on. It's just time and patience. It's different ways of taking in the world.

Jill: Why do you think it's important to have integrated deaf and hearing theatre?

Alexandria: It's the power of storytelling. That's the biggest benefit of all, the different ways the same stories can be told. I read or someone told me that throughout human history, at the core there are only three or four stories. There are so many different interpretations of these stories, from different perspectives—culture and gender and so on. But there are only three or four basic stories. Wow! So, for deaf and hearing, both benefit from integrated theatre because so much of what deaf artists can bring to the space is their experiences, and their exceptional skills in taking in the world. It's so different from hearing artists who have their own view of the world, which is based on more access, more opportunities, experiences, education, all that. The exchange in itself is really rich. The benefit is cultural exchange. My perspective as a deaf person, a lot of my daily life and work is interacting with hearing people. I interact with hearing people a lot more than hearing people interact with deaf people, so I do know a thing or two about hearing people. [LAUGHS] You know what I mean? How do I present that knowledge? How do I say, "Umm, wait a minute. Let's communicate more efficiently." How do we empower each other? This isn't a me problem, this is our problem. You know, how do we solve this together? The interpreter isn't for me, it's for us. Because guess what, friends? You don't know sign language! If you knew sign language on a conversational level, we wouldn't need an interpreter. So that's a paradigm shift towards more equality. On a deeper level, it's about the human desire to connect, engage, learn about what scares them, and how to move through and get past that. How to get around that, how to shift that fear into more curiosity about the world and about different perspectives. Start to understand what is missing from how we tell stories. Who's not in this room? Who are we not including? More awareness of taking in the world. Just recently, I was told about one director who was told their work had really improved within the past few years. The director was asked, "What changed you?" The director said, "I worked with deaf actors. I worked with deaf actors, and that opened my mind, that experience." If only that one person changed, great. I'm ecstatic because it takes every single person to spread that shift forward. Of course, it'd be nice if they all at the same time had that paradigm shift, boom! But that's a dream, really.

Jill: What do you hope to see happen going forward in the theatre community, in terms of inclusivity and accessibility?

Alexandria: More exposure, more opportunities, more education, more training, and less haggling for interpreters or access, or all that oppression that historically and currently exists.

Jill: Is there any area we haven't touched you feel I should ask about that?

Alexandria: One thing that hasn't been mentioned that is really important to emphasize. As with any culture, any community, the language and society keep changing and evolving. It's really, really important to have resources like this book to become part of that ongoing anthology, that ongoing open conversation. It's a living, breathing process. Because I encounter a lot of people who have very old thinking and old biases from the 1970s and 1980s in terms of words, labels, identifiers, and I say, "No, no, don't do that, that's not okay. That's not how we introduce ourselves nowadays." The level of empowerment has shifted over time because resources, technology, and access are changing. That applies to language and sign, and what that means, what it looks like, all that. I think it's really important that people read this book but also to remember that in their lives, they should always ask the deaf person, "How do you prefer to communicate? What works best for you?" Not just assume, "You lipread. Great. Let's move on." Deaf people are very diverse. Always approach each person as an individual. If you're in a room where there are many diverse deaf people, how do you make that space fit as broad a range as possible? That's challenging, but when everyone shares that goal of a more equitable space, then everyone will likely feel more comfortable with the process. No one said it would be easy! What we do is not easy. Not easy.

APPENDIX C: FURTHER READING

DEAF HISTORY AND DEAF STUDIES

Banks, Michelle. 2006. *Reflections of a Black Deaf Woman*. DVD.
Bauman, Dirksen, ed. 2008. *Open Your Eyes: Deaf Studies Talking*. Minneapolis: University of Minnesota Press.
Gertz, Genie, and Patrick Boudreault, eds. 2016. *The SAGE Deaf Studies Encyclopedia*, 3 vols. Thousand Oaks, CA: SAGE Publications, Inc. https://doi.org/10.4135/9781483346489.
Groce, Nora. 1985. *Everyone Here Spoke Sign Language: Hereditary Deafness on Martha's Vineyard*. Cambridge, MA: Harvard University Press.
Harlan, Lane, Robert Hoffmeister, and Ben Bahan. 1996. *A Journey into the Deaf-World*. San Diego: DawnSignPress.
Ladd, Paddy. 2003. *Understanding Deaf Culture: In Search of Deafhood*. Bristol, UK: Multilingual Matters.
McCaskill, Carolyn, Ceil Lucas, and Joseph Hill. 2011. *The Hidden Treasure of Black ASL*. Washington, DC: Gallaudet University Press. See also the short documentary informed by this book, *Signing Black in America*. https://www.youtube.com/watch?v=oiLltM1tJ9M.
Van Cleve, John Vickery, and Barry A. Crouch. 1989. *A Place of Their Own: Creating Deaf Community in America*. Washington, DC: Gallaudet University Press.

DEAF THEATRE

The DeafHistory.eu website contains historical information on European Deaf Theatre companies: https://deafhistory.eu/index.php/deaf-history/deaf-arts. Racheal Missingham has written an MA thesis on "Australia's Deaf Theatre: Past, Present, and Future." Queensland University of Technology (2021).

© The Author(s), under exclusive license to Springer Nature Switzerland AG 2024
A. Head, J. M. Bradbury, *Staging Deaf and Hearing Theatre Productions*, https://doi.org/10.1007/978-3-031-61446-0

For Deaf theatre in the United States, the only book for the general public still in print is Stephen Baldwin's *Pictures in the Air: The Story of the National Theatre of the Deaf* (Washington, DC: Gallaudet University Press, 1993). A more scholarly resource is Kanta Kochhar-Lindgren, *Hearing Difference: The Third Ear in Experimental, Deaf, and Multicultural Theater*. (Washington, DC: Gallaudet University Press, 2006).

OTHER RESOURCES INCLUDE:

Bangs, Donald. 1989. What is a Deaf Performing Arts Experience? In *The Deaf Way: Perspectives from the International Conference on Deaf Culture*, ed. Carol J. Erting et al., 751–761. Washington, DC: Gallaudet University Press, July 9–14, 1989.

Conley, Willy. 2001. Away from Invisibility, Towards Invincibility: Issues with Deaf Theatre Artists in America. In *Deaf World: A Historical Reader and Primary Sourcebook*, ed. Lois Bragg. New York: Routledge.

———. 2023. *Plays of Our Own: An Anthology of Scripts by Deaf and Hard-of-Hearing Writers*. New York: Routledge.

Giordano, Tyrone. 2016. Actors. In *The SAGE Deaf Studies Encyclopedia*, ed. Genie Gertz and Patrick Boudreault, 5–8. Thousand Oaks: SAGE Publications. https://doi.org/10.4135/9781483346489.

Miles, Dorothy. 1974. A History of Theatre Activities in the Deaf Community of the United States. MA thesis, Connecticut College.

Mow, Shanny. 1987a. Theater, Community. In *Gallaudet Encyclopedia of Deaf People and Deafness*, ed. John Vickery Van Cleve, vol. 3, 288–289. McGraw-Hill Professional.

———. 1987b. Theater, Professional. In *Gallaudet Encyclopedia of Deaf People and Deafness*, ed. John Vickery Van Cleve, vol. 3, 289–291. McGraw-Hill Professional.

Rholetter, Wylene. n.d. Arts, Performing. In *The SAGE Deaf Studies Encyclopedia*, ed. Genie Gertz and Patrick Boudreault, 48–51. Thousand Oaks: SAGE Publications. https://doi.org/10.4135/9781483346489.

Steketee, Martha Wade. 2016. *NEA Roundtable: Creating Opportunities for Deaf Theater Artists*. The National Endowment for the Arts.

Tadie, Nancy Bowen. 1979. A History of Drama at Gallaudet College. PhD diss., New York University.

Zachary, Samuel J. 1995. Cleveland Signstage Theatre: America's Professional Resident Theatre of the Deaf. In *A Deaf American Monograph*, 127–133. The National Association of the Deaf: Silver Spring.

DeafBlind Theatre and Protactile

Bradbury, Jill Marie, John Lee Clark, Rachel Grossman, Jason Herbers, Victoria Magliocchino, Jasper Norman, Yashaira Romilus, Robert T. Sirvage, and Lisa van der Mark. 2019. Protactile Shakespeare: Inclusive Theater By/For the DeafBlind. *Shakespeare Studies* 47: 81–115.

Bradbury, Jill Marie, and Gallaudet Video Services. 2019. *Protactile Romeo and Juliet: Theater by/for the Deaf Blind.* https://www.youtube.com/watch?v=btB_nePm860.

Clark, John Lee. 2015. My Dream Play: A DeafBlind Man Imagines a Pro-Tactile Theatre. *Scene4 Magazine.* Accessed November 15, 2023. https://www.scene4.com/archivesqv6/2015/apr-2015/0415/johnleeclark0415.html.

granda, aj, and Jelica Nuccio. 2018. *Protactile Principles.* Tactile Communications LLC. Accessed November 15, 2023. https://www.tactilecommunications.org/ProTactilePrinciples.

Sign Language Poetics

Bauman, Dirksen, Jennifer Nelson, and Heidi Rose. 2006. *Signing the Body Poetic: Essays on American Sign Language Literature.* Berkeley, CA: University of California Press.

Taub, Sarah F. 2001. *Language from the Body: Iconicity and Metaphor in American Sign Language.* Cambridge, MA: Cambridge University Press.

Valli, Clayton. 1993. Poetics of American Sign Language Poetry. PhD diss., Union Institute.

Wilcox, Phyllis Perrin. 2000. *Metaphor in American Sign Language.* Washington, DC: Gallaudet University Press.

Sign Language Musicality

Jody Cripp's *Signed Music* website has many resources for those interested in learning more about sign language musicality, including links to his own publications. https://wp.towson.edu/signedmusic/.

The Journal of ASL Studies has a special issue on musicality and sign language. Video transcripts are available. https://journalofasl.com/special-issue-music/.

Shakespeare in Sign Language

Novak, Peter. *The ASL Shakespeare Project.* http://www.aslshakespeare.org/.

Deafinitely Theatre. *Shakespeare Found in Translation.* Video documentary of 2012 production of *Love's Labour's Lost.* http://www.bslzone.co.uk/watch/shakespeare-found-translation/.

Deafinitely Theatre transformed their production of the play for the 2012 Globe to Globe Festival. A short documentary is available at: http://www.bslzone.co.uk/watch/deaf-world-deafinitely-theatre-translate-loves-labours-lost/.

ACCESSIBILITY FOR DEAF AUDIENCES

For theatre organizations in the United States, the Leadership Exchange in Arts and Disability Office of the John F. Kennedy Center for the Performing Arts has developed several tip sheets. https://www.kennedy-center.org/education/networks-conferences-and-research/research-and-resources/lead-research-and-resources/.

For theatre organizations in the United Kingdom, the Arts Council of Wales has developed a handbook containing a helpful checklist and suggestions about media outreach. https://arts.wales/sites/default/files/2019-10/Developing%20Audiences%20toolkit.pdf.

Index

A
Accessibility, 6–12, 14, 15, 22, 23, 32, 34, 37–41, 40n11, 43–46, 48, 55, 57, 60, 68, 72, 73, 75, 76, 78, 79, 82, 87, 88, 91, 97, 99, 99n5, 100, 104, 106, 108, 109, 111, 112, 131, 132, 136, 138–141, 143–150, 152, 153, 157–162, 166–169, 172–176, 178–179, 182, 183, 186, 188, 189, 191, 192, 194–196, 198, 200, 205–214, 217, 218, 220, 222–224, 226–228, 230, 240, 245–247, 249, 254, 256–260, 264, 266–268, 273, 283, 285, 287, 288, 292–295, 297, 302, 305, 306
    audience accessibility, 40, 99, 100, 256, 302
Americans with Disabilities Act, 7, 9, 29, 32, 73, 149
Angels in America: Millennium Approaches, 18–19, 18n8, 36, 68–77, 88–91, 94, 100–102, 133–137, 174–179, 237, 240
Arden, Michael, vii, 16, 44, 74, 155, 157, 203, 208, 222, 227, 228
Arsenic and Old Lace, 24, 24n5, 28
Assistant director, 37, 64, 66–68, 89, 91, 100–102, 104, 111, 129, 132, 134–136, 175, 178, 197, 205, 231, 261
Auble, Erin, vii, 34, 90, 207
Audism, 4, 14, 66, 92, 115, 157, 163, 265
Auditions, 63, 65–68, 77, 88, 93, 96–97, 101, 103–112, 114, 120, 123, 182, 183, 196, 208, 217–220, 231, 232, 239, 241, 247, 260, 261, 268, 290, 297–300
    callbacks, 65, 66, 101, 104–109, 111, 112, 114–117, 182, 183
Autocorrect Thinks I'm Dead, 28, 30, 266

B

Baldwin, Stephen, xi, 29
Banks, Michelle, vii, 26, 27, 29, 30, 167, 173, 211–221
Baron, Michael, vii, 17, 28, 74, 167, 169
Barton-Farcas, Stephanie, xi, 33
Big River, xi, 27, 28, 38, 39, 153, 187, 238, 274, 290
BIPOC, 198, 217, 219, 229
Blocking, 33, 35, 37, 45, 89, 96, 98, 102, 117, 123–137, 142, 143, 163, 166, 173, 177, 191, 235, 256, 280, 283
Bove, Linda, 26–28, 38
Bragg, Bernard, 268

C

Cabaret, 43, 44, 46
Captioning, x, 7, 9, 10, 15, 38, 45n13, 46–48, 73, 74, 76, 83, 87, 88, 99, 104, 132, 143, 144, 146–150, 152, 160, 166–169, 174, 175, 177, 192, 196, 197, 214, 217, 223, 224, 226, 241, 246, 247, 256, 257, 260
  closed captioning; GalaPro, 146, 147, 214, 224, 227; I-Caption, 146
  closed captions, 47, 144, 146, 147, 295, 296; GalaPro, 45, 45n13, 144; I-Caption, 147
  creative captioning, 87, 166
  open captions, 11, 14, 46, 57, 73, 74, 76, 86, 87, 89, 90, 132, 143, 144, 146, 156, 159, 168–171, 173, 174, 176, 178, 226, 240, 284, 288, 295, 296
Cardona, E.J., 234, 270
Castille, Joshua, vii, 27, 30, 41, 154, 221–235, 255, 266, 270
Casting, 14, 53–54, 58, 60, 101, 103, 104, 111, 182, 218, 231–233, 240, 254, 260, 261
Casting director, 218
Caverly, James, vii, 17, 28, 30, 47, 168, 171, 173, 191, 195–196, 204–205, 208–209, 216
Cheslik, Brian, vii, 196, 209–210
Children of a Lesser God, xi, 26, 28, 239, 252, 290
Choreography, 123, 156, 191, 201, 215, 234, 250
Chou, Aimee, vii, 28, 30, 191–192
Circuit Playhouse Theatre of the Deaf, 25
CODA, xii, 3, 25, 53, 54, 71, 75, 92, 101, 169, 170, 172, 175, 217, 240, 241, 270, 290
Co-director, 17, 28, 64, 65, 67, 68, 104, 111, 129, 132, 160, 161, 197, 205, 209, 218, 237, 268, 269
A Contemporary Theatre, 41, 230
Costumes, 33, 34, 36n9, 37, 67, 82, 84–86, 97, 133, 159, 166, 174, 179, 205, 213, 237, 251, 260, 276, 302
Counterpart, 113–118, 120, 121, 124, 126, 129, 131, 132, 134–136, 158, 162, 165, 166, 177
Covell, Victoria, vii, 44, 196
Cues, 58, 100, 102, 117, 125, 128, 130, 136, 140, 234, 235, 249, 304
Curious and Curiouser, 257

D

Dameron, Jules, 30, 225, 229, 231
Daniels, Bob, 29
Deaf Austin Theatre, 28, 31

INDEX   313

DeafBlind, 3, 4, 30, 112, 153, 190,
    198, 208, 219, 255
Deaf consultant, 14, 66–67, 83–85,
    98–100, 106, 109, 111, 112,
    120, 128, 143, 145, 149, 178,
    182, 232
Deaf culture, 6, 8, 14, 63, 65, 77, 79,
    81, 92, 93, 100, 105, 106, 109,
    115, 118, 119, 123, 128, 129,
    155, 160, 163, 166, 170, 177,
    182, 192, 206, 213, 225, 253,
    254, 267, 291, 303, 304
Deaf gain, 1, 1n1, 278, 286
Deaf Studies, 2, 4, 150
Deaf theatre, 2, 8, 21–24, 21n1,
    23n3, 26–32, 59, 68, 101, 120,
    193, 197, 211, 222, 229, 280,
    282, 289
Deaf West Theatre, xi, 16, 26–28, 31,
    38, 39, 41, 152, 153, 186, 190,
    193, 221, 229, 232, 235, 238,
    256, 271, 272, 274, 290
Director of artistic sign language, 11,
    14, 27, 31, 53, 55–60, 64,
    66–68, 84, 85, 89, 91–102,
    91n3, 99n5, 105, 106, 109, 111,
    120–122, 124–126, 128, 129,
    132, 134–136, 143, 149, 162,
    167, 173–175, 178, 181, 197,
    204–206, 212, 213, 215, 217,
    218, 232, 233, 235–237, 239,
    241, 243, 247, 248, 254,
    258–265, 269, 272, 291,
    293, 297–303
Diversity, 195, 200, 214, 219, 231
Double casting, 34
Dual staging, 32, 33, 130–132, 162,
    165, 169, 176, 178
    disconnected persona, 40–43, 113,
        131, 154, 157, 162, 165, 169

double casting, 33–35, 37, 39, 113,
    130, 153, 226, 256
interpreter-character, 43, 44, 46, 73,
    113, 131, 169, 236
shadowing, 33, 35–39, 36n9, 43,
    76, 113, 130, 153, 154, 157,
    162, 172, 176, 178, 191, 222,
    226, 257, 296
signing-centered, 46–48, 132
SimCom, 45 (*see also* SimCom)
voice of, 33, 38–39, 113, 131,
    153–155, 157, 158, 161, 162,
    165, 169, 217, 296
Durant, Daniel, 27, 153, 156, 158

E
Edmond, Treshelle, 154, 156
Equus, 26, 239, 255

F
Fairmount Theatre of the Deaf,
    25, 31, 32
Fidelio, 28, 221, 230, 234
Fingerspelling, 57, 128, 178, 233,
    241, 287
First rehearsal, 97, 100, 117,
    119–122, 133, 182, 183
Focal point, 126, 127, 129, 156, 158,
    279–281, 283
*For colored girls who have considered
    suicide / when the rainbow is enuf*,
    xii, 211, 214–216, 290
Frank, Sandra Mae, 17, 27, 28, 74,
    153, 156, 158, 167, 169,
    218, 238
Frelich, Phyllis, 26, 27, 239
Front of house, audience accessibility,
    99, 100, 138–150

G

Gallaudet University, 8, 22, 24, 28, 28n6, 30–32, 221, 235, 242, 274, 275, 280–283, 286, 288
Gesture, 51, 57, 58, 74, 95, 96, 104, 110, 164, 194, 226, 235, 251, 272, 289
Giordano, Tyrone, vii, 24n5, 38, 39, 186–187, 192–193, 197, 205–206, 208
Glasser, Sacha, vii, 28, 207–208
Gloss script, 59, 95, 124–125, 212, 262, 263
Graybill, Patrick, vii, 235–241

H

Haggerty, Luane Davis, vii, xi, 27, 33, 196–197
Harvard, Russell, xii, 27, 44, 155, 156, 158, 227, 230, 238
Hayes, Ashlea, 296
Hays, David, 25, 56, 238–240
Hensley, Amelia, vii, 27, 154, 162, 168, 171, 173, 190, 197
Hlibok, Bruce, 26, 29, 30
Holt, Monique, vii, 27, 29, 30, 228, 242–252, 259
The Hunchback of Notre Dame, 221, 225, 234, 255, 266, 270

I

Inclusion, 7, 10, 11, 13–15, 54, 68, 78, 88, 97, 99, 104, 106, 108, 140, 152, 153, 160, 161, 168, 175, 182, 194–196, 207–208, 214, 217, 219, 220, 222, 231, 233, 239, 244, 247, 253, 263, 264, 268, 272, 273, 286, 288, 297, 299
Integrated theatre, vii, xi, xii, 4, 6, 7, 9–14, 25–27, 33, 35, 49, 53, 56, 59, 63, 64, 66, 76, 85, 96, 108, 118, 138, 144, 150, 152, 160, 168, 175, 185, 186, 190–194, 197, 201–207, 211–213, 216, 219–221, 235, 238, 241–244, 251–254, 256, 266, 267, 269, 274–276, 289, 291, 303, 305
Interaction web, 69–71, 73
Interborough Repertory Theatre, 27
Interpreter, 3, 9, 14, 36n9, 37, 38, 65, 66, 78–81, 85, 92, 93, 96, 99, 99n5, 100, 104–112, 115–118, 120–124, 126, 140–144, 148–150, 153, 170, 182, 196–201, 204, 209, 213, 214, 216–218, 223, 226, 232, 233, 239, 240, 242, 246, 248, 252, 257–263, 265, 267, 270, 272, 276, 287, 288, 291, 292, 295, 297, 299, 301–303, 305, 306
Intersectionality, 244
In the Heights, 33, 34
Into the Woods, 266, 270
ISM, 30, 211, 216, 220

K

Kelstone, Aaron, vii, 30, 189–191, 201–202
Kennedy Center American College Theatre Festival, 176, 241
Kiwitt, Cath, vii, 197, 199, 201, 204
Kotsur, Troy, xii, 27, 239, 256
Kurs, DJ, vii, 38, 230, 274

L

Levels, 82, 89, 128, 136, 156, 158, 163, 281

Lighting, 28, 58, 67, 85–87, 97, 110, 128, 156, 158, 159, 164, 173, 175, 176, 179, 205, 207, 213, 235, 237, 240, 241, 245, 249, 251, 259, 260, 269–271, 275, 281, 282, 286, 302, 304
  blue lighting, 86
  cue lights, 86
  stopping signal, 86
Lipreading, 1, 4, 48, 74, 110, 116, 234, 265
Lobster time, 202
Lopes, Gregor, 230

M

Mainstreaming, 2, 7–13, 32, 55, 99n5, 178, 241, 274, 278, 289
Mainstream theatre, xii, 8, 9n5, 30, 31, 86, 99n5, 120, 143, 148, 149, 266, 278
Makeup, 84, 85
Manualism, 4, 21, 24n4, 155
Martha's Vineyard, 167, 169, 171, 242, 244
Matlin, Marlee, 27, 53, 247
Merkin, Lewis, 26, 239
Milan Conference, 24n4, 74, 155, 157
Morrill, Andrew, 30, 168, 171, 173, 259
Mosaic Theater, 288
Mow, Shanny, 26, 29, 202
Musicals, 26–28, 58, 85, 88, 95, 123, 128, 129, 201, 202, 215, 216, 230, 234, 235, 238, 250, 251, 263, 270, 271, 273, 283, 284, 291, 303
The Music Man, xii, 17–18, 28, 47, 48, 74, 167–174, 194, 211, 214–218, 220, 222, 274, 283, 287, 290
My Third Eye, 29, 237

N

National Technical Institute for the Deaf, ix, 18, 18n8, 25, 28, 30–34, 36, 43, 76, 89, 90, 95, 100, 176, 178, 235, 236, 238–240, 252, 289
National Theatre of the Deaf, x, 25–29, 31, 32, 53, 56, 190, 193, 198, 235–243, 257, 266
Native Son, 286, 288
New York Deaf Theatre, 25, 29–31, 244, 252
Non-negotiable principles, xii, 14, 15, 46, 65, 78, 88, 109, 139, 140, 181, 182
Novak, Peter, 83, 191, 261
Nutter, Guthrie, 162, 163, 166, 225

O

Oedipus, 28, 41, 190, 290, 296
Olney Theatre Center, 17, 28, 47, 48, 167, 211, 274
One Flew Over the Cuckoo's Nest, 236, 237
Onyx Theatre, 25, 30, 211, 220
Oralism, 4, 24, 24n4, 25, 32, 74, 76, 155, 170, 275
Oregon Shakespeare Festival, 242, 243, 248, 266, 270, 272, 273
The Oresteia, 281
Orr, Hayden, vii, 193, 198
Our Town, 242, 245

P

Paris, Malik, vii, 34, 193–194, 198
Post mortem, 182–184
Pre-audition period, 63–77, 91, 93, 100, 106
Primeaux-O'Bryant, Mervin, 30, 168
Projections, 29, 86–87, 89–91, 137, 146, 176

Props, 58, 77, 85, 143, 173
Protactile, 3, 30–31, 304
Protactile Theatre, 30–31

R
Read-through, 119–122, 125, 133
Representation, 53–55, 60, 69, 78, 92, 97, 153, 167, 194, 203, 276
Robinson, Christopher, vii, 187–189, 199–200, 202–203, 206, 210
Rochester Institute of Technology, 18, 18n8, 34, 36, 43, 90, 289
Runge, Nicki, 168, 169
Rush, Serena, vii, 194, 241

S
Santini, Joseph, vii, 190, 191
Saunders, Crom, vii, 253–265
Scene partner, 45, 106, 113, 114, 116, 118, 120, 121, 126, 129, 135, 137, 140
Scene work, 133, 136–137
Scheduling, audience accessibility, 148
Schlecht, Ryan, 161, 163
Schneiderman, Iosif, 27
Scott-Flaherty, Alexa, vii, 189, 194–195
Seago, Howie, vii, 17, 26, 28–30, 41, 42, 159, 160, 162, 222, 226, 243, 265–274
Seating, audience accessibility, 83, 88, 89, 99, 100, 128, 143, 148, 279, 282, 302
Sets, 29, 37, 67, 76, 82–83, 85, 86, 88–91, 94, 97, 128, 132, 136, 143, 147, 156, 158, 161, 163, 167, 171, 173, 207, 213, 241, 254, 256, 260, 274–276, 278, 279, 281–284, 286, 288, 296

Shakespeare, 17, 23, 27, 44, 58, 59, 83, 161, 162, 164, 166, 242, 244, 248, 250, 251, 253, 259, 260, 266, 274, 289
ASL Midsummer Night's Dream, 17, 28, 159–167, 266, 268, 269
Cymbeline, 243, 266
Hamlet, 22–24, 59, 289
Henry IV, 22
Henry IV: Part I, 290
Julius Caesar, 282, 283
King Lear, 44, 227, 290
The Merchant of Venice, 288
A Midsummer Night's Dream, 17, 27, 94, 164, 281, 282
R+J: The Vineyard, 48
Richard III, 55, 228, 242, 248
Romeo + Juliet, 41, 42, 221, 222, 226, 227, 232
Romeo and Juliet, 31, 251
The Taming of the Shrew, 22
The Tempest, 26, 290
Titus Andronicus, 244, 245, 259, 263, 286
Twelfth Night, 83, 289, 290
Twelfth Night in ASL, 83, 191, 253, 261
Sightline, 9, 37, 82, 89, 98, 102, 128–129, 131, 132, 135, 136, 143, 163, 166, 188, 279, 288, 301, 304
Sign box, 84, 128, 166
Signed English, 5
Sign language linguistics, 4, 5, 48–53
Black ASL, 5, 77
classifier, 51, 250
eye gaze, 50, 127, 129, 250
facial expression, 42, 45, 50, 58, 84, 85, 128, 158, 230, 257, 263, 282
handshape, 5, 49–51, 250

International Sign Language, 5
mouthing, 45, 50, 51, 58, 59, 165, 166
Sign language musicality, 48–53, 52n17, 58, 88, 173, 263, 303
sign language music, 53
Sign language poetics, 48–53, 59
onomatopoeia, 51
rhyme, 51
rhythm, 51, 52
visual vernacular, 51, 230
SimCom, 5, 45
Sinnott, Ethan, vii, 29, 55, 167, 171, 274–290
Snyder, Lindsey, vii, 55, 200, 207
Sound, 78, 78n1, 86, 87, 166, 236, 241, 278
Sounds of Silence, 29
Sound Theatre Company, 17, 28, 30, 112, 159, 161, 266, 268
Spectrum Deaf Theatre, 26
Speech, 4, 24n4, 110, 155, 163
Split visual attention, 10, 37, 38, 58, 144
Spring Awakening, xi, 16, 18, 27, 28, 74, 94, 151–159, 216, 221, 222, 225, 234, 238, 257, 269, 271, 274, 279, 290
Stage manager, 80, 86, 120, 121, 138–141, 143, 144, 161, 175, 176, 259, 288, 301
Stage sign language, 25, 42, 56–58, 66, 76, 84, 93, 96, 98, 99, 99n5, 142, 144, 157, 173, 174, 179, 202, 241, 279
A Streetcar Named Desire, 256

T
Tablework, 98, 101, 117, 121, 124–126, 134, 136, 137
Tech week, 65, 86, 93, 133, 137, 138, 141–142, 234, 293
Tester, Christopher, 168, 216
Thuman, Teresa, vii, 17, 269
Ticketing, audience accessibility, 148
To Kill a Mockingbird, xii, 266, 267, 273
Translation, 11, 56–59, 66, 93–96, 98–101, 104, 105, 117, 121, 122, 124–126, 133, 134, 136, 152, 160, 162, 168, 173, 175, 187, 191, 204, 212, 215, 216, 219, 244, 250, 252, 259, 261, 263, 270, 301, 303
Tribes, 221, 252

V
Vaidya, Vishal, 170, 171
Video script, 95, 99, 104, 105, 109, 218, 252
Viscript, 252
Visionaries of the Creative Arts, 30, 31, 211, 219, 221
Visual communication rules, 80
Visual gestural communication, 244, 251

W
Wailes, Alexandria, vii, xii, 27, 239, 260, 290–306
Waterstreet, Ed, 26
Wiegand, Annie, vii, 28, 275
Will & Co., 27
Winchester, Kai, 161, 163

Printed in the USA
CPSIA information can be obtained
at www.ICGtesting.com
CBHW071635280924
14997CB00012BA/698